USEFUL ENEMIES

DAVID KEEN
USEFUL ENEMIES
WHEN WAGING WARS IS MORE IMPORTANT THAN WINNING THEM

YALE UNIVERSITY PRESS
NEW HAVEN AND LONDON

For information about this and other Yale University Press publications, please contact:

U.S. Office: sales.press@yale.edu   yalebooks.com
Europe Office: sales@yaleup.co.uk   www.yalebooks.co.uk

Set in Minion Pro by IDSUK (DataConnection) Ltd
Printed in Great Britain by TJ International Ltd, Padstow, Cornwall

Library of Congress Cataloging-in-Publication Data

Keen, David, 1958-
    Useful enemies : when waging wars is more important than winning them /
David Keen.
    p. cm.
    ISBN 978-0-300-16274-5 (cl : alk. paper)
1. War—Causes. 2. Protracted conflicts (Military science) 3. War—
Psychological aspects. 4. War crimes. 5. Violence—Social aspects. 6. Politics
and war. I. Title. II. Title: When waging wars is more important than winning
them.
    U21.2.K427 2012
    355.02'7—dc23

                                                                        2012003457

A catalogue record for this book is available from the British Library.

10 9 8 7 6 5 4 3 2 1
2016 2015 2014 2013 2012

Contents

Acknowledgements

Writing this book was harder than I expected, but I hope that reading it will be a little easier. In part, I am trying to bring together – and find a new audience for – a large body of research that has so far found outlets only in rather specialist publications or in the academic textbook *Complex Emergencies*. The book also draws on considerable new first-hand research – notably on the causes and functions of 'permanent emergency' in Sri Lanka and the United States.

In this task, I have been enormously assisted by Phoebe Clapham at Yale, a brilliant and courageous editor. I owe thanks to Clive Liddiard for his copy-editing, a task undertaken with dedication and fortitude under great pressure. My thanks also to Paula Clarke, who did a great job on the proofreading and index. I would like to say a particular thank-you to James Macdonald Lockhart (at Antony Harwood Ltd), my kind and patient agent, for his perceptive editorial input and steadfast encouragement.

In the hectic final stages, I am especially indebted to my aunty Ann for her energy and all-round support. I would like to thank Stuart Gordon for his very helpful comments on the Afghanistan chapter, though unfortunately he – like my equally helpful anonymous reader – cannot be held responsible for any major gaffes on my part. I am grateful to Mareike Schomerus for sharing, prior to publication, her fascinating paper on the Lord's Resistance Army in South Sudan. Particular thanks are extended to the Leverhulme Foundation for the Major Research Fellowship awarded to me, something that helped enormously in researching and writing this book. Thanks also to Elliott Green for stepping in for me with great skill and adaptability at LSE. I would also like to thank my (Masters and PhD) students at LSE for their stimulating company – and of course, the lifeblood of my department, Sue Redgrave, Drucilla Nelson and Stephanie Davies.

In Sierra Leone, I was helped greatly by Wael Ibrahim, Karen Moore, Mark Bradbury, Ricken Patel, Comfort Ero and Dennis Bright among many others. I offer a particular thank-you to James Vincent, who helped me tremendously during my early research on the war there. In Guatemala, I was greatly assisted by Alessandro Preti, Roddy Brett and Marcus Lenzen In Serbia, I benefited greatly from the kindness and assistance of Marie-Thérèse Mauro and David Shearer. In Sudan, I owe my greatest debt to Peter Cutler. In the US, I have benefited from the patience and insights of numerous war veterans and activists and I thank them warmly. In Sri Lanka, I enjoyed the company of Nicholas Crawford and many kind staff at the World Food Programme. Most importantly, I thank all the people who gave time for interviews, many of whom had suffered enormously and yet still found the strength and patience to offer their perspectives and analysis.

The book has benefited from the insights of colleagues and mentors too numerous to mention. But I would like to say a special 'thank you' to Mark Duffield, Alex de Waal, Amrita Rangasami, Fabrice Weissman, Frances Stewart, Valpy FitzGerald, John Ryle, David Jones, Paul Richards, Mats Berdal, Adekeye Adebajo, John Harriss, Hugo Slim, Megan Vaughan, Barbara Harriss-White, Tony Vaux, Nicholas Stockton, Amartya Sen and Tim Allen.

I owe special thanks to so many friends, including Cindy, Simon, James, Wolfgang, Kaori, Haro, Eric, Edward, Chandima, Jeremy, Helen, Tim, Elisa, Natalia, Maemunah, Frederik, Huw, Thomas, Georgia, Nira, Andreas, Joel, Rajeka and Hartmut. I warmly thank my family – my mum and my sister and also Joanne in the US. I would also like to thank everyone associated with St Antony's football team, past and present, for their friendship, for helping to keep me (almost) sane, and for tolerating my dwindling powers. I am very grateful to Jennifer and also everyone at Waterways nursery; also to Dr Li for his needles and fascinating conversation. Special thanks, too, to my main Oxford life-support system, Clare and Martin.

I would like to offer a big 'thank-you' hug to Sophia, already a renowned artist and still only four. Like children everywhere, she can paint a better world. Most of all I would like to thank – and dedicate this book to – Vivian, my true love, compass, halcyon and shining star. Thank-you for guiding and sustaining me – and keeping me, with your special grace, from the rocks!

Introduction

In 1995, at one of the peaks in Sierra Leone's civil war, a young man from Kailahun district in eastern Sierra Leone told me what had happened when five armed rebels entered his village:

> My younger brother was wearing a shoe boot, so they said he was a soldier. I denied it. So the armed men said we were trying to hide the government troops. I told them my brother was not a soldier. So they said I was covering for a government soldier, and in due course they will kill me. But I begged for mercy, so they never killed me. So they called up my younger brother and laid him on a long table in front of everyone and cut his throat and killed him. They asked me to clap and laugh. Having no power, I just did what they told me.[1]

This kind of appalling atrocity became commonplace during Sierra Leone's eleven-year war, which began in 1991 when a rag-tag rebel force spilled over from Liberia. The rebels, who said they were fighting against corruption and injustice, were led by Foday Sankoh, a former soldier in the Sierra Leone army and a one-time professional photographer. They were also backed by Charles Taylor, a Liberian rebel leader who later became Liberian president. For most observers, Sierra Leone's war was at once senseless and deeply confusing – and it is not hard to see why. A teenage boy recounted a rebel attack near Koribundu in the south of the country:

We decided to go to our grandfather's place, a chief. When we got there, the rebels came. My grandfather was killed by the rebels in front of the house. They put him in front of the house. They gathered his wives, and they shot him. They asked the wives to laugh.

One woman recalled how she and her cousin were put in a tiny wooden cage and rebels would drop cassava and boiled bananas into the cage – as if they were animals.[2] The woman was raped by rebels, who accused her of being a spy – part of a pattern of widespread sexual violence in the war.

In the face of such atrocities, attempts to explain or understand seem to run the risk of excusing the inexcusable. The senselessness of the atrocities is underlined when we realise that they alienated the very civilians whose support the rebels claimed to be cultivating. There were countless incidents that revealed the rebels' propensity for 'losing hearts and minds', and the rebels' cruel actions usually spoke much louder than their sometimes high-sounding words. One woman told me that rebels attacked her home town of Koidu, Kono District, in October 1992, taking diamonds and stealing food from local stores. She added sceptically: 'They said they'd come to redeem us from the past government.' A team of researchers noted in 1991: 'In Sumbuya [in southern Sierra Leone], villagers gathered voluntarily in the village *barri* [meeting place] to lend an ear to the rebels' plea for democracy; it turned out that the village was being looted behind their backs even as the high ideals were being espoused.' Many rebels also subjected civilians to forced labour.

Sadly, the habit of abusing civilians – and the gift for losing hearts and minds – was soon to be adopted by the rebels' ostensible opponents, the government soldiers. Explaining these soldiers' abuses is another challenge, and – as with the rebels – some of the perpetrators were children. On the outskirts of the capital, Freetown, I spoke with an eleven-year-old boy at the Kissy home for recovering child soldiers. The boy, who would have been eight at the time he was recruited into the government army, recalled how he had consumed gin and gunpowder, how he had learned to fire an AK-47, and how he had carried out acts of indiscriminate violence: 'When we go to a village, if they say there are no rebels, we leave', he said. 'But if we find rebels there later, we treat everyone as a rebel.' Somehow, the violence was not entirely real to him:

he was smiling winningly as he spoke of many terrible things, often laughing and periodically pretending to fall asleep.[3] If this was not some kind of madness, what is?

Revealingly, the cruelty of the rebels and government soldiers often extended to the abuse of their own fighters. Rebel recruits were frequently forced into atrocities against their own families – and branded with tattoos to increase their exposure to reprisals if they tried to 'desert'. Once recruited or abducted, rebel children were sometimes given cocaine or crack and sent in first against government forces. Meanwhile, rank-and-file government soldiers were often bullied and were routinely deprived of the most basic necessities.

The rebel force that spilled into Sierra Leone's border region from war-torn Liberia in March 1991 consisted of just a few hundred fighters. Yet this localised conflict somehow mushroomed into a conflagration that displaced more than half the country's population.[4] How was this possible? The result seemed out of all proportion to the cause.

The extremity of the rebels' violence also seems to defy explanation. How can you ever 'understand' the countless atrocities in this war, the amputation of children's arms and legs, the rapes, the cutting out of tongues, the relentless acts of cruelty by drugged-up rebels in Rambo-style headbands? It is difficult to take in the full horror of such violence, let alone explain it.

If the disproportionate displacement and the level of atrocity were at once horrific and mystifying, another deeply troubling aspect of the war was the stark fact that it endured for more than a decade. The economic devastation was enormous, and every reasonable person seemed to be against the war. Even when the considerable weight of a West African military force was thrown behind the counterinsurgency in 1998, rebel factions – containing large numbers of children and many who were high on drugs – managed to launch a devastating attack on Freetown in January 1999. After the advent of democratic government in 1996, and again after the West African force's victory in 1998, peace proved merely the prelude to more war.

Some people in the country began to speak ominously of collusion by government soldiers – an explanation for the war's longevity that itself raised many difficult questions. Why, in particular, would a fighter willingly support his enemy? Some civilians began to whisper that both 'sides' in the war were less keen on confronting each other than on carrying out violence against those who were unarmed. But again, this was an explanation that, from a military point of view, seemed to defy reason: would such tactics not simply propel civilians into the eager arms of the opposing side?[5]

That said, stories of attacks on civilians by both sides in Sierra Leone became so frequent and so detailed that they could no longer be dismissed as rumour; so, too, did stories of collaboration. Civilians reported that rebels and soldiers were coordinating their movements and abstaining from direct confrontation with each other. Government soldiers' weapons were being swapped for rebel diamonds. It seemed as though nothing helped the insurgency in Sierra Leone quite so much as the abusive and collusive counterinsurgency.

If this was a war, then, it was not war as we have commonly understood the term. A growing body of evidence suggested that this enduring conflict was actually something rather different from a contest between two sides; something more sinister; something somehow just beyond the grasp of outside observers and indeed of most of those who were suffering in Sierra Leone. A senior worker with the Ministry of Health told me: 'Our world is breaking apart, and we do not even know what is causing it. This is what is the most scary. You don't see the light at the end of the tunnel. You can't even see the tunnel.' As in several other wars, the incomprehensibility of the conflict might also have been part of the strategy.[6]

When government forces joined with rebels to form a military junta in May 1997, some suggested that covert cooperation between enemies had now come out into the open and into the capital. That gallery of rogues was kicked out by West African forces early in 1998, but they returned with a vengeance in January 1999. The devastating attack on Freetown at that time was usually attributed to 'rebels', but the invaders were actually a combustible combination of Revolutionary United Front (RUF) rebels and disgruntled government soldiers. Both elements were looking to reinstate the 1997–98 junta – effectively a joint rebel and soldier–rebel (or 'sobel') regime – and they were seeking vengeance against the civilians, civil defence forces and West African soldiers who had ousted this junta.

When we turn to other countries in Africa (and to other relatively poor parts of the world), a similar sense of horror and incomprehension is hard to avoid. Many of the wars in these countries have endured for decades or longer. In the Democratic Republic of the Congo (DRC), violent conflict has been going on – to varying degrees – since 1996. In the decade from 1998, an estimated 5.4 million people died in the DRC as a result of violence and humanitarian crisis;[7] meanwhile, rape has been notoriously widespread. In Sudan, a civil war that pitted southern rebels against the government lasted from 1955 to 1972 and then resumed from 1983 to 2005 – effectively a fifty-year war 'interrupted' by a decade of peace. Among the atrocities during this long war was the creation of a man-made famine in the south, a famine that I witnessed in 1988. Just when Sudan's catastrophic civil war was finally drawing to a close after a 2002 ceasefire agreement, another vicious war erupted in Darfur, with results that are now widely known. And then there is the case of Uganda, where war endured for some two decades after 1986 – a war that still rages in other countries where Ugandan rebels have taken refuge: Sudan, the DRC and the Central African Republic. As with the RUF in Sierra Leone, Uganda's rebel Lord's Resistance Army has generally been far inferior in strength to the Ugandan army (with many of the rebels again being children).

Angola's war lasted, with brief respites, from 1975 to 2002; Sri Lanka's endured (again with respites) from 1983 to 2009; and Guatemala's spanned the thirty-six years from 1960 to 1996. A 2007 article on Colombia noted that the country 'had been effectively in a state of civil war for at least 42 years and there are no signs that this will end soon'.[8] The armed conflict continues today.

Recently, it is true, there have been some significant grounds for hope in many parts of the world. In fact, the 2007 Human Security Brief noted a sharp fall in the number of wars and the number of war deaths in Africa since 1999, and a big rise in the number of wars brought to an end through negotiated settlements. Two factors seem to have been especially helpful. First, there has been an increased diplomatic push for peace – for example, within the UN and the African Union.[9] Secondly, the post-Cold War period seems to have been an unusually violent one, reflecting in part a troubled and violent transition to democracy in many parts of the world. We do not yet know whether the recent lull is temporary or not.[10] There are certainly many devastating wars still raging. Moreover, we seem to be entering *another* wave of democratisation (notably in the Middle East and North Africa), which could be bringing a similar wave of instability in its wake. Worryingly, the Human Security Report noted that 'campaigns of one sided violence', as well as aggregate human rights abuses around the world, have actually become more numerous since the end of the Cold War. It would seem that, if and when peace does eventually arrive, it frequently does not fix the problem of violence. In fact, post-war violence has sometimes reached levels matching or even exceeding those in wartime.[11]

While it may be comforting to think of bizarre and atrocious civil wars as a problem 'over there', many of the puzzling features of 'faraway' wars – including Sierra Leone's – find uncomfortable echoes in wars that directly involve Western powers. Longevity is one such. Think of the Cold War, which lasted forty years and (to judge from large-scale remaining missile deployments and diplomatic tensions between the West and Russia) may not quite be over. Think of the apparently endless 'war on terror' (appropriately re-dubbed 'the long war' by the George W. Bush administration). Or think of the various individual wars – notably in Iraq and Afghanistan – that have endured within these wider global wars. The plot thickens – as it did in Sierra Leone and Uganda – when these wars endure for an extended period despite a severe imbalance in military forces.

Wars directly involving Western powers have also seen a great deal of violence of the kind that predictably creates new enemies. The widespread killing of civilians in Vietnam was known to have propelled large numbers into the arms of the Communists.[12] In the early 1970s, the carpet-bombing of Cambodia by American B-52s – with around 100,000 tons of bombs dropped – was described, in Ben Kiernan's study *The Pol Pot Regime*, as 'probably the most important single factor in Pol Pot's rise'.[13] It encouraged recruits to the Khmer Rouge Communist rebels, who used the American bombing as the main theme in their propaganda and insisted that the defeat of Lon Nol was the way to stop it.[14] The bombing also added plausibility to the Khmer Rouge claim that Phnom Penh was about to be bombed by the Americans, a claim they used to encourage the mass exodus in 1975 that precipitated mass killings.[15]

Other 'proxy wars' within the Cold War have also exhibited a great deal of militarily counterproductive violence. In El Salvador, for example, the wave of state-sponsored terror in 1979–81, ostensibly to defeat the rebels, actually increased the rebels' power as they drew on a pool of activists motivated by state abuses.[16] The danger of provoking a violent backlash is underlined when we remember that provoking an overreaction – and thereby winning more recruits – has often been part of the *intention* of rebels and terrorists.

Significantly, a number of key elements in the US-led 'war on terror' have also helped to reproduce the enemy. According to the former head of MI5, Eliza Manningham-Buller, the attacks on Afghanistan and Iraq substantially increased the terror threat in Britain, and one study found that 'jihadist' terror attacks jumped sharply after the invasion of Iraq with most (but not all) of the increase a result of the wars in Iraq and Afghanistan.[17] The deaths of large numbers of civilians in those countries are also widely recognised as having stoked the fires of insurgency. On the war in Afghanistan from 2001, Sir Richard Dannatt, Chief of the General Staff, 2006–09, commented:

> A lot of the people we were killing were effectively the farmers that had AK47s put in their hands by the Taliban leadership . . . Part time Talibs and not very well trained ones and we killed huge numbers of them, and I don't think that was to our liking at all. We were conscious that really with everyone we killed, we were probably actually fuelling the insurgency.[18]

It is tempting to dismiss such apparently bizarre and counterproductive behaviour in a wide variety of wars with labels like 'chaos'[19] and 'mistakes'.[20] My own view is that, when cases of bizarre and paradoxical behaviour begin to mount up, we really need to rethink some of our most basic assumptions. The same applies when similar 'mistakes' are made over a prolonged period or even in successive wars. At some point, we need to consider that the exception may actually have become something very close to the rule.

Having witnessed many of these conflicts (or their results) at first hand, and studied them in my role as a sociology and politics specialist, I have begun to realise that many conflicts cannot be explained on the basis of the conventional assumption that war consists of two sides aiming to defeat one another. In this book, therefore, I aim to let go of this widely held assumption and instead investigate the real factors that sustain and reinforce so many brutal wars.

Rather than focusing on military 'mistakes', and asking how we can 'get it right' (for example, by killing *only* the bad guys), this book suggests that militarily counterproductive tactics in wartime may not be a problem so much as a solution. It argues that when the expressed goals in a war are not being achieved, a number of *unexpressed* goals are nevertheless being fulfilled. And it proposes that we need urgently to understand the many functions of violence, which extend well beyond winning (and consequently well beyond the period of outright war as well).

When war 'refuses' to conform to our preconceptions, it has often proven tempting to go to the other extreme and conclude that 'faraway wars' approximate to chaos and anarchy. The most influential work on these lines was probably Robert Kaplan's notorious 1994 article 'The Coming Anarchy', which was widely circulated in US government circles and which portrayed young men in West Africa as 'loose molecules in a very unstable social fluid, a fluid that was clearly on the verge of igniting.[21] In his book on Sierra Leone's war, Greg Campbell describes Freetown as 'a writhing hive of killers, villains and wretched victims'.[22] Journalists in the country often presented a sensationalist angle, and at times aid agency copy mirrored this. 'They're ripping out tongues, gouging eyes and hacking off hands. Christmas in Sierra Leone', said one Médecins Sans Frontières (MSF) advertisement in Britain's *Daily Telegraph*.[23] The temptation to portray the world in terms of gathering chaos is a longstanding one, and writers in this tradition would seem to have a secret weapon: the worse the analysis, the more the impression of chaos appears to be confirmed.

But this temptation should be resisted. It is not just unhelpful intellectually, but deeply harmful in a practical sense. All too often, this model of 'chaos' has dovetailed with the popular template of 'ethnic war' (and its close cousin, 'ancient ethnic hatreds') to wreak havoc on conflict-affected societies. A tragic example was Rwanda in 1994. Here, the world's media (and indeed the UN secretary-general) tended to present mass violence as a spontaneous 'Hutu versus Tutsi' conflict that was driven by senseless hatred – a damaging misrepresentation that helped to delay international recognition that this was actually a carefully planned genocide. In the crucial first four weeks of the Rwandan genocide, both the UN Security Council and the UN Secretariat focused their attention on the 'civil war' in Rwanda, virtually ignoring the genocide and the possibility of organising peacekeepers to prevent or reduce it.[24]

This book suggests that a great many wars are resistant to ending for the simple (but hidden) reason that powerful actors (both local and international) *do not want* them to end. If that sounds like a conspiracy theory, in many ways it *is* a conspiracy theory. But while powerful actors *may* seek selfishly to prolong a war (or to find a new one to replace it), the theory does not stand or fall by such Machiavellian behaviour. Very often, powerful actors may simply pursue other priorities that conflict with the expressed goal of winning (actions that may have the *effect* of reproducing the enemy, or that may simply take time, energy and resources away from 'winning').

As Hannah Arendt noted back in 1971, governments are motivated not just by winning wars but by the desire to be *seen to be* winning in the eyes of their own electorates.[25] This latter goal may be very different from actually winning (and indeed a *pretence* of winning may remove any small chance of addressing the issues that are, in the real world, impeding victory).

Crucially, an overt and publicly expressed intention to defeat some demon enemy – whether RUF rebels in Sierra Leone or the Viet Cong in Vietnam or the Taliban in Afghanistan – has repeatedly created huge opportunities for diverse actors within the counterinsurgency to engage in politically and economically advantageous abuse with minimal international criticism (and very often with significant international encouragement and assistance).

Meanwhile, the institutional interests of Western militaries and related industries have also fed into tactics that reproduce the enemy, as well as into the reproduction of war through a constant 'discovery' of new enemies. The arms industries in the West and the military industrial complexes in many less developed countries are intimately linked. Both feed off a sense of 'permanent emergency'. Meanwhile, the subordination of Western aid to concerns like 'security' and 'economic liberalisation' has helped to sustain a great many abusive governments, even as the 'greed' and 'irrationality' of rebels are loudly condemned.

Further eroding the primacy of 'winning' have been the diverse psychological functions of violence, which have themselves routinely encouraged attacks on powerless groups with no relation – or minimal relation – to rebels or terrorists. The book examines the distribution of shame in wartime and at war's end, and shows how shame has fed into further violence.

To pre-empt misunderstanding, I am not attempting to argue that all wars are the same, or that winning has become – or has ever been – irrelevant in warfare. Of course, there are wars (perhaps more scarce than we imagine) where winning *is* the overriding priority. This usually reflects the existence – and the widespread perception – of a genuine threat to the existence of a nation or a community. One immediately thinks of the Allied effort to defeat Nazi Germany, an endeavour that continues powerfully to shape Western ideas of what war *is* and *ought to be*. Even here, the picture was not quite so simple: the political and economic advantages of preparing for war, at least on the Nazi side, were considerable; the mass extermination of the Jews in many ways distracted from the war effort; and mass reprisals by the Nazis predictably created new rebels in occupied areas.[26] Moreover, some of the Allied violence – like the firebombing of German cities and the nuclear bombs on Hiroshima and Nagasaki – was itself indiscriminate and vindictive.

I want to stress that winning is only *one part* of war (and sometimes a surprisingly small part). A genuine desire among the American people and many US officials to 'defeat' terrorism can be argued to coexist with interests – both in America and in, say, Afghanistan, Pakistan and Somalia – that have 'downgraded' winning in relation to other goals (with some people actually favouring the prolongation, rather than the cessation, of conflict). Complexities abound: even violence that is perpetrated for economic gain will naturally produce a desire (within the victimised community) for survival, and the best way to survive may sometimes be 'winning' (or at least *not losing*). Thus, one side may seek (primarily) to exploit, while the other side seeks (primarily) to win. A good case is Sudan, where economic motives were very important in fuelling attacks on the south, but the resulting desire to survive and 'win' eventually culminated in the creation of a new state.[27]

Taking seriously the multiplicity of agendas in wartime means looking at the economic functions of war – war as a continuation of economics by other means – and it means looking at political and psychological functions too. While these various functions are difficult to separate rigidly, there is a focus on economic functions in chapters 1 and 2, and a great deal on economic agendas in chapters 3 (on Vietnam) and 4 (on Afghanistan). Political functions are directly addressed in chapters 5, 6, and 7, while chapter 8 looks at the US war economy and chapter 9 focuses on the psychological functions of violence, especially the role of shame.

To get a better sense of what some of this means 'on the ground', it is worth going back to the strange and vicious war in Sierra Leone.

CHAPTER 1

Resource Wars

It was the summer of 1995 and, in a rather unaccustomed act of semi-bravery, I had decided to take a small propeller plane from the capital Freetown to Sierra Leone's second city of Bo, which was itself relatively secure but was also surrounded by ferocious fighters. We soared over the leonine mountains from which Sierra Leone takes its name, and I looked down at the forests and roads below. Although nervous of flying, I find that the prospect of roadblocks 'manned' by drugged-out and machine-gun wielding children makes for excellent therapy.

Soon the young man next to me was introducing himself as a student and informing me of the professions and extracurricular activities of our fellow passengers. 'That man is a teacher,' he said, gesturing towards the back of the plane, before adding in a whisper, 'but he is also trading diamonds.' Nodding towards a middle-aged man on the other side of the plane, my acquaintance continued in his confidential tone: 'That man is an aid worker . . . but he is also dealing in diamonds. They are very portable.' Sensing a pattern, I observed that this kind of commerce seemed to be common. 'Oh, yes!', the young man replied with an air of quiet triumph. 'The pilot is also trading diamonds!'

At this point, my young companion switched the topic to himself. In addition to being a student, he observed cautiously, he was also a businessman. Perhaps, he suggested, I might care to liaise on the export side? I will not insult the reader's intelligence by revealing the nature of this young man's trade. But I was beginning to suspect that I was the only mug on the plane who was failing to profit from the trafficking in precious stones.

The more I inquired into the war in Sierra Leone (and at this point I was talking mostly with the victims of attacks), the more I came to realise that much of the violence was economically motivated. Apparently inexplicable and counterproductive behaviour – whether on the part of rebels or government soldiers – began to make more sense when viewed through an economic lens.[1] Soldiers' collusion with rebels took the form not only of minimising military confrontation with rebels, but also of mining diamonds in areas where rebels were also mining. There were several instances of coordinated attacks against civilians. Most surprising of all was the willingness of some government soldiers to exchange arms and ammunition for rebel diamonds – a trade that amounted to arming the enemy.

In these circumstances, informants began to talk of a 'sell-game' – a football match that had been fixed in advance. A local aid worker, whose work had brought him into contact with government soldiers, as well as with youths linked to the rebels, told me that government troops

> ... would sit down in security meetings and discuss where to attack, and usually when agreement was made, this message was sent across to the guys in the bush, the rebels, that you have to be ready. Most of the military were selling the game – abandoning weapons ... They would exchange the weapons for diamonds.

More and more people were talking about the soldier-rebels or 'sobels'. One internal report of the aid agency Catholic Relief Services noted that the army 'showed no signs of being on a war footing. Non-commissioned officers had taken up residence as town chiefs. They forcibly took local women as "wives" and used the village manpower to cultivate cash crops and dig for diamonds.'[2] Sierra Leone's diamonds had been part of the attraction for Charles Taylor, the Liberian rebel – later to be president – who helped to sponsor the initial Revolutionary United Front (RUF) incursion into Sierra Leone in 1991 and who trained with RUF leader Foday Sankoh in Gaddafi's Libya.[3] Soon, control of mining areas became a key goal of *many parties* in this complex war.[4] A French aid worker involved in rehabilitation work in 1993 said a lull in fighting had prompted soldiers to stage ambushes – so as to justify their presence in diamond-rich areas. Where civilians opposed illegal mining by armed groups, violence was used to intimidate – or simply eject – the civilians.

When reports began to accumulate of government soldiers abusing civilians, those soldiers tended to be reclassified as 'deserters', rebels or 'sobels'. In Orwellian mode, government abuse almost became impossible *by definition*.

In Bo, I had the chance to speak to a worker at an important bauxite mine called Sieromco, a young man who went into hiding at the mine when he heard civilians call out that rebels had attacked. While in hiding, the mineworker had recognised some of the 'attackers' as government soldiers who had earlier arrived by helicopter – ostensibly to defend the mine against rebels. Now their military fatigues had been supplemented by rebel-style 'Rambo' bandanas. (The impunity of soldiers who undertook such impersonation was sometimes reinforced by the rebels' habit of claiming 'credit' for attacks they had not actually carried out.)

After the attack, the official government line was that 250 rebels had attacked Sieromco and the nearby Sierra Rutile mining site. This prompted the Sieromco worker into some sceptical arithmetic: 'We had seventy-one men [government soldiers] at Sieromco. In Rutile they had around 150. Twenty-seven rebels entered [a figure the mine worker had been given by refugees from the nearby village of Bendoma]. We were told later that the strength of the rebels was around 250. You add it up.' These mines were, in theory, well protected: they were a high priority for the government, which relied heavily on export earnings from them. Yet mine employees reported that not a single shot was fired when rebels 'attacked'.

What had happened at the time of the May 1997 coup was that a covert and symbiotic relationship between rogue government soldiers and rebels had finally come out into the open. Coup leader Johnny Koroma had been part of the 'sobel' element in the army,[5] and upcountry collusion had now come to the capital. It soon became clear that the newly installed rogue soldiers and RUF rebels – as well as many of the coup's business backers – were intent on defending what were effectively 'joint venture' diamond operations upcountry, operations that had been challenged by civilian defence forces and by the country's democratic government from 1996.[6] They also seemed concerned to prevent any legal recriminations, and attacked courts and buildings holding public records.[7]

While astonishing at one level, the upcountry collaboration of rebels and soldiers was in line with some long-established patterns in Sierra

Leone (and many other poor countries, for that matter).[8] In peacetime, Sierra Leonean government officials had repeatedly been sent out to control the smuggling of diamonds and other valuable commodities. But these officials, generally underpaid and often under-motivated, had routinely been drawn into collusion with the very networks they were supposed to be suppressing – a case of gamekeeper habitually turning poacher. In effect, a chronically weak state had been persistently unable to confront or control a largely illegal economic system based on lucrative international trading – and in wartime this process mutated in dangerous ways.

Underpaid and under-motivated government soldiers – with very little reason to remain loyal to a state that was generally displaying an extreme contempt for their welfare – were now being sent out to confront elusive rebels who were drawing sustenance from smuggling (notably diamond smuggling). 'Sell-game' – and the widespread abuse of civilians by government soldiers – was the result. Often, rank-and-file soldiers would see their superiors making substantial private profits and would then feel entitled to feather their own more modest nests.[9] Resisting the lure of diamonds and other resources was not made any easier when the difficult task of confronting elusive and vicious rebels was offloaded onto a hastily assembled rag-tag army that itself included many children.

We frequently assume that 'the two sides' in a war have diametrically opposed objectives. But in Sierra Leone, government soldiers and rebels came from a similar 'demographic'; they also shared many goals, including those of staying alive, getting access to some resources and enjoying a sense of power that the gun could bring.

Internationally, a number of betting scandals in cricket and football have reminded us that when we think we know what 'game' is being played we can be very much mistaken. The war in Sierra Leone had strong elements of a 'fixed' sporting fixture, and the assumption that the overriding aim within government circles was defeating rebel 'bad guys' actually created space for a wide variety of parties to engage in their own exploitative 'games' under the cover of a self-righteous war. Meanwhile, international support for an abusive military regime contributed damagingly to this impunity.

Part of my interest in flying to Bo in 1995 was that Sierra Leone's second city had become a focus of efforts by civilians to stand up to what was emerging as a *twin threat* from rebels and rogue government soldiers. Adapting a familiar English saying in a way that is common in Sierra Leone, one local human rights worker told me: 'We are between the deep blue sea and the devil.' Faced with this double jeopardy, civilians had organised themselves into civil defence organisations that were based on ancient hunting societies (or *kamajors*), while both soldiers and rebels had retaliated by intensifying their atrocities and by restricting food supplies to towns like Bo.

Unfortunately, the democratic regime under President Tejan Kabbah (installed in 1996) did not deal adequately with continuing grievances in the army. The army was already smarting from having been sidelined when, in another bizarre alliance, civil defence forces joined with the South African mercenary company Executive Outcomes to confront rebels and rogue soldiers. In Bo, a curfew was established and it was *the army* that could not venture out at night. The alliance between civil defence forces and mercenaries eventually permitted the 1996 peace agreement and Kabbah's elected government.

President Kabbah got a minimal response from Britain and the US when he requested help with training the national army.[10] Meanwhile, the International Monetary Fund (IMF) pressed successfully for a reduction in security spending. Military rations were cut in half, and Kabbah was talking about reducing the army to 3,000–4,000 (from perhaps 10,000 or 12,000).[11] Although donors were promising significant sums of money for the rehabilitation of Sierra Leone as a whole, they were still offering very little for those who might be demobilised from the army (or from the rebels and civil defence forces, for that matter).[12] In February 1997, following pressure from the IMF, Executive Outcomes left the country, creating a major security vacuum.[13]

The claimed numerical strength of the army was actually significantly higher than the actual strength, and senior officers were pocketing salaries and rations for these 'ghost soldiers'. Moreover, salaries and rations for 'real soldiers' were still subject to diversion.

On 25 May 1997, a group of disgruntled soldiers arrested a number of senior officers and then used grenades to blast open Pademba Road prison, an overcrowded and unsanitary compound in Sierra Leone's ramshackle capital, Freetown. The soldiers released some 600 inmates and gave arms to freed soldiers and ordinary criminals. One of those released was Major Johnny Paul Koroma, who was thirty-three at the time and had been trained at Sandhurst military academy in the UK before serving in Sierra Leone's civil war. He had been locked up for allegedly plotting a coup the previous year. Koroma quickly emerged as leader of the 1997 coup-makers.

One aid worker told me how he had seen some of the 1997 coup-makers take out their frustrations on senior officers: 'I saw them tie down one of the senior officers, Major Henry, and accuse him of stealing from ordinary soldiers. These guys freed Johnny Paul [Koroma] and he stopped them from killing senior officers and even politicians.' Koroma told me later about his encounter with the soldiers who released him from Pademba Road prison:

> A group of soldiers stormed the prison and they got me out . . . They said you must be our leader. They said if you are going to escape, we will kill you and your family. Their first intention was to kill all the senior officers and politicians. I stopped them . . . The problem is with the officers . . . When I was in Sandhurst [military academy], British guys were saying you have good and bad officers but you don't have good and bad soldiers. That is true . . .

The lasting enmities that civil wars create are not to be underestimated, and Sierra Leone's war had seen government soldiers apparently pitted against a vicious group of rebels for the previous six years. Yet virtually the first thing that Major Koroma did on taking over power was to ring up the rebel leader, Foday Sankoh, and invite him into the government! Particularly given that there had been no peace process to speak of, the offer was deeply surprising to most observers. Sankoh, for his part, was quick to give his blessing to soldiers he had ostensibly been fighting for years, and in a phone conversation with Koroma, he called on his own rebel fighters to come out of the bush and join the soldiers in Freetown. Sankoh was in detention in Nigeria at the time, but still had access to communications. With the help of a speakerphone and a cassette recorder, his message was relayed over the radio in Sierra Leone.[14]

In such a bitter war, this call was surely unlikely to go down well with Sankoh's foot-soldiers. Yet thousands of rebels began – apparently without hesitation – to descend on the capital in solidarity with the new government.[15] Koroma commented: 'We had to extend an olive branch to the RUF so we could stop the fighting. They came out within seventy-two hours.' One former rebel told me that his colleagues had already infiltrated Freetown. Many observers felt that the coup must have been planned and carried out with the active collaboration of the rebels.[16]

Upcountry, the rebels' bizarre behaviour was observed by a delegate from the ousted democratic government, who had been captured by the rebels some two months earlier. On the day of the coup, roughly a thousand rebel fighters had assembled and travelled to the small town of Pendembu. Again, one does not normally expect armed rebels to head straight for an army barracks (unless they are going to attack it). But this rebel group drove directly to the major army barracks at Daru, clearly anticipating a friendly reception. There, rebel and government troops began parading together. A joint party then drove to Freetown. While there was a degree of wariness of the opposing faction,[17] the rebels and soldiers seemed more concerned about a possible attack by a *kamajor* civilian defence force: some thirty RUF rebels and thirty government soldiers together shouted into the bush, demanding that the *kamajors* 'watch out'.

It was a strange – and for many civilians a rather queasy – reconciliation between such apparently implacable enemies, now joined together in unholy matrimony. But arguably *any kind* of reconciliation is helpful in the midst of such a destructive civil war. The new junta quickly stated that the war was over, and the sight of two enemies parading together might reasonably be taken as an indication that peace was on the horizon.

In the event, despite the overt cooperation of the two opposing sides, violence *intensified*. The rebel/government forces carried out a series of vicious attacks on the *kamajor* civil defence and their relatives, and there were sustained waves of looting – both upcountry and in the capital. One young man living in the capital at the time told me: 'Vast numbers opposed the junta in Freetown, but for safety it was better to keep indoors and keep a sealed mouth. Early morning you would see corpses out on the street.' If this was peace, it was one that surpassed most people's understanding.

Fast-forward to January 1999. The joint-junta had by this time been ousted from power by the combined military forces of West African 'peacekeepers', and there were some 12,000 or 15,000 of these protecting the new democratic government, which had been restored with the full backing of the international community. The reinstated Kabbah government was now also being protected by civil defence forces and a reconstituted and reformed national army. Meanwhile, the disgraced coup-makers were riven by internal tensions – not least between the RUF and army elements.

And yet, in late 1998 and January 1999, a dishevelled group of rebels and rogue soldiers – many of them children, many of them traumatised, and many of them high on cocaine – were somehow able to seize control of much of the country before taking Freetown, where they went on a killing spree. After these massacres, the government's senior pathologist registered the burial of 7,335 people. The sudden and unexpected collapse of the capital – and the extreme nature of the violence – only added to the impression among many Sierra Leoneans that this was a senseless and incomprehensible war. Others still saw the war in conventional terms – as a contest between rebels and government forces. And a third group of observers – in many ways better informed – were beginning to detect some kind of criminal conspiracy. What none of these frameworks offered, however, was an explanation for the sheer fury of the January 1999 attackers, for their murderous rage against civilians, or for their surprising sense of self-righteousness. I later had the chance to interview a young man who had taken part in the attack on Freetown. 'I was the first into Freetown on 6 January', he said proudly. 'I don't mind who knows it!' Some of the attackers later seized hostages, and one of those held hostage remembered their attitude to the January attacks: 'No remorse', he said. 'For some, it was like an achievement.' At any rate, the January 1999 attack represented an astonishing reverse, particularly as the West African force had some 12,000–15,000 soldiers in Sierra Leone in 1998. How could this happen?

In answering this question, it may be helpful first to revisit some of the basic dynamics of war in Sierra Leone. A traditional view of war, as we have seen, is that two sides are battling for victory. In a civil war, we also tend to imagine that either side will have a different vision of how it wishes society to be constructed. Meanwhile, we may suppose that civilians can fall victim to this struggle when 'caught in the crossfire'. But in Sierra Leone the ideological contest, while not entirely absent, was remarkably unclear. Civilians were *intentionally* victimised. And battles were usually avoided.

A different way of thinking is needed. Broadly, the war in Sierra Leone shows what can happen when a series of military organisations – exhibiting varying degrees of internal dysfunction – are sent into a resource-rich environment. In these circumstances, war may not resemble a contest so much as a 'black hole', a hole that threatens to consume each military force that is dispatched into it. In Sierra Leone, several successive military organisations were deflected (to varying degrees) from their original purpose (or at least from their original *stated* purpose). It started with the rebels, whose weakly articulated ideology was quickly corrupted by diamonds and other valuable resources. Then came the government soldiers, who were poorly paid, deprived of essential supplies by corruption among senior officers, and increasingly distracted from counterinsurgency by diamonds and other resources. Before long, the civil defence forces had themselves become embroiled in the diamond business – and in looting. As with the government army, corruption at senior levels of the civil defence fed into abuses lower down. One confidential report on the civil defence forces noted: 'the belief that their own commanders are misappropriating supplies with impunity leads many to ask what is wrong with them harassing and appropriating community supplies at a local level'.[18]

Also helping to explain the rapid advance towards Freetown of rag-tag rebels in late 1998 was a fourth variation of this process: namely that members of the West African military force, known as ECOMOG, were themselves becoming dazzled by diamonds.

Through late 1998, the rebel-soldier ex-junta forces made quick progress, wresting control of the Kono diamond district from the West African ECOMOG forces and then moving relentlessly towards Freetown. Despite some serious ECOMOG resistance in Kono and some heavy ECOMOG casualties there, ECOMOG soldiers were widely accused of being distracted from military priorities by diamond mining, with some ECOMOG soldiers even accusing their own officers.[19] Once again, there was also active collaboration with the enemy: a UN Panel of Experts reported in 2000 that it 'heard an overwhelming number of reports on Nigerian ECOMOG troops exchanging weapons with the RUF for cash, diamonds, food or other goods'.[20] One young aid worker from Kono district in the east told me:

Nigerians were mining diamonds there. If their attention was on military matters, the RUF would never have taken Kono in 1998. Nigerians were more interested in the mines ... The RUF infiltrated in substantial numbers. In 1998, the RUF was capturing lots of towns

from the Nigerians. They used Nigerian tanks to drive through to
Makeni . . . Enticement was a big tactic. Nigerian soldiers would fall
for them [RUF women] and be enticed. There were lapses in their
alertness.

The Sierra Leonean army had meanwhile been slimmed down to around
3,000, and it included significant numbers of soldiers absorbed from the
junta that was ousted by West African troops in February 1998. That
contributed to tensions between the army and ECOMOG – tensions
that added to the problems in confronting resurgent junta forces. In
addition – and partly in response to a growing chorus of criticism – the
number of ECOMOG troops was, by the end of 1998, being scaled
down.[21]

In contrast to ECOMOG, the ex-junta forces were *drawing strength*
from the diamond economy and from international actors seeking to
get their hands on the diamonds. While some ECOMOG soldiers were
using weapons to acquire diamonds, the rebels were using diamonds to
acquire weapons – not only from ECOMOG, but also from abroad. The
ex-junta forces got equipment and training from Ukrainian and South
African mercenaries, and their business backers included South African
and Israeli diamond interests.[22]

When a solution to Sierra Leone's war did eventually emerge between
2000 and 2002, it hinged on getting away from the previous preoccupa-
tion with rebels as the sole cause of the war. One key element was the
dispatch of British military forces. British troops helped to protect
Freetown, sent a resolute signal to the RUF, and confronted the rogue
army faction known as the West Side Boys.[23] Britain's willingness directly
to confront the rebels themselves has often been exaggerated, however.[24]
And a key contribution came from the British-led effort to retrain and
reorganise the *national army* – an army that had been such a crucial
cause of instability.[25]

A second element contributing to peace was a major step-up in the
UN peacekeeping effort: the UN force was given a stronger mandate
and was expanded to the point where it became the largest in the world;[26]
meanwhile, the resources available within this greatly expanded
international effort were themselves a significant incentive for peace-
able behaviour, particularly in the context of such a small country.[27] A
third factor was the military involvement of neighbouring Guinea (in

association with *kamajors*), which severely weakened the rebels; and a fourth was the international effort to rein in a 'war economy' that had sucked in numerous factions in Sierra Leone. A key factor fuelling this war economy – as in Angola's enduring war further south – had been the willingness of the de Beers international cartel, in particular, to 'mop up' any diamonds that might fall outside its worldwide buying operation – an operation that underpinned diamonds' artificially high prices on world markets.[28] But de Beers was coming under pressure to dissociate itself from 'blood diamonds', and the UN was now pushing for tougher regulations. Suspicions that al Qaeda was laundering funds by buying West African 'blood diamonds' added to this momentum.[29]

In June 2000, the UN passed a resolution demanding that all states take measures to prohibit the direct or indirect import of rough diamonds from Sierra Leone, and requiring the government of Sierra Leone to implement a certificate-of-origin system for diamond exports, so that diamonds from RUF areas could be distinguished from other diamonds.

This was no panacea: some diamonds from the RUF were still getting certificates within Sierra Leone; and smuggling into Liberia remained an option.[30] Another problem was that sanctions on Liberia itself were significantly weakened by richer countries' interests: China and France blocked timber sanctions for two years (until May 2003), reflecting their own import interests.[31] Even so, the long-established smuggling into Liberia (where de Beers had been buying) was addressed when increased diplomatic pressure, notably from the US, was applied to Liberia to stop its dealings with the RUF. In March 2001, Liberian diamond exports were banned by the UN Security Council and a travel ban was imposed on senior Liberian officials.

A holistic approach to Sierra Leone's war, taking seriously the war economy and the abuses within the counterinsurgency, had finally brought this terrible war to a close.

***

If we look closely at a number of other civil wars, we can see that the model of war-as-a-contest can be similarly misleading. Again, we need to understand the war economy. We need to understand the prevalence of militarily counterproductive tactics. And we need to understand the abuses, often hidden or systematically downplayed, that have flourished within the counterinsurgency.

In many civil wars, rival factions have exhibited a strong inclination to avoid direct confrontation with each other and a preference for directing their violence at civilians.[32] This has frequently helped the enemy in two ways: first, by allowing it to operate, and, second, by encouraging (attacked) civilians to side with the enemy.

In the DRC, Rwandan troops proved surprisingly reluctant to confront their sworn enemies (who had participated in genocide).[33] In Cambodia, there was covert cooperation between Khmer Rouge leaders and officers in the Cambodian army in the 1980s.[34] In Angola, government soldiers traded with rebels.[35] And so it goes on.

Shelton Davis notes that in Guatemala's civil war indigenous groups joined the guerrillas more in search of defence against the army and death squads than from ideological motives.[36] David Stoll observed:

> The army's violence backfired. Instead of suppressing the guerrillas, it multiplied a small band of outsiders into a liberation army, mostly Indians drawn from local communities. By the end of 1980, government atrocities seemed to have alienated the entire Ixil population [Ixil was a key region for the rebels].[37]

When I visited Guatemala in 2002, former rebel leader Rodrigo Asturias told me about his government soldier opponents:

> ... they were sometimes more interested in attacking civilians than armed rebels ... Despite being very desirable to attack a guerrilla concentration, it was very costly – and particularly when going against well-trained troops who'd been perfecting military strategies for a long time, using traps, holes in the ground, mines. They could lose a whole thirty people.

In Uganda from the mid-1980s, the government alienated civilians by forcing them into camps, which duly became centres for rebel and militia recruitment.[38] In Chechnya, rebels received a powerful boost from Russia's aggressive intervention in December 1994.[39] It is true that repression against civilians can in some circumstances terrorise people into quiescence. But such violence does usually generate resistance – sometimes with a delay. As Frances Stewart and her colleagues observed, 'In Indonesia, the viciousness of the Indonesian armed forces' response to the original, small-scale Acehnese rebellion [in 1977] boosted support for the movement when it re-emerged [in 1989].'[40]

Consider also the case of Turkey, sometimes mentioned as a case of repression that 'worked'. In the early 1990s, after the forcible evacuation of Kurdish villages in south-eastern Turkey in response to activity by the separatist PKK (Kurdistan Workers' Party), some 3 million Kurds were displaced, most of them into urban areas where their living conditions were dire. It is true that the PKK military forces were gravely weakened – and the PKK leadership more conciliatory – by the turn of the century. But PKK violence and government repression continued. One detailed 2011 study noted: 'These displaced Kurds in shanty towns became more radicalized. Paradoxically, the evacuation strategy, formulated to destroy the PKK in the rural areas, turned into a new opportunity structure for PKK recruitment, and it transformed the PKK into an urban organization.'[41] Moreover, '. . . the state harshness that has prevented the rise of legitimate Kurdish political actors has helped the PKK perpetuate itself as the dominant influence in Kurdish politics'.[42]

Enemy reproduction has been routine in Sudan. From 2003, the western Sudanese region of Darfur saw government-sponsored militia attacks that predictably radicalised civilians – and thereby created more rebels.[43] In December 2003, the International Crisis Group noted: 'The latest attacks occurred deep inside the Fur tribal domain, against unprotected villages with no apparent link to the rebels other than their ethnic profile.'[44] A few months later, the organisation noted: 'The government's heavy-handed counter-insurgency campaign has facilitated a major recruiting drive for the rebels, as suggested by the scarcity of young men in the refugee and IDP camps.'[45]

In the late 1980s, I was able to investigate a forerunner of the Darfur catastrophe. This was a man-made famine that resulted in some of the highest death rates ever recorded. The famine took place in the relatively lawless 'borderlands' that span Sudan's northern regions (normally, but in some ways misleadingly, labelled 'Arab')[46] and in the southern regions that harboured a rebellion by the Sudan People's Liberation Army (SPLA).[47] Prefiguring the later crisis in Darfur from 2003, the most important cause of this famine was merciless raiding by northern Arab militias, in this case mostly Baggara cattle herders. As today, Arab groups were used as an instrument of counterinsurgency by a Sudanese government that was severely strapped for cash.

The Dinka ethnic group, in particular, was seen by Khartoum as guilty by association with the SPLA rebels, and the rebels themselves stood in the way of exploiting some vast oil reserves that could potentially pay off Khartoum's huge international debts.

As later in Darfur, the problem (from a counterinsurgency point of view) was that raids on people not linked to the rebels – whether southern civilians or people from the Nuba ethnic group – tended to make them more radical. In fact, these raids had the effect of encouraging support for the rebel SPLA – even in areas that had (before the raids) been relatively neutral.[48] And this also tended to spread the war to new geographical areas.[49]

Whether the creation of new rebels represented 'failure' is a moot point, however. Spreading rebellion to new geographical areas had the effect of legitimising the exploitation of new groups of civilians under the cover of war – exploitation that included stealing cattle and gaining access to southern grazing land. The raiding also offered the prospect of access to oil – significantly, many of the areas of greatest famine were also the areas of greatest oil (areas that remain subject to violence even today). And finally, there was widespread profiteering from price changes that accompanied – and helped to drive – the famine in the south. These damaging market trends included sharply rising grain prices (as the southern Sudanese were desperate for food), plummeting cattle prices (as the southern Sudanese were desperate to sell cattle in order to buy food), and falling labour prices (which could even reach 'zero' in conditions of renewed slavery).

Consider also the war in the Democratic Republic of the Congo, which has been even more destructive than those in Sierra Leone and Sudan. The figure of 5.4 million dead in the decade from 1998 bears repeating. Here again, economic motivations have played a key role – and exploitation by regional powers has been critically important.

A UN Panel of Experts found that, in eastern DRC, Ugandan commanders had been arming and training militias from the Hema ethnic group.[50] It was not so unusual to find a regional power supporting an ethnic faction in a neighbouring country; in fact, this has been a pretty common way in which wars spread. What was especially shocking – and sinister – in this case was that the Ugandans were also training the Lendu militias that were fighting the Hema![51] While this looked like a particularly senseless policy, the UN Panel observed, 'There are strong indications that some UPDF [Ugandan armed forces] elements may spark violence so as to remain in the region in an attempt to control the gold-rich area and the potentially coltan-rich areas of Nyaleki [in north-eastern DRC].'[52] (Coltan is valuable, in large part, because it is an essential component of mobile phones and laptops.) It is clear that the illegal exploitation of a variety of natural resources in the DRC was enriching Ugandan military commanders, as well as 'elite' Ugandan civilians.[53] Ugandan officers were reported to be paying for valuable minerals with salaries that had been intended for ordinary Ugandan soldiers.[54] Ugandan commanders also turned a blind eye to their own soldiers' racketeering – apparently as a way of rewarding them.[55]

Rwanda had also become deeply embroiled in the Congolese conflict – and at one level, this was entirely understandable. In 1994, militiamen from Rwanda's Hutu ethnic group had taken part in the murder of some 800,000 Rwandan citizens (mostly from the Tutsi ethnic group, but also some Hutus). (Ethnicity was partly a colonial construction, but ethnic labels had become a dangerous reality, and there were even official identity cards that specified your ethnicity.) When Tutsi rebels seized power in Rwanda and put a stop to the 1994 genocide, Hutu militias (ably assisted by France) took refuge in eastern DRC, where they were planning to resume their murderous campaign inside Rwanda. It was natural that the Rwandan army would want to track down and neutralise this vicious group of militiamen: if ever there was an incentive to confront a group of armed men, then surely this was it. What only a few observers noticed, however, was that Rwandan soldiers were increasingly exhibiting a marked *lack of desire* to confront the Hutu militias in the DRC. Rwandan soldiers were making little effort to engage them in battle, and they were also reported to be stalling on attempts to disarm the Hutu militias. Some Rwandan soldiers were even reported to be supplying arms to these 'genocidaires'.[56] Again, it just didn't make any sense.

But, as so often, this apparently bizarre behaviour begins to make more sense if we consider the economic motivations at play. In particular, the war in the DRC was generating huge resources for the Rwandan army, which is estimated to have made a profit of at least $250 million over an eighteen-month period in 1999–2000 and (according to the UN Panel) is supposed to have used Rwandan military aircraft and the planes of notorious Russian criminal and arms dealer Victor Bout.[57] The 2001 UN Panel noted:

All military experts consulted suggested that the official defence budget of Rwanda cannot alone cover the cost of their war and presence in the Democratic Republic of the Congo. The Panel concurs with [Rwanda's] President Kagame, who described the conflict in the Democratic Republic of the Congo as 'a self-financing war'.[58]

The UN Panel of Experts looked at the DRC 'battlefront'[59] (which was fluid but ran roughly north-west to south-east, dividing government forces from rebels and their Ugandan and Rwandan allies). Then it compared this 'battlefront' with those zones in the east that were controlled by (feuding) rebels and their respective Ugandan and Rwandan allies. In the period from mid-1999 to 2002, skirmishes in the Ugandan- and Rwandan-controlled zones numbered ninety-six, while the number of battles in what was supposedly the main battlefront numbered only nine. Moreover, these battlefront skirmishes were becoming less common as time went by.[60] The final report of the UN Panel, dated October 2002, observed:

> The claims of Rwanda concerning its security have justified the continuing presence of its armed forces, whose real long-term purpose is, to use the term employed by the Congo Desk of the Rwandan Patriotic Army, to 'secure property'. Rwanda's leaders have succeeded in persuading the international community that their military presence in the eastern Democratic Republic of the Congo protects the country against hostile groups in the Democratic Republic of the Congo, who, they claim, are actively mounting an invasion against them. The Panel has extensive evidence to the contrary.[61]

One example was a May 2000 letter from Jean-Pierre Ondekane, chief of the military high command for RCD-Goma (a faction of the Rwanda-supported Rally for Congolese Democracy) urging all army units to maintain good relations 'with our Interahamwe [genocidaires] and Mayi-Mayi [community-based militias] brothers' and 'if necessary to let them exploit the sub-soil for their survival'.[62] In early 2002, a thirty-year-old Interahamwe combatant living in Bukavu, eastern DRC, told a UN officer:

> We haven't fought much with the RPA [Rwandan Patriotic Army] in the last two years. We think they are tired of this war, like we are. In

any case, they aren't here in the Congo to chase us, like they pretend. I have seen the gold and coltan mining they do here, we see how they rob the population. These are the reasons for their being here. The RPA come and shoot in the air and raid the villagers' houses but they don't attack us any more. If you are lucky, and you have a big brother in the RPA, he might be able to get you some food and ammunition.[63]

In general, the reports of the UN Panel – much more revealing than the bureaucratic and deferential statements that are often produced within the UN system – showed just how misleading it can be to assume that the overriding aim of warring parties is military 'victory'. Significantly, violence has been strongly concentrated in resource-rich zones, and many of the most lucrative areas have been controlled by forces from acquisitive neighbouring countries.

If Uganda was interfering damagingly in the DRC, Uganda's own civil war demonstrated again just how dangerous it can be to assume that winning in wartime is the overriding objective. Back in 1986, atrocities against the Acholi people had helped to spur a rebellion in northern Uganda,[64] and the main rebel movement that eventually emerged was known as the Lord's Resistance Army (LRA). In the decades that followed, the Ugandan government – with an estimated 30,000 soldiers deployed in northern Uganda in 2002[65] – somehow proved unable to suppress a movement whose core fighters numbered perhaps between 1,000 and 4,000. This 'failure' occurred despite the fact that the rebels lacked a coherent political ideology and that their ancillary forces consisted, to a large extent, of children.[66]

In his ground-breaking study of this war (called *Social Torture*), Chris Dolan shows that the Ugandan civil war cannot realistically be portrayed as 'government versus rebels', and he reveals how government tactics actually fed strongly into continued violence. By 2003, there were some 800,000 displaced people in northern Uganda, most of them forced into government camps by government troops (including through the use of shelling). While the camps were ostensibly designed to protect civilians from the rebels, the 'safety' they provided was extremely precarious and it often related more directly to safety from *government* attacks. In practice, the forcible nature of the relocation – and the miserable conditions in these camps – further alienated the Acholi population, and the camps encouraged military recruitment into a range of armed

groups, including the government army, various militias and, significantly, the rebels themselves. That helped to sustain the rebellion
and the war more generally. Importantly, the replenishing of rebel
ranks from the camps took place in a context where Acholi civilians had
every reason to *reject* a rebel group whose abuses included the widespread abduction of children. Again, a violent official backlash against
terror helped limit a *popular* backlash. Meanwhile, whenever a peace
settlement appeared on the horizon in Uganda, talks would break
down – often because of some provocation from the government side.[67]

The mass relocation also yielded a windfall of Acholi cattle for many
linked to the Ugandan authorities.[68] An idea of the various economic
interests involved is given in a detailed investigation by Ugandan
journalist Andrew Mwenda. A major part of the problem was that war
in northern Uganda became profitable for many army officers. Siphoning
soldiers' salaries was common, and, as Mwenda notes:

> The supply of logistics to the fighting troops soon became the quickest
> route to riches. Commanders allied with civilian business people to
> inflate prices of supplies (if they supplied any logistics at all) and make
> huge profits. Other officers did not report the dead and missing in
> their units, and instead continued to receive salaries of these 'ghost
> soldiers' for their personal enrichment.[69]

With the Ugandan army poised for a major incursion into Sudan in
early 2002 (ostensibly to confront the LRA rebels there), an audit of
the 4th Division in northern Uganda showed that, of the expected
7,200 troops, only 2,400 actually existed. Mwenda notes that the relatively low numbers of troops actually deployed to the north (which
compared unfavourably with the 12,000-strong Presidential Guard
Brigade) 'demonstrates that the President had limited interest in seeking
a military victory'.[70]

In Uganda (as in many other cases), greed and abuse more generally
did not spring out of nowhere: they were nurtured by anxieties and
grievances among many of the perpetrators. An often overlooked factor
in Uganda was the very high rate of HIV infection among army officers,
with one estimate putting the figure at 40 per cent. IMF austerity
measures had encouraged the state to withdraw from free healthcare
and education, and these officers were under severe pressure to cover

their own treatment and to provide for their own families, particularly if the officers should die. Mwenda sees these conditions as feeding Ugandan army dissatisfaction.

While the rebels of the LRA acquired an increased incentive to make peace when they lost support and protection from Khartoum after Sudan's 2002 ceasefire agreement, the Ugandan government seemed to have fewer incentives to make peace. Achieving peace might bring some personal satisfaction (notably to President Museveni), but there have been powerful incentives acting in the opposite direction. Some of these apply to the army and, as Mwenda notes, 'the Ugandan army has tended to exploit every mistake the LRA makes in its political posturing to claim the rebel group is not committed to peace, thereby justifying a resumption of hostilities'.[71]

The Ugandan army's role in Sudan has hardly been more creditable than its role in northern Uganda. Ostensibly, Ugandan soldiers were sent to Sudan to defeat the LRA rebels hiding across the border from Uganda. But rather than confronting the LRA rebels, the Ugandan army has concentrated on exploiting civilians and natural resources (especially, in this case, teak logging).[72] In a thorough and fascinating investigation inside Sudan, Mareike Schomerus cites a common joke in UN security circles in 2006: 'Why is the Ugandan army in Sudan? To make sure the LRA does not get destroyed.' One respondent told her there was:

> . . . a lot of fighting between SPLA [by that time part of the government in Sudan] and LRA, but not LRA and UPDF [Ugandan army]. UPDF did not engage in battle that much. It was very funny. The UPDF even supported the LRA.[73]

While Khartoum's support for the LRA has historically been a significant factor in the latter's survival, the covert support of the Ugandan army has certainly been another.

Meanwhile, Ugandan soldiers' abuses have often been conveniently blamed on the LRA, and the soldiers have sometimes worn uniforms that make them resemble the rebels. Like the RUF rebels in Sierra Leone, the LRA – apparently seeking to elevate its own importance and to boost its reputation for ferocity – has often claimed 'credit' for attacks it did not actually carry out.[74]

While we have seen several examples of a 'sell-game' in Africa, the importance of economic goals during conflict is not confined to that continent. In Sri Lanka, for example, a major network of economic interests grew up around the counterinsurgency in the course of that country's decades of civil war. This included all those dependent on military salaries, as well as those with powerful interests in an ongoing conflict (including kickbacks from arms acquisitions).[75] While the Tamil Tiger rebels were successful – and sometimes ruthless – in getting money to sustain their struggle (not least from the Tamil diaspora), they often exhibited less 'personal' greed than did many of those associated with the counterinsurgency.[76]

Part of the problem – as is so often the case around the world – has been the presence of militias with a rather shadowy attachment to the government. With the army under a certain amount of international pressure to observe human rights, relying on militias – as in so many countries – has offered a way to conduct a kind of 'dirty war' at least partially under the international 'radar'.[77] The government's strategy has involved forging a divide within the radical Tamil opposition, and in 2004 this strategy bore fruit when a group of eastern Tamils, under Colonel Karuna, broke away from the Tamil Tigers (or the Liberation Tigers of Tamil Eelam (LTTE) to give them their full name). According to a secret 2007 cable from the US embassy in Colombo:

> Paramilitaries such as the Liberation Tigers of Tamil Eelam (LTTE)-breakaway Karuna group [operating in the east] and Eelam People's Democratic Party (EPDP) [operating in the north] have helped the Government of Sri Lanka (GSL) to fight the LTTE, to kidnap suspected LTTE collaborators, and to give the GSL a measure of deniability . . . President Rajapaksa's government, strapped for cash, has cut direct payments to paramilitaries initiated by former President Kumaratunga and instead turns a blind eye to extortion and kidnapping for ransom by EPDP and Karuna.[78]

The paramilitaries – as well as army officers and indeed the LTTE – have been able to make money by taxing trading and by charging high fees for 'allowing' people to move around.[79] Those who believe that civil war is relentlessly 'ethnic' should note that, even in the ethnically divisive context of Sri Lanka, these paramilitary crimes are mostly against fellow

Tamils. Lacking the Tigers' access to funding from the Tamil diaspora, the paramilitaries seem to be much more dependent on criminal income. As in Uganda, the war itself fed into military recruitment, with camps for internally displaced people providing recruits to Karuna (including children) and other factions, often with the tacit approval of the military.[80] Informants told the US embassy that the Colombo government allowed Karuna's cadres to recruit children forcibly within internally displaced person (IDP) camps in the east with the tacit approval of the military. Karuna's cadres were also reported to have plundered supplies for IDP camps and to have run prostitution rings based on the camps (notably to 'take care of' Sri Lankan government soldiers).

In the Philippines, a combination of corruption and profiteering from conflict grew so intense among some senior officers that it prompted outright mutiny in 2003. The ringleader of the so-called 'Oakwood mutiny' said that not only were senior officers corrupt, but that they actively assisted the Moro Islamic Liberation Front and Abu Sayyaf terrorist groups in the south.[81] Mutinous soldiers in the Philippines have accused senior officers of exaggerating the terrorist threat, of selling weapons to rebels, of helping terror suspects to escape from jail, and even of carrying out their own terror bombings.[82]

In Indonesia, conflict and military profiteering have often been hard to disentangle. When, in 1999, armed conflict broke out (along religious fault-lines) in the Maluku island region, a major obstacle to the conflict's resolution was the Indonesian military's interest in remaining in the region and ensuring a successful military candidate for the local governorship, thereby helping to promote military interests in the oil fields on Seram island. One study found that the military had become the main source of weapons and ammunition for *both sides* (Muslim and Christian) in the Maluku conflict.[83] Meanwhile, in oil-rich Aceh, Indonesian government soldiers were also accused of collaborating with the enemy, notably through weapons sales.[84] Soldiers have been heavily involved in illegal logging and the drugs trade.[85] ExxonMobil is thought to have paid the Indonesian military US$6 million a year for 'security' services, a powerful incentive for a continued military presence in Aceh.[86] In a general comment, one Indonesian human rights activist said in 2005: 'The [business] involvement of army officers is a fundamental trigger for conflict, abuses of power, crime, and human rights violations.'[87] Human Rights Watch noted that not only could the military's business interests lead to looting and extortion, but they also constituted an incentive to prolong conflict and justify a military presence.[88]

While Middle Eastern conflicts are usually discussed in terms of national or religious 'enmities', rather than economic interests, the latter should not be ignored. In Syria, the army obtained massive Soviet support during the Cold War – in the form of weapons, money and training. This peaked in the 1970s, but fell away from the mid-1980s and then disappeared altogether. One International Crisis Group report noted: 'The army sought compensation for its losses essentially by pillaging Lebanon and turning corruption and racketeering into a full-fledged industry.'[89]

But given all these economic motivations, what role has been played in contemporary international aid? The next chapter shows that abusive and 'greedy' counterinsurgencies have routinely been fuelled by international aid that turns a blind eye to this abuse, while donors focus almost exclusively on the abuses and 'greed' of the rebels.

CHAPTER 2

Aiding Resource Wars?

We can see, then, that economic goals have been important in many wars. In some ways, this might seem to accord with Paul Collier's emphasis on 'rebel greed' as the key driver of civil wars. But what has routinely been ignored within the international community (and in Collier's influential work) is the role of greed within the counterinsurgency.[1] The dangers in fuelling regime abuse through inappropriate aid policies (including those aimed at 'winning hearts and minds') have been similarly downplayed. A further blind spot centres on the continuing importance of grievances – not least in fuelling the greed of rebels and government actors alike.

To understand how international blind spots can be so harmful, it is helpful to go back to the case of Sierra Leone. Here, an international (and, to a degree, national) focus on devilish and 'greedy' rebels created a damaging degree of impunity for counterinsurgency actors who were engaged in their own abuses. This case also shows quite starkly how some elements of international aid may reinforce abuse.

For many years, international donors and the UN system kept silent about the horrendous abuses by government soldiers in Sierra Leone, while the RUF received nearly all the blame. The 'situation reports' of the UN Development Programme and of UN inter-agency missions, for example, routinely used the language of 'rebel attacks'.[2] Even where abuses by government troops were referred to, they were usually presented as temporary aberrations that were being rectified by men of good will within the government. This was an example of the habitual reluctance of UN agencies to criticise member governments. While the

German ambassador, Karl Prinz, did speak up on the military regime's excesses, he was an exception and was quickly kicked out of the country by the regime.

A key reason for international reticence was that Sierra Leone's military government was obligingly adopting a programme of financial 'liberalisation' (and prompt debt repayment) that was favoured by Western donors.[3] In this sense, the ideological battles of the Cold War were not quite over.[4] While wars normally boost inflation (notably when governments print money to fund them), Sierra Leone's government was magically keeping inflation at very low levels in the middle of a vicious civil war. The International Monetary Fund made it clear that it was impressed.[5] Yet it was precisely abuses by the army – the looting and illegal mining by severely underpaid soldiers – that *allowed* this 'economic miracle', since the war became largely *self-funding*, enabling the government to avoid the (inflationary) printing of money.

It is clear, also, that aid was helping to prop up Sierra Leone's abusive military government (1992–96). The most important part of this aid were loans on favourable terms, and the major international financial institutions – as usual – were lending without any major concern for human rights. Governments and multilateral donors like the European Community were buying back debt, pushing for a rescheduling of the debt, and providing development aid. But again, human rights featured only at the margins. The potential leverage was certainly considerable. In fact, after soldier/rebel attacks had brought aluminium and rutile-exporting operations to a halt in early 1995 (the attacks on Sieromco and Sierra Rutile), foreign aid came to provide more than half the national operating budget.[6]

For much of the war, Freetown was something of a 'bubble' of relative security – and even, in some ways, of prosperity and modernity – that could easily mislead visitors about the situation in the country as a whole. The European Community (EC) and the African Development Bank were funding work on Freetown's electricity supply, and the capital also saw improvements in fuel availability, water supply, roads, schools and hospitals.[7] One senior US humanitarian official told me: 'The government have cleaned up the city. Sierra Leonean friends say at least there's electricity in Freetown … They have tried to add to the country's attractiveness. It's just the war that has got in the way.'[8] But Father Michael Hickey, an engaging priest with decades of experience in the country, responded angrily: 'The EC is providing the electricity and roads. They're making the government look good. It's a sham. And then the government forces are just beating up on everyone.'

Aid was also altering the local economy in ways that some people felt were undermining the political will to solve the conflict. Some groups in urban areas, notably Freetown, were able to benefit from the cheap labour of the displaced and from rents that had been boosted sharply by massive population influxes and further fuelled by the influx of aid staff themselves. One man who fled to Freetown in 1995 complained that elites in the capital were benefiting economically, while being protected militarily:

> The UN can pay anything, so everyone wants his house to be rented by the UN or another company. There are many houses here, but people prefer to keep it empty in the hope that the UN will pay … They are rented out by lawyers, doctors, academics, people owning more than one house.

He said rents had risen by some ten times in a little over a year: 'And yet people shout and say they want the war to come to an end; but how can it happen when you are benefiting? Deep in your heart, you do not want the war to end. These are the key people in the society …'

Opposition to the war was also said to have been undermined by the benefits flowing to traditional chiefs and other local notables when they served as intermediaries between aid agencies and the displaced. These benefits were often greater if the chiefs left for major urban areas; but when chiefs migrated in this way, it tended to reduce the opportunities for those chiefs to help organise resistance in rural areas. Stealing relief was one way in which soldiers could profit from the war, and some aid agencies had to pay them 'protection money' for relief convoys.[9] The priest who criticised the focus on Freetown went so far as to state:

> The aid business is a way of life. It's an income. It's keeping the country going … There's a division of things in the NPRC [the military regime]: 'We'll make use of the diamonds [upcountry]. You live off the aid in Freetown.' There's a vested interest in keeping the chaos going, and attracting the aid.

As is common, aid favoured urban and government-held areas, and this could fuel violence among *non-recipients*. As one Sierra Leonean academic noted, 'those fleeing organised banditry were forced to choose between becoming brigands themselves or joining the teeming ranks of the destitute, starving or dying'.[10] Some local people reported that recruitment into the government army had been helped by the inadequacy of relief in rural areas. So in these areas, the problem, in many ways, was not the presence but the absence of aid.

Of course, there were many ways in which international aid – especially emergency aid – did mitigate the suffering in Sierra Leone, and there was also much more to the war economy than siphoning off international aid. Nevertheless, the international community largely ignored its responsibility to speak out, whether on human rights abuses or on the widespread diversion of aid. As is commonly the case, maintaining 'access to the beneficiaries' was an overriding priority for most aid agencies. One British aid worker told me: 'It's not really a food emergency at heart. It's treated as one because this is what aid agencies do.'

Perhaps most damagingly of all, emergency aid seems to have served as a substitute for effective diplomatic action to address the humanitarian crisis. This is a pattern that has proved equally damaging in Sudan, Rwanda, Uganda, Bosnia and many other places. The efficacy of donor pressure in Sierra Leone – when it was eventually applied in the run-up to the 1996 elections, and then again from around 2000 – rather underlined the failure to use it more consistently, or at an early stage in the war.

The case of Sudan is an even starker illustration of the dangers of ignoring abuses within the counterinsurgency – and of the dangers of aid that feeds those abuses. A key problem during the early years of Sudan's second civil war (and accompanying famine) was the uncritical international support for Khartoum. In the 1980s, Sudan was the largest recipient of US foreign aid in sub-Saharan Africa. Cheap wheat was essential for the maintenance of political control in urban areas, and fully 80 per cent of Sudan's wheat came in the form of foreign aid. At the end of 1988, Western donors were still providing around half the government's recurrent expenditure. So again, significant leverage did exist. There was, however, a great reluctance to use it. As a result, information on the escalating human rights abuses in the south – and on the escalating food needs – was typically discounted by major international donors. The needs in the south were said to be 'unknow-able', and stories of militia abuses were described as 'anecdotal' or as 'tribal violence'. Yet at the same time, thousands of people with direct experience of these abuses were now camped on the donors' doorstep, in the slums around the capital, Khartoum. Oxfam's Mark Duffield, now a leading critic of the 'securitisation' of aid, told me at the time: 'It was just too hot for them. The European Community was backing the government.' So, too, was the US government under President Ronald Reagan.

Crucially, with the Cold War not yet over, international engagement with the war and the famine at this time was compromised by links that were persistently made between the rebel SPLA and the Communist 'menace'. The rebels' ties with neighbouring Ethiopia fed these fears. Western donors also worried that if they 'got tough', Sudan would move closer to Gaddafi's Libya. In a context where the Sudan government was seen as a strategic ally, donors liked to defer to 'Sudanese sovereignty'. This manoeuvre could be made to sound quite politically correct. But when it came to pressuring Khartoum to carry out *economic* reforms (and the kinds of 'structural adjustment' packages favoured by the World Bank and the IMF), explicit connections were made between future aid and Sudan government policy.[11] Suddenly 'sovereignty' did not seem to be such a problem.

Given the reluctance to exert pressure over human rights, humanitarian aid again was treated as a substitute for diplomatic engagement. But emergency aid can rarely address the *causes* of violence. In fact, the position was worse than this – because the Khartoum government was able to turn emergency relief to its own advantage. For example, Khartoum raised a great deal of revenue by charging an extortionate rate when relief agencies exchanged their foreign currency. Or again, trains that were earmarked to carry emergency relief were actually used to smuggle military supplies to government garrison towns in the south.

To my surprise, I was able to obtain detailed data on this transport scandal from an official at Babanousa railway station – and all for the price of a smile and a used Michael Jackson cassette. To judge from this pleasant young man's openness (as well as from many other such encounters), there was remarkably little shame around the use of these trains to prosecute the war and deepen the famine. In fact, this abuse of international law was even turned to Khartoum's advantage in the propaganda war. For when rebels (predictably) attacked these trains, the government turned around and accused the rebels of blocking humanitarian relief! Also contributing to the obstruction of relief were the actions of people on the ground in Babanousa: relief threatened to lower grain prices in the south; for economic as well as strategic reasons, traders and army officers used their influence (and money) to prioritise the delivery of commercial grain and military goods.[12]

Due to a combination of commercial considerations, government obstruction and security restrictions, most of the international relief for starving southern Sudanese ended up on the edges of the famine zone (which, as noted, coincided to a large extent with the richest oil deposits). This was a pattern of aid that contributed significantly to the depopulation of this coveted area. The manipulation of relief was repeated in the 1990s, when UN-supported 'peace villages' became a mechanism for controlling displaced people from the south and the devastated Nuba Mountains region and for exploiting their labour on farms owned by northern Sudanese; meanwhile, rebel-held areas of the Nuba Mountains were being systematically deprived of relief.[13] The aid system, as so often, was reinforcing the war system.

When it came to the DRC and neighbouring countries, international blind spots were again damagingly in evidence. This illustrates once again that, while major donors have grown fond of referring to 'peace spoilers', they have often been rather blinkered when it comes to *identifying* those spoilers. In particular, *governmental* 'spoilers' were damagingly absent from international radar screens in the DRC – just as they had been in Sudan and Sierra Leone.[14] At the turn of the twenty-first century, Uganda and Rwanda were being praised by international donors for their enlightened domestic policies and economic achievements, even as they were plundering the DRC and indeed waging war on parts of their own populations[15] – again an echo of the bizarre international reverence for the 'financial magicians' who had brought down inflation in Freetown while wreaking havoc in upcountry Sierra Leone. The Rwandan regime had considerable international sympathy that had been encouraged by collective guilt over the international community's non-response to the 1994 genocide. But this guilt was now feeding renewed suffering – and some began to talk of new genocides *within the DRC*, including mass mortality among the Hutu refugee population. Hundreds of thousands were deprived of humanitarian relief, and in 1996–97 an estimated 232,000 Hutu refugees were killed in the DRC, primarily at the hands of the Rwandan army and its Congolese rebel ally, the Alliance of Democratic Forces for the Liberation of Congo (ADFL).[16] One careful analysis noted: 'There was little in the way of public protest in the West, and the silence that greeted the massacre of refugees was overwhelming.'[17]

The World Bank did not seem too bothered about neighbours fuelling conflict in the DRC. It was happy, for example, to praise Uganda's economic performance and to promote the case for debt relief. As in Sierra Leone, it was the spoils of war – to a significant extent – that were underpinning Ugandan economic 'success'. The UN Panel noted:

> ... the illegal exploitation of gold in the Democratic Republic of the Congo brought a significant improvement in the balance of payments of Uganda. This in turn gave multilateral donors, especially [the] IMF, which was monitoring the Ugandan treasury situation, more confidence in the Ugandan economy. [And] it has brought more money to the treasury through various taxes on goods, services and international trade.[18]

In fact, tax revenues in Uganda had risen sharply in the five years to 2001, with the best-performing sectors being related to the agricultural and forestry sector in the DRC. The World Bank must have known that something was not right, but it did not highlight these links. Moreover, the UN Panel observed: 'Notes exchanged between World Bank staff clearly show that the Bank was informed about a significant increase in gold and diamond exports from a country that produces very little of these minerals ...'[19] Meanwhile, as an investigation by Roger Tangri and Andrew Mwenda noted, 'the Congo has proven to be a veritable treasure trove for a small number of high-ranking [Ugandan] army officers who, together with their civilian business partners, have become rich from smuggling and resource plunder.[20]

The UN Panel of Experts also named a number of international companies whose trading in Congolese minerals was helping to fuel the conflict. But this exercise was not followed up with any enthusiasm. While there were some lawsuits in Germany, there was little effort to prosecute big companies that were involved in resource extraction in the DRC. Moreover, diplomatic pressure was exerted on the UN

Secretariat and members of the UN Panel to drop allegations against particular companies.[21]

The problem of foreign meddling was to prove a persistent one. One detailed investigation, published in 2007, found that the conflict in DRC 'had enabled foreign countries to set up systems of exploitation that could continue functioning through Congolese proxies even after the Rwandan or Ugandan armies had withdrawn'.[22]

Significantly, international pressure over human rights in eastern DRC was much more muted than in Sudan's Darfur from 2006. In a trenchant critique, Ugandan academic Mahmood Mamdani asked: 'Could the reason be that in the case of Congo, Hema and Lendu militias – many of them no more than child soldiers – were trained by America's allies in the region, Rwanda and Uganda?'[23] Mamdani's thesis has its problems: it is worth stressing, for example, that Darfur's crisis was itself severely neglected in the early phase (particularly in 2003). Nor is it necessary to minimise the crisis in Darfur (a charge some have forcefully levelled at Mamdani)[24] to make the point that the DRC received disproportionately little international attention. But Mamdani's critique of the neglect of the DRC is a cogent one.

In a context where political and economic pressures on the relevant actors were very weak, strange and magical powers were attributed to international emergency and agricultural aid within the DRC. In fact, this aid was increasingly held to be capable of 'conflict resolution' and of promoting 'development', even in the midst of a vicious and destructive war.[25] Meanwhile, as the incisive and courageous aid worker Nicholas Stockton has shown, the basic life-saving function of emergency aid was woefully neglected: at one point, aid agencies sought food for only 1.4 million people, but reported that fully 16 million were in need.[26] As Zoe Marriage shows in her book *Not Breaking the Rules, Not Playing the Game*, the proliferation of aims around international aid (everything from conflict resolution to avoiding the creation of 'dependency' among aid recipients) meant that it was very hard to hold agencies accountable for any single failure – even for failure to deliver life-saving assistance. Meanwhile, the weak response inside the DRC contrasted with the large amounts of international aid that were being channelled to Rwanda and Uganda as a reward for their 'good governance'.[27]

Soon the international blind spot in relation to *governmental* abuse was being extended – in a way, logically so – to the Congolese national army. Many different factions were incorporated into a reformed national army as part of the 2002 peace agreement. But individual militia commanders were usually able to retain control of their foot-soldiers, and they were able to use the threat of violence to continue to make large profits from 'taxing' Congo's resources, usually withholding the benefits from central government.[28]

The earlier reluctance on the part of Rwandan soldiers to engage with the militias responsible for the Rwandan genocide (the *genocidaires*) was increasingly being matched by a similar reluctance on the part of the reformed Congolese national army. Corruption within the national army was rife, moreover. When salaries were siphoned off, the rank-and-file would often 'pay themselves' through looting and using armed force to extract natural resources on exploitative terms.

Poor or non-existent pay was also encouraging government army soldiers to take bribes from the Democratic Forces for the Liberation of Rwanda (FDLR), the militia linked to the Hutu *genocidaires*. Government soldiers often tolerated the presence of FDLR soldiers and sometimes helped them to tax and loot civilians.[29] With international donors reluctant to provide funding for the DRC army, many soldiers found themselves living in straw huts and there were also significant outbreaks of cholera and tuberculosis.[30]

The army was desperately in need of support to tackle corruption and to ensure regular payments and supplies for its soldiers. Donors began to move into these areas, but most remained very wary of involvement in military organisations.

Donors were also very slow to challenge Ugandan army corruption relating to Uganda's civil war[31] and to criticise government abuses, such as the mass relocation of civilians to 'protection' villages.[32] Once again, the focus was very much on the bad qualities of the rebels – this time, for the most part, their 'fanaticism'. Meanwhile, as in relation to Sudan, a number of incisive observers accused aid agencies of colluding with the government's policy of forcible relocation (or 'villagisation'). One consultant's evaluation concluded in 1999: 'WFP [World Food Programme] may have too readily fallen in line with government policy, in effect becoming both provider and legitimizer of a villagization policy.'[33] Chris Dolan sees the provision of aid as playing into a process of 'social torture': like doctors in a situation of torture, he argues, aid organisations actually kept people alive for further abuse. He suggests that WFP and many NGOs working the camps were 'complicit bystanders': they assisted a villagisation policy 'whose benefits in terms of protecting the population were never demonstrated, and whose costs to the population were manifest'.[34] Although many have returned to their homes, renewed conflict in the north-eastern Karamoja region has seen the Ugandan army engaging in abuse of civilians and looting.[35]

It is fair to say that, in relation to Colombia, the role of economic goals has been widely remarked upon. However, perceptions here have often been as myopic as in Sierra Leone, Sudan, the DRC and Uganda. A common practice, both within and outside Colombia, has been to label the Revolutionary Armed Forces of Colombia (FARC) as 'narco-terrorists'. These rebels have indeed raised a huge amount of money from the cocaine trade. But allegations of 'rebel greed' are much harder to support. As Mats Berdal points out in a more general observation, armed groups need income in order to wage war; the fact that they are raising money does not, in itself, prove that money has become their main goal.[36] Most outsiders do not realise that looting for individual benefit is severely punished by the FARC. In fact, it is nearly inconceivable. Corruption among the leadership has been relatively rare – especially considering the huge sums handled by the guerrillas.

By contrast, as Colombian academic Francisco Gutiérrez Sanin shows, greed – and profiting from the coca crop – has been rife within paramilitary forces (usually seen as part of the counterinsurgency).[37] Serving in the paramilitary forces has been a potent means of upward social mobility, and huge personal profits have been made from narco-trafficking.[38] In contrast to the position with regard to rebel groups, these profits do not need to go directly into the treasury of the organisation. One result has been a kind of 'splintering' that has constantly impeded the military effectiveness of the paramilitaries, who have generally preferred to attack civilians than to attack the rebels. There have been many conflicts over money between different paramilitaries – and many conflicts between different ranks inside particular paramilitary organisations.[39] There have also been major land-grabs by the paramilitaries, funded in part by the drugs trade.[40] Gutiérrez Sanin argues convincingly that abundant natural resources do not necessarily feed into potent military organisations in the way that Paul Collier seems to imply. Whether or not we like a particular ideology, it is often ideology that creates some degree of military discipline and a willingness to risk one's life.

So how did Colombia's rebels get their reputation for 'greed'? Well, some of them do drive fancy cars. But a more important explanation is that in Colombia (as also in Afghanistan, for example) it has proven *politically convenient* to label rebels as greedy – or, more specifically, as 'narco-guerillas' or 'narco-terrorists'. Unfortunately, the more readily rebels are stigmatised as greedy, the easier it becomes for greed to flourish – largely unaddressed for many years – within the counterinsurgency. In Colombia, largely on the strength of their enthusiastic participation in an international 'war on drugs', various governments for many years received a huge injection of international aid and military support, in particular from the US.[41] One thing that seems to have placed a limit on the war in Colombia was a belated recognition in 2002 that it was necessary to deal with the paramilitaries, rather than simply to assume that they would disappear once the 'insurgent' problem had been solved.[42] Demobilisation schemes for the paramilitaries were no panacea, as we shall see; but they had a significant impact in reducing civilian deaths.[43]

We can see that, whether we look at conflict in Colombia, Sri Lanka, Sudan, the DRC or Sierra Leone, there are few grounds for assuming that 'greed' is a rebel phenomenon. In fact, there are many cases (including Colombia and, as we shall see, Afghanistan) where rebels have displayed more discipline and more ideological intensity than their opponents. Importantly, this can contribute to a degree of military success. In cases like Afghanistan, where the counterinsurgency forces enjoy far superior resources, the ideological element in the insurgency appears to have levelled the playing field a little, contributing to a stalemate.

Those who assume – whether for reasons of convenience or laziness – that all greed is rebel greed might usefully cast their minds back a little further, for example to the English civil war in the 1640s. The English Parliamentarians (the 'rebels') actually had quite strict controls on plunder, and they felt – with some justification – that this had helped them to win the hearts of the people. The Royalists, by contrast, lost popular support when they plundered; and, as the war progressed, a squeeze on Royalist supply lines encouraged an increase in these abuses, which Royalists themselves sometimes acknowledged to be counterproductive.[44]

***

We can see, then, that international blind spots have often contributed powerfully to humanitarian crises, usually by reinforcing the impunity of governmental 'spoilers'. Aid has played a troublesome part here: in many different countries, international aid has reinforced an abusive government, while the international community has simultaneously oversimplified complex war systems into the much-condemned brutality and 'greed' of the rebels. This 'statist' bias has been reflected in a much greater willingness, generally, to sanction abusive rebel movements than abusive governments.[45]

Those processes have naturally given rise to criticism (particularly in the 1990s), and this, in turn, contributed to the emergence of a framework borrowed from medical interventions. Aid workers were increasingly urged, as the title of a much-read 1999 book by Mary Anderson suggested, to *Do No Harm*.[46] And it became common for aid agencies to build some kind of 'conflict sensitivity' into the design of their aid programmes. However, in practice, the priorities of major donor governments (often strategic in nature) continued to mean that such concerns were often wilfully set aside – and this tendency became more pronounced after 9/11. In fact, the so-called 'war on terror' has reinforced major international blind spots when it comes to aid that fuels corruption and conflict. The case of Afghanistan is taken up in chapter 4, while chapter 6 looks at how various 'global wars' – most recently the 'war on terror' – have fed into damaging impunity for those who can claim their local war as part of some internationally approved wider war.

If many of the lessons of the 1980s and 1990s have been cast aside, the practice of strategic amnesia is actually much older than this. In the following chapter, I look at some of the international blind spots in relation to the Vietnam War. The critical lessons of this conflict – in particular the problems when greed infuses a counterinsurgency – seem themselves to have been largely ignored, both at the time and subsequently. In fact, we seem to be experiencing a form of serial amnesia that allows an apparently endless repetition of very similar mistakes. In particular, aid is being repeatedly reinvented as a way of legitimising disastrous wars and of 'rescuing' failing counterinsurgency. While greed in the government structures has largely doomed this strategy to failure, our ability to forget this lesson – and resuscitate our own optimism – is impressive indeed.

CHAPTER 3

Vietnam: Useful Enemies
and Useless Allies

I recently came across a book published in 1968 and now largely forgotten. The author noted:

> After twenty years of fighting, war has become a way of life for the leadership of the ARVN [South Vietnamese army]. They are in no hurry to pursue the enemy, for from their point of view the goal is not to defeat the enemy, but to maintain their position, receive promotions, and enhance their personal fortunes. Combat, at best, is an extra-curricular activity to be engaged in as a last resort.[1]

It sounds like the work of a radical researcher or journalist. But *The Betrayal* was written by US General William Corson, who grew up in the slums of Chicago, won a university scholarship aged just fifteen, and eventually became commander of the US Marine Corps' Combined Action Platoons in South Vietnam. It is a masterly account of the political economy of the Vietnam war – and one written, incidentally, around two decades before the 'political economy of war' had supposedly been 'discovered', largely in the context of African wars, by academics such as myself![2]

The involvement of American troops in Vietnam began in 1965 as, in the aftermath of occupation by the French and the Japanese, the US sought to prop up an ailing – and ostensibly 'democratic' – South Vietnamese government against a Viet Cong Communist rebellion that was supported from North Vietnam. While we have noted in the introduction that armed groups in many civil wars are surprisingly reluctant

to confront each other, the Cold War saw this kind of 'stand-off' acted
out on a larger scale. The Soviet Union and the United States were reluctant (for obvious reasons) to confront each other directly, and the
majority of 'Cold War wars' were fought in relatively poor countries,
usually without the involvement of US or Soviet troops. Vietnam was
one exception; Afghanistan (on the Soviet side) was another. But even in
these cases, the commitment of superpower troops carried – and was
seen to carry – significant political risks.

After failing to quell the Communist rebels in Vietnam (and with
popular protest growing in the US), American troops were finally withdrawn in 1973 and Saigon fell to the Communists in 1975. The US
tactics in the war, which involved aerial attacks on North Vietnam and
the South Vietnamese countryside, as well as the 'rounding up' of civilians in the south, reflected a broader failure to understand how the war
might look from the perspective of a Vietnamese villager. Meanwhile,
the chronic unreliability of the South Vietnamese government and
soldiers was, for the most part, simply wished away. Yet for a great many
South Vietnamese officers and officials, war itself seemed more advantageous than winning.

As Corson put it, 'one thing the GVN [Government of South Vietnam]
seeks to avoid [is] the end of the war and the withdrawal of US forces'.[3]
He added: 'The GVN's power is based on the US presence, and since
that in turn is based on the level of violence it is to their advantage to
orchestrate the war at the appropriate level.'[4] Meanwhile, Vietnam's
flourishing war economy was fuelled in large part by US aid.

In many ways, this was an early instance of the kind of blind spots we
have noted in relation to many more recent wars. The general approach
of the Americans was in line with approaches to more recent conflicts, in
that it focused heavily on the bad qualities of rebels (who were usually
not presented as greedy, but certainly as fanatical) and exhibited damaging
blind spots in three key areas: grievances among the rebels; greed within
the counterinsurgency; and grievances within the counterinsurgency.

With grievances being largely ignored, it proved tempting to attribute
America's problems in Vietnam to the enemy's resilience. Others
pointed to tactical mistakes or to the constraints imposed by domestic
pressures within the US. Much less widely remarked at the time – and
subsequently – was just how severely the counterinsurgency effort was
compromised by the low priority attached to winning on the part of

America's allies in South Vietnam. So far from being obsessed with defeating the Communists, America's allies placed greater importance on staying in power, protecting themselves from physical danger, and making money. The Communists (often recruiting from the same families as the South Vietnamese army) were actually much more disciplined than their opponents. Like the Taliban in a later period, they were much better at reining in 'greed' than was the regime they were facing; and in both cases superior discipline contributed strongly to military success.

The South Vietnamese army had been established under French rule and had played a mostly non-combatant role in relation to the Viet Minh rebellion at that time. In the war against the Viet Cong, while fatalities among the South Vietnamese forces did reach significant levels,[5] much of the army continued this 'non-combat' tradition. Meanwhile, as General Corson noted, corruption was nurturing the Viet Cong and radically undermining subsequent US efforts to win 'hearts and minds':

> The people smell the decay of GVN corruption, which permeates all of South Vietnam and makes a joke out of activities urged by the United States in the name of promoting a democratic society ... The absurdity of the situation lies in the fact that while we champion the cause of democracy as the justification of our presence in Vietnam, we overtly support a government whose actions completely deny this *raison d'être*.[6]

Does that sound vaguely familiar? The case of Afghanistan is one that we shall return to. But at this earlier point, the contradictions were stark. Moreover, the frequent reluctance on the part of the South Vietnamese troops to engage with the enemy was a significant incentive for civilians to cooperate with the Communists. In a typically trenchant comment, General Corson noted:

> What is often overlooked in evaluating the ARVN leadership is that the desultory fashion in which they pursue the enemy is not lost on the people. They know all too well that the ARVN is in no hurry to engage the enemy and that they [the people] therefore must seek some form of accommodation with the enemy in order to survive.[7]

A good idea of how all this worked on the ground is given by Neil Sheehan's account of the war in his acclaimed book *A Bright Shining Lie*. Sheehan focuses on Hau Nghia province, just north-west of Saigon. The provincial capital, Bau Trai, was controlled by the South Vietnamese and the Americans, but it was dangerous, mostly because of out-of-control South Vietnamese soldiers who consumed large quantities of alcohol. Of Colonel Phan Trong Chinh, commander of the South Vietnamese army's 25th Division in Hau Nghia province, Sheehan comments: 'He not only did everything he could to avoid attacking the guerrillas himself, he went to pains to keep anyone else from doing so.'[8] The colonel also forced the provincial chief, Major Nguyen Tri Hanh, to send troops where there was no enemy. On the other hand, he was happy to target civilian villages with air strikes.[9]

The incentives operating within the South Vietnam military were, on the whole, not conducive to confronting the enemy. As conflict specialist Stathis Kalyvas notes, 'South Vietnamese officers saw artillery shelling as an easy way to show that they were aggressive without running the risks of actual "search and destroy" operations.'[10] Meanwhile, the South Vietnamese government seems to have been more concerned with preserving its elite troops (to protect against a coup) than with winning a war.[11]

In Vietnam, the shortcomings of a military approach led many parts of the US government to put considerable faith in developmental interventions that would somehow 'plug the gap'. Yet both the military and the aid approach suffered from a weak understanding of local realities. While US officials in the 1960s and 1970s sometimes spoke of the need for a 'political' approach, they typically displayed only a very limited interest in local political realities. While the US focused on 'eliminating the enemy', the way in which corruption, exploitation and civilian casualties were *producing* the enemy was disastrously set aside. (This lack of interest in the local political economy extended to numerous subsequent studies of the Vietnam War, notably within military academies.[12] While the international politics and the military tactics of the Vietnam War have yielded thousands of books, the political economy of that war has been addressed less extensively.)

The war saw a massive onslaught on highly populated areas – an onslaught that was designed to eject the civilian population, and thereby to deprive the Viet Cong of both assistance and civilian cover. This involved declaring 'free-fire zones', which one American adviser to the

South Vietnamese army's 25th Division justified by saying: 'If these people want to stay there and support the Communists, then they can expect to be bombed.'[13] Guenter Lewy, generally a defender of the US military intervention, notes: 'The prevalent but uncodified policy was that of compulsory relocations and displacement by military pressure through combat operations, crop destruction and the creation of specified strike zones.'[14] The places into which people were rounded up were known as 'strategic hamlets'. General Corson referred to a 'rootless urban proletariat' numbering 3–4 million, living in squalid conditions on the edge of major towns and cities.[15]

In Vietnam, heavily populated areas were subject not only to bombing and shelling, but also to crop destruction:[16] 'Herbicides poisoned crops, and tanks and armored personnel carriers crossed and recrossed paddy fields until every stalk of rice had been chewed up.'[17] Unsurprisingly, the devastation of the environment – including rice harvests – with crop-destroying chemicals helped the Viet Cong.[18]

The American forces aimed to kill Communist rebels faster than replacements could be sent by Hanoi from the north. In effect, it was an earlier incarnation of the idea – which came once more to prominence in George W. Bush's 'war on terror' – that there was a limited number of 'bad guys', whose destruction would solve the problem.

Tempting as it may be to point the finger at the brutality of recent wars in the developing world, we should note that when governments like Sudan, Uganda, Sri Lanka, Indonesia and elsewhere have used forcible relocation as a key counterinsurgency tactic, they have been following the path pursued by American forces in Vietnam, who were themselves following in the footsteps of British forcible relocations in Malaya, Kenya and earlier, in the Boer War, as well as internment by American forces in the Philippines.[19] As a saying in Sierra Leone has it: 'When you point the finger, three of your fingers are pointing at yourself.'

Apart from General Corson, another American who *did* try to engage with important political realities was John Paul Vann, the principal subject of Sheehan's *A Bright Shining Lie*. In July 1962, Vann retired from the US army after twenty years of active service. But less than three years later he was back in Vietnam, working for the US Agency for International Development (USAID).[20]

Vann was one of those who denounced the US strategy of indiscriminate bombing and shelling of the countryside. He pointed out that this strategy was self-defeating: indiscriminate violence was actually creating more Viet Cong, particularly since the farmers who were being attacked by the US actually had an alternative army (backed by an alternative government) that was offering them revenge.[21] General Lewis Walt, commander of the III Marine Amphibious Force, told his men that 'The injury or killing of hapless civilians inevitably contributes to the communist cause.'[22]

We know from studies of a range of conflicts – notably by Stathis Kalyvas – that violence against civilians tends to be counterproductive in winning popular support, particularly in circumstances where civilians have a choice between two rival parties. One reason is anger, which can easily push an individual into the opposing camp. Another is rational calculation. Civilians are typically risk averse, and they will usually try to 'stand aloof' from an armed conflict. For example, they will often withhold support from rebel groups if they feel that this will allow them to avoid government retaliation. However, where civilians are being attacked indiscriminately, there may actually be little incentive to withhold their support from 'the other side'. If 'innocence' is no protection, why not join an insurgency?[23]

This dynamic certainly applied in Vietnam – and Vann's views on Vietnam were soon to be vindicated. General William Westmoreland's 475,000-strong American army was not able to control the situation, and the US war plan was dramatically discredited by the infamous 'Tet Offensive', when Viet Cong forces launched several attacks within Saigon and penetrated the US embassy compound in early 1968.[24] The offensive turned out to be an opportunity as well as a problem: as General Corson noted, 'During the Tet offensive the ARVN leadership looted and stole as though they were conquerors.'[25]

Significantly, Vann's pessimism – like Corson's – was fuelled by his familiarity with the strengths and weaknesses of the two opposing Vietnamese forces. In 1965, Vann wrote to a friend in Denver that the bombing of the North would not alter events in the South because 'regrettably, we are going to lose this war'. He added: 'We're going to lose because of the moral degeneration in South Vietnam coupled with the excellent discipline of the VC [Viet Cong].'[26] In May 1971, Vann became USAID's senior adviser for the region comprising Central Highlands and adjacent provinces on the Central Coast. Oddly for a USAID official, he was given authority over all US military forces in the area. He also covertly shared command of 158,000 Vietnamese troops via his relationship with a South Vietnamese general.[27]

A key premise behind American policy (a premise shared, for the most part, by South Vietnamese government officials) was that there were few, if any, genuine grievances on the rebel side. But this was quite inaccurate. Genuine grievances articulated by the rebels centred both on historical inequities (notably in landholding) and on current government policy. In his book *War Comes to Long An,* Jeffrey Race provides an admirable summary of damaging and unpopular South Vietnam government policies:

> ... the policy of maintaining the existing landholding system; the policy of military service far from one's home; the policy of persecuting former Vietminh [who had fought against the French and the Japanese]; the policy of denying local organs sufficient authority to punish offending soldiers and officials; the policy of building strategic hamlets; and the policy of maintaining a government recruitment pattern which denied advancement to those from majority elements of the rural population.[28]

Corson illustrated the South Vietnamese army's insensitivity through the case of one villager who had had two out of three sons killed in military service. The law exempted his remaining son, but the son was called up anyway. Both father and remaining son ended up joining the Viet Cong, and three months later the father was killed in a fire-fight with General Corson's own battalion.[29]

As David Hunt notes, the architects of 'winning hearts and minds' in Vietnam 'could not grasp that they were dealing with a highly politicized rural population and the blizzard of propaganda leaflets they scattered across the countryside could not undo ties between peasants and the NLF [National Liberation Front rebels]'.[30] The Viet Cong, for all their ruthlessness and numerous acts of brutality, were actually offering some concrete and practical solutions to many people's daily problems.[31] 'Taxation' by the Viet Cong was often less onerous than 'taxation' and land rents taken by South Vietnamese landlords and government officials.[32] In fact, the rebels were gaining popularity by leading something of a social revolution in the South Vietnamese countryside, notably through establishing their own school system. This was in a context where it had been extremely difficult for children from the peasantry to proceed beyond primary education.[33] The Saigon government was busily building elementary schools at US government urging (incidentally, accompanied by massive corruption). But such schools did not tackle the problem of closed access to secondary schools and higher education.[34] General Corson commented:

> Intelligent, capable children of peasants and the urban poor who are fortunate enough to attend schools complete their education only to find the next set of doors to learning are closed. Their dissatisfaction is readily exploited by the Vietcong. How well our stupidity serves the enemy![35]

Vann himself went so far as to say that he would himself have become a Communist had he grown up in Vietnam.[36] But these voices were unusual. In general, both the Viet Cong's resilience and its popular support were severely underestimated by the Americans.[37]

One of the more unrealistic assumptions was that, once the peasants were removed to the strategic hamlets, the provision of aid would help to win their 'hearts and minds'. Washington claimed that displaced people from these free-fire zones were 'refugees from Communism' and were 'voting with their feet'; these people were supposed to be 'cared for' and 'indoctrinated' so that they would one day go back to their villages as loyal citizens. But would some bags of rice and other material benefits be enough to win them over to the same party that had recently bombed them? Few thought to pose the question in this way.

In any case, using 'development' for counterinsurgency was based on a misconception: namely, that incrementally reducing poverty would reduce support for the rebels. In reality, the biggest problems were corrupt government and a hugely unequal distribution of land – and the South Vietnamese government and its American allies were doing very little about these critical issues.[38] General Corson referred to 'the rather forlorn hope' that a new school, bridge or pig farm would give the peasant what he really wanted.[39] Another analyst, no friend of the Viet Cong, noted:

> Aid measures like building roads and schools, digging wells, medical care, etc., were incremental rather than distributive. While the VC

offered to redistribute status, wealth and income, the [South Vietnam government] efforts were perceived as the preservation of the social status quo.[40]

There were some Americans who did realise the role of grievances in this war. In fact, some US officials in Vietnam were of the view that even if the US army were to occupy the whole country and crush the guerrillas, the rebellion would break out again after the American soldiers had gone home.[41] But in general the peasants' grievances were woefully neglected.

If the grievances nurturing rebellion were severely downplayed, so too was the 'greed' within government structures. One of the reasons that local corruption was not more widely understood – or counteracted – was that corruption was something of a taboo topic within the US military and aid bureaucracy in Vietnam. Neil Sheehan reports that most of the American advisers in Vietnam avoided the subject because they knew it was not welcome at the US embassy or at General Westmoreland's headquarters.[42] This damaging neglect seems to have been wrapped in some rather benevolent language. For example, one justification given for the very weak oversight of international aid was 'the development of indigenous management'.[43] Meanwhile, Westmoreland told US advisers who did register complaints that they should 'exercise care in reporting corruption lest they get a reputation as spies and lose leverage with their counterparts'.[44] Instability was generally seen as far worse than corruption, particularly after the coups of 1963–65.[45] David Hunt comments: 'The [Vietnamese] generals in control of the state apparatus were thus granted a blank check.'[46]

With corruption endemic, there was a shortage of influential South Vietnamese who could legitimately point the finger at others. In fact, one American adviser was of the view that 'The system was designed to ensure that no pot was in a position to call another kettle black'.[47] So what, exactly, were the elements of the war economy?

One was simple theft. This included looting by government soldiers, which could take place in villages (for example, when rebels were pushed back) or at the camps.[48] As General Corson noted, 'if the peasant who has managed to get out of the way of the war arrives with some money or livestock, the ARVN/GVN vultures quickly fleece him'.[49] Another element in the war economy was the reassertion of old exploitative relationships in places where the rebels had been pushed back. When US Marines took an area as part of a major military push in 1965, they had assumed that South Vietnamese troops would follow to maintain security. But that was not the case. 'The ARVN came not to stay, but to loot, collect back taxes, reinstall landlords, and conduct reprisals against the people', recalled Corson. 'These actions, along with the Marines' absence, enabled the Vietcong to regain control in the supposedly cleared areas.'[50] The return of absentee landlords meant the return of burdensome and often illegal land rents.[51]

'Protection money' was also profitable for government officials. At village level, policemen would sometimes demand payment from farmers for not reporting them as Viet Cong.[52] Meanwhile, detention centres for suspected Viet Cong became a focus for extortion,[53] and many captured guerrilla operatives were bought out of their cells – sometimes even before the Americans knew that a valuable catch had been made.[54]

Money could also sometimes buy 'protection' from the guerrillas, and some businesses made these payments; the Viet Cong even provided receipts. Some of the money coming in from corruption went out in protection payments to the guerrillas.[55]

General Corson noted that, within the South Vietnamese army, 'promotions can be bought along with specific assignments which provide the opportunity to make fortunes in Vietnam's inflated war economy'.[56] This suggests not only lucrative opportunities for those appointed, but a substantial flow of funds to those doing the appointing.

As in many subsequent conflicts, 'ghost soldiers' were a major source of income. They made winning the war both less desirable and less feasible. General Corson shows how South Vietnamese generals prof-ited from a system that saw commanders pocketing the salaries of soldiers who had been killed, as well as those of soldiers who had deserted. This gave the officers a perverse incentive to keep their mili-tary units under-manned – and Saigon's units were indeed chronically short of men. Other soldiers unavailable to fight were those who had paid bribes to commanders so that they could go back to their families. These soldiers were known as 'potted trees', since they were now back in a domestic 'pot'. At one point, Hau Nghia provincial chief Hanh called up a military unit in which 140 men were supposedly being paid, but only fifty showed up. One estimate suggested that as many as a quarter of the soldiers on the official rolls may not have existed – a huge racket. With perhaps 100,000 soldiers deserting in any given year, the opportunities for using out-of-date registers were very considerable.[57]

Further profits could be made from supplying goods and services to the foreign troops. There was a major scam around doing American soldiers' laundry, for example, and prostitution was rife.[58] In addition, a huge drugs industry grew up around the foreign troops – another source of profit and distraction for South Vietnamese officials.[59]

Trading with rebels was a further source of profit. In practice, the Viet Cong were able to buy all manner of things from government officials. Feeding into such practices was the fact that the 'two sides' were not always entirely distinct. As Sheehan noted, 'Viet Cong penetration of the Saigon side had always been a major problem, and it became an ever graver one as the fortunes of the regime declined and men and women turned their coats to hedge against the future.'[60] The sale of some items (like antibiotics and batteries for mine detectors) was prohibited, but proceeded nonetheless. These items fetched some of the highest prices; indeed, this appears to have been part of the point of prohibiting them. Since trafficking with guerrillas carried the theoretical possibility of a death sentence, someone who had engaged in this trafficking on a small scale could then be blackmailed by the Viet Cong into a larger-scale collaboration.[61]

There were reports that South Vietnamese soldiers were selling off their own gasoline, stripping parts off their own helicopters, and even firing artillery simply so that they could retrieve and sell the brass casings. Selling gasoline intended for South Vietnamese and US troops was a huge commercial operation with widespread involvement of civilian officials.[62] There were also substantial profits to be made from manipulating exchange rates and import quotas.[63]

US aid was inserted into a context of endemic corruption, which it duly exacerbated. A related problem (as later in Afghanistan) was that aid did not easily transfer into legitimacy. As David Hunt put it in an important assessment:

> Washington supplied troops, weapons, and economic aid but did not find a way to transfer legitimacy to Saigon authorities. Playing on the American need to respect their sovereignty, Vietnamese generals eventually gained a free hand to dispose as they pleased

of the vast resources the United States was pouring into the country. The resulting corruption further discredited them in the eyes of the population.[64]

General Corson noted:

> ... the materials to build the 'Refugees from Communism' camp at Cam Lo had been usurped by persons unknown, forty truckloads of cement given by the United States to the GVN to build floors in the refugee huts had mysteriously disappeared. And peasants were dying from lack of food and water.[65]

By 1970, an estimated half a million tons of rice had been stolen, along with large quantities of cement and roofing to rebuild houses after US bombing and shelling.[66] Relief food was being sold to refugees when it was supposed to be free.[67] Money, materials and medicine went missing on a massive scale.[68] Bizarrely, the displaced people had to prove their entitlement to relief as 'refugees from Communism', but they were excluded from this status if their hamlet was one that the Viet Cong controlled.[69] A 1967 US government report revealed that more than half of the refugees had received no assistance.[70] Schools financed by USAID were sometimes put up very shabbily and cheaply, with the contractor profiting.[71] Even the aid designed as compensation for war damage was subject to a 'rake-off', with local officials sometimes demanding a bribe to pass the money on.[72] Meanwhile, corruption was further stimulated when government officials found their salaries eroded by inflation, which itself was fuelled by all the resources and personnel that the Americans and their allies had pumped into the country.[73]

As later in Afghanistan, aid not only fuelled corruption, but also helped to fund the enemy. General Corson observed angrily:

> ... the chief of Quang Ngai province was reported to have 'confessed' to a group of Revolutionary Cadres that he had, among other instances of malfeasance, paid 500,000 piasters for his job and recovered his purchase price within six months. The province chief is the means that makes corruption work. He determines what, where, how and why monies and materials are to be made available in the province. Like simple-minded schoolboys, American officials turn over supplies

and money to province chiefs on the rose-colored presumption that these items will be used for their intended purposes. It matters not that American troops have captured tons of supplies financed by U.S. tax dollars and in turn sold by the province chief to the Vietcong – the charade goes on.[74]

A so-called 'rural reconstruction' effort in Thua Thien province, which was close to North Vietnam and saw heavy fighting, was studied by James Trullinger. Reconstruction efforts reinforced hostility to the government and local notables who were linked to it, giving further assistance to the rebels. For example, the introduction of high-yielding rice created a dependence on fertilisers and pesticides, and a few suppliers were able to make large profits from these inputs. These suppliers also had an arrangement with the rice buyers, lowering the price that farmers got for their rice. Government infrastructure projects generally served the interests of a few prominent individuals: for example, irrigation channels were often constructed (using free labour) so as to help the larger landowners. The Viet Cong capitalised on these grievances and even presented themselves as a way to escape from the village development programmes. An immunisation programme for water buffalo was blocked when the Viet Cong persuaded peasants that it was an attempt to kill their cattle as punishment for supporting rebels.[75] As later in Afghanistan, the *sheer presence* of the Americans was seized on by rebels as a reason why ordinary people should support them and reject the invaders.[76] For government officials and village chiefs, even being seen in the presence of the Americans could lead to an important loss of face in the eyes of ordinary people.[77] Something that severely compromised the 'neutrality' of development initiatives in many parts of Vietnam was the way these were used to get information on the Viet Cong for the express purpose of targeted assassinations.[78] In any case, Viet Cong control of the countryside was frequently a major obstacle to development projects.[79]

With such a range of profits being made from war – and even from wartime 'reconstruction' – continuing the war was 'an enabling context'.[80] Conversely, when aid was eventually cut, this profitable stalemate lost some of its allure. After the North Vietnamese finally took Saigon in 1975, one South Vietnamese army colonel said: 'The cutbacks in

American aid that reduced the flow of personal profits to the Vietnamese leaders affected their motivation to fight in 1975. From their point of view, it made more sense "to take your winnings and run".[81]

As in many more recent conflicts, 'greed' in the counterinsurgency was strongly nurtured by grievances. Low government salaries fed corruption, as has been noted. Meanwhile, corruption at the top of the army was feeding into the looting and abuse of civilians by lower ranks, and it also made troops more reluctant to confront the enemy and more prone to the abuse of civilians. General Corson noted that, while promotion within the Viet Cong was based on fighting ability, the situation in the South Vietnamese army was very different:

> The ARVN officer corps is derived solely from the wealthier social class because each officer is required to possess a French-style second baccalaureate (college degree) ... Because the ARVN soldier comes from either the urban poor or the peasant class, he also suffers from his officer's indifference. One might think that the ARVN soldier, because of his background would identify and be sympathetic with the peasant, but this is not the case. The ARVN soldier has a lot to complain about – he has been drafted under a law which enables the sons of the rich to escape the draft indefinitely, his term of service is indefinite, his pay irregular, and if he is a member of a unit serving in the countryside he has nothing to look forward to but being the target of unending Vietcong hit-and-run attacks, while those in favored units, who have been able to avoid combat since 1954, are used merely as palace guards. Because of this and many other inequities, the ARVN soldier takes his resentment and anger out on the people. He rapes, loots, and pillages in the manner of a conqueror rather than a protector ... this kind of behavior on the part of the ARVN soldier has made the Vietnam War unwinnable. It is not possible to convince the people that the GVN is on his side when his own family is subject to more danger and violence from the ARVN than from the VC.[82]

Poor conditions (and a policy of non-local military service) encouraged a very high desertion rate in the South Vietnamese army.[83] In these circumstances, disciplining these soldiers was sometimes seen as impractical. The provincial chief of Hau Nghia, Major Nguyen Tri Hanh, believed there was nothing that the government could do: the soldiers were in a state of despair, had lost faith in their officers, and would mutiny if any attempt were made to discipline them.[84]

Although South Vietnamese corruption and the shortcomings of Saigon's army did not go unnoticed, there was no systematic attempt to make aid conditional on improvements. As Corson put it:

> Americans who become indignant over the fact that the ARVN does not carry their fair share of the burden are misdirecting their displeasure. The plain fact is that the United States has never made this a condition for our assistance.[85]

The US could also have put pressure on Saigon by talking to opposition figures and to the Viet Cong itself. This would have helped, in Corson's words, to show the South Vietnamese government that 'they need us more than we need them'.[86]

If America's allies were not intent on winning, there are many indications that winning was not an overriding priority even for the Americans themselves. If self-protection was an important goal for the South Vietnamese army, it was not an irrelevant goal for the Americans either. Colonel James Herbert, the senior American adviser in Long An in 1967–69, said the main reason that revolutionary forces had not been defeated was the way counterrevolutionary forces had been deployed:

> In general, the employment of forces over here – ARVN, PF [popular forces], and US – has been to put them in such places as to provide the forces some protection, but not to provide protection to the people in the hamlets.[87]

Colonel Herbert added that it was hard to demand that ARVN commanders

> ... deploy their forces so as to protect people and not just to be in big mud forts to protect themselves ... Now it turns out that in general when American forces come over here they go into bigger outposts and bigger bases, and do not deploy their forces so as to provide security for the people in the hamlets. So you can see the position of the advisor here: it is very difficult to get the Vietnamese to do what the US doesn't do.[88]

US politicians and officials seem to have entered – and subsequently esca-
lated – the conflict without any serious conviction that their actions would
lead to victory. As one detailed study noted, 'those making decisions to
increase U.S. involvement were aware that victory would probably not be
the result'.[89] Rather than paving the way for victory, the bombing of North
Vietnam brought international condemnation, loss of opportunities for
ending the war, popular discontent at home in the US, a reinforcement of
Ho Chi Minh's political control in the north, a hardening of the North
Vietnamese position, and a drain of resources away from what some saw
as the need for 'tactical close air support' for US and South Vietnamese
troops in the south.[90] We also saw in the introductory chapter how carpet-
bombing Cambodia helped to create many new 'enemies', as Cambodian
peasants were propelled into the arms of the Khmer Rouge.

The fact that US tactics in South Vietnam, North Vietnam and
Cambodia all predictably created new enemies should also call into
question the assumed aim of 'winning'. Unless we wish to label these
actions 'irrational' en masse, it would seem that – even in Washington
– winning was not the overriding goal.

Hannah Arendt made a perceptive study of leaked US documents
known as *The Pentagon Papers*, and concluded:

> The bombing of North Vietnam … was begun partly because theory
> said that 'a revolution could be dried up by cutting off external sources
> of support and supply.' The bombings were supposed to 'break the will'
> of North Vietnam to support the rebels in the South, although the deci-
> sion makers themselves (in this case [John] McNaughton [one of the
> key strategists behind the bombing campaign]) knew enough of the
> indigenous nature of the revolt to doubt that the Viet Cong would 'obey
> a caving' North Vietnam, while the Joint Chiefs did not believe 'that
> these efforts will have a decisive effect' on Hanoi's will to begin with.[91]

From 1970, the use of bombing – notably in Cambodia – was also
pushed as a way of 'substituting' for American combat units being withdrawn from Vietnam. The impetus to bomb Cambodia was redoubled
after the 1973 Paris peace agreement had banned bombing in South and
North Vietnam.[92]

The military intervention in Vietnam wilfully pushed aside the fact
that the Vietnamese had been fighting foreign invaders for almost two

thousand years,[93] and Arendt noted: 'nearly all decisions in this disastrous enterprise were made in full cognizance of the fact that they probably could not be carried out: hence goals had constantly to be shifted.'[94] As General Corson put it: 'By leaping from one purpose to another the politician has, so far, not sat still long enough for the people to demand an accounting or a straight answer.'[95]

If winning was not an overriding aim, what were the key goals? This is a big topic, and cannot adequately be addressed here. But it is clear that a significant influence on political decision-making was the idea, operating strongly in the White House, that 'This is a bad year for me to lose Vietnam to Communism.'[96] General Corson noted:

> The [US] politicians saw in Vietnam, or so they thought at the time, a chance to pull off a cheap victory against the Communists. When their initial judgments about Vietnam were found to be in error, there was no way to confess their error without risking defeat at the polls.[97]

As Arendt put it:

> ... when all signs pointed to defeat in the war of attrition, the goal was no longer one of avoiding humiliating defeat but of finding ways and means to avoid admitting it and 'save face'. Image-making as global policy – not world conquest, but victory in the battle 'to win the people's minds' – is indeed something new in the huge arsenal of human follies recorded in history.[98]

Particularly given that American tactics could not realistically win the 'hearts and minds' of the Vietnamese, attention naturally turned to managing the 'hearts and minds' of Americans. In many ways, winning was less important than appearing to win – or at least *not appearing to lose*. The parallels with Afghanistan today are again uncanny. One example of carving an image of victory from a reality of quagmire was the so-called Hamlet Evaluation System. This elaborate monitoring scheme appeared to show that security was improving in the years before 1968, and a key indicator of 'improvement' was taken to be the growing proportion of people now living in government-controlled zones. But the main reason for this 'positive' trend was the forcible expulsion of civilians from areas of rebel strength through the infliction of massive violence.[99] In Orwellian mode, massive violence and forcible displacement was thus neatly reclassified as an improvement in security! Meanwhile, this violence was itself creating large numbers of new Viet Cong, with rebel numbers rising significantly from 1966 to 1968.[100] The measurement process seems to have been designed to support the existing military strategy; yet this was a strategy that, when it came to defeating the enemy, was simply not working.[101] Even the massive setback of the 'Tet Offensive', which saw numerous attacks within Saigon itself, was often 'explained away'.[102]

Incentives within the US military were also conducive to an aggressive strategy that few senior officials seem to have believed would actually work. As David Hunt notes, 'Promotions for artillery and air-unit commanders went to those who fired off the most rounds and launched the most bombing sorties.'[103] Even the killing of civilians could be counted as part of the 'score' or 'body count' by which the performance of American soldiers was often assessed.[104] Significantly, rapid rotations made it difficult for the Americans to learn from experience in Vietnam; yet these rotations were strongly encouraged by a sense that higher-ranking officers all needed their 'turn' in Vietnam if they were to get promoted.[105] As Corson put it:

> The intellectual recognition of the subtleties and nuances of the Vietnam war was displaced by the emotional requirement to 'get my command – be it a company, battalion, regiment, or division.' Peacekeepers may be blessed, but war makers get promoted … Each of the military services has seen in Vietnam an opportunity to 'get theirs'.[106]

Rivalries between different arms of the military fed into aggression, too, with each element trying to establish a 'high-profile' role. In his well-known book *Sideshow*, William Shawcross noted:

> The US Air Force emphasized the important of strategic bombing over tactical bombing (close air support for ground troops) in part to guarantee its independence from the army. The Air Force had no real strategic mission in Korea but it immediately saw possibilities in Vietnam.[107]

Noting that some senior soldiers were complaining about the lack of 'approved' targets in South Vietnam, Corson observed: 'By definition an insurgent force lacks an air force. The bombing of North Vietnam is the means to allow our own air forces ... to get a piece of the Vietnam action and to enhance their own positions.'[108]

As so often, the mere existence of a powerful war machine seemed to demand its use, and the wider war around Vietnam illustrated this very starkly. In particular, the November 1968 halt to bombing over North Vietnam freed hundreds of planes for bombing missions in Laos. The American ambassador to Laos told Fred Branfman, an American educational adviser in Laos who documented the bombing of that country: 'You gotta understand, Fred – we had all those planes coming in to Laos. What could we do? We had to bomb villages.'[109] Over 2 million tons were dropped on 1 million people in the zones where the Pathet Lao rebels were strong – equivalent to the tonnage dropped on Europe and the entire Pacific 'theatre' during the Second World War.[110]

CHAPTER 4

Afghanistan

The defeat of the Taliban was announced in 2001. But as British administrator and ethnographer Sir Olaf Caroe warned, back in 1958, 'Afghan wars become serious only when they are over.'[1] After the Taliban government was ousted, the Russian general staff lost no time in pointing out (from their own bitter experience in the 1980s) that entry should not be confused with victory.[2] Yet gaining control of major cities in 2001 was repeatedly, and mistakenly, equated with winning the war – a 'victory' that left international forces in control of Kabul and surrounding areas, but had most of the 'defeated' insurgents returning home with their rifles.[3]

Ten years after it was first confidently announced, the defeat of the Taliban was still nowhere to be seen. Following 'defeat' in 2001–02, remnants of the Taliban were able to recover in Pakistani safe havens, and by 2005 had begun raiding in earnest into Afghanistan.[4] In many ways, the Taliban seemed quite content to destabilise the Afghan state, rather than attempt a direct 'takeover', and the rebels focused on controlling Pashtun regions of both Pakistan and Afghanistan.[5] While optimism has routinely been recycled among Western politicians, it has been increasingly difficult to substantiate. In his well-respected 2009 book *Accidental Guerrilla*, David Kilcullen described the overall trend in the conflict as extremely negative.[6] Although in 2010 more territory was held in Helmand and Kandahar by NATO forces, by early 2011 many indicators (including the number of insurgency attacks, civilian and foreign troop casualties, and the area of territory controlled by the Taliban) were refusing to point in the 'right' direction.[7] One 2011 study by Frank Ledwidge, called *Losing Small Wars*, was uncompromising in its assessment: when it went into Helmand in 2006, the British army's objective, Ledwidge recalled, had been to provide security in the province's fourteen districts; but 'five years later a force three times the size of the initial deployment clings on to three districts, and even in those the situation is appallingly difficult.'[8] Meanwhile, an August 2011 report by the International Crisis Group was similarly downbeat: 'Insurgent attacks have risen steadily, with the UN and international NGOs [non-governmental organisations] deeming more and more districts unsafe for travel.'[9]

In many ways, the puzzle of the war's longevity mirrors similar puzzles surrounding many wars in Africa and elsewhere. While estimates of the Taliban's (fluctuating) size vary, Kilcullen's study suggested a rebel force of maybe 32,000–40,000 men, of which perhaps 8,000 or 10,000 were full time and just 3,000 or 4,000 were 'hard-core fanatics who are not reconcilable under any circumstances'.[10] For several years, the size of international and national counterinsurgency forces reflected a lack of any serious planning to deal with the Taliban after the 'post-conflict era' had been declared from 2001–02. In early 2007, there were 32,000 US and allied forces under NATO command and another 8,000 coalition troops in counterterrorist operations.[11] Meanwhile, the national army numbered just 34,000.[12] Eventually, these various forces were boosted significantly, and by 2011 the Afghan National Security Forces (army and police) topped 300,000, while there were some 130,000 NATO troops (and a further 10,000 under direct US command). Although there have been some controversial equipment shortages (for example, of rescue helicopters) these NATO and US troops have nevertheless had access to some of the most sophisticated military equipment in the world.[13] Yet victory over the insurgents remains perpetually elusive.

Why has the Afghan war persisted for so long? Part of the answer would seem to be a reluctance to negotiate. While many diplomats on the ground have favoured some kind of negotiation with at least elements of the Taliban,[14] it has generally been very difficult to negotiate – or to be seen to be negotiating – with a group that has been publicly labelled 'terrorist'.[15]

That leaves the option of winning. But a key problem with this option has been that diverse actors shaping the counterinsurgency have attached a rather low priority to winning. Part of the mechanism here was the insistence – useful on the domestic political front – that victory had *already* been achieved in 2001, and the corresponding low commitments of resources to Afghanistan. In a 2007 article, one Afghanistan specialist noted that the country was getting less aid per capita than any other state with a recent post-conflict building effort, with significant underinvestment in reconstruction and state-building.[16] Actual aid given was often significantly below the amounts pledged. Another Afghanistan specialist referred to a 'bargain basement' or 'minimalist' approach that erroneously equated peace with ousting the Taliban.[17] Another article noted in 2007, 'The United States is spending more money every 72 hours on the war in Iraq than it is spending on Afghan reconstruction this year.'[18]

The lack of priority attached to defeating the Taliban on the part of local and regional actors seems to have taken many Western observers and officials by surprise. While the war itself has been a disaster, we need to recognise that a number of local and regional actors have been 'succeeding' (in terms of their most important goals) in the midst of what looks like a 'failure' to quell the Taliban. Meanwhile, even many Western politicians and officials appear to have achieved important goals (like limiting political 'fall out' and maintaining budgets) in the face of this collective 'failure'.

Part of the explanation for the war's intractable nature is that, despite the casualties that have been inflicted on Taliban fighters, the foreign occupation has itself helped the Taliban in various ways. For one thing, the extended and expanding military occupation has helped the Taliban to portray itself as the latest in a long line of Afghan movements resisting foreign (and non-Muslim) invaders.[19] Correspondingly, President Hamid Karzai has often been portrayed as a Western puppet.[20] The civilian casualties and other abuses inflicted by Western troops have also helped the Taliban.[21] In Helmand, where British forces took the lead in counterinsurgency operations, a shortage of troops seems to have encouraged a reliance on air strikes and heavy weaponry.[22] One observer noted the propensity for charging off into the desert with a Land Rover and a large machine-gun.[23] Yet such tactics clearly conflict with the goal of protecting the population.[24] It is true that US General Stanley McChrystal, who took over as commander of US and NATO forces in Afghanistan in June 2009, pushed strongly for a policy of 'zero civilian casualties', arguing that these casualties generated recruits for the Taliban – and McChrystal did succeed in bringing the casualties down.[25] But use of air strikes and artillery subsequently increased again,[26] and there have been well-publicised recent cases of civilians being killed by international forces.[27]

American researchers Thomas Johnson and Chris Mason, drawing on considerable experience in Afghanistan, observe:

> At the strategic level, the Taliban is fighting a classic 'war of the flea,' largely along the same lines used by the mujahideen twenty years ago against the Soviets, including fighting in villages to deliberately provoke air strikes and collateral damage. They gladly trade the lives of a few dozen guerrilla fighters in order to cost the American forces the permanent loyalty of that village, under the code of Pashtun social behavior called *Pashtunwali* and its obligation for revenge (*Badal*), which the U.S. Army does not even begin to understand.[28]

Even if it had been possible to kill *only* insurgents, the killing could still produce additional insurgents due, in part, to strong local codes of revenge.[29]

Another way in which the international forces have sought to weaken the Taliban has been by attempting to eradicate the production of poppies (used to make opium), a crop that has been helping to finance the rebels.[30] But this has been something of a blunt instrument – not least because many *non-rebel* Afghans rely on poppy production for their livelihoods, and the Taliban has been able to present itself as a defender of these livelihoods.[31] It sometimes even offered compensation to those so affected.[32] Where drug-trafficking warlords have been ushered into power and crops have been targeted, it can look like a policy of rewarding rich drug dealers and punishing poor farmers, particularly since crop eradication can raise prices and put more money in the hands of drug traders.[33] There has also been a problem of bias: for example, in Helmand province (which produces a large quantity of poppies) the international effort to eradicate poppy production has become highly politicised, with fields that belong to favoured groups being left alone and the fields of less well connected groups being targeted. The Taliban has also exploited grievances arising from this bias.[34]

The NATO occupation has also given a boost to the Taliban *within Pakistan*, first when Taliban elements fled from Afghanistan, and secondly when drone strikes against the Taliban inside Pakistan led to casualties among Pakistani civilians.[35] The Taliban has argued that foreign forces have spilled blood on both sides of the border.[36] In September 2009, US Vice President Joe Biden noted that, despite an over-whelming international focus on Afghanistan rather than Pakistan, Taliban fighters were actually much stronger in the latter. Biden also pointed to a fundamental problem with counterinsurgency in the context of a mobile enemy and porous borders: 'There's a balloon effect. We squeeze it, and it pops out somewhere else. Are we prepared to go to other countries where al Qaeda can pop up?'[37] Such wars have a way of widening, even *within* countries: in a 2009 article, Steven Simon and Jonathan Stevenson noted, 'The very success of the [US] targeted-killing programme in Waziristan [a Pakistani region on the border with Afghanistan] led survivors to move into Baluchistan and would seem to necessitate an expansion in that direction.'[38] Meanwhile – and this is a crucial point – the safe havens for the Taliban in Pakistan mean that, even if the military campaign within Afghanistan were extremely successful, it would not be able to eliminate the main insurgent groups in that country.[39]

If the presence of foreign troops has given the Taliban an important 'cause', the announcement of those troops' impending departure has also, paradoxically, boosted the Taliban. Given waning political support among Western publics for such an extended military campaign, the Taliban insurgents – as well as a variety of 'fence-sitters' in Afghanistan – have for some time realised that the NATO alliance is on its way out.[40] Moreover, US President Barack Obama and British Prime Minister David Cameron have both made clear their intention to remove their troops from the country. Yet this impending departure represents a huge disincentive for ordinary Afghans to turn unambiguously against a Taliban that will certainly remain present and influential once Western forces have left, and that has already shown its willingness to 'retaliate' against those who cooperate with the 'reconstruction' efforts sponsored by Kabul and the international forces.

Pakistan nurtured the Taliban and helped its rise to power in Afghanistan. Pakistan's Inter-Services Intelligence secretly supporting the Taliban, and the Afghan rebels' resurgence in 2006 would not have been possible without this support.[41] Despite US pressure on the Pakistan government, the expressed intention of withdrawing Western troops seems actually to have strengthened Pakistan's support for

Taliban elements. As Rudra Chaudhuri and Theo Farrell noted in early 2011, 'Western intelligence accepts that the July 2011 deadline for the beginning of US force withdrawal reinforced Pakistani support for the QST [Quetta Shura Taliban] and the HQN [Haqqani Network], viewed by Pakistan as its proxies in the Afghan endgame.'[42] Pakistan, which helped the Taliban to rise to power in the first place,[43] fears a raging civil war in the wake of Western withdrawal, and for Pakistan there is little sense in targeting Pashtun Taliban actors who are traditionally closer to Pakistan and who are likely to play a part in any future Afghan government.[44] Significantly, the Afghan government in Kabul, where Tajiks have had a disproportionate influence since 2001, is considered to be close to Pakistan's great rival, India, which has given the Kabul government US$1.3 billion as an aid package.[45] Pakistan's overriding concern is with India – and with avoiding any sense that India is using Afghanistan to 'surround' it. Pakistan has also been concerned to neutralise Pashtun and Baluch nationalism within its own borders, and has done so in part by supporting Islamist militias among the Pashtun.[46]

As if all this were not bad enough (from the point of view of Western forces), the Western intervention has provided another major 'boon' for the Taliban: both the NATO military campaign and the associated aid effort have powerfully fuelled corruption and Afghanistan's war economy more generally. The backing of Western forces has combined with substantial resource flows to prop up a variety of abusive actors linked to the Afghan government. This has helped to undermine attempts to build a modern, legitimate and responsive state and has enabled the Taliban to paint itself not only as 'holier than thou', but also less corrupt. The difficulties in harnessing aid to counterinsurgency can be seen as a sub-set of a larger and well-documented problem: it is very hard to channel large amounts of aid through corrupt and abusive regimes without reinforcing corruption and abuse. Meanwhile, major political and economic interests in continued conflict have been nurtured within the Afghan regime.[47] Moreover, a large injection of Western resources has actually helped to fund the insurgency.

When a Western 'war for peace' refuses to end, common reactions have been to call for *more troops*, to call for *more aid*, or even to call for *more wars* (and hence more distractions). While hawkish elements have tended to favour more troops or more wars (or both), rather more 'liberal' elements in Western governments have often advocated *more aid.* In a prolonged war, Western officials (and even aid workers) commonly suggest that what is needed is a shift from a purely or largely military approach towards one that favours some kind of 'development' as a way to win 'hearts and minds'. We saw this in Vietnam, and the impulse to inject aid into an ailing military campaign has been reinvented in Afghanistan. With the war against the Taliban faltering, a large increase in aid spending has been pushed through in a bid to 'win hearts and minds' (a goal so commonly referred to that it now has its own acronym – WHAM). In the summer of 2009, the US government indicated that it planned nearly to double (to $1.2 billion) the main fund for projects that military commanders use to 'win hearts and minds'.[48]

The hope of the US-led coalition in Afghanistan has been that a 'development-oriented' approach will wean Afghans from the Taliban more effectively than crude military force. That may look sensible in theory. But there is a great deal of evidence that throwing money at the problem has actually been making it worse.

In the rush to wage war on 'terror' (with bombs, bullets, money, food, schools ... anything), important lessons that many aid workers (and even politicians) had learned about international aid – notably the dangers of fuelling violence and the importance of 'Doing no Harm'[49] – seem to have been thrown overboard with some abandon. More specifically, the way that poorly directed aid fed into war economies in Ethiopia, Sudan, Sierra Leone, Somalia and elsewhere has apparently been erased from the collective memory. Another hard-earned lesson from Africa and elsewhere that has now seemingly been set aside is that aid cannot realistically substitute for diplomatic failures.[50]

In Afghanistan (as so often elsewhere) aid has regularly been ascribed almost magical qualities – notably, the ability to bring conflict to an end; yet most available evidence points to the centrality of serious diplomatic engagement (backed by carefully calibrated aid 'conditionality'). In the context of Afghanistan, Goodhand and Sedra refer to 'narcissistic beliefs in the transformative potential of aid'.[51] It is as if the Vietnam-style 'quagmire' in Afghanistan somehow demands resuscitation of the habitually failing paradigm of aid-as-counterinsurgency – even though we have little reason to believe that it can work (or has worked before in comparable circumstances). The nurturing of corruption among abusive allies mimics a similar process in Vietnam, but the parallel is typically ignored. It all adds up to an attack of collective amnesia that continuously reinvents unrealistic solutions that have already been discredited.

Meanwhile, with the Taliban being vilified internationally, a focus on the bad qualities of the rebels (often blamed for the drugs trade, as well as for terrorism) has tended to squeeze out proper consideration of 'greed' within the counterinsurgency. This one-eyed view – which mirrors a similar myopia in Vietnam, as well as in many more recent conflicts – has once again distracted attention not only from government avarice, but also from the various grievances that have fuelled violence, whether within the insurgency or the counterinsurgency.

***

If recent Western interventions have inadvertently helped the Taliban, it is also worth remembering the days when the Taliban was *intentionally* assisted. Taliban forces originally emerged from refugee communities – and *mujahadeen* forces – that were supported by the West in Pakistan as part of a Cold War struggle against the Soviet-backed Kabul regime in the 1980s. At this time, the *mujahadeen* were also getting major backing from the Saudis in particular – assistance that was mediated, in part, by a Saudi billionaire called Osama bin Laden.[52] (Many of the weapons provided to *mujahadeen* were used in the civil wars of the 1990s and have more recently fallen into the hands of the Taliban.[53] One USAID official told me in 2007, 'The stingers [anti-aircraft missiles] have really stung us!')

The Taliban benefited from the violence and exploitation that followed the Soviet departure in 1988–89. There was also a sense among the *mujahadeen* – and Afghans more generally – of having been deserted by the West. Significantly, the Western-based alliance that ejected the Soviets from Afghanistan did not survive Moscow's departure, and the former *mujahadeen* were soon riven by internal conflicts. Western aid fell sharply, and Soviet aid to Kabul also collapsed. In these circumstances, disorder in Afghanistan mutated from a struggle between the Western-backed *mujahadeen* and the Soviet-backed Kabul government into fighting between rival warlords who looked increasingly to *internal* revenue-raising, including looting, demands for 'protection money', and the taxation of opium.[54] With external aid falling in the context of a government attempt to 'buy off' warlords and enlarge the security

forces, the government resorted to printing money, which caused inflation and further encouraged opium growing – in part, so that ordinary
Afghans could afford the rising cost of food.[55]

In the 1990s, with the economy undermined by warring factions, the
country's already fragile central administration and much of the army
went into deep decline. In these circumstances, it was impossible to rein
in the autonomy of local warlords. Even within the national army, ficti-
tious 'ghost soldiers' became widespread. As Antonio Giustozzi, an
astute Italian who has done as much as anyone to improve understanding of this complex country, explains:

> ... local military leaders, now appointed to command 'official' armed
> units, inflated the number of troops in their ranks and pocketed the
> difference in the salaries paid, burdening the coffers of the rulers with
> a massive military expenditure which did not even translate into real
> military strength.[56]

All this left the Kabul government in a very weak position when the
Taliban advanced in 1997–98.[57] Strange as it may sound, conditions of
endemic conflict between rival warlords were also encouraging many
people to turn to the Taliban as a *better alternative*. The Taliban has been
demonised as a source of terrorism and an abuser of human rights
within Afghanistan – and not without reason: Afghanistan did indeed
serve as a base for al Qaeda under the Taliban; and many of the Taliban's
actions have indeed been extremely abusive (not least in relation to
women). But it is also important to recognise that the Taliban was only
able to rise to power because it could offer certain things that many
people considered valuable. Most notable here was relative security
(after the country's collapse into warlordism), and this included safer
conditions and fewer roadblocks for traders (many of whom supported
the Taliban),[58] as well as a reprieve from having one's sons forcibly
recruited by one warlord or another.[59] In many ways, outsiders'
'blind spots' in relation to the Taliban and other demonised groups
seem to mirror similar blind spots in relation to war more generally.
Merely condemning the Taliban – like condemning war – does not
get us very far, and we need to understand the functions of the Taliban
and other rebel groups, just as we need to understand the functions
of war.

The Taliban's functions have arisen quite naturally and logically from the *dysfunctions* of the Afghan state. 'Despite the role of foreign sponsors,' Giustozzi has written,

> the insurgency would not have succeeded in becoming anything more than a mere annoyance if it had not been able to exploit the intrinsic weaknesses of the Afghan state, both as it was originally conceived and as it was 'rebuilt' from 2001 [that is, after the Taliban government was ousted].[60]

This emphasis on state weakness takes us back, in many ways, to the situation in Sierra Leone, where a rebel force of just a few hundred was able to displace over half the country's population because of grave weaknesses within the Sierra Leonean state.

Of course, there has been a huge international effort to strengthen the Afghan state, much of it with the best of intentions. Strikingly, the Afghan army and police got fully US$29 billion between 2002 and 2010 – more than half the total international aid.[61] But the performance of the army and police has been poor. In 2008, NATO reckoned that 62 per cent of Afghan National Army units were incapable of conducting battalion-level operations, even with some support from international forces. The national army has been plagued by corruption, poor leadership, drug use, ethnic rivalry, absence without leave, and high desertion rates (as high as 55 per cent in some units in the south).[62] Insurgent infiltration is reported to be another problem.[63] It did not help that, in a situation prematurely and optimistically labelled 'post-war', many members of the Afghan national army were originally recruited for the task of reconstruction, rather than for counterinsurgency.[64] Meanwhile, alongside the major international effort to expand the army, there has been little attempt to *reform* the security services so as to make them accountable to civilian authorities.[65] Other problems loom on the horizon: while expanding the army has been a priority, such a large military may not be financially sustainable – and in Afghanistan an inability properly to fund the military machine has, in the past, been a major source of instability.[66]

While a functioning police might have compensated for the army's weaknesses, Afghanistan's police force appears to have been even more corrupt, drug-ridden and ill-disciplined than the army.[67] As Chaudhuri and Farrell noted in 2011, 'Often, the police are little more than a militia of the local powerholder; they commonly prey on the population, and through their extortion and violent abuse of civilians can turn local people towards insurgency.'[68] Barnett Rubin noted that many Afghans 'report that kidnappers and robbers wore police uniforms'.[69]

The 'failings' of the Afghan state are not simply accidents or mistakes: they reflect powerful structural factors that are extremely difficult to transform. By 2010, Afghanistan was the second most corrupt country in the world (after Somalia), according to Transparency International.[70] This is not going to change overnight. Many of the state's shortcomings reflect the power and significant autonomy of warlords who were brought into the state administration in 2001 – essentially as a reward for their role in ousting the Taliban.[71] Although the American air force was certainly important in defeating the Taliban at this time, the modest commitment of foreign ground troops left a key role for local anti-Taliban militias and helped them to become key players in the post-Taliban power game.[72] Some of these continued to get CIA and US military funding.[73] Many of the returning warlords had earlier been ousted by the Taliban precisely because of their predatory activities, so there are *longstanding* grievances against resurgent warlords.[74] As Barnett Rubin put it: 'Rearming warlords empowered leaders the Afghan people had rejected.'[75] These warlords have also created problems for 'reconstruction' – not least when they have withheld customs revenues from central government in Kabul.[76] Another rather fundamental problem is that Afghan President Hamid Karzai has often given important local positions to members of minority tribes (not least to limit the possibility of local warlords rising against him).[77] But this has helped further to undermine government legitimacy, and the Taliban has been able to denounce unrepresentative and corrupt local rulers.[78]

While Western observers have tended to link the drugs economy with the Taliban – a variation of the 'greedy rebel' thesis – many government actors have themselves been involved in the drugs trade on a massive scale.[79] As Ahmed Rashid wrote in 2007:

> The lack of developmental activities in the south has resulted in part from [President] Karzai's failure to purge corrupt or drug-trafficking officials from powerful positions. This has fuelled disillusionment among Pashtuns, the dominant ethnic group in southern and eastern

Afghanistan, many of whom are now offering to fight for or at least offer sanctuary to the Taliban.[80]

Barnett Rubin noted in 2007: 'Police chiefs in poppy-growing districts are sold to the highest bidder: as much as $100,000 is paid for a six-month appointment to a position with a monthly salary of $60.' Of course, the balance of power in Afghanistan is far from unchanging. From 2003, the Tajiks and Uzbeks of the anti-Taliban Northern Alliance began to lose their stranglehold over central government, with Hamid Karzai pushing back against the Northern Alliance warlords.[81] But popular perceptions of rule by a small (if shifting) elite remain entrenched, disarmament has often proceeded more slowly among units affiliated with the Northern Alliance,[82] and warlords connected to the Karzai family have themselves been abusive. In Helmand province, the international community backed local warlords in 2001–05, and this contributed to a perception that the government authorities lacked legitimacy. After that, the warlords were rather precipitously removed, and this seems to have created a security vacuum in which the ousted warlords fed the continuing violence in the area.[83]

A key problem is that aid has been seen by many Afghans as reinforcing a much older pattern, whereby elites do not need to cultivate popular support and prefer to rely on outside support of various kinds.[84] Andrew Wilder at Boston's Tufts University notes:

The most destabilizing effect of aid ... is its role in fueling massive corruption, which in turn is eroding the legitimacy of the government. Our research suggests that we have failed to win Afghan hearts and minds not because we have spent too little money, but because we have spent too much too quickly, often in insecure environments with extremely limited implementation and oversight capacity.[85]

Particularly important in drawing people to the Taliban has been the failure of the Afghan state to provide security – and many Afghans believe the main cause of insecurity is their corrupt and predatory government.[86] One Afghan official in the southern province of Uruzgan said: 'In this area the family and friends of Karzai get everything. All aid in these areas is to make them more powerful. They are corrupt and cruel people, but donors continue to support them.'[87]

American journalist Ann Marlowe makes a similar point even more graphically:

> American commanders will tell you of governors, police chiefs, district governors, and district police chiefs so corrupt, abusive, and vicious that the Taliban are a desirable alternative. We are talking about Afghan government officials who sell famine aid for their own profit, rape boys and women, run drugs in police cars – and often conspire with insurgents to kill Afghan civilians and security forces, and even American troops.[88]

On the basis of detailed research on the ground, Stuart Gordon, formerly of the Royal Military Academy Sandhurst and now at the London School of Economics, notes that signs of development have been taken by some non-beneficiaries as evidence that aid has been captured by elites. Thus, 'the distribution of aid in such a fragmented and polarized polity often marginalized groups and increased the sense of alienation rather than giving hope of potential change'.[89] In Paktia province in the east, the US-led Provincial Reconstruction Team has been funding aid projects since 2003. Andrew Wilder quotes a tribal elder in the region:

> Paktia has lots of problems, but the issue of lack of clinics, schools, and roads are not the problem. The main problem is we don't have a good government ... Without a clean government, millions of dollars are stolen. If you increase the amount of money it will also be useless because the government will simply steal more. There's a growing distance between the people and the government and this is the main cause of the deteriorating security situation.[90]

The Taliban has been promising to tackle corruption and to improve justice and security,[91] and many Afghans see the rebels as better able than the government to deliver security and justice.[92] In fact, the Taliban has already been providing guerrilla law courts through southern Afghanistan, meeting some of the local needs for mediation and dispute resolution.[93] Meanwhile, with international interventions having generally neglected reform of the courts and the justice system, citizens' trust in the police and government courts has fallen in many parts of the country.[94] Many local people contrast Islamic law not with secular law but with corruption and impunity.[95]

One window on the nature and effects of continuing corruption in Afghanistan is Kandahar province, a key Taliban stronghold in the south of the country. Here, the international forces chose to work closely with Ahmed Wali Karzai, brother of the president, in a bid for stability. But security has actually deteriorated over time.[96]

A thorough and enlightening investigation in Kandahar district by Carl Forsberg of the Washington-based Institute for the Study of War concluded: 'The governance situation in Kandahar undermines any attempts to fight the insurgency.'[97] Forsberg explained further:

> The local population sees the government as an exclusive oligarchy devoted to its own enrichment and closely tied to the international coalition. Anti-governmental sentiments are exploited and aggravated by the Taliban. Many of the local powerbrokers who are excluded from [Ahmed] Wali Karzai's network see the Taliban insurgency as the only viable means of political opposition.[98]

Ahmed Wali Karzai, who was killed by one of his own bodyguards in July 2011, had enjoyed particularly close ties with the CIA and US special forces. Significantly, he was able to convince rivals that he had the support of the coalition. For its part, the CIA came to rely on him as a fixer for renting property and as a provider of a key proxy force, the Kandahar Strike Force.[99] The International Security Assistance Force (ISAF) also needed him for intelligence and contracting support. Bolstered by external support, Ahmed Wali Karzai was able to use his own militias to get a significant cut from business activities in Kandahar, transferring much of this money abroad.[100] Benefiting from international contracts – and strongly influencing the distribution of these contracts – became a vital part of Wali Karzai's power strategy. In an important statement, Forsberg observes:

> An underlying dynamic driving Kandahar politics, which has become more important after 2006, has been the consolidation by the Karzai and Sherzai families [a rival network] of patronage networks whereby they gain the loyalty of militia commanders in exchange for distributing lucrative contracts from international actors. The Sherzai and

Karzai families have secured a duopoly on the distribution of major contracts from the international community. Obtaining private security contracts became extremely desirable for militia commanders in Kandahar, who could secure enormous compensation and in some cases legitimize their militias. The politics of contract patronage has undermined security in Kandahar by generating armed militias operating outside formal Afghan structures which are committed to protecting their own profits and the political interests of their commanders.[101]

In Kandahar district, many militias were integrated into the police, and this was presented as part of 'state-building'. But some of the militiamen subsequently engaged in crime and extortion *as policemen*. Meanwhile, this process of absorbing militias into the police has helped to give militias a veneer of legitimacy, even when they have remained under the control of former (and often abusive) commanders.[102] Police chiefs quickly learned not to impinge on Ahmed Wali Karzai's huge commercial interests.[103] Meanwhile, as Forsberg notes:

> Local powerbrokers have intentionally kept the official police force weak. This allows them to manipulate the police force to their ends and forces ISAF to rely on their [the powerbrokers'] private security companies. Because many of these companies are controlled by or allied with Ahmed Wali Karzai, this ensures both revenue and influence.[104]

One incident brings this manipulation into sharp focus. In June 2009, forty members of Ahmed Wali Karzai's CIA-trained Kandahar Strike Force turned up at the Kandahar police headquarters demanding the release of a criminal they had been working with. The protest culminated in the killing of the police chief, Matiullah Qateh, who had been relatively well regarded by the Canadians (who have played a key role for NATO within Kandahar). Significantly, Qateh's replacement was Mirwais Noorzai, a loyal ally of the Karzais, who was subsequently accused of turning a blind eye to massive electoral fraud in Kandahar in 2009. (During the 2009 Afghan presidential elections over 250,000 votes were reportedly cast in Kandahar, but more than 177,000 of these were deemed to be fraudulent.[105])

In Kandahar province, as elsewhere, the international effort to demo-bilise former soldiers – a process known as disarmament, demobilisa-tion and reintegration (DDR) – was, in many ways, a major threat to the authority of the Afghan warlords (mostly ex-*mujahadeen*). Militias' profits from checkpoints and extortion were severely reduced. But there were also new opportunities. The militias' survival often came to depend on getting a lucrative contract from the ISAF international forces. If the smaller players in Kandahar were to get such a contract (and thereby secure wages higher than the army or police), they needed good rela-tions with the two dominant networks – and this helped both Ahmed Wali Karzai and the rival Sherzai family to build their political bases.[106]

Ahmed Wali Karzai also had connections with large security firms like Watan Risk Management and Asia Security Group, which have been run by the extended Karzai family and which have enjoyed lucrative contracts with the occupying forces. Moreover, Ahmed Wali Karzai was able to play a key role in the distribution of aid, including by NGOs (it appears to have helped that he had worked with them in Pakistan in the 1980s and 1990s). As Forsberg notes, 'Local leaders desiring NGO or state assistance found Ahmed Wali Karzai a chief mediator for securing desired resources.'[107] Ahmed Wali Karzai seems to have realised that maintaining his position – and his legitimacy in international eyes – would demand some success in elections. As has also been observed in other contexts (such as the former Yugoslavia),[108] those who benefited from war were often able to use their wealth and 'muscle' to carve out a political role, using international resources provided for 'reconstruction'.

If contracts to serve ISAF have entrenched abusive elites, it is also the case that international forces have sometimes been used more directly for political purposes. In his 2010 report, Forsberg commented on night raids in Kandahar city by coalition forces and the Kandahar National Directorate of Security (NDS), which is loyal to Karzai family interests:

> There is a widespread belief that night raids are ordered by Ahmed Wali Karzai for political ends, targeting his political opponents rather than dangerous insurgent leaders. As long as the perception remains that a small elite is using the NDS and coalition forces to further their own power at the cost of significant constituencies, it will be difficult to reconcile much of the population with the government.[109]

Forsberg comments further: 'The use by Ahmed Wali Karzai and his allies of private paramilitary forces to subordinate rivals is deeply incompatible with ISAF's governance objectives.' This is part of a more general problem: in their study of war in Afghanistan, Tim Bird and Alex Marshall observe: 'Intelligence passed by Afghans to the coalition was often slanted to further private feuds.'[110]

The case of Kandahar strongly suggests that while the Afghan state has been 'weak' in significant respects, these weaknesses actually correspond to important 'strengths' on the part of various local actors throughout the country. A significant 'shadow state' lurks on the fringes of state institutions, simultaneously undermining them and drawing strength and resources from them.[111] As the long war drags on in Afghanistan, increasing numbers of people have been led to ask 'what went wrong?'. But, as so often in the context of contemporary wars and 'state failure' and the perplexing 'failure' of aid interventions, we may be better off asking 'what went right?' – and 'for whom?'.

While many Western politicians and observers have overestimated the West's ability to transform Afghan politics and society, it is also striking (as in Vietnam) that whatever leverage the international community *does* possess has rarely been put to use. Forsberg notes: 'ISAF contract and other forms of funding, including development aid, are the foundation of Kandahar's political economy. As such, ISAF has tremendous power to shape local dynamics through the calculated use of its funds.'[112] However, this demands not only a willingness to tackle corruption, but also a reasonable degree of unity among the various elements of coalition forces (for example, in relation to local warlords like Ahmed Wali Karzai).[113] A telling episode came when donors proved slow to support the IMF after it suspended credit in September 2010 due to massive fraud at the Kabul Bank.[114] One neglected instrument against corruption is the possibility of arresting, under the US Foreign Corrupt Practices Act, those criminal suspects who have dual citizenship.[115]

Probably the most shocking aspect of the international intervention in Afghanistan is the way it has provided material support for the Taliban – the very rebels it is intended to destroy. While the bible invites us to 'love thine enemy', this seems to have been taken to an extreme in Afghanistan. The need to protect the foreign intervention from the rebels has itself helped to fund the rebels. As one intelligent analyst noted in December 2009: 'One of the major sources of funding for the Taliban is the protection money.'[116] This is not a radical journalist digging for dirt; it is US Secretary of State Hillary Clinton in a statement to the Senate Foreign Relations Committee. According to a June 2010 US House of Representatives report: 'Such protection payments are alleged to be widespread across a number of different industries in Afghanistan: reconstruction projects, telecommunications systems, poppy cultivation and smuggling, and transportation.'[117] An investigative team assembled by General David Petraeus, called Task Force 2010, estimated that some $360 million provided by US taxpayers had ended up with the Taliban, criminals and powerbrokers with ties to both.[118]

Andrew Wilder and his team at Tufts University heard many reports of the Taliban 'being paid by donor-funded contractors to provide security (or not to create insecurity), especially for their road-building projects'.[119] In fact, a symbiotic relationship has grown up between the Taliban and the security firms that are being paid so handsomely to provide protection against it. As UN Special Representative Peter Galbraith has noted:

> The U.S. spends hundreds of millions on Afghan security companies who use the proceeds to pay off the Taliban not to attack, or, in some cases, to stage attacks so as to enable the local warlord (a.k.a. security contractor) to hire more men at higher prices.[120]

According to the 2010 US House of Representatives report, many of the Taliban attacks on security firms 'are really negotiations over the fee'.[121] While the warlords who often control security companies may claim daily gun battles with the Taliban, some seem to be able to 'obtain' a surprisingly small number of attacks, particularly given the large number of truck trips.[122] In March, the US Defense Department awarded a $2.16 billion contract with local truckers to supply American troops (equivalent to around 10 per cent of Afghanistan's gross domestic product).[123] The above-mentioned US House of Representatives report noted that many people within this trucking community

> believe that a large portion of their protection payments to local warlords for convoy security subsequently go to the Taliban or other anti-government elements, the forces that actually control much of

Afghanistan and many of the key routes used for transportation of U.S. supplies.[124]

Colonel David Haight, commander of the Third Brigade of the US's 10th Mountain Division, said of these payments: 'The American soldier in me is repulsed by it. But I know that it is what it is: essentially paying the enemy, saying "Hey, don't hassle me." '[125]

The security companies themselves can be pretty frank about these arrangements. The head of the Mirzada Transport Company said: 'Every truck costs about $200 as a bribe I pay on the route – to police or Taliban.' Sometimes the Taliban has kidnapped drivers, asking between $10,000 and $50,000 for their release.[126] Notes from a July 2009 meeting of HNT (Host Nation Trucking) truckers referred to a request to carry more arms on the trucks, estimating that this would stop the flow to the Taliban of some $1.6 to $2 million a week.[127]

Apart from fuelling corruption, funding the Taliban and fostering vested interests in 'permanent emergency', patterns of aid and other resource flows have stoked resentments and created incentives for violence on the part of those who feel excluded. As Wilder puts it:

> In an ethnically and tribally divided society like Afghanistan, aid can also easily generate jealousy and ill will by inadvertently helping to consolidate the power of some tribes or factions at the expense of others – often pushing rival groups into the arms of the Taliban.[128]

The summary of a major conference at the UK's Wilton Park in March 2010 noted:

> There is a definite perception that donor money is following the violence and drugs to the South and South-West, creating a form of 'peace penalty' for those living in other parts of the country. It was felt that this was exacerbated by the resource-strained PRTs [Provincial Reconstruction Teams] in those areas.[129]

Significant sums have also gone east, but many relatively peaceful parts have been neglected.[130] In many ways, stable northern communities have been sent a 'signal' that peace does not pay.[131] A related problem is that first raising and then not meeting expectations fuels resentment and insurgency.[132] Meanwhile, a 'dollar bubble' in Kabul has exacerbated longstanding disparities in wealth between the capital and rural areas.[133] Within Kabul, inequalities have also been heightened, as some have benefited from aid and the international presence, while others have suffered from rising prices, including for food and housing.[134]

It is easy to forget that the Taliban itself – and many Taliban-controlled areas – have been excluded from aid. The international community has not been trying to negotiate access with rebels here, despite many attempts to do so in other countries and a mandate from the UN's Office for the Coordination of Humanitarian Affairs that calls for such negotiations.[135] The International Committee of the Red Cross is something of an exception in its ability to sustain some kind of relationship with Taliban leaders.[136] In addition to former US Secretary of State Colin Powell famously speaking of NGOs as 'force multipliers',[137] senior UN figures have publicly welcomed the prosecution of the war and the US-led military 'surge'. In an incisive analysis, Donini notes that there is

> ... no clarity on humanitarian needs, and an extremely politicized environment where aid agencies are pressured into supporting the Coalition and the government's political and military agendas. As a result, there is little understanding of, and respect for, humanitarian principles by the Taliban and other insurgents who tar the UN and NGOs with the occupiers' brush.[138]

In many ways, NGOs have walked into this quagmire – notably by presenting their relief and reconstruction activities as part of a broader political or peacemaking project. Indeed, criticisms after the Rwandan genocide that aid and diplomatic interventions were insufficiently 'joined up' seem to have fed into some of the more unhelpful forms of politicisation of contemporary aid.[139]

Yet another problem in Afghanistan is that aid operations have sometimes exposed civilians to retaliation. Violence has included Taliban attacks on reconstruction projects and on the people implementing them. The Taliban has targeted schools, teachers and health centres, as well as NGO staff.[140] This means that associating oneself with government/donor development projects can be very dangerous – and once international forces leave, the threat of Taliban retaliation may increase. According to Thomas Johnson and Chris Mason, the message from the

Taliban, delivered in person or by 'night letter', is: 'The Americans may stay for five years, they may stay for ten, but eventually they will leave, and when they do, we will come back to this village and kill every family that has collaborated with the Americans or the Karzai government.'[141] (This mirrors similar dynamics earlier in Vietnam.)[142] Evidence from Helmand underlines these difficulties. Here, the idea was that British forces would turn certain parts of the province into 'beacons of development' that would entice other parts into a political settlement with the government authorities. This was a model that seems to have helped counterinsurgency in Malaya, but the thin foreign administrative presence in Afghanistan does not remotely resemble the colonial administration in Malaya.[143] In areas where the Taliban has been incompletely 'cleared', local people have generally been reluctant to engage with the reconstruction process.[144] Often the Taliban has returned to 'cleared' areas, prompting the British task force commander to comment that his forces' repeated sorties felt like 'mowing the lawn'.[145] Stuart Gordon notes that many people would only engage in government/international reconstruction if they could actually buy Taliban security, or if they could use their own militias to prevent Taliban retaliation; yet paying the Taliban and building up local militias are hardly activities that are consistent with 'state-building'.

After Andrew Wilder and his team carried out more than four hundred interviews in Afghanistan, Wilder noted:

> The underlying assumption is that aid projects, such as building schools, clinics, and roads, will win the hearts and minds of Afghans, give them more faith in their government, and turn them away from the Taliban. The logic sounds reasonable. But the problem is that there is little evidence to support it.[146]

He added:

> While many projects have clearly had important humanitarian and development benefits, we have found little evidence that aid projects are 'winning hearts and minds', reducing conflict and violence, or having other significant counterinsurgency benefits. In fact, our research shows just the opposite. Instead of winning hearts and minds, Afghan perceptions of aid and aid actors are overwhelmingly

negative. And instead of contributing to stability, in many cases aid is contributing to conflict and instability.[147]

A key problem – again mirroring Vietnam – is that rebellion has fed on perceptions of injustice, corruption and bad governance (as well as help from Pakistan) rather more than on poverty and 'underdevelopment'. Goodhand and Sedra point out that many of the poorest areas of Afghanistan, like central Afghanistan, are relatively unaffected by insurgency,[148] while Barnett Rubin notes: 'The argument that poverty and underdevelopment, rather than Pakistani support, are responsible for the insurgency does not stand up to scrutiny: northern and western Afghanistan are also plagued by crime and insecurity, and yet there is no coordinated antigovernment violence in those regions.'[149]

Another major difficulty is that, since aid has been proclaimed by top US government officials to be an arm of counterinsurgency, it is not surprising that aid agencies have been *perceived* as an arm of counterinsurgency. So the idea that a 'humanitarian' enterprise will win hearts and minds has arguably been undermined at the outset. Further, with aid agencies often seen as part of a Western political agenda, those aid agencies have tended to 'bunker themselves in', taking extensive security precautions and often preferring to use local aid workers rather than expatriates (employing what is sometimes called 'remote management').[150] But this 'bunkering' itself makes genuine development more difficult, as it becomes harder to respond to Afghans' needs and priorities.[151] UN veteran Antonio Donini charges that UN agencies and non-governmental organisations 'are allowing their universe of responsibility to be defined by political and security considerations rather than by the humanitarian imperative to save and protect lives'.[152] 'Non-governmental organisations' is sometimes rather a misnomer, since many receive substantial funding from Western governments; whether taking government money or not, they have found themselves in an extremely difficult position. Some – notably the International Committee of the Red Cross and MSF – have channelled a certain amount of assistance to areas of Taliban strength. Most agencies, though, have focused on government-held areas. This adds to the risk that they will be perceived as parties to a war effort, endangering not only their reputation for neutrality, but also their staff.[153]

'Winning hearts and minds' has also been impeded by the sheer difficulty of carrying out effective development projects in the middle of a
conflict zone. It is easy to get the impression that the British have been
promoting 'development' in Helmand province for many years. But a
2011 study of Helmand by Robert Egnell provides a valuable corrective:

> Despite great efforts and sacrifices, the limited and thinly spread combat
> forces were simply not equipped to tackle an insurgency that controlled
> the majority of the province. The British and their coalition partners
> were in fact holding very little territory, which impeded any genuine
> progress in the areas of economic development and governance – both
> considered essential aspects of ISAF's campaign plan.[154]

In 2005, the British government sent a team of experts to Helmand to
plan a three-year state-building effort, but the obstacles were huge – a
vast land mass, virtually no infrastructure, a flourishing drugs economy.
The timeline and level of resources were never remotely realistic. The
UK was trying to hold an area half the size of England with a little over
1,000 combat troops.[155] Until mid-2009 DfID had few staff in Helmand
and few 'quick impact projects' were completed in the rebellious towns
in the north of Helmand despite considerable pressure from the British
Ministry of Defence.[156] Six-month rotations of civil and military elements
also weakened the knowledge-base on Helmand's complicated politics.[157]

In an important statement, Jonathan Goodhand and Mark Sedra
observe: 'To a great extent, the nature of the political settlement and the
security environment are what determine the possibilities for development rather than vice versa – to pretend otherwise is to put the development cart before the political horse.'[158] Where some development *has*
been possible (as in the north-east of Afghanistan), there have been
some signs of greater support for international actors, but not of
increased *government* legitimacy.[159] A slow and fragile consolidation of
government presence in Central Helmand River Valley reflects a heavy
concentration of international troops there, underlining the failure of
earlier underfunded efforts.[160]

Invited to plug the gaps in a foundering 'war on terror', the aid world
now risks legitimising some highly destructive and probably unwin-
nable wars. Convincing Western publics to give priority to aid spending
– in other words, spending on *other people* – is a tough 'sell' in tough

times. Given that the global financial crisis has come in the context of a continuing 'war on terror', government aid departments (like the UK's Department for International Development (DfID) or USAID) have been tempted to defend their budgets by suggesting that aid – if carefully targeted at key fragile states like Afghanistan – can contribute powerfully to national security in the West. In the UK, success in defending the official aid budget has been matched by treasury insistence on staff cuts within the government's aid department. In USAID, staff levels have been cut quite drastically in line with a growing reliance on contracting out – in line with a more general privatisation of state functions under George W. Bush in particular.[161] A threat of redundancy has made dissent (or free thinking) particularly difficult – so unrealistic solutions, like 'aid as counterinsurgency', become harder to challenge. Certainly, criticism of the war effort in Afghanistan has become highly taboo. Meanwhile the combination of big budgets and reduced core staff has created incentives to spend large amounts of money with relatively little oversight while at the same time reducing the ability to manage or monitor this large spending.[162] Despite (and perhaps in part *because of*) a huge diversion of funding and huge corruption, there has been very little serious official evaluation.[163]

If parts of Afghanistan with significant numbers of 'terrorists' have received disproportionate amounts of aid, this pattern has been mirrored at a global level. In particular, there has been a growing concentration of aid on the so-called 'arc of crisis', a region encompassing Pakistan, Afghanistan, Iraq, Iran, Yemen and Somalia that is seen as yielding the bulk of support for international terrorism, notably 'Islamist terrorism'.[164] It is true that some other 'fragile states' are also getting a lot of aid – effectively part of the deal struck by the UK's DfID with other government departments. But some of the imbalances are stark. On one estimate, people in the DRC have received at best $10 of aid per person per year, while people in Iraq have, in some years, got twelve times that amount.[165]

***

Let us return for a moment to General William Corson's sobering assessment of the US role in Vietnam:

The people smell the decay of GVN [Government of South Vietnam] corruption, which permeates all of South Vietnam and makes a joke out of activities urged by the United States in the name of promoting a democratic society ... The absurdity of the situation lies in the fact that while we champion the cause of democracy as the justification of our presence in Vietnam, we overtly support a government whose actions completely deny this *raison d'être*.[166]

We can see by now that the same passage is largely accurate if we substitute 'Karzai government' for 'GVN', and 'Afghanistan' for 'Vietnam'. As in Vietnam, conflict has been manipulated for economic and political gain by powerful local actors. As in Vietnam, there has been massive appropriation of international aid. And as in Vietnam, it has become ever clearer that aid is unable to make up for a failing military policy. The problem has not been a lack of precedents, but a lack of learning.

In Afghanistan, as in Vietnam and other wars we have looked at in Africa and elsewhere, the assumption of a war between 'two sides', where the overriding aim is victory, turns out to be a deeply and damagingly misleading one. Peter Galbraith, the UN secretary-general's deputy special representative to Afghanistan in 2009, observed:

> Americans view the war as a contest between the U.S.-backed Karzai government and the Taliban insurgency. The reality is more complex. In the Pashtun south where the insurgency is strongest, local power brokers and officials have relations with the Taliban, who are tribesmen and relatives. They make deals with each other to run drugs, trade weapons, eliminate rivals, and rig elections. Both sides collaborate in order to profit from massive U.S. expenditures.[167]

While the conception of war as a contest is clearly not simply an 'American' one, the importance of Galbraith's comment is clear. While it is true that some militias have taken on the Taliban aggressively,[168] many Afghan civilians have described the war less as a conflict between the insurgents and an internationally supported government than as a mutual business enterprise, where belligerents use insecurity as a cover for personal and political ambitions.[169] No wonder this war – like so many before it – has refused to end as quickly or as neatly as advertised.

Even for Western politicians (as we saw in Vietnam), the point is not necessarily to win. More important, once again, may be to avoid a 'humiliation' that will be electorally damaging, and at the same time to preserve a sense that the war is going well – that 'we are winning' – and that a solution is imminent (even as the conflict heads into its second decade).

From the point of view of the US military, so long as casualties are not 'too high' and so long as there are accessible targets, then the situation may be seen as satisfactory. During the original US-led attack on Afghanistan in 2001, reporter Bob Woodward noted: '[Deputy Secretary of Defense Paul] Wolfowitz said that the Taliban were getting reinforcements but [General Tommy] Franks [head of US Central Command] thought that had a good news side – it would create more targets.'[170] There is always the possibility of creating a distraction, moreover. At a meeting of the US National Security Council on 25 September 2001, Donald Rumsfeld suggested: 'Look, as part of the war on terrorism, should we be getting something going in another area, other than Afghanistan, so that success or failure and progress isn't measured just by Afghanistan?'[171] That was one of the many dubious 'logics' for attacking Iraq. When (after years of conflict) Iraq came to be widely seen as an expensive mistake, another useful distraction appeared in the shape of Obama's renewed focus on … Afghanistan.

When the West's 'righteous' wars drag on (whether in the war against Communism or in the war against terrorism), Western government officials typically have a handy bag of reasons at the ready. One is that the terrain is not conducive to counterinsurgency. (Unfortunately, while the US government tried to strip the jungles in Vietnam – using the cancer-causing chemical compound known as Agent Orange – Washington has not been able to do much about the mountains in Afghanistan.) Another explanation is that the enemy is more powerful, pervasive, ruthless, mobile, elusive, determined and/or cunning than we originally thought. A third is that we have made mistakes (like too many dead civilians) that we are now, so to speak, 'correcting'.

While none of these reasons for prolonged warfare is irrelevant, there is another possible explanation that has been damagingly neglected, and that in many ways is both simpler and more convincing: the reason these wars have endured for so long may just be because a shifting coalition of influential actors *does not want them to end*. That brings us back, whether we like it or not, to the *functions* of war – and the functions of violence in what may prematurely be labelled as 'peace'. Of particular concern here are the functions of war and wartime violence for the local allies of major Western powers (especially the US). If these allies do not actually want to win, the war in question will be doomed to failure. But optimism can still be relentlessly reinvented – not least in the wishful thinking that aid is about to 'turn things around'.[172] As in Vietnam, a failing military solution has led to an increasing emphasis on 'developmental' solutions. Meanwhile, another source of optimism has been the idea that 'corruption' is being addressed (or is about to be), so that aid will now begin to yield the long-promised harvest of hearts and minds.

We have seen the problems besetting aid as counterinsurgency, and the solution of 'tackling corruption' seems equally problematic. A key difficulty is that tackling endemic corruption is not just difficult, but is also potentially hazardous for 'stability'. As Chaudhuri and Farrell observe, 'Afghan politicians depend on the well-entrenched patronage system for survival and capacity to govern. Hence, tackling corruption targets the bedrock of the Afghan government'.[173] Insofar as there is an awareness of this among international actors, it inhibits corruption drives (as it did in Vietnam). A second problem is that, even if corruption could be sharply reduced, there might be an increase in the number of 'spoilers' willing and able to destabilise the emerging state. If anything, this underlines the problems with launching this kind of war in the first place: corruption will undermine the war effort, and if corruption is tackled strongly and vigorously, this may itself be an additional source of instability.

In a judicious comment on reconstruction efforts in Helmand province, Stuart Gordon noted: 'at a provincial level the reconstruction programme appears not to have countered negative perceptions resulting from collateral damage, civilian casualties, house searches, etc'.[174] Logically, it would take a lot to do so.

So what, exactly, has been gained from all this violence? Some people are much richer. And some people have achieved important political goals. But the war itself has been a counterproductive failure. The value that terrorists frequently attach to provoked aggression was noted in the introduction. The most effective strategy against many forms of terrorism seems to be to allow popular revulsion to take its course, without putting such revulsion into reverse with a violent retaliation.[175] Yet, as Bruce Riedel (a CIA officer in 1977–2006) observes, 'Prompting America to invade Afghanistan was exactly what Osama bin Laden was hoping for on September 11th. His son has told us in retrospect "my father's dream was to get America to invade Afghanistan".[176] Meanwhile, the benefits of this international intervention for most Afghans remain very unclear, particularly given that the entire political settlement is premised on an international presence for which deadlines have already been announced.[177] The international 'reconstruction' in Afghanistan was dramatically underfunded and built around an exclusive political settlement that reinforced the power of abusive warlords and incentivised rebellion. The warlords' power was also frequently increased by the presence of international forces and the lucrative contracts aimed at sustaining these international troops. Even when reconstruction efforts were significantly increased, they were routinely sabotaged or appropriated by abusive warlords, and indeed by the Taliban. Believing you can win a war in Afghanistan is always something of a folly. While Western troops have fought bravely and have been sent into extremely dangerous environments to confront a variety of enemies (including those defending the drugs trade as well as the Taliban), a key reason why Western forces (like many before them) have not been able to 'win' in this vast and rugged country is that so many people – both Afghans and interested foreigners – have attached a low priority to this endeavour. I was going to say 'a surprisingly low priority', but for how long can we afford to be surprised in these matters?

CHAPTER 5

The Political Functions of War

… the consciousness of being at war, and therefore in danger, makes the handing-over of all power to a small caste seem the natural, unavoidable condition of survival. (George Orwell, *Nineteen Eighty-Four*)

The model of 'war as a contest' tends to blind us not just to the economic functions of war, but also to its political functions. These political functions have been important – and often overlooked – in countless wars, whether they directly involve Western powers or not. While there are frequently significant reasons to want to win a war (for example, idealism, self-defence, prestige, promotions, electoral pay-offs), very often it is war itself – rather than winning – that is most useful. A state of war may be helpful for building a political constituency and for suppressing dissent.

Within the West, wars have long served as 'unifiers' and as means of absorbing discontent, and even gaining electoral advantage.[1] There are some well-known examples from the modern era. In the UK, Prime Minister Margaret Thatcher received a huge boost to her popularity from the Falklands War with Argentina. In the US, George Bush Sr got a similar political windfall from his UN Security Council-authorised 1990 attack on Iraq after Saddam invaded Kuwait, and in February 1991 a report in the *New York Times* observed:

It remains unclear what the Persian Gulf War will do to the political geography of the Middle East, but so far it has transformed the psyche of the United States. The sour, deeply divided nation of a few months ago, worried about economic decay and political paralysis, has received a remarkable lift from the war. Despite the presence of a sizeable minority opposed to the fighting, there has been a surge of patriotic rallies, flag-waving and professions of unity unmatched by anything in this generation.[2]

A little over a decade later, Bush Jr also received a significant boost to his popularity through a foreign war – this time by invading Afghanistan in response to the attacks of 9/11.

It may even be that deaths in wartime serve a function in generating a sense of nationhood. That, certainly, is the argument in Carolyn Marvin and David Ingle's provocative book *Blood Sacrifice and the Nation*.[3] Marvin and Ingle see the flag and the nation as deriving their meaning – and their enduring hold on people's loyalties – from the sacrifices made in their name. In a disturbing passage, the authors note: 'We tell ourselves that the purpose of war is to kill the enemy. And it is. But what keeps the group together and makes us feel unified is not the sacrifice of the enemy but the sacrifice of our own.'[4] Paul Kahn pursues a related argument in his insightful book *Sacred Violence*:

> Viewing the battlefield from a certain distance, it is not even clear who is the object of sacrifice: the enemy and the conscript suffer the same threat and burden of physical destruction for the sake of making present sovereign power.[5]

Kahn argues that after 9/11 the use of violence to sanctify the nation and the sovereign power – a demand to kill and be killed – has reasserted itself over what he calls the 'counter-religion' of international law. Governments' authority is defined and dramatised by the right to take life, whether of enemy soldiers or of one's own, and if a government is unable to sustain the impression of a genuine foreign threat, then the death of one's own soldiers may come to be seen as a senseless killing rather than a heroic martyrdom. Kahn suggests that this was the case in Argentina at the time of the Falklands War and that the US government today risks being seen as killing its own in senseless wars that do not enhance security. In these circumstances, the incentive to portray the enemy as a threat to the existence of a political community is all the greater.[6]

These arguments take a bit of digesting. But we may agree that war
has important political functions, even if we have a problem with the
idea that we are 'sacrificing our own'. The function of war as a 'unifier'
goes back a long way. In his eloquent book *Killing Civilians*, Hugo Slim
notes that 'the early Crusades were as much about the diversion of
destructive feudal energy within European nations as they were about
the sanctity of Jerusalem'.[7] The Crusades offered an outlet for a heavily
armed European nobility (particularly in France), whose predations had
been curbed by a truce in the year 957, which forbade violence between
Christians.[8] Some 900 years later, in 1859, on the eve of French military
intervention to eject Austria from Italy, French President Napoleon III
(also Emperor) told his cabinet that war would 'bring together under
the mantle of glory the parties that are steadily drifting away from one
another day after day'.[9] Next door, in Germany, Otto von Bismarck,
prime minister of Prussia in 1862–90 and overseer of German unifica-
tion, gained unrivalled influence over foreign and domestic policy –
notably, as Chancellor of the German Empire from 1871 – in large part
as a result of his military successes.[10] There were hints of a more ruthless
approach to internal dissent, too. By 1905, Kaiser Wilhelm II was anticipating, with some pleasure, that in the event of a European war: 'First
we will neutralise the socialists, shooting them down and cutting off
their heads in a bloodbath, if necessary, and then we will fight the war
abroad.'[11] The two tasks were regarded as inseparable, in any case, as
internal disorder was widely held to be caused by foreign enemies.[12]

When the First World War did break out, the hope was commonly
expressed in Germany that it might heal troublesome internal divisions.
Historian Paul Lerner described the atmosphere in Germany at the time:

> Medical writers ... reported that the war was improving the mental
> and nervous health of the civilian population. In these accounts war
> fostered feelings of communal solidarity that, many hoped, could
> overcome decades of division, continuing the Bismarckian strategy of
> using external conflict to forge domestic unity.[13]

War was also often seen as a health-giving antidote to illness, hypochon-
dria and moral weakness arising from industrial growth and city life.[14]
As Lerner noted, 'Psychiatrists valorized, in the words of one such, "the
mighty healing power of the iron bath [*Stahlbad*] for nerves dried up

and languishing in the dust from years of peace and monotonous voca-
tional activity".[15] One German nationalist wrote in 1913: 'Let us regard
war as holy, like the purifying force of fate, for it will awaken in our
people all that is great and ready for self-sacrifice, while it cleanses our
soul of the mire of petty egotistical concerns.'[16] Again, we see the limitations of the view that war is all about winning: the point here was not
that war must be won through self-sacrifice, but that war was an *opportunity* for self-sacrifice. Psychological disturbance arising from war was
typically labelled 'war hysteria', a label carrying significant stigma and
enduring feminine associations.[17] Industrialisation had also brought
incipient class conflict, and historian Robert Weldon Whalen, noted in
his book *Bitter Wounds*: 'By 1914, epic politics, in which the idea of
violent explosion took on a cathartic appeal, seemed to the German
governing classes a promising way to direct attention away from
domestic discord.'[18]

In both Russia and Germany, the First World War created a threat of
revolution, stemming largely from mass casualties, economic crisis and
a loss of face among ruling elites who had failed either to protect their
people or to achieve military victory. But while revolution duly occurred
in Russia, in Germany the Communists were defeated. By channelling
popular grievances and First World War veterans' frustrations into
nationalism and racism, rather than into class politics, the Nazis married
an anti-Communist and strike-breaking agenda with a project of
rebuilding Germany's military and economic strength and eliminating
those elements (notably, the Jews) who, they alleged, had plotted to
bring about Germany's demise. The Nazis and the Jewish 'enemy' proved
useful to a business and aristocratic elite in Germany – in large part
because Nazi ideology deflected the blame for defeat and economic
crisis away from the political and military leadership.[19]

The political functions of wars in developing countries are no less
striking. Yet they have routinely been glossed over by conflict analysts,
who have tended to assume that the aim in these wars is to win. Political
functions have also sometimes been overlooked in analyses that emphasise 'greed' (and especially 'rebel greed').

Today Darfur has become a household name for all the wrong reasons.
But in 1987 it was just another obscure region within the seemingly infi-
nite land-mass of Sudan. One thing that surprised me at the time was
that I found out considerably less about Darfur when touring this vast

area than I did subsequently, when shut up in a small and extremely hot room-cum-cupboard hundreds of miles away in the capital, Khartoum. Part of the problem in Darfur was that I was travelling with a Red Cross water purification team that was not entirely successful in purifying *its own* water supplies: most of our team succumbed to something, and my own fever stopped me making much sense of the rather dense set of data they were kind enough to provide.

Back in Khartoum (fully alert and consuming enormous quantities of tea that seemed to put a distinct 'high' into re-hydration), I was able to study detailed reports by Save the Children Fund field officers. These gave a good indication of who did – and did not – receive relief grain in Darfur during the drought famine of 1984–85. Those who received very limited amounts included people living far from urban areas – and especially pastoralists. A key problem was that those whose livelihoods and location exposed them most markedly to famine tended to be groups that lacked political clout in relation to the local authorities that were helping to shape relief distributions.

I returned to Sudan the following year. This time I was not just a scruffy student but a scruffy consultant linked to the European Community – a much grander individual altogether. The project was evaluating international assistance to combat the terrible famine in southern Sudan. My immediate boss, Peter Cutler, was known for his work on Ethiopia, where he had developed a 'model' that allowed him to predict the way famines would spread geographically (as food moved into the 'epicentre' of famine and people moved out). Peter was very keen on predictions and 'the future' in general. At the end of the evening in Khartoum, he would sit in our hotel room and visualise what he and I were going to achieve the following day. It seemed to help. In the medium term, Peter had his eye on a nuclear bunker in Venezuela, as he figured it would be a safe haven in the event of Armageddon. (He later went into the ecologically sound carpet cleaning business after predicting – accurately – that 'green products' would become very profitable.)

What was of more immediate concern to us in 1988 was the man-made famine evolving in the south and spilling into Darfur and neighbouring Kordofan. With data gathered from the famine region, we were able to show that the southern Sudanese famine was actually departing from Peter's model. More specifically, high grain prices were not spreading out from the 'epicentre' of the famine in the expected manner. The main reason was that artificial restrictions on the movement of grain into the starving south were creating huge disparities in the price of grain (and of livestock) over quite short distances.

Some of the main 'victims' in the 1984–85 drought famine were now emerging as principal 'villains' in the famine that was devastating the south. Arab pastoralist groups in the west of the country (Darfur and Kordofan) had lost out in the distribution of drought relief. More generally, the process of 'development' in Sudan had left most people on the geographical peripheries either disadvantaged or dispossessed – or both. In what Sudan expert Alex de Waal calls the 'inner periphery', expanding commercial farming – much of it funded by the World Bank – led to the confiscation of land from small farmers and the restriction of herders' migration routes. Many of the Arab pastoralists were suffering even before the drought disaster.[20] On the 'outer periphery' (often the most violent part, and including Darfur and the south), a key problem was simple neglect.[21] The rumblings of discontent that have arisen from both neglect and dispossession have consistently been managed in Sudan through policies of 'divide and rule'.

By the mid-1980s, the Sudanese state was actively redirecting the frustrations of Western Sudanese Arab groups against groups in the south that were deemed 'guilty by association' with the SPLA rebels. Taking a leaf or three from the old colonial policy of 'divide and rule', a resource-stretched government in Khartoum was trying to exercise control over a huge land-mass by playing off the malcontents of one disadvantaged group against those of other groups that were still more disadvantaged. The vicious and cynical tactic of encouraging militia raids on the south was, in many ways, a reinvention of British colonial policy at the end of the nineteenth century and the beginning of the twentieth. For the British had often tolerated, and even encouraged, Arab raiding and slaving against rebellious southerners, and were influenced here by Arab pastoralists' own propensity to rebel (something that persisted through the years and almost led to the overthrow of the Khartoum government in 1976, for example). After Sudan's civil war resumed in 1983, Khartoum's militia strategy helped to prevent the kind of alliance of marginalised groups for which rebel SPLA leader John Garang had long hoped. Meanwhile, the financial benefits of war and famine played a significant part in consolidating the support base of a succession of different governments in Khartoum.

Incidentally, I was left in no doubt about the potency of the militias' weaponry when I visited a horrifying camp for starving southern Sudanese who had fled militia attacks. Out of curiosity, I accepted an invitation to go with some of the militiamen who were 'guarding' the camp when they went on a lakeside duck-hunting expedition. They used machine-guns and the ducks did not stand a chance.

Apart from absorbing discontent in western Sudan, the militia strategy had four other important political advantages. First, it invited the label of 'ethnic violence', helping to engender a sense among international actors that there was little they could do. Secondly, it allowed the government to avoid an unpopular military draft. Thirdly, it created a counterbalance to the power of the army. (If you mention the word 'army' in many developing countries, political leaders will often think 'coup'.)[22] Finally, it offered – as noted – the prospect, for a heavily indebted government, of access to oil. The state-sponsored violence in Sudan, so far from being simply irrational or an interruption to development, was a kind of 'permanent emergency' – in Mark Duffield's phrase – that offered an 'escape hatch' to ruling elites who were pursuing their own vision of 'development' and who were themselves under complex political and economic pressures.[23] Mass violence – and even genocide – was in this sense 'functional'.

However, from a purely military point of view, the militia strategy was problematic (as we have seen). In particular, the use of militias resulted in attacks on civilians who were unconnected to the rebels, and it helped spread rebellion to new areas by radicalising civilians.[24] For those facing the possibility or reality of militia attacks, the rebel SPLA could offer a degree of protection, a degree of relief from passivity, and the possibility of revenge.[25] Thus, the violence of war – notably the largely indiscriminate militia attacks – was itself the main driver of recruitment to the SPLA, as a detailed study by Saskia Baas confirms. As one of Baas's respondents told her: 'Instead of staying and being slaughtered like a goat, I thought I can die as a hero.'[26] Significantly, the lack of government 'scorched earth' policies in the east of Sudan created lower incentives to join the rebels there.[27] But in Darfur from 2003, indiscriminate violence again encouraged rebel recruitment – just as it had in the south.[28]

The Sudanese state – wracked by numerous wars in the south, west and east – has been variously described as 'weak', 'collapsed', 'failed' and 'failing'. There is some truth in these labels. But what they tend to disguise is the remarkable continuity in rule by a relatively small elite in Khartoum, where politicians and other elite members tend to maintain civil relations with their rivals – not least because they may soon be in alliance.[29] Omar al-Bashir became head of state after a military coup in 1989, and he continued to rule through the 1990s and 2000s. This makes him more enduring than Britain's Tony Blair or Margaret Thatcher. On top of regime stability, there has also been a great deal of continuity among senior Sudanese security officials.[30] In many ways, this adds up to a political 'success story'. Meanwhile, a policy of perpetual warfare (with the focus sometimes switching bewilderingly between south, west and east) has not only proven quite consistent with that success, but has *actively contributed* to it. From the 1980s, the political mobilisation of Islam – so destructive in relation to the south – served important political functions for unpopular elites in search of a northern (and indeed an international) constituency.[31] When the long war in the south finally drew to a close (with a ceasefire in 2002), this owed a great deal to increased international pressure (especially from the US) and to a 'buy-in' arrangement that allowed the SPLA in the south (and affiliated southern elites) to gain access to a significant share of the oil (albeit still relying on the north for oil export pipelines).[32] Strikingly, the Khartoum government was soon fuelling another war in the west. For their part, the southern SPLA rebels also tried to 'instrumentalise' disorder in the west, giving support to rebels there and using this as a bargaining chip in the north–south peace negotiations.[33] There is nothing very 'pure' or even stable about this peace process: it represents a realignment of interests and a 'bargain' quite heavily dependent on continued international involvement.[34]

In central Africa, too, strategies of divide and rule have created widespread devastation. Some 800,000 people were killed in the 1994 Rwandan genocide, which went on to precipitate a catastrophic war in neighbouring DRC, after more than a million Hutus moved there when Tutsi-based rebels seized power in the Rwandan capital Kigali and finally put a stop to the genocide.[35] Significantly, the DRC was itself 'ripe' for armed conflict: its long-time leader, Mobutu Sese Seko, was himself a master of divide and rule: like President Siaka Stevens in Sierra Leone, and many others with a knack for survival, Mobutu would constantly move his officials around, punishing and even jailing anyone who hinted at disloyalty. He played off the country's numerous ethnic groups against each other and kept the army weak (sometimes using French and Belgian troops instead). A strikingly inefficient bureaucracy proved remarkably efficient in keeping Mobutu in power.[36] But his legacy was a resource-rich country wracked by poverty and 'protected' by a demoralised and avaricious army that quickly collapsed over a period of seven months in 1996–97 when faced with Rwandan-backed rebels.

As with war and famine in Sudan, the catastrophe in Rwanda was commonly attributed to ancient ethnic hatreds. Top UN officials proclaimed that authority had collapsed and tribalism had erupted. But authority was actually all too real in Rwanda, a small and highly central-ised country. A more fundamental cause of the genocide was the Rwandan elite's strategy of divide and rule in the face of impending democratisation. Conditions of economic austerity – and collapsing coffee prices – proved a disastrous context in which to attempt a radical redistribution of power. While it is true that democracies rarely go to war with each other (an argument used in the US to support the *violent* promotion of democracy), the case of Rwanda illustrates that the *process of democratisation* can itself be an important cause of violence and war.[37] Promoting democracy and economic liberalisation – so often seen as a panacea for ending the 'craziness' of war – can actually propel powerful interests *into* violence, and we need to be thinking much more clearly about how to prevent such backlashes. In Rwanda, even the prospect of holding human rights abusers to account – another part of the orthodox prescription for 'peace' – may have played a role in precipitating geno-cide, as abusers tried to hold onto power and escape the courts.[38]

Back in October 1990, Rwandan Tutsi refugees in Uganda had deserted their posts in the Ugandan army and invaded northern Rwanda, with Ugandan support, as the Rwandan Patriotic Front (RPF). Ominously, many Tutsi within Rwanda were quickly rounded up in response – a move that was justified by a 'rebel' attack on the Rwandan capital, Kigali, that turned out to be the work of the Rwandan military. As Gérard Prunier noted:

> ... in order to dramatise the perceived gravity of the situation, [the government] staged a fake attack on Kigali by 'enemy troops' during

the night of 4/5 October. Beginning at 1 a.m., shooting started in the capital, lasting with varying intensity till around 7 a.m. Thousands of shots had been fired, but miraculously there was not a single casualty and there was very little damage to buildings. The international press was deceived and the French ambassador Georges Martre duly reported 'heavy fighting in the capital', thereby achieving the desired effect in Paris. Within the next few days, French troop numbers [supporting the government] had been increased to 600 although the government had started a campaign of massive arrests in Kigali (and to a lesser extent in the provincial capitals) and news of civilian massacres in the countryside had started to filter out.[39]

Prunier goes on to observe:

It soon became obvious that these arrests did not target supporters of the RPF (there were very few and even these few were not all known to the police) but indiscriminately swept up educated Tutsi, opposition-minded Hutu, anyone who was in the bad books of the power elite ...[40]

After some three years of war, the 1993 Arusha agreement saw Tutsi rebels reaching an accommodation with a single-party Rwandan regime that had held sway over Rwanda since the mid-1970s and that was dominated by a small group of Hutus from the north-west of the country, the *Akazu* (or 'little house'). However, a group of Hutu extremists (including high-ranking soldiers) tried to sabotage the peace process and to destroy the emerging democratic opposition by (successfully) inciting large numbers of the majority Hutu ethnic group to engage in the mass killing of Tutsis (as well as the killing of some Hutus who were in the political opposition or were deemed to be 'Tutsi collaborators'). The bitter pill of democracy was not made any easier to swallow by provisions in the 1993 peace agreement that gave 40 per cent of rank-and-file army posts to the invading RPF rebels, as well as 50 per cent of the officer posts.[41]

In many ways, the genocidal strategy in Rwanda can be understood as an attempt to use nationalism and racism to deflect class tension, rather as the Nazis had done – in a very different context and over a longer period – in post-First World War Germany.[42] As in Germany, there was also an element of displaced violence: picking on an internal enemy when the external enemy (in this case, the Tutsis coming in from Uganda) had proved too strong.

A further parallel with Germany was the difficulty of demobilising the Rwandan army at war's end. The Rwandan army was to play a key role in the 1994 genocide: it promoted fear and hatred of Tutsis;[43] it argued that the 'ethnic problem' was being neglected in favour of a politics of rich and poor; and, most importantly, it was responsible for massacres and assassinations, sometimes leading the way in attacks on civilians, often commanding the *interahamwe* militias that became notorious for massacring Tutsis, and frequently attacking the Hutu opposition. The war with the Tutsi-based RPF rebels seems to have fed this fury: in Butare, southern Rwanda, those soldiers who had arrived from the war-front were reported to be among the most ruthless in the genocide, and this applied particularly to those who had been wounded. Soldiers were also fearful of demobilisation: having been rapidly expanded in wartime, the army now faced the unwelcome prospect of redundancy following the 1993 peace agreement between the Rwandan government and the Tutsi rebels. In this combustible context, cynical Hutu politicians spread rumours that soldiers would be sacked and, in a crumbling economy, would never find work again.[44] The soldiers' reluctance to give up the privileges of military service was a significant factor encouraging them to lend support to the mass killing.

After the genocide, with Rwanda and its new Tutsi-led army intervening in the DRC (ostensibly in pursuit of those responsible for genocide), fears around military demobilisation continued to feed into violence. In 2002, Fabienne Hara of the International Crisis Group noted: 'About half of Rwanda's oversized army is now reliant on occupied territory to survive. A formal peace agreement and withdrawal from Congo would mean demobilising huge numbers of men into a tiny, poor country.'[45] When the Rwandan army did 'withdraw', many soldiers simply moved into pro-Rwandan militias, which continued to prey on the natural resources of the DRC.[46]

If Rwanda underlined the perennial lure of 'divide and rule' and the difficulty in demobilising a war machine, so, too, did the simultaneous catastrophe in the former Yugoslavia. Again, a process of democratisation combined with significant economic crisis to precipitate mass violence; and again, many influential observers deemed this to be a case of 'ancient ethnic hatreds'. As in Sudan and Rwanda, this misleading label served as a convenient alibi not only for local politicians and warlords, but also for powerful elements within the international community – including the United States government – that wished to insist (or imply) that that there was little or nothing the international community could do to help (other than provide humanitarian aid).[47] In the former Yugoslavia, as in Sudan and Rwanda, the idea of 'ancient ethnic hatreds' obscured periods of 'ethnic peace', as well as long traditions of intermarriage. (In Sudan and Rwanda, this intermarriage also hinted at the precarious status of southern Sudanese and Tutsis, respectively, since intermarriage typically involved women from these groups.)[48] Revealingly, some studies of former Yugoslavia have suggested that ethnic hatred was often more a *product* of violence than a *cause* of it. In fact, violence was used to drive a wedge between people who had often been living quite happily with each other. As one liberal analyst put it: 'The war had to be so bloody because the ties between us were so strong.'[49] In Bosnia, articulate moderates – 'those who refused to hate'[50] – were a particular target of the paramilitaries.[51]

Underpinning the catastrophe in the former Yugoslavia was a process of political adaptation. With Communism collapsing in Eastern Europe, ethnic nationalism emerged as the easiest and most effective means of gaining and keeping a political following.[52] Milošević, a prominent Communist official, successfully adapted to the changing political climate by building a constituency among the Serbs, using a potent combination of paranoia, nationalism, intimidation and corruption.[53]

An important factor in Milošević's success – and in the violence that overran the former Yugoslavia – was the support of officers from the old Yugoslav National Army, an army that faced being disbanded as Yugoslavia crumbled. Significantly, officers' pensions remained unsecured, and many of them seem to have seen a greater Serbian state as their best hope of financial security.[54] Military spending on the Yugoslav national army (JNA) was cut almost in half between 1986 and 1991,[55] and Balkans expert Mary Kaldor notes that this contributed to 'a growing sense of victimization and paranoia about internal and external enemies within the JNA'.[56] Meanwhile, the existing war machine was falling into dangerous hands, as Kaldor observes:

> The JNA and the TOs [Territorial Defence Units, or regional armies
> for the republics and provinces] disintegrated into a combination

of regular and irregular forces augmented by criminals, volunteers and foreign mercenaries competing for control over the former Yugoslavia's military assets.[57]

After Bosnia and Herzegovina had declared independence from the Yugoslav federation, the Yugoslav national army formally withdrew. But in the event only some 14,000 troops actually left, while around 80,000 transferred to the Bosnian Serb Army.[58] The latter had inherited the national army's equipment and weapons stores, which had originally been put in the hills of Bosnia-Herzegovina because this area was expected to be at the heart of any guerrilla-based defence of Yugoslavia.[59]

In the end, the international community backed an ethnic carve-up of Yugoslavia,[60] which had the effect of rewarding ethnic nationalists. Those who gained from the war were often able to consolidate their access to resources in the tense peace that followed.[61] In Serbia, Milošević was able to hold onto power despite a range of international sanctions. In fact, a state of more or less permanent warfare, while it precipitated the sanctions, seemed actively helpful in clinging onto office. Milošević was soon involved in war with NATO over his incitement of ethnic violence in Kosovo.

The Kosovo conflict also prompted renewed international sanctions, and in the summer of 1999 I had the opportunity to go to Belgrade to try to get a better understanding of their impact. One thing that struck me was that sanctions imposed on Serbia and Montenegro from 1992 – and renewed over Kosovo – had in many ways *given a boost* to Milošević's cabal, which was able to profit economically from the artificially high gaps between prices inside and outside the Federal Republic of Yugoslavia.[62] Wartime inflation was devastating the middle classes, while a small elite prospered – not only from sanctions, but also from corruption, pyramid schemes and simply printing money. All this effected a radical redistribution of wealth *among the Serbs*, underlining the limitations of trying to portray the conflict as a simple fight *between* ethnic groups. Meanwhile, the Milošević cabal was also able to extract *political* benefits from sanctions, by presenting them as another example of the 'international conspiracy' against the Serbs. With Milošević controlling most of the key media, he was able to get across the message that sanctions were not his fault, but rather the fault of the international community. Having risen to power through his skill in encouraging a sense of 'siege' among the Serbs, Milošević was able to consolidate his hold on power by perpetuating this sense of siege. Some diplomats felt that sanctions ceased to help Milošević only when he effectively ran out of plausible wars to wage. Significantly, the use of targeted sanctions – restructuring travel and access to bank accounts – eventually helped to encourage politicians and officials to defect from Milošević.

In Asia, a disturbing case of divide and rule – and of politically functional conflict – is that of Sri Lanka. Here, conflict – once again – has typically been presented as 'ethnic': a common view is that the Tamil minority was engaged in a protracted (twenty-six-year) political and military struggle against the Sinhalese majority. But, as in Sudan, Rwanda and former Yugoslavia, this 'ethnic' interpretation misses important class dimensions in the conflict, and also glosses over the political functions of endemic conflict. As in Sudan, war provided an outlet for marginalised groups at the expense of even more marginalised groups. Rajesh Venugopal, an academic at the London School of Economics, argues convincingly that war and high levels of military mobilisation have served something of a hidden function in de-fusing longstanding social tensions (notably in the south).[63]

Significantly, there had been a major expansion of education in the 1970s and 1980s. It helped to turn Sri Lanka into one of the 'success stories' of international development. Literacy rates rose and infant mortality fell. Unfortunately, the availability of jobs (particularly the more sought-after public-sector jobs) simply could not keep up with the numbers of qualified candidates.[64] The army took up much of the slack, with an extremely rapid expansion in the 1980s and 1990s. Crucially, the military absorbed very large numbers of young Sinhalese males from rural areas, who had shown their potential for destabilising the state in the Janatha Vimukthi Peramuna (JVP – People's Liberation Front) rebellions of 1971 and 1987–89. The latter rebellion was so serious that it almost brought the government down.[65]

Venugopal comments:

Sri Lanka's social democratic state, which went through a long phase of expansion from the 1940s to the 1970s, has, since the 1980s, experienced atrophy and compression. Since the early 1990s, however, the only part of the state that has consistently grown has been the military.[66]

In 2007, a detailed report for the International Crisis Group noted: 'Today the national budget is no longer capable of funding any significant development projects; almost all revenue goes to public sector salaries and pensions, debt payment and the military.'[67]

If war has often been good for business, the incentives may go both ways. In Sri Lanka, some business interests pushed strongly for peace when conflict in the north – long regarded as acceptable and compatible with growth in the rest of the country – also began to be seen as a major tax burden (due mostly to military spending) and an unacceptable deterrent to investors and tourists; some also hoped to boost business with a land link to India via the war-torn north.[68] But not everyone wanted peace. After a ceasefire agreement in 2002 between the Sri Lankan government and the Tamil Tigers, the JVP party was able to capitalise on popular fears of a loss of sovereignty. It expressed particularly vehement opposition to any agreement with the Tamil Tigers over the distribution of aid to victims of the 2004 tsunami. While peace had been presented as 'good for the economy', the JVP was also capitalising on widespread frustration at the lack of an economic 'peace dividend'. The government tended to make a strong link between its 'economic reform' agenda and its 'peace' agenda, but this had the effect of undermining the peace process, as Venugopal shows.[69] The JVP was a key actor, campaigning simultaneously against the peace process and the government's liberalisation policies. The latter had removed important subsidies for agricultural inputs, and also threatened the state employment on which vast numbers of rural Sinhalese – and government patronage networks more generally – had come to depend.[70] World Bank and International Monetary Fund mechanisms for ensuring 'popular participation' in economic reforms were condemned by many in civil society as a sham.[71] In these circumstances, the JVP made a dramatic electoral comeback in the parliamentary elections of 2004, and this helped to wreck the peace process.[72] From early 2006, the JVP was pushing hard for a military solution to the conflict and was goading the government into a resumption of the war, which duly occurred in August 2006.[73] Mahinda Rajapaksa, who became prime minister in 2004 and president in 2005, was increasingly in thrall to Sri Lanka's nationalist parties, including the JVP, on whom he depended for a working majority.

The destabilising effects of elections in 2004 and 2005 were part of a much older story, with any party that pursued some kind of peace becoming vulnerable to what has been called 'ethnic outbidding' – essentially, the practice whereby parties would try to gain a following by stressing their nationalist credentials.[74]

In a subtle analysis of this mechanism, Jonathan Spencer notes that a combination of a first-past-the-post electoral system and the broad geographical separation of Tamils and Sinhalese had fostered a political system in which both Sinhalese and Tamil politicians looked to their own ethnic groups for a political constituency. Feeding into this 'ethnicised' politics was a feeling among many Sinhalese that Tamils had been unfairly favoured under British rule. Significantly, politicians from different ethnic groups had not been brought together in an anti-colonial movement of the kind that brought together Muslims and Hindus in India. All this led to what Spencer calls 'a zone of permanent opposition in the north' of Sri Lanka, where Tamil parties were dominant, and 'a zone of competition in the south', where mostly Sinhalese politicians fought for votes and where the energy of party thugs, who physically attacked their opponents, was sometimes redirected into attacking Tamils.[75] In such a context, democracy itself could be profoundly destabilising, and Spencer observed in 2008:

> In the aftermath of the events of 11 September 2001 many commentators succumbed to the temptation to picture a world divided between liberalism, pluralism, tolerance and peace on the one hand, and illiberalism, intolerance and violence on the other. The stark choice for the world, we were told, lay between democracy and terror. But, in this case, I would argue that the origins of the 'ethnic' divide between Sinhala and Tamil, and much of the peculiar nastiness of the past 20 years of conflict, lie in the institutional structure and working dynamic of representative democracy in Sri Lanka.[76]

If the support of Sinhalese nationalists helped to propel Rajapaksa to the presidency in December 2005, also important was a boycott of the presidential elections orchestrated by the Tamil Tigers. To many, it seemed as if the Tigers themselves wanted a resumption of all-out war.[77] The Tigers attracted a great deal of support – locally and within the Tamil diaspora – for standing up to the abuses of the Sri Lanka government. But over the years the Tiger leadership, like some politicians in Colombo, had found that continued conflict conferred significant political advantages in relation to their own 'constituency'. Significantly, it had usually been abuses by government forces – and related paramilitaries – that pushed civilians towards the Tamil Tiger rebels, who were frequently brutal and practised forcible recruitment of children,[78] but nevertheless came to represent many Tamils' best hope of standing up to an oppressive government. The Tigers had used a good deal of violence to establish their supremacy over other Tamil organisations, and over a long period war had provided cover for this intra-Tamil violence, as well as carrying the strong implication that 'moderation' was unrealistic. Commenting in December 2009 on the overall course of the war in Sri Lanka, one informative report by University Teachers for Human Rights (Jaffna), a human rights organisation in the north, noted:

> ... the LTTE's [Tamil Tiger] repression of its own population succeeded best when the violence of the State was at its worst. The LTTE understood this and it formed a part of its calculations in breaking off every peace process and restarting war. Under heightened levels of violence, the people were on the move or were too busy trying to keep their families safe and fed. Whenever the violence diminished, people talked more to each other and began to wonder why they accepted this level of repression that often involves surrendering their children to the LTTE for cannon fodder. If governments had understood this, they would have had some ready political options for dealing with the LTTE. But they were so undisciplined that whenever war began, they lost all control and rushed headlong into indiscriminate violence against the Tamil people.[79]

We might add that Colombo's violence was rarely *entirely* indiscriminate. Co-option of Tamils into the government and into the various paramilitaries was common, for example. Even so, that element of indiscriminate violence was also part of the ongoing terror, and the 2009 catastrophe saw Tamils being forcibly detained *en masse*, while vicious counterinsurgency tactics killed perhaps 40,000 Tamils,[80] the majority of them civilians.

The careful reader will notice, perhaps with some sense of relief, that there has so far been no mention of Sierra Leone in this chapter. That happy situation cannot be allowed to persist, however, and I include here a brief word on the role of 'divide and rule' in Sierra Leone's war. It is striking that ethnicity played a relatively minor role in the war, and this helped to constrain the politics of divide and rule. Even so, the counterinsurgency in Sierra Leone was sometimes used to absorb the energies of some of the more marginalised elements.

When (in the early 1990s) government troops were rapidly recruited from the streets of the capital in particular, some observers suspected that this tactic was a way of 'packing off' urban criminals and potential troublemakers to an upcountry war. A Freetown businessman recalled: 'The government took pickpockets and so on, and put them in the army. Many of them used to attack and rob with knives. Now they had the extra power of the bullet.' A human rights campaigner told me: 'They were drop-outs and robbers. You've legalised their trade.' Whatever purposes may have been served by this approach, as we have seen, it cannot be regarded as a serious effort at counterinsurgency. More generally, many youths began to regard the country's war – and not without some justification – as an elite attempt to deflect the threat of a rapidly expanding and highly discontented youth by inciting one faction of youth against another. One young man who had not taken part in the fighting commented: 'Youths are saying we should not be drugged to fight our brothers for the old politicians.' At the outset of war, many suspected that maintaining a state of emergency offered the old All People's Congress (APC) party a way of resisting the democratisation that was sweeping the world at that time and gathering momentum in Sierra Leone itself.[81]

***

We can see, then, that the political functions of war – whether in richer or poorer countries – have included: weakening a political opposition; gaining electoral advantage; absorbing the energies of discontented groups; and sabotaging an emerging democracy.

Though this chapter has focused on those functions (and particularly on the tactic of 'divide and rule'), the political functions of war are actually extremely complex and a more wide-ranging investigation is called for. While space here is limited, four other political functions are worth noting.

First, war tends to legitimise a large allocation of resources to the military in many countries, which has political and economic pay-offs for powerful sectors of society.[82] This issue, touched on in our discussions of demobilising armies in Rwanda and Yugoslavia, is taken up in more detail in chapters 7 and 8.

Secondly, restless groups have often been absorbed not just into civil wars, but into wars *in other countries*. The case of England and Ireland in the 1640s illustrates some of these dynamics (even if these were not, strictly, separate countries at the time). For example, after the first English civil war of 1642–46, Parliamentarian soldiers vociferously demanded payment of their arrears. In April 1647, Parliament offered to disband part of its army and to pay the arrears. But, as so often in more recent conflicts, the economy was in dire straits and the plan to demobilise soldiers was potentially destabilising. In these circumstances, Parliament said it would send a large contingent of Parliamentarian soldiers to Ireland (at the time ruled from London) to suppress a continuing Catholic pro-Royalist revolt (which had begun in 1641).[83] Conrad Russell comments: 'In Ireland, they would be safely out of the way while a settlement was negotiated, and the officers were to be purged before they went.'[84]

While an angry and increasingly politicised Parliamentarian army was not to be so easily defused,[85] the conflict in Ireland still played a part in absorbing its energies. The 'counterinsurgency' saw mass expulsions and mass killings, usually linked to a new plantation scheme centred on the east of Ireland.[86] Some of the best estates in Ireland were taken by Parliamentary soldiers,[87] and large numbers of local people were forced to move to the more infertile lands of the west.

Significantly, the disaster in Ireland also served the function of rewarding the investors who had backed the Parliamentarians and their reformed, salaried New Model Army in the first place. Commercial investors took some of the best estates, and as historian Tristram Hunt notes: 'a large part of the New Model Army funding had been secured from the City [of London] on the promise of Irish land. The City institutions were now calling in their debts.'[88] Thus, the radicalism of what some were to call the 'English revolution', often acclaimed as a milestone in the history of parliamentary democracy, had actually been bankrolled, in part, through the promise of mass expropriation.

Coming much closer to the present day, the 1980s saw a number of regimes in the Middle East and North Africa taking advantage of a distant war to absorb the energies of restless domestic elements when they discreetly encouraged some of their militants (the so-called Islamists) to join the anti-Soviet *jihad* in Afghanistan. Michael Scheuer, former chief of the CIA's bin Laden unit, noted:

> The Saudis, the Kuwaitis, the Egyptians, the Algerians, the Tunisians emptied their jails of Islamic militants on the condition that they accepted a ticket to Karachi or Peshawar and then ended up in Afghanistan, hoping that they would kill Soviets and die in the process.[89]

Western countries themselves may not be entirely exempt from such calculations. In 2010, I met a Home Office official whose job it was to combat terrorism in the UK. After referring to the 7/7 London attacks, I asked him why there had not been *more* attacks in the UK – for example, in retaliation for the Iraq invasion. He said many of the worst 'known troublemakers' were currently absorbed in fighting 'over there' – in Iraq and Afghanistan. While the 'war on terror' has, in general, been ineffective in reducing terrorism, this particular mechanism (a troubling one that I have never seen publicly discussed) at least merits investigation.[90]

A third additional – and by no means obvious – political function of war arises when war is used by counterinsurgency forces to destabilise a regime that they are supposedly defending. This paradoxical situation becomes more comprehensible when we realise that many soldiers may feel less loyalty towards a current regime than a previous one. That was certainly the case in Sierra Leone in 1992–96, when many senior officers were covertly supporting the RUF rebels as a result of the loyalty they felt to the previous APC government, toppled in a 1992 military coup.

One of those trying to draw attention to this phenomenon was Chief Sam Hinga Norman, who had played a key role in setting up the burgeoning civil defence movement that stood up to rebels and rogue government soldiers. A tall and charismatic man, Chief Norman was nevertheless trying to keep a low profile in a run-down Freetown apartment block when I met him in 1995. As a retired army officer (like coup leader Koroma, he had trained at Sandhurst in the UK), Chief Norman had good contacts in the army. We met during a power cut, but Chief Norman's eyes shone brightly as he told me how army officers appointed under the old APC government were now trying to destabilise the military government: 'Their role is incitement against the [military] regime.

They say to soldiers, "Why are you so low?" There's a volcano. And you can't get rid of these inciters because they'll create problems. It's a pretty kettle of fish!' Former APC officers, mostly from the north of the country, were also trying to organise against the civil defence movement and were widely held to be working in tandem with deposed APC politicians. Some former APC officers seem to have been sent to the warfront as a punishment for lack of loyalty and as a means of getting them away from Freetown and reducing the risk of a coup.[91]

At the risk of exhausting both topic and reader, let me add a fourth – and crucial – additional political function of violence. This is war's possible function in intimidating a broad swathe of the population – well beyond the rebels or the named enemy.[92] This was evident in Guatemala's civil war (from 1960 to 1996). As Shelton Davis noted:

> Most observers are in agreement that the purpose of the Guatemalan army's counterinsurgency campaign was as much to teach the Indian population a psychological lesson as to wipe out a guerrilla movement that, at its height, had probably no more than 3,500 trained people in arms.[93]

One donor representative with long experience in Guatemala told me: 'There was never a huge guerrilla movement – it was more used by the army so they could do what they wanted. They could have destroyed them like this ...' (and she snapped her fingers). More than a straight fight between government troops and rebels, the civil war served a function not just in suppressing the guerrillas (the named enemy), but also in providing cover and legitimacy for violence against a broad range of political activists and human rights workers. The findings of the Guatemalan Commission for Historical Classification are worth quoting at some length:

> ... from 1978 to 1982 citizens from broad sectors of society participated in growing social mobilisation and political opposition to the continuity of the country's established order. These movements in some cases maintained ties of a varying nature with the insurgency. However, at no time during the internal armed confrontation did the guerrilla groups have the military potential necessary to pose an imminent threat to the State. The number of insurgent combatants

was too small to be able to compete in the military arena with the Guatemalan Army, which had more troops and superior weaponry, as well as better training and co-ordination.[94]

And the report concludes:

… the State deliberately magnified the military threat of the insurgency, a practice justified by the concept of the internal enemy. The inclusion of all opponents under one banner, democratic or otherwise, pacifist or guerrilla, legal or illegal, communist or non-communist, served to justify numerous and serious crimes … the vast majority of the victims of the acts committed by the State were not combatants in guerrilla groups, but civilians.[95]

The traditional distinction between 'war' – in Guatemala's case, from 1960 to 1996 – and 'peace' tends to conceal as much as it reveals. The Commission for Historical Clarification notes that, up until 1970, the victims of military operations were mainly peasants, members of rural unions, teachers, students and guerrilla sympathisers. In 1971–77 repression was more selective, but victims again included union leaders.[96] Between 1978 and 1985 the victims were much more numerous and were principally Mayan and 'in the majority of cases, the identification of Mayan communities with the insurgency was intentionally exaggerated by the State'.[97] After that, repression became more selective again.[98] In many ways the extremity of the anti-Mayan violence in 1978–85, which has plausibly been labelled as genocide, has tended to obscure an underlying continuity and, in a sense, an underlying rationality: the targeting of politically inconvenient opponents under the cover of a wider war. This tactic, as we shall see, has extended into 'peacetime', where a 'war on crime' and a 'war on drugs' have proved convenient.

The political functions of 'counterinsurgency' in Colombia resemble those in Guatemala in many respects. With Colombian paramilitaries often backing and bribing particular politicians, paramilitary violence was used to intimidate political opponents and local voters through massacres and selective murders.[99] Given the threat of rebel violence and crime more generally, the paramilitaries' 'alternative order' sometimes even won them a degree of popular support.[100]

As Chris Dolan shows, in the case of Uganda the point of all the forcible displacement into government 'protected villages' was not so much to defeat the insurgency – if anything, it had the opposite effect – as to send a sharp and intimidating message to the Acholi people as a whole (and to other potentially restive groups, such as the Teso ethnic group) about the dangers of political activity. This 'social torture', like individual acts of torture, was counterproductive in defeating or eliminating terror – in part because it *nurtured* the LRA rebels, and in part because it *constituted* an additional terror. But as an intimidating message that underscored the power of Uganda's long-term rulers, it may nevertheless have been disturbingly successful.[101] It may be helpful to put Chris Dolan's insights here alongside Paul Kahn's argument in his book *Sacred Violence*. Kahn emphasises the political functions of individual torture, and particularly its function in underlining the authority of the government by reducing potentially heroic 'martyrs' among the enemy to a condition of degradation. He also asks why war is commonly considered acceptable when torture is not, particularly since 'the internal logic of combat is torture: to create such an asymmetry in force that the enemy has no capacity to injure but can only suffer injury'.[102] Dolan is highlighting that asymmetry of force in Uganda, as well as the systematic degradation inflicted on the Achola. He stresses that calling this 'war' rather than 'social torture' obscures as much as it reveals. It is important to note, moreover, that at election times (for example in 1996), President Museveni would often play on southerners' fears of terrorism in the north and of a possible return of northerners to power. The war also helped to delegitimise opposition politicians, especially from the north, in the name of 'security'.[103] Andrew Mwenda notes:

> Over the years, the war provided the justification for the broader assaults on individual freedoms. Newspapers and radio stations would be illegally closed and journalists detained and harassed. The justification in all these cases was 'security'. Opposition politicians who threatened the president were emasculated, harassed and sent into exile, and their supporters incarcerated for months on grounds that they were supporting the LRA rebellion.[104]

A related process – and a precedent – had earlier unfolded during the so-called 'Mau Mau Emergency' in British-ruled Kenya in the early

1950s, which also involved forced villagisation. A careful study by Bruce Berman noted that the rebellion was strongly fuelled by government emergency measures, including the attempt to use 'development' and forced relocation as instruments of counterinsurgency.[105] Moreover:

> The collective violence of the Kenya Emergency cannot be adequately explained as originating in an armed rebellion. While small numbers of young Kenyans began to move into the forests on the fringes of the reserves as early as July and August 1952 in response to the demands being made by Europeans for a state of emergency, the underground movement possessed neither coherent plans, organization or training for guerrilla combat nor a significant stockpile of modern arms ... *The Emergency, in reality, was a pre-emptive attack carried out by the incumbent colonial authorities against a significant segment of the African political leadership of Kenya and its supporters* [emphasis in original].[106]

Discovering the most important fault-lines in any particular conflict is made more difficult by the fact that a misreading is often *intended*. For example, the manipulation of ethnic divisions by elite groups will 'work' better when people see – and are encouraged to see – ethnic fault-lines as natural and inevitable.[107] Similarly, where war is serving some kind of hidden function in suppressing internal opposition, this tactic will 'work' better when most citizens can be convinced that war is actually a response to some real threat (internal rebels, some kind of a danger emanating from abroad, or preferably both). Given that abusive governments typically like to exert a high degree of control over the media, and even over international aid organisations (notably through the threat of expulsion), finding good information on the real fault-lines of conflict will not be easy. Meanwhile, media control can help limit the political 'fallout' from military reverses, and in any case a degree of disorder upcountry may not be seen as an economic or political threat to elites in a Khartoum, a Freetown or a Colombo.[108]

It would seem, in short, that a reviled enemy (whether external or internal) and a 'state of emergency' are almost ideal circumstances for abusive and corrupt governments that seek some degree of legitimacy and popularity.

CHAPTER 6

Wars within Wars

While war is generally seen as a contest between two sides, it may sometimes more usefully be seen as an 'enabling environment' for diverse local conflicts. This applies to both civil wars and 'global wars', like the Cold War and the 'war on terror'.

Well before Sierra Leone's civil war, there had been a long-running dispute between ruling families in Kailahun district in the east, a dispute that centred on chieftaincy positions.[1] A Methodist minister who was working in Kailahun at the time of the rebel incursion told me that chiefs appointed by the ruling party became a particular target for violence once war broke out, adding:

> When the rebels came from Liberia, the main chiefly families in Kailahun were in a position to stand by the soldiers and drive the rebels back. They are known to be good fighters. For the rebels to overtake them tells you a lot. Each [family] saw it as an opportunity to gain ascendancy, so they did not stand as a team to destroy the rebels. They stood by the rebels to destroy the houses of the other factions. The war has been going on long before we realised it, in the sense that people had their differences.

In their own investigation, Philippa Atkinson and her colleagues observed: 'Some people collaborated with the rebels out of desire to wreak revenge in old feuds ... Long-lasting family feuds were brought to the surface with the knowledge that pointing a finger could mean death.'[2] There are parallels here with the pursuit of personal vendettas under cover of witch-hunts, for example in seventeenth-century Salem, North America.[3]

Yale scholar Stathis Kalyvas emphasises that civil war has tended to serve as a vehicle for local feuds, but he adds that such wars do not simply represent an *accumulation* of local feuds. A study by Benjamin Paul and William Demarest of the small town of San Pedro in Guatemala illustrates the point. Here, local cleavages – both political and religious – were actually of long standing, but it took a war to ignite these disputes into outright violence: 'What disrupted the peace in San Pedro was not the presence of differences and divisions, but the army's recruitment of agents and spies that had the effect of exploiting these cleavages.'[4]

Just as local feuds tend to grow more violent within the context of an 'enabling' civil war, so, too, national disputes tend to become more violent and more destructive within the context of an 'enabling' global war that provides cover and legitimacy for these disputes. Thus, conflicts at various levels tend to overlap dangerously and to interact: there are wars within wars, and systems within systems.

Since at least the Second World War, civil wars have usually been waged within the context of a wider, global war, like the Cold War or the 'war on terror'. In this context, major powers have routinely turned a blind eye to violence by allied actors (especially allied governments), while civilians have frequently fallen victim to this process. At the national level, civilians may be deemed by their own governments to be illegitimate (and not deserving of rights or protection) because of their (actual or presumed) association with some demonised enemy;[5] and where that enemy has also been demonised internationally, the abuse has typically been reinforced.

Whether in the Cold War or after, the standard framework in the West has been to dismiss the grievances of rebel groups (who may be labelled 'Communist', 'greedy', 'criminal', 'terrorist', 'fanatical', 'geno-cidal' or some combination of these) and to articulate very publicly the absolute importance of militarily defeating this embodiment of evil.

Unfortunately, this reflex has tended to create a kind of 'open season' for greed and political repression within the machinery of counterinsur-gency (which may sometimes extend beyond the state borders to include neighbouring countries). Meanwhile, any leverage that the West may have in relation to an abusive regime and its international allies has routinely been thrown away amidst a loudly proclaimed project of eliminating a demonised enemy.[6] These overlapping war systems are all the more pernicious because the proclaimed intention of eliminating the enemy may often itself be a cover for exploitation and repression, as we have seen. The priorities of pro-Western politicians and their soldiers have rarely centred solely on defeating that enemy, while international actors, too, have typically had goals that complicate – and even impede – the declared goal of 'winning'.

The Cold War meant a 'green light' for government repression in Vietnam, El Salvador, Guatemala, Indonesia, the Philippines and a great many other countries. Often, there was little incentive for repressive governments to reform (for example, implementing land redistribution), since inflows of aid were guaranteed so long as domestic Communists had a presence.[7] Some governments were able to play the superpowers off against each other. Meanwhile, there was also Western encouragement for abusive rebel groups in Nicaragua, Angola, Mozambique and elsewhere. Famine, too, found a sinister friend in the Cold War: in Ethiopia, for example, international responses to the 1984–85 famine were impeded by Cold War politics (notably Western fears of driving the regime further into the Soviet camp).[8] Meanwhile, the evolving famine in Sudan was deepened when Western governments turned a blind eye to militia raiding – and the blocking of relief – that was sponsored by Khartoum, a Cold War 'ally' that Western governments were reluctant to criticise.[9] In effect, the southern Sudanese became 'illegitimate civilians', both nationally and internationally. Even after the Cold War, the enduring ideological assumption that 'liberalising' governments are good governments has created space for widespread abuses, as we saw in Sierra Leone.

The 'war on terror' has reinvented and reinvigorated many of these damaging dynamics. When George W. Bush famously said that 'either you are with us, or you are with the terrorists', this was usually interpreted (correctly) as a message of intimidation towards those hesitating to sign up to his 'war on terror'. But another problem with this 'pick a side' approach has become increasingly clear: namely, that those who are deemed to be 'with us' have been able to use this status to carve out a great deal of impunity for abuse. In fact, many exploitative and repressive regimes have managed to secure huge inflows of Western aid – and even lavish praise – while engaging in such abuse.

In Algeria, heightened international fears around 'Islamism' in the 1990s helped fuel regime abuse in a number of ways. Powerful elements of the Algerian military found, in the 1990–98 civil war against 'Islamists', the means of forestalling democratic rule by the Islamists (who were winning the – interrupted – elections in 1992), of attracting foreign aid and loans (to combat the 'Islamists'), of engaging in crime under cover of war (for example, the trade in cars stolen from France), and of positioning themselves within a lucrative privatisation process (notably in relation to the oil and gas industries).[10] In his study of the Algerian war, Luis Martinez was led to ask: '... are the Islamist groups and the military not in the process of becoming "complementary enemies" finding in the violence of war the way to achieve their aspirations?'[11]

Sudan has positioned itself rather ambiguously, but often very cleverly, within emerging post-Cold War global conflicts. After the Cold War had helped to shield the Khartoum government from Western criticism in the 1980s, Sudan's relations with the US soured in the 1990s. This stemmed, in large part, from Khartoum's support for Saddam Hussein's 1990 invasion of Kuwait. Sudan's close ties with the Middle East (including Iran and Iraq)[12] and, increasingly, with China and Malaysia, helped to sustain the abusive military government in Khartoum in the 1990s. In effect, Khartoum was able to carve out renewed impunity in the context of, first, the growing tension between the 'Arab world' and the West (a forerunner of 'the war on terror') and, second, the growing rivalry between China and the West (a mutation of the Cold War).

The US, however, had not given up on restoring its influence in Khartoum, and in the aftermath of 9/11 Washington and Khartoum enjoyed something of a 'rapprochement'. Significantly, Khartoum gave the US government access to banking details on Osama bin Laden (who had lived in Sudan from 1991 to 1996), as well as information on other al Qaeda operatives. Khartoum also courted favour with Washington by, first, detaining Islamist militants on their way to join insurgents resisting the US-led occupation of Iraq from 2003, and, second, by supplying information on Islamist groups in Somalia. Disturbingly, Sudan's intelligence chief, Major-General Salah Gosh, was even flown by executive jet in April 2005 to meet CIA officials in Virginia.[13] Yet this was the same Salah Gosh who had been accused by US Congress members of directing attacks on civilians in Darfur. John Prendergast and Colin Thomas-Jensen commented:

Cooperation accelerated after the 9/11 attacks on the United States, and Sudanese intelligence officials deftly exploited this relationship to deflect US pressure on other fronts. When President Bush asked his cabinet for robust options to sanction the Sudanese government because of Darfur, the US intelligence community squashed any actions that might upset the US-Sudanese relationship.[14]

Too much international protest over Darfur was also seen as jeopardising the north–south peace agreement that the US government had done so much to nurture. In these circumstances, particularly during the intense government-sponsored violence in 2003, many victims of violence in Darfur became, to a significant extent, 'illegitimate civilians', whether in the eyes of Khartoum or Washington. Washington's view began to change as the campaign in the US to highlight genocide in Darfur gathered steam in 2004, but much of Darfur was already in ruins by that time, and even the US declaration of 'genocide' did not translate into very substantial sanctions or protection on the ground.[15] Meanwhile, the *Arab* victims of Arab pastoralists' violence tended to remain unremarked and unassisted, and the continuing grievances of some of the attackers were largely neglected.[16]

The case of Libya also shows how systems of violence can overlap and interact. Muammar Gaddafi, Libya's 'brother leader', had long been seeking to clamp down on domestic Islamists, even claiming that they were supported by 'Zionists' and 'US imperialists'. After the 1988 Lockerbie plane bombing, Gaddafi also faced UN sanctions, which threatened to ignite Islamist opposition. The events of 9/11 gave him a new opportunity, and Gaddafi was able to secure something of a green light for his habitual internal repression by positioning himself as an unlikely ally in the 'war on terror'. In George W. Bush's brave new world, where you were 'either with us or with the terrorists', Gaddafi was 'with us'.

After 9/11 (and facing the threat of an Iraq-style attack by the Bush regime), Gaddafi announced the end of his programme for weapons of mass destruction and allowed international access to the relevant sites. The Bush administration had hoped that attacking Iraq would send a message to any state with plans for weapons of mass destruction, and in the case of Libya at least the tactic may actually have worked. Gaddafi stated explicitly that, with George Bush in charge, no one could know whether they would be a target or not[17] (a point that seems to have applied equally to Vice President Dick Cheney, who famously missed the quail during a 2006 hunting trip and shot a fellow hunter). Gaddafi was also courted as a source of oil, a customer for Western arms, and an unlikely advocate of Tony Blair's 'Third Way' between capitalism and socialism.

In December 2003, the UN Security Council lifted sanctions on Libya, and less than a year later the European Union ended its embargo on weapons sales to Tripoli. All this opened up major opportunities, in particular for arms companies and US oil companies.[18] The EU granted export licences for more than 800 million euros' worth of arms exports to Libya.[19] Britain was even happy to export 'toxic chemical precursors' (which can be used to make chemical weapons) to the country (a courtesy also extended to Sudan, where in 1998 the US had bombed a Khartoum factory that was suspected of producing chemical weapons).[20] Political scientist Luis Martinez commented: 'for the oil companies and the weapons industry, the Libya of Colonel Qadhafi turned from a "pariah state" into a Mediterranean "eldorado".'[21]

One of Gaddafi's assets in this remarkable turnaround was his knowledge of the Islamist groups that he had been attempting to suppress within Libya for many years.[22] A wave of Islamist violence had threatened the regime in the late 1990s. When Gaddafi had blamed this on 'imperialist' and 'Zionist' powers, he was trying to build an international support base in the Arab world. But he was generally unsuccessful in this endeavour.[23] Gaddafi cleverly adapted to the new international climate, and after 9/11 the Islamist opposition within Libya was deftly rebranded as the work of al Qaeda.

Another of Gaddafi's assets in his rapprochement with the West, strangely, was precisely his experience and expertise in sponsoring international terrorism. Over the years, Gaddafi had not only supported the 1988 Lockerbie passenger-plane bombing, but had also lent his support to a wide range of terrorist groups around the world, including the Irish Republican Army (IRA), Abu Sayyaf in the Philippines, and even the Revolutionary United Front (RUF) in Sierra Leone. After 9/11, Gaddafi proved his newfound 'usefulness' by helping to secure the release of hostages held by Islamist groups in Algeria and the Philippines, for example.[24] Like President Bashir in Sudan, Gaddafi benefited from supplying the West with information on his erstwhile friends. At my university, an expert in information technology once told me that the most lucrative corporate jobs combating viruses sometimes go to those who have created viruses themselves; Gaddafi seems to have been exploiting a similar logic.

In addition to Sudan and Libya, a number of other abusive regimes in Africa have been able to carve out a degree of impunity from the 'war on terror'. A particularly disturbing case is Somalia, which hit the headlines when famine spilled over from southern Somalia into Kenya and Ethiopia in 2011. For many months, this catastrophe was presented within a depoliticised framework that highlighted 'drought'. In fact, as Somali scholar Abdi Ismail Samatar has pointed out: 'The African Union, the UN, the EU and the US continued to describe the famine as a drought until July 18 [2011].'[25] While drought was certainly a factor, the role of conflict went damagingly unremarked. And when it was belatedly acknowledged, this was usually through a vague reference to 'civil war' or to the abuses of the Islamist rebels in Somalia. An October 2011 report by Matt Bryden for the prominent US pressure group Enough stated: 'it is ultimately al-Shabaab's [the Islamist rebels'] twisted ideology, repressive methods, and indifference to the suffering of its own people that lies behind this catastrophe.'[26] While the rebels played a major part, this famine also owes a great deal to the US-led 'war on terror' and to various forms of violence that have been deemed acceptable – even desirable – within a 'war on terror' framework.

In 2006, a coalition of local Sharia courts ended the fifteen-year domination of Mogadishu by Somali warlords. The resistance of many militias crumbled as the Union of Islamic Courts (UIC) gained ascendancy in much of the country and restored a significant degree of order. Most Somalis seem to have welcomed the UIC as blessed relief from the warlords, and Samatar observed that 'the vast majority of Somalis supported the UIC and pleaded with the international community to engage them peacefully.'[27] But the US government, which had been cooperating with several of the incumbent warlords in apprehending suspected terrorists,[28] suspected that the UIC was itself harbouring East African terrorists. In fact, there were growing fears that Somalia was becoming a haven for al Qaeda.

These fears were rather exaggerated: most Somali experts estimated that there were no more than half a dozen terror suspects on Somali territory. But the damage done by this atmosphere of suspicion and paranoia was real enough. For one thing, US statements against – and lack of support for – the UIC government meant that some of the less radical Islamists lost influence to the radicals.[29] In these circumstances, Ethiopia was able to play cleverly on US fears of a 'new Taliban', and in December 2006 – with Washington's explicit approval – Ethiopian forces invaded Somalia, defeated the Islamist UIC government, and installed a new regime in Mogadishu (known as the Transitional Federal Government, or TFG).[30] At this time, Ethiopian forces shelled heavily populated neighbourhoods in Mogadishu, while TFG militias terrorised the population of the capital.[31] More than a million people were displaced, and many were propelled along a path that was to culminate in outright famine in 2011.[32] Meanwhile, the newly installed TFG regime proved deeply abusive and corrupt. According to a detailed report by the International Crisis Group in February 2011:

> A cabal within the [TFG] regime presides over a corruption syndicate that is massive, sophisticated and extends well beyond Somalia's borders. The impunity with which its members operate and manipulate the system to serve their greed is remarkable. They are not fit to hold public office and should be forced to resign, isolated and sanctioned.[33]

Such concerted pressure was never brought to bear, however. Instead, the TFG was shored up by international support in the context of a much-highlighted 'al Qaeda threat'. As Mark Bradbury noted in an authoritative report:

> … the Ethiopian invasion (unsanctioned by the UN), US airstrikes, the rendition of suspected Islamic militants, the closure of the Kenyan border to Somali refugees, the indiscriminate shelling of civilian neighbourhoods in Mogadishu by Ethiopian forces, the mass displacement of civilians from Mogadishu, assassinations, and arbitrary detentions all elicited very little reaction or condemnation from foreign governments and multi-lateral agencies … The international backing for the TFG and muted international response to abuses by it, illustrated the extent to which the 'global war on terror' had taken priority over human rights, humanitarian principles, and international law.[34]

In these circumstances, unsurprisingly, the TFG showed little genuine interest in power-sharing. The former 'Islamist government', now recast as 'Islamist insurgents', was subjected to a series of American missile strikes against 'high value terrorist targets'.[35] As so often in the past, however, this kind of aggressive approach proved profoundly counter-productive. In a cogent analysis, Harry Verhoeven observed: 'the decision by the White House to place Al-Shabaab [the Islamist rebels] on the list of terrorist organisations [in March 2008] has further radicalised Somalia's Islamist youth'.[36] Particularly destabilising was a May 2008 US Tomahawk missile strike that killed the leader of al-Shabaab, Aden Hashi Ayro. Al-Shabaab responded by declaring that all American, Western and UN officials and organisations were now on its expanded list of targets, something that placed aid agencies in much greater danger.[37] The assassination also encouraged a fragmentation of the Islamists, which further reduced the security of humanitarian agencies.[38]

In 2008 retired Colonel Thomas Dempsey, former director of African Studies at the US Army War College, told a US Senate hearing on the Horn of Africa that military strikes in Somalia had created widespread mistrust of the US in Africa, adding:

> The collateral damage, including loss of innocent civilian lives, which is an unavoidable consequence of military strikes, no matter how carefully targeted or surgically delivered, threatens to undermine the moral authority of our counterterrorism efforts and arguably contributes to the ongoing recruitment efforts of the terrorist groups themselves.[39]

Meanwhile, TFG leaders and security forces (which were being supported by the 'international community') were themselves blocking and looting relief, arguing that this relief was helping 'the terrorists'.[40] Some government supporters were also attacking aid workers.[41] These abuses from both sides helped to starve the population of Mogadishu, as well as people displaced from the capital.[42] At the same time, some UN and donor-state diplomats were downplaying the crisis, lest it embarrass an internationally favoured TFG government that was said, rather optimistically, to be engaging in 'state-building'.[43]

It is true that al-Shabaab has banned most agencies from working in the zones it controls and has carried out attacks on humanitarian workers. It has also confiscated food and other goods and restricted people's freedom of movement. All these actions have contributed significantly to famine, and there is an urgent need for governments in the Middle East, in particular, to exert whatever leverage they can on the rebels.[44] That said, there is something a bit too easy about blaming – once again – the 'fanatical rebels' (in this case, 'Islamic extremists'). Al-Shabaab's antipathy towards Western-led interventions (including Western-led relief operations) has not arisen out of nothing, but rather reflects, in large part, a backlash against the US/Ethiopian interference in Somalia and the ousting of a government that was, in many ways, both popular and successful. It would seem to be a case of Hannah Arendt's concept of 'action as propaganda' – essentially the use of violence, usually by totalitarian regimes, to shape the world in a way that makes propaganda look more plausible.[45] In this case, the military intervention by US-backed Ethiopian forces helped to create a radicalised and anti-humanitarian al-Shabaab. As the stereotype of the 'fanatical Islamist rebel' became more and more plausible, this seems progressively to have edged out any lingering international recollections of the relative peace that the UIC had brought to Somalia before the Ethiopian intervention.

International aid also seems to have been compromised by the 'war on terror'. At the beginning of 2010, the World Food Programme (WFP) suspended aid to south-central Somalia, citing insecurity. But the UN agency had also been under strong pressure from the US government, a major donor, not to provide relief that could find its way into the hands of 'terrorists'.[46] US food aid to Somalia fell foul of US anti-terrorist legislation in 2009,[47] and Somalia expert Ken Menkhaus notes that relief to areas of rebel strength was effectively criminalised, as the US government sought to ensure that no relief would reach terrorist groups.[48]

Unfortunately, impunity linked to the 'war on terror' has radiated outwards from Somalia to affect neighbouring Ethiopia as well. Ethiopia is a key US ally in Africa, particularly given its role in confronting 'Islamists' in Somalia. Ethiopia has attracted huge aid resources from the West, and this assistance (and related international approval) has given Addis Ababa a great deal of political space in which to deepen the repression of its own people.[49]

In the Ogaden region, the Ethiopian government has confined aid agencies to the edge of the war it has been waging since 1994 against the Ogaden National Liberation Front, allowing the government to conduct reprisals 'behind closed doors'. These reprisals, intensifying since 2007, have included forced displacement and a commercial blockade against the Ogadeni population, which is mostly Muslim and ethnic Somali.[50] Aid agencies were accused of supporting the rebels, while the aid agency Médecins Sans Frontières (MSF) has been particularly critical of what it sees as a weak response within the UN system.[51]

The Ugandan government, too, has derived damaging impunity from the 'war on terror' – not least because of its involvement in Somalia. Uganda has provided 'peacekeepers' to support the US-backed Transitional Federal Government in Somalia, and has also hosted European Union training of TFG soldiers.[52] As so often, these mechanisms are variations on a well-worn theme: it may be recalled that repressive governments in the Philippines and South Korea, for example, gained important US support from supplying troops for the war in Vietnam.[53]

The provision of 'peacekeepers' for Somalia was only the latest in a series of efforts by the Ugandan government to curry favour with the US as an ally against 'terror'. In the 1990s (and before 9/11), the US was already turning its attention to 'Islamic extremism' as part of the new, post-Cold War definition of the enemy. Sudan's government was seen as part of this emerging threat, and in these circumstances – as Andrew Mwenda shows – Washington increased its support to the rebel SPLA in southern Sudan, using Uganda as a channel for this assistance. The Sudanese government retaliated by supporting the Ugandan rebel LRA. While Khartoum's abuses against southern Sudanese people were all too real (as we have seen), Uganda's role in the US anti-terror drive itself proved to be an opportunity for manipulation and abuse. Ugandan President Yoweri Museveni was able to present himself as confronting Sudanese government 'terror', as well as LRA rebel 'terror' in Uganda and Sudan, and in these circumstances he was able to secure very substantial economic and diplomatic support from the US. The US government also stepped up its logistical and intelligence support for the Ugandan army, and encouraged Ugandan forces to pursue the LRA inside Sudan. Yet this flew in the face of existing evidence on just how ineffective and acquisitive the Ugandan army was proving to be when confronting named enemies in the DRC and in northern Uganda.[54]

The Khartoum government, anxious to be seen as 'anti-terrorist' in the wake of 9/11, gave explicit permission for Uganda's 'anti-LRA' operations in 2002, operations that had been going on unofficially for many years prior to that and that offered a continuing opportunity for economic predation.[55]

In fact, Museveni was able to obtain a free hand for a wide variety of dangerous 'security' projects – not only the invasions of Sudan from 1997, but also the mass displacements and expropriations in northern Uganda, the Ugandan-backed incursion of Tutsi RPF rebels into Rwanda in 1990–93 (which helped to precipitate genocide in 1994), and the Ugandan invasion of the DRC in 1998.[56] For a country with a reputation in the West for 'good government', this represents a formidable record. Uganda's strategic alliance with the West was underlined when Uganda (like Rwanda) signed up to the so-called 'coalition of the willing' that supported the US-led invasion of Iraq.[57]

Within Latin America, the global drive against 'terror' has probably proved most damaging in Colombia. Combining perniciously with the 'war on drugs', a pre- and post- 9/11 'war on terror' has propped up abuses by counterinsurgency actors, while at the same time minimising the attention paid to grievances that have helped to inform rebellion. Most of the spending under the US-backed Plan Colombia (announced in 1999) has been military spending, in contrast to the US's Alliance for Progress scheme in the 1960s, when the proportion was only around 10 per cent. The radical land and tax reforms envisaged in the 1960s were also dropped amidst a fashionable emphasis on the need for a military solution to the problems of drugs and 'terrorism'.[58]

In the Middle East, Israel has been able to exploit the 'war on terror' to underscore its longstanding impunity in the face of its abuse of Palestinian civilians and its periodic aggression in Lebanon. While the economic context for Israel's abuses is rarely discussed, it is significant that the country has pioneered 'home security' industries, and that its economy – increasingly geared towards counterterrorism industries – has flourished amidst widespread violence in the region. In 2006, Israel was the fourth-largest arms dealer in the world – larger than the UK – and the country's large imports of US weaponry have encouraged Israel's own arms industry to look for markets abroad.[59] Israel has also been extremely active in exporting counterinsurgency advice and technology (including to dictatorships, as well as abusive counterinsurgencies like those in Guatemala, Turkey and Sri Lanka).[60] Klein notes that while wars around the world have often sent shocks through financial markets, the Tel Aviv Stock Exchange actually rose in August 2006, despite a devastating war with Lebanon. This is not quite the whole story, as the markets did fall in the summer of 2006 when the war was starting, but the general point still holds. As an enthusiastic report from Wyatt Investment Research points out: 'Less than three months after the war, the Tel Aviv stock market hit all time highs. The war put only a slight damper on growth, and after it ended, almost every sector of the economy came out stronger than before ... Israel truly is a success story.'

The report went on: '... violence has done very little to derail the tech sector's growth ... On November 4 2008, the Israeli Defense Force made their first major incursion into Gaza ... Despite this surge in violence, the Tel Aviv Stock Exchange traded more on news of Lehman Brothers' collapse than battles next door.'[61] In fact, the Tel Aviv stock market rose strongly after the renewal of the Gaza conflict.[62]

Many of Israel's 'home security' and 'defence' products can truthfully be proclaimed to be 'tried and tested' locally, and each new war brings a chance to advertise high-tech killing products.[63] Israel's changing economy has also subtly – but substantially – affected its attitudes to peace. In the early 1990s, the damage inflicted when Arab countries boycotted Israel provided a significant incentive for peace accords in the form of the 1993 Oslo agreement.[64] But Israel's growing reliance on high-tech exports – including its defence-related exports – has seen a growing focus on Western markets rather than Arab markets; and these exports generally do not require Arab labour either. This seems to have created a greater indifference to Arab opinion (and sanctions), while also incentivising border 'closures' (which limit the 'flow' of Palestinian labour into Israel and simultaneously create great suffering).[65] Meanwhile, hardship arising from the opening up of the Israeli economy and the loss of many traditional manufacturing jobs tended to strengthen Israeli nationalist parties while also angering the Arab minority within Israel.[66]

Yemen provides another illustration of the way in which impunity for local abuses can flourish in the context of a 'war on terror'. It also illustrates how the expressed desire to eradicate the enemy may conceal a degree of mutual interest.

Yemen's tribal periphery has become a refuge for several leaders of a shadowy group known as Al Qaeda in the Arabian Peninsula (AQAP).[67] While Yemen was already seen as an ally in the 'war on terror', the country's own terrorist problem came under much greater international scrutiny when the attempted bombing of a US passenger jet on Christmas Day 2009 was linked to AQAP. International concerns about Yemen deepened in October 2010, when explosives were found in the toner cartridges of two printers on board cargo planes whose flights originated in Yemen. The separate packages were discovered in the UK and Dubai just hours before they were set to detonate.[68]

In this climate of heightened fear, Yemen's long-time president, Ali Saleh, seems to have realised that AQAP represented in many ways a rather useful enemy. Saleh was able to appeal to the West for massive economic assistance to ward off the threat of AQAP.[69] Meanwhile, AQAP also offered a pretext for internal repression, including intimidation of the media. All this helped Saleh to prop up an extremely corrupt political system.[70]

In these circumstances, the Yemeni government's desire to eliminate AQAP – and other 'enemies' – has been very much open to doubt. After the Yemeni government announced the killing of Abdullah al-Mehdar, he was officially described as one of the country's most wanted militants and the suspected leader of an al Qaeda cell. But *Guardian* journalist Brian Whitaker noted pithily: 'The word in Yemen is that Mehdar was just a troublesome tribal figure who didn't join al-Qaida until he was dead.'[71]

Whitaker added in January 2010 that in the 'Houthi war' (a rebellion in northern Yemen led by former member of parliament Hussein al-Houthi), 'the army has supposedly been just days from victory ever since September [2009]'.[72] That war in the north has seen government abuses that have themselves been encouraged by the 'war on terror'. Michel-Olivier Lacharité, with the aid agency MSF, notes:

> There was very little media coverage of the Yemen conflict between 2004 and 2007. The lack of war images and reports was due to the Yemeni government's extremely tight control over information exercised through physical persecution of journalists and legal prosecution of the regime's opponents. These prosecutions stepped up in 2001, helped by Yemen joining the 'Global War on Terror', which signified its alignment with the United States.[73]

In late 2009, MSF did draw attention to government air strikes and poor health service provision (and also put Yemen on its list of 'top ten humanitarian crises'), but the government immediately suspended permission for all MSF activities, and the aid agency quickly issued an apology.[74]

In a pattern familiar from Vietnam, Afghanistan, Somalia and elsewhere, Western intervention in Yemen seems to have ignored (and worsened) corruption within the government and the counterinsurgency, while also ignoring (and worsening) grievances among the rebels. The two problems are linked, since – again mirroring Vietnam, Afghanistan and Somalia – government corruption has fed strongly into rebel grievances.

As so often, large-scale international aid has created 'perverse incentives' for the local elite, reducing the need for it to be responsive to its own constituents.[75] As Phillips puts it, 'By seeking to strengthen the existing power hierarchies, donors may unwittingly reduce the incentives for the Yemeni elite to become more responsive to the deep sociopolitical ruptures it is perpetuating.'[76] Among the most profitable activities for government actors have been large-scale diesel smuggling and the shadowy operations of the Yemen Economic Corporation, which was originally funded by soldiers' contributions and which proved to be the main beneficiary of a privatisation drive at the end of Yemen's 1994 civil war.

Like the Viet Cong, the Taliban and al-Shabaab, AQAP has made good use of bad governance. Phillips comments drily: 'Much of AQAP's potency rests on its ability to offer – or be perceived to offer – more to the tribes than what the government is offering. Given the current turbulence of Yemen's domestic politics, this is not an overwhelming task.'[77] Among the grievances that AQAP has exploited has been the draining of oil revenues from poor regions of the country.[78] A related grievance has been the use of oil money, from the late 1980s, to undermine the willingness of tribal leaders to advocate on behalf of their constituents; many of these leaders moved to the cities, where they could strengthen their ties with the central government, often neglecting their own people.[79] Falling oil revenues have themselves put a major strain on this system.

In another echo from other wars, the legitimacy of the Yemeni government has been further undermined by US air attacks. As Phillips observes, 'AQAP's political appeal is … heightened by the US air-strikes that help the group to paint the Yemeni regime as an American puppet.'[80]

Also moving towards 'centre stage' in the 'war on terror' has been Pakistan. Here, a series of governments have been able to secure massive resources – and a high degree of impunity for internal repression – by positioning themselves cleverly in relation to wider, 'global' wars. After India and Pakistan became independent at the end of the Second World War, it was Pakistan that was chosen as America's 'anti-Communist' ally. Pakistan fell from grace with the 1965 India–Pakistan war, but large-scale US aid was revived by Pakistan's role in the anti-Soviet struggle in Afghanistan in the 1980s, and then again (after a lull in the 1990s) by 9/11 and the renewed need for help with war in Afghanistan.[81] Between 2002 and 2006, the US supplied Pakistan with over a billion dollars a year in military aid, and Pakistan has also benefited from the rescheduling of its huge debt.[82] Total US aid topped $4.5 billion in 2010, a huge sum in a country (population 180 million) where less than 2 million people pay taxes.[83] It has been a cosy arrangement for Pakistan's top brass, as well as for US military industries that supply the military exports. Since the birth of Pakistan, Western assistance has helped to stave off political reform. As one analyst put it:

> The army dealt with the Americans without reference to other Pakistani institutions ... Grave matters of state security were taken out of the hands of the always untrustworthy political class ... This phenomenon also contributed to the myth that the army was Pakistan's most competent institution – a myth because civilian institutions never had a chance to grow, nor were they encouraged by outsiders who lavished funds on the military.[84]

Playing on Western fears of a 'Talibanised' Pakistan run by 'atomic mullahs', Pakistan repeatedly promised to take on the Taliban.[85] But those 'confronting' the Taliban in Pakistan's border region have generally been poorly trained and woefully equipped for the task.[86] Meanwhile, most of the military aid has been spent on defence relevant for deterring India – for example, fighter jets, anti-ship missiles and air defence radar – rather than on 'counterterror' operations.[87] In fact, as Lawrence Wright notes in *The New Yorker*,

> As much as half of the money the U.S. gave to the I.S.I. [Inter-Services Intelligence] to fight the Soviets was diverted to build nuclear

weapons. The father of Pakistan's bomb, A.Q. Kahn, later sold plans and nuclear equipment to Libya, North Korea and Iran. A month before 9/11, Pakistani nuclear scientists even opened a secret dialogue with Al Qaeda.[88]

Pakistan's military benefited hugely from US aid during the Cold War – most notably in the 1980s, when funds were directed through the military's shadowy Inter-Services Intelligence directorate to help the Afghan *mujahadeen* wage war on the Soviet-installed government in Kabul. Today, the military's willingness to eradicate a Taliban or al Qaeda enemy is still very much open to doubt. The well-known Pakistani writer Ahmed Rashid commented in 2007: '... the Pakistani military, arguing that only it can combat Islamic fundamentalism, believes that the threats posed by Al Qaeda and the Taliban encourage continued international support for General Pervez Musharraf's regime and for military rule.'[89] Notoriously, Osama bin Laden was able to live in considerable comfort less than a mile from the military academy in the Pakistani city of Abbottabad, a city where the Intelligence Bureau, Military Intelligence and the ISI, as well as local police, had a presence. Significantly, the US government declined to inform the Pakistan government about the planned raid on bin Laden's residence, apparently fearing that the operation might be jeopardised. Lawrence Wright commented in *The New Yorker* in May 2011:

> What would happen if the Pakistani military actually captured or killed Al Qaida's top leaders? The great flow of dollars would stop, just as it had in Afghanistan after the Soviets limped away ... The Pakistani army and the I.S.I. were in the looking-for-bin-Laden business, and if they found him they'd be out of business.[90]

Washington has clung to the hope that the defence bonanza it is providing will somehow encourage Pakistan – and particularly its military and its intelligence agencies – to cooperate in the struggle against not just the Pakistan Taliban, but also the Afghan Taliban. But quite apart from the perverse incentives around capturing bin Laden, there is another fundamental problem here. Pakistan sees its long-term interests in Afghanistan as demanding a *strong* Pashtun/Taliban group in Afghanistan – principally as a way of countering India's influence in Afghanistan. The problem goes beyond *non-cooperation* by Pakistan: many credible Western analysts believe the Pakistani military and its intelligence agencies are actually the main forces *behind* the Afghan Taliban (as well as Lashkar-e-Taiba – LeT – militants in Kashmir).[91] A degree of antipathy to the US within the Pakistani military has also been encouraged by the 'stop–go' nature of US assistance over the years – not least a sense of being used for war in Afghanistan in the 1980s and then discarded.[92]

Significantly, while the Pakistani military has targeted members of the Pakistani Taliban in South Waziristan and elsewhere in Pakistan's Federally Administered Tribal Areas (FATA), the military has refused to take action in North Waziristan, headquarters of the Haqqani network that has been involved – as part of a broad Taliban coalition – in the cross-border insurgency in eastern Afghanistan. This inaction, in turn, has been used as an argument for more hardware: the Pakistani military claims it is stretched thin by existing deployments, and that it needs more equipment like helicopters.[93]

Even when it comes to the military campaigns that *have* been waged within Pakistan, there is a suspicion that war itself may be more interesting than winning: the Pakistani military displaced some 600,000 of its own citizens in 2009 offensives in the Swat Valley and South Waziristan without capturing or killing any significant number of senior Taliban leaders.[94] There is also reason to believe that the tactics adopted, having created such suffering, will not be successful in reducing the strength of extreme Islamist groups.[95] Apart from the mass displacement, attacks by unmanned drones in Pakistan have produced a lot of civilian casualties.[96] Many of the displaced have not even been registered for assistance because they do not come from areas recognised by the government as the location of counterinsurgency operations.[97]

Even when attempts have been made to bring Pakistan 'into line' on Afghanistan, they have ended up underlining the ability of local actors to subvert the global 'war on terror'. The most notable initiative was the US's 2009 Enhanced Partnership with Pakistan Act, which made continued military assistance conditional on Pakistan ceasing support for militant groups outside the country (including Afghanistan) and on effective civilian oversight of military budgets, strategy and promotions.[98] This move prompted a major backlash by the Pakistani military, which was then appeased by having the conditions watered down and by being offered an additional $2 billion in military aid.[99] The Pakistani tail seems to be wagging the American dog, but the military-industrial complexes of both countries benefit in any case.

Elsewhere in Asia, the 'war on terror' has been helping a range of other abusive regimes. Indonesia billed its military campaign in Aceh from 2003 as a signal that Jakarta was 'serious about terrorism',[100] and the campaign also involved the use of 'embedded journalists', mimicking the US-led invasion of Iraq.[101] In the Philippines, as Eva-Lotta Hedman observes:

> ... the events of 11 September 2001 and the onset of the so-called Global War on Terror encouraged an intensification of Manila's 'forward movement' in the southern Philippines, with the new president, Gloria Macapagal-Arroyo, keen to demonstrate her loyalty and usefulness to the Bush administration in Washington. With US military assistance and active involvement, the AFP [Philippines armed forces] extended their counterinsurgency and counterterrorism campaigns in Muslim areas of Mindanao and parts of the Sulu Archipelago.[102]

This represented more of Hannah Arendt's 'action as propaganda', since it helped to reinforce the problem to which it claimed to be responding. Hedman notes: 'The response of the armed groups mobilized in parts of Mindanao and the Sulu Archipelago – most notably the onset of a terrorist bombing campaign in cities across the country – was deemed an ample post-facto justification for the prosecution of the Global War on Terror in the southern Philippines.'[103]

Among the most disturbing cases of a 'war within a war' has been Sri Lanka. From the 1950s, the US directed significant aid at Sri Lanka – in part because of Cold War rivalries. After the Tamil Tigers were formed in 1976, rebels were sometimes labelled 'Communist terrorists'. While the easing of superpower tensions meant that it was no longer useful or plausible to dub the Tigers 'Communists', the 'war on terror' did sustain the profound utility of the 'terrorist' label. Moreover, this new international context helped to maintain the status of the Tamils as, in effect, 'illegitimate civilians': the Tamil population as a whole has been exposed to renewed and large-scale state violence that has received significant international support.

Both the US and the European Commission declared the LTTE a terrorist group,[104] and US law prohibits contact with a listed terrorist group, even for the purpose of distributing food, and individual aid officials can be prosecuted if food falls into the hands of 'terrorists'.[105]

During Colombo's military onslaught on the east and north, US government intelligence proved important in putting a military squeeze on the Tamil Tigers. In a detailed report for the *New Yorker*, John Lee Anderson noted: 'Sri Lankan diplomats and military officers acknowledged to me privately that U.S. satellite intelligence had been crucial when, in 2008, Sri Lanka's Navy sank seven Tiger ships loaded with military cargo.'[106] The Tigers lost tens of millions of dollars' worth of *materiél* – a major blow. At the time, the ships were cruising in international waters up to a thousand miles from Sri Lanka. In August 2010, at a self-congratulatory naval conference in Galle, south of Colombo, Gotabaya Rajapaksa, defence minister and the president's brother (and a man who keeps four sharks in a large aquarium at the bottom of his garden), thanked the US for helping to locate the Tigers' ships.[107]

Alongside the targeting of the Tigers themselves, there was a significant degree of international toleration of abuses against civilians. For one thing, the 'war on terror' seems to have created an ambivalence within the US government in relation to the abuses of the paramilitaries – often Tamil – enlisted by the Sri Lankan government against the LTTE rebels. A secret 18 May 2007 cable from the US embassy in Colombo, while noting that addressing paramilitaries' human rights abuses was a top priority for the embassy, observed that 'it is perhaps understandable that the GSL [Government of Sri Lanka] wants to use every possible means in its war against LTTE terror ...'[108] When Karuna's paramilitary faction (having broken away from the Tigers in 2004) joined the counterinsurgency in the east from 2006, international protests were muted.

In general, the framework of a 'war on terror' encouraged repeated concessions (in upholding international law and humanitarian principles) to the Sri Lankan government. This was most glaringly in evidence at the point, in September 2008, when Colombo effectively kicked aid agencies out of the north. Asked if there were protests from influential international governments at the expulsion, one experienced UN staff member who was working in Sri Lanka told me:

No, they [the government] have the support of the Americans, the Pakistanis and the Indians for their strategy. The Americans wanted to avoid civilian casualties – they pushed to allow the humanitarian corridors to go in, but only to the extent that it did not conflict with war objectives.

In the shadow of Guantanamo Bay, it was also difficult for US leaders to criticise the Sri Lankan government's policy of indefinitely detaining Tamil civilians in camps. While the British government did exert strong pressure in 2009 for disbanding these internment camps, the positioning of the war within an 'anti-terrorist' framework always implied the need to strike a 'balance' between liberty and security (with Tamil civilians as the likely victims of such a compromise).

The Sri Lankan case is a particularly complex one, and the Colombo government has been especially shrewd in playing to several audiences simultaneously. While the 'war on terror' framework plays well with many Western governments, at the same time the Sri Lankan government has explicitly aligned itself, so to speak, with the Non-Aligned Movement (and Russia and China), and has portrayed itself as defending national sovereignty and as standing up to the West and the declining colonial countries of Europe. An NGO worker commented: 'The government has played as much as it can on the global war on terror, but also at the same time they use the defence that this is a purely national problem, not an issue that has international implications.' In the war's final year, with the US and UK governments belatedly stepping up their public pressure for international humanitarian law to be observed, China supplied a billion dollars' worth of military aid, including fighter jets. Russia and Pakistan provided artillery shells and small arms, and Iran supplied fuel.[109] Colombo also had a fleet of Israeli Kfir combat aircraft.[110] A variety of soft loans, including from the IMF, also reduced the potential for individual Western governments to exert leverage – a potential that had already been eroded by their 'anti-terrorist' agenda. Meanwhile, major aid donors – as in Afghanistan – were anxious to spend their aid budgets if at all possible. Jonathan Goodhand, a Sri Lanka specialist and an academic at London's School of Oriental and African Studies, succinctly summed up the complex circumstances contributing to impunity in Sri Lanka:

There is a realisation among Sri Lankan elites that international concerns about terrorism, the state-centric bias of larger donors, disbursement pressures [donors' desire to spend their aid budgets], vested institutional interests and the growing importance of non-traditional donors in many ways load the dice in their favour, enabling them to create policy space for themselves.[111]

The weak (or non-existent) criticism by aid agencies of human rights abuses in Afghanistan and Iraq in the context of a 'war on terror' – for example, the massacres of prisoners of war in Afghanistan in November 2001 and the torture at Abu Ghraib – was used by the government in Sri Lanka (as well as by governments in Russia, Colombia, Algeria and Pakistan) as evidence of 'double standards' on the part of aid agencies that tried to criticise *them*.[112]

In the wake of the 2009 Sri Lankan emergency, patterns of judicial accountability also seem to owe something to Western strategic priorities. Amnesty International's Steve Crawshaw commented:

> Quite recently the Security Council unanimously voted for the case of Libya to be referred to the International Criminal Court in the Hague. The contrast between that and the complete and utter silence and inaction on scores of thousands dead in Sri Lanka is absolutely striking. I think it is inexplicable and morally quite indefensible.[113]

We can see, then, that civil wars and wider 'global wars' have intersected in a number of important ways, and that this has routinely created significant windows of impunity for abusive actors who are able to manipulate these overlapping war systems. More specifically, high-profile global conflicts like the Cold War and the 'war on terror' have created a large degree of impunity for allies who are deemed useful in these wider wars. This has helped those allies to abuse and exploit their own populations, while international criticism or sanction remains damagingly limited. Worse, such regimes have frequently received encouragement and tangible assistance. It is 'illegitimate civilians' who have paid the price.

CHAPTER 7

The Politics of Permanent Emergency[1]

Vavuniya, northern Sri Lanka, April 2009: At a camp for Tamils who had just endured horrific violence further north, government soldiers were very reluctant to let us talk to the new arrivals. If any of our group of visitors showed any sign of departing from the official 'tour', a soldier would immediately peel off to accompany him or her, effectively deterring any contact with the displaced people. In these constrained circumstances, one option was to talk to the soldiers themselves. While that, too, was discouraged, I did have a short but interesting conversation with a young government soldier.

'Now that the army is defeating the Tamil Tiger rebels,' I suggested, 'it will be possible to reduce the size of the army, so that young men like yourself can go home.' 'Oh, no,' the soldier replied quickly, 'there is still a lot of work to do – many pockets of resistance, and we have to prevent terrorism!' He said the army would not be shrinking any time soon.

It turned out he was right. Shortly after military victory over the Tigers (or LTTE)[2] was announced in May 2009, the government declared that it would be *increasing* the size of the army by 50,000.[3] Such an increase was said to be necessary because of the role the military would be playing in the huge 'developmental' challenges in the wake of the war.[4]

The prospect of 'development' seemed a long way away in April 2009. With thousands of Tamils arriving every day in Vavuniya, the Sri Lankan government announced that it had carried out what it called the 'greatest humanitarian rescue operation in history'.[5] The official story was that these civilians had been rescued from the Tamil Tiger rebels, who had been holding them hostage, and that now the grateful civilians were arriving in the safety and freedom of government-held areas.

It was true that the Tamil Tigers had been using civilians as a 'human shield' in the north. In the face of a massive government onslaught, they had forced many civilians to retreat with them to a narrow strip of seaside land in the north-east. It was true also that government strikes against the area occupied by the Tigers had sent waves of civilians to Vavuniya. But there were also several problems, to put it rather mildly, with the government 'line'.

First, if Tamils were arriving into safety and freedom, why the large quantity of barbed wire around the camps? Some 300,000 Sri Lankans were actually being forcibly detained in the camps in and around Vavuniya. Secondly, the nature of the civilians' injuries indicated that most were the result of shelling; this did not tally with attempts to pin all the blame on the Tigers, who relied mostly on gunfire. Thirdly, the stories of displaced people could not be entirely suppressed. Some told of being forced east not simply by rebels, but by government shelling. Some remembered how hospitals had been shelled by Colombo's forces. Some told of the inadequacy of humanitarian relief over a long period and the severe restriction in food supplies sent by sea to the civilians who had been crowded into the seaside death-camp that was Mullaitivu. Some told how medical care was even now being withheld, and how evacuees from Mullaitivu were dying on government buses. Some told of the detention and disappearance of males, as the government sought to 'root out' the terrorists from among the civilians. Most horrifically of all, civilians and aid workers began to tell of the mass slaughter of civilians by government forces in Mullaitivu – in what the government had declared to be a 'no fire zone'.

It turned out that this 'no fire zone' was a cynical attempt to assemble the Tamils in one place, while 'reassuring' the international community that the government intended to protect civilians. The 'no fire zone' was also used by the Sri Lanka ministry of defence to justify the killing of civilians who did not assemble there (on the grounds that they had thereby shown their allegiance to the Tiger rebels).[6]

From the government's point of view, securing compliance – especially international compliance – for the terrible events in the north was a complex task. However, the Sri Lankan government proved remarkably adept at this cynical undertaking. In particular, it created an elaborate network of bureaucratic obstacles that served to intimidate aid workers and restrict the flow of news. Journalists were systematically denied access to conflict areas, and aid agencies – as we have seen – were kicked out of the north in September 2008, when the government told them their safety 'could not be guaranteed'. One NGO worker who had recently arrived in the country recalled the September evacuation:

> I was surprised and shocked it was so easy. It took only a few days …
> I don't understand why it was so easy to tell everyone to leave. Some expats were really upset with headquarters in Colombo, saying they should have reacted in a stronger way.

MSF's Fabrice Weissman remembered international diplomats' reactions to the expulsion: 'Asked to pressure the authorities, the Indian and western embassies said they were powerless.'[7] Reflecting on the ejection of the aid agencies, one experienced UN worker gave an interpretation of the government's motives that was widely shared by aid workers:

> When the military were pushing the LTTE to coastal areas, there were no more WFP [World Food Programme] convoys … They allowed vessels by sea. The government doesn't want people to see the devastation of the land.

In Killinochi, local Tamils tried to stop the aid agencies from going, arguing that this was leaving them exposed to massive violence.[8] Several sources expressed the belief that the Sri Lankan government had learned lessons about information control from other contemporary and recent crises (including Afghanistan, Sudan and Israel/Gaza). Significantly, a large number of Israeli military advisers were in the country to advise the government. The Sri Lankan government had also learned lessons from its earlier military campaign in the east, in 2006–07, where aid agencies had been similarly intimidated; donor governments had also been muted in their response, and many had simply withdrawn.[9] Of particular importance in intimidating aid staff was the killing in August 2006 of seventeen employees of the famine-assistance organisation Action Contre La Faim in their office in Muttur on the east coast, a few hours after pro-government forces recaptured the town.[10] MSF protested about the killings and pushed for improved medical responses to those caught up in conflict in the east, but the aid agency quickly received an expulsion order.[11] While aid agencies have often been prepared to sacrifice speaking out in the interests of access, most were not even getting access – or at least not to the zones of most intense conflict. As MSF's president, Marie-Pierre Allie recalls: 'In 2009, still under threat of expulsion from Sri Lanka, MSF signed a Memorandum of Understanding enjoining it to remain silent – but still did not gain access to the combat zones.'[12]

Other governments were also reported to be learning lessons from Colombo's tactics in what some were calling 'a model counterinsurgency'.[13] One UN worker noted: 'This is the training ground for any state that wants to behave like this. Fifteen years ago the UN was stronger and principles weren't up for negotiation to that extent.' Another UN worker said: 'There's a different level of negotiation that actually becomes begging. There's a need for stronger advocacy at all levels.'

Even aid agencies operating in Vavuniya, on the fringe of the conflict zone, had to sign 'gagging clauses', ensuring that they would not engage in advocacy or highlight human rights abuses – a growing trend in many countries.[14] Many could not even discuss publicly the adequacy – or inadequacy – of services they were providing.[15] Government fears around aid workers talking with the displaced people were reflected in severe restrictions on aid agencies' attempts to engage in counselling or 'trauma' work – an official phobia that had similarly restricted counselling work in Sudan's Darfur.

For a government that had just brought off 'the greatest humanitarian rescue operation in history', there seemed to be a great deal to hide. Human Rights Watch had managed to do a report by going undercover. As a researcher, I myself only got permission to go to Vavuniya because I was working for the World Food Programme, one of the agencies that was seen in a relatively favourable light by the government in Colombo. A key factor here was that this UN agency had, in effect, removed from the government the burden of providing food to the hundreds of thousands of people in Vavuniya, thereby playing an uncomfortable role in Colombo's strategy of mass displacement. In meetings in the capital, several government officials made clear that they approved strongly of WFP, a welcome that made me feel a little queasy.

Another official restriction was that aid workers and other visitors were not allowed to drive through to Vavuniya. We had to engage in what became known as 'the kiss', a time-consuming and sometimes humiliating manoeuvre, in which travellers would be compelled to leave their vehicle at a checkpoint to the south of Vavuniya, undergo a search, and then move to a *different* vehicle before proceeding north. In preparation for leaving Vavuniya via this notorious checkpoint, I made two sets of notes and went to great lengths to conceal them in separate bags – partly to avoid detection and partly, I suspect, to make myself feel more important.

Even the aid that did get through to the north was often subject to extreme manipulation. One aid worker who travelled on a relief convoy in January 2009 recalled that both sides in the war had used convoys as cover: 'They [the government army] did it to us, and the LTTE [rebels] used the convoy to move around.'[16] The rapidity of the influx and the inadequacy of preparations gave the impression that this was a sudden and unexpected population movement, and in April 2009 aid agencies were frantically engaged in an 'emergency' response. Yet the influx had actually been part of government planning. Slow aid agency preparations reflected a reluctance to collude with ethnic cleansing, as well as a variety of practical obstacles created by the Sri Lankan government. But the government's intentions were reasonably clear. As one Human Rights Watch report noted:

> In September 2008, the Sri Lankan authorities informed the UN and humanitarian organisations that they were in the process of drawing up contingency plans to keep up to 200,000 displaced people from the Vanni [the north][17] in new camps in Vavuniya district, in case a mass outflux from the Vanni materialised.[18]

Since Sri Lanka's war – and war economy – has served a variety of functions, it was not going to be easily demobilised. In particular, the planned role for an *expanded* military in 'post-conflict reconstruction' should be seen in the light of the military's recent role in absorbing discontented elements within the south. Sri Lanka, as we have seen, has become a highly militarised society, and many people, particularly in poor, rural areas, have come to depend on income from military organisations (which include not just the formal military, but also the paramilitaries and the home guards).

That plan to use the military for 'development' did not spring out of nowhere, incidentally. In many ways, it sat rather comfortably within regional norms, since militaries in South East Asia have often professed a developmental role.[19] The Thai military, for example, promoted rural development as part of its anti-Communist insurgency in the 1950s and 1960s.[20] The militarisation of development in Sri Lanka also sat fairly comfortably with aspects of the global 'war on terror' – in particular, the assumption that 'development' (whether in Afghanistan or Palestine) can somehow replace the resolution of deep political differences (and, in the case of Palestine, that it can somehow conjure a solution in the absence of greatly increased pressure on Israel).[21] After eastern Sri Lanka had experienced severe conflict in 2006–07, 'development' had similarly been put forward as a means of conflict resolution (with troop numbers also kept high). It turned out to be a peculiar kind of 'top-down' development that discouraged popular participation for fear that it could be a platform for political organisation and dissent.[22] In September 2009, after all the devastation of the previous months, President Rajapaksa announced: 'They [the Tamils] want to start their paddy fields, go back to their farms … without development, there won't be peace.'[23]

Whether any genuine and lasting 'development' will prove possible in the highly militarised environment of northern – or eastern – Sri Lanka is extremely doubtful, particularly with the army continuing to drain the treasury. Few have publicly recognised that there were many aspects of *previous* development that helped to *engender* the conflict – notably the colonisation schemes that drew on international aid to move Sinhalese into traditionally Tamil and Muslim areas.[24] Meanwhile, although the context has been labelled 'post-war', the activities of aid agencies have still been tightly controlled. Northern and eastern Sri Lanka saw a proliferation of 'high security zones', with soldiers exerting near-total control over civilians; the government later announced there was a 'single peace zone', which seems to mean that military camps and installations are everywhere.[25] Major General Mahinda Hathurusinghe, the security commander of Jaffna, noted: 'The LTTE inculcation of the youth – this is a big problem for us.' He added that the army needed to maintain a presence in the north to make sure that Tamil radicalism did not start again, with infiltration and electronic surveillance being key means to this end.[26]

Meanwhile, the Sri Lankan military – almost entirely Sinhalese – has developed its own material interests in the north. One aid worker commented in 2009: 'The military are going to war. They have lost a lot

of men. They will want their share, their fiefdoms afterwards.' Many
Tamils believe that this military presence is a permanent one, and that
the north of the country will be flooded with Sinhalese soldiers and
their families, rather on the model of China in Tibet.[27] Referring to the
process of 'development' in the north and east, a July 2011 International
Crisis Group report said: '… many Tamil residents feel it is more like the
extraction of the spoils of war than a real effort to improve livelihoods
and build trust'.[28]

The catastrophe in the north was preceded by a government offensive
in the east from 2006, and the experience of 'reconstruction' here has
not been encouraging. 'Disappearances' have been common here – even
after the outright conflict abated. Meanwhile, government initiatives
that were advertised as devolving power actually resulted in the election
of a number of 'stooges' who were heavily dependent on Colombo.[29]
As one international development official told the International
Crisis Group in 2008: 'The clear sense you get from government is
that the east was won through war, not a negotiated settlement, and that
the winner of the war has the authority to determine policies and assert
its identity'.[30] Whether in the east or the north, there are grave doubts
about what kinds of 'democracy' and 'devolution' are going to be
possible.

For its part, the government in Colombo has made significant
electoral gains from its 'glorious victory' over the Tamil Tigers, and
many of the government's emergency powers have actually been
strengthened in the wake of victory. In July 2011, the International Crisis
Group noted: 'Constitutional reforms strong-armed through parliament have removed presidential term limits and solidified the president's power over the attorney general, judiciary and various
"independent" commissions'.[31] Anti-terrorism legislation continues to
allow detention on a wide range of pretexts, and opposition to the
government continues to be portrayed as unpatriotic. After the war,
suppression of freedom of speech continued to flourish under what one
local analyst in 2008 had called 'A State of Permanent Crisis', a situation
where 'both conflict as well as the assumption of extraordinary
powers and measures by the State have become normalised as a part of
everyday life'.[32]

Meanwhile, a solution for the north remains far away. When the
government crushed the Tigers, a local aid worker told me:

The war won't be over. If they give a political solution, it can be. But they didn't give before. Do you think they will give it now? The [Tamil] bargaining position is zero. Another group will come and the LTTE will also be strong. The way the government is treating the Tamils will make another liberation movement.

In September 2009, another local aid worker voiced his scepticism at the idea of a 'military solution':

We have not solved the problem. We have militarily defeated the armed group. But all the factors that led to this conflict are still there … Even the opportunities for reconciliation, the government is not using them. We are heading for a big disaster. There won't be rebellion soon because the Tamils will be very passive and Tamil politicians will be compliant. But the government is still not sending any message to the Tamil community that they are equal citizens, especially confining them in camps. There has not been a significant move on the hearts and minds.

Several others interviewed in Sri Lanka expressed the view that some kind of guerrilla action was likely to continue. It was felt that many LTTE soldiers and sympathisers will have sought to avoid almost certain death or capture within the narrow, so-called 'no fire zone' on the north-east coast, and have probably slipped away southwards. While Sri Lanka lacks the kind of natural resources that fund many rebel movements, the Tigers received major support from an extensive Tamil diaspora – and this source of strength for potential rebels has not gone away. One senior diplomat told me:

The LTTE has lost a conventional war and probably will never come back and have territorial control. But that does not mean they are out of the equation – for example as an exile movement with the diaspora controlling – and the ability to exercise terrorist attacks is unknown.[33]

Beyond the immediate question of the displaced, the manner in which governance issues are addressed will be particularly important. One NGO worker observed:

> The LTTE is resurgent in Batticaloa and Ampara [in the east], different
> cells hiding and coming up. It's far, far from over ... In the east ... people
> feel less secure than when the LTTE was there. There are lots of abduc-
> tions, extortions, white vans ... We need pressure from the interna-
> tional community – what sort of governance is going to be put in place?

Significantly, there are local precedents for the revival of defeated rebels.
After all, the Sinhalese nationalist JVP, having suffered a crushing military defeat during the 1987–89 rebellion, managed to bounce back and
became a potent political force.[34]

An increase in prostitution and in violence against women has been
reported in a context where large numbers of male Sinhalese soldiers
live among decimated Tamil communities that have a large proportion
of female-headed households. Some women have been stereotyped as
the widows of 'terrorists'.[35] Significantly, the LTTE, for all its faults, was
known for imposing a strict moral and sexual discipline,[36] and some
Tamils have suggested that LTTE rule was actually preferable because of
this element of discipline.[37]

Pessimism as to the long-term prospects for peace was expressed with
particular poignancy by Lasantha Wickramatunga, editor of the *Sunday
Leader*. In January 2009, Wickramatunga was shot and killed by motor-
bike assassins on his way to work in Colombo. In a posthumous editorial, he predicted his own death, noting, 'When finally I am killed, it will
be the government that kills me ... It has long been written that my life
would be taken, and by whom. All that remains to be written is when.'[38]
He also observed:

> ... a military occupation of the country's north and east will require
> the Tamil people of those regions to live eternally as second-class citi-
> zens, deprived of self-respect. Do not imagine you can placate them by
> showering 'development' and 'reconstruction' on them in the post-war
> era. The wounds of war will scar them forever, and you will have an
> even more bitter and hateful Diaspora to contend with.[39]

Some idea of how deeply these wounds may run is conveyed in the
account of a young pastor who managed to get a group of orphans
out of the 'kill zone' on the beach at Mullaitivu in May 2009. He told
journalist Jon Lee Anderson:

At the end, we were walking out through fire and past dead people, and the soldiers were laughing at us and saying, 'We have killed all your leaders. Now you are our slaves.' You can imagine how I feel about my country.[40]

***

Driving from Guatemala City to Huehuetenango in the east takes you through volcano country. The trick is to squeeze between the side of the cliff and the onrushing buses. Since the latter go at breakneck speed, it is not especially reassuring to hear that many of the drivers lighten the burden of long journeys with a heavy ingestion of alcohol.

Arriving – to my relief – in Huehuetenango, I was pointed towards a member of the civil intelligence service working in the town. I was interested in the persistence of violence in 'peacetime' Guatemala, and I had heard that he would be a good person to talk to. He told me:

Organised delinquency is well structured. They have information and are protected or have some kind of relationship with some people in the government. Robbery of banks, kidnapping (sometimes millions of dollars for just one individual), narco-trafficking, car-stealing, smuggling. There's also quick kidnapping to force someone to pull out money from a bank – this tends to be more common delinquency … There's a culture of war that hasn't really dissolved. In delinquency gangs, participants have been soldiers, or guerrillas, or ex-PACs [members of the civil patrols who had collaborated in counterinsurgency], so they all have a culture of war and they have all been trained for what they're doing. When they commit an assault, it's what they know how to do!

Several others stressed that this kind of 'training' helped to explain the persistence of violence. But during my visit in 2002 – six years after the peace agreement – it became increasingly clear to me that violence in 'peacetime' Guatemala was not just the work of those who had somehow grown used to it: it was a much more systematic violence that protected a particular – and extremely unequal – social order. After a war that lasted from 1960 to 1996 (with left-wing rebels pitched against government forces that had the support of the United States), the 1996 peace agreement contained provisions for far-reaching social and economic reform. But hopes that it would lead to a radical transformation of the

country – to radical land- and tax-reform, for example – were largely
disappointed, as were hopes that those guilty of major human rights
abuses would be held to account.

***

Many of the civil patrol leaders, with blood on their hands, were determined to hold onto the authority that war had bestowed on them.
Women were a particular target for their violence, especially if these
women tried to highlight past abuses.[41] Patrol leaders were also drawn
into protecting the privileges of others: many were recruited as armed
guards to protect landed estates from incursions by poor farmers.
Despite the long years of revolutionary war, these poor people continued
to be excluded from much of the best land, and many had to work as
labourers on large plantations (mainly coffee, sugar, bananas and cotton).
Private security was booming more generally, boosted not just by the
supply of ex-soldiers and ex-civil patrollers, but also by rising crime.

Post-war violence also reflected the fact that Guatemala's thirty-six-
year war had never been entirely about 'winning' or defeating the rebels.

Conditions amounting to a 'permanent emergency' in Guatemala are
easier to understand if viewed in the light of the widespread violence
against trade unionists, radicals and human rights activities that took
place alongside – and under the cover of – the long war against the guerrillas. In 'peacetime', this campaign of political intimidation was
renewed, much of it masquerading as a 'war on crime'. An underlying
function of the violence was now to maintain a highly exploitative
system, to block the radical potential of the 1996 peace agreement, and
to keep the indigenous Indian population – the Mayans – subservient.
Many senior and retired officers adopted the attitude that the war went
on, peace or no peace.[42] Since the wartime rebels, like the various post-
war 'enemies', had frequently been referred to as 'criminals' and 'subversives', there was actually considerable continuity in official statements.[43]

In Guatemala City, I had the chance to talk to the head of the
Guatemalan civil intelligence, Edgar Gutiérrez. He stressed that crime
was not simply a way for low-level ex-fighters to keep occupied: involvement in crime – and in the so-called 'war on crime' – had also been a
feature of shadowy structures linked to the highest levels of the military.
Clandestine intelligence organisations were being used to fight organised crime, and 'this same apparatus and method have been used to

intimidate the human rights organisations'. The 'war on crime', the 'war on drugs' and the 'war on political subversives' were also providing cover for widespread criminality and corruption among elements linked to the old counterinsurgency. The army's attempts to secure finance from various kinds of relationships with organised crime (including drugs) had been a marked feature of the long civil war. After the peace agreement was signed in 1996, elements of the military had continued to pursue links with organised crime. Criminal groups often benefited from relationships with former military officers, as well as from current state officials, while these officers and officials extracted a 'cut'.[44]

Another function of 'permanent emergency' was that these various post-war 'wars' were providing a rationale for maintaining high military spending.[45]

The damaging collusion between elements of the old counterinsurgency and criminal elements had an emotional aspect that has often been overlooked. During the civil war, business interests had found the military to be a useful weapon against Communism and political radicalism. But when a shift in the US government's position meant that war was jeopardising access to US markets,[46] business interests began to break with the military and increasingly tried to put all the responsibility for the abusive counterinsurgency onto the military. A variety of sources reported that the military's sense of having been 'used' in this way was feeding into soldiers' involvement in crime and corruption – not least among army generals who had retired (or been forcibly retired) in the period before and after the 1996 peace agreement. These generals were sometimes darkly referred to as *La Cofradia* (The Brotherhood).[47] Adding to the sense of disillusionment within the military was the attempt, within Guatemala and internationally, to redefine as misguided and abusive the 'righteous' struggle against Communism. One senior analyst close to the Guatemalan military told me:

Those depending on the army came to see it as an obstacle – their repressive tactics were stopping markets in the US and vacations in Miami and whatever. Now there's a huge protest in the officers' corps against the moneyed classes because they feel betrayed. They were doing their dirty work and then their backers decided they were no longer useful ... The army became very resentful that the elites were creating an image that the army was fighting the guerrillas while the

rest (including the private sector) were the victims ... It is significant
enough, the sense of betrayal.

Whereas the interests of business had once been linked rather directly
to the continued repression and exploitation of labour on large plantations, a diversification of the Guatemalan economy created significant
interests in 'peace' (or at least in the absence of outright war). This
reflected not only the costs of international censure, but also the
economic costs and tax costs of the war itself. But, as so often, once a
war machine is mobilised, it is not easily demobilised or discarded.

In fact, some of the dwindling US support for security structures had
been 'clawed back' – first, in the context of a post-Cold War 'war on
drugs' and next in the post-9/11 re-emphasis on 'security'.[48] In effect,
these structures had found a new global 'war' that could legitimise them
and bring them resources.

While Guatemala's 'permanent emergency' has certainly been one of
the worst in Latin America, it also finds strong echoes elsewhere on the
continent. The good news is that outright warfare has greatly diminished in Latin America since the end of the Cold War, while levels of
growth and development have often been healthy. However, high levels
of violence – whether crime, state violence, or some combination of the
two – continue to plague many countries on the continent.[49]

Facing budget cuts in the 1990s, the armed forces of Argentina, Brazil,
Chile and Bolivia presented themselves as an important arm of the 'war
on drugs', operating on the reasonable expectation that this would bring
them more foreign aid. One 1998 study, focusing on Latin America,
noted that officers 'are crafting institutional and individual strategies to
meet an expanded definition of "threats to national security", even as
they take advantage of new opportunities to pursue profits'.[50] Patterns of
violence in a number of countries indicate, in a parallel with civil wars
in many countries around the world, that the interests of Latin American
security organisations do not always involve the elimination of the
problem they say they want to eliminate. In the course of Peru's civil
war, which began in 1980 and wound down after 2000, government
soldiers became complicit in the drugs trade.[51] In Mexico, there have
been longstanding symbiotic relationships between senior military
officers and the drug cartels;[52] such is the corruption in the Mexican
police that the entire police force of Veracruz, a major drugs conduit on

the east coast, was dissolved simultaneously in December 2011.[53] Not only has the bribery and corruption of state officials been routine, but military staff and logistics have also been used for drugs production and transportation.[54] In Bolivia, police, security and military forces have sometimes competed to enhance their respective domains by undermining each other's efficiency.[55]

Beyond the 'war on drugs', some officials have spoken of a 'war on poverty', while others have seen 'security' as dependent on 'development'. This mirrors the touting of aid as an arm of the global 'war on terror'. Many Latin American militaries have themselves been involved in development projects (for example, the participation of the Mexican army in literacy campaigns). In the aftermath of Guatemala's civil war, the abusive civil patrols were renamed 'Peace and Development Committees'.[56] But while some of these activities are constructive, they have been accompanied by a more disturbing sub-current. In 1998, two respected analysts noted that there had arisen

> ... a troubling public discourse that recasts socioeconomic and collective action problems – poverty, migration waves, displaced workers, and ecological degradation – as 'threats to national security' ... Potential enemies of the nation now range from guerrillas and paramilitary organizations to drug traffickers and foreign economic competitors in a globalized market.[57]

One Latin American country where war continued through the 1990s and even beyond was Colombia. As in Guatemala, the persistence of violence into 'peace' or 'quasi-peace' from 2002 needs to be understood in the light of wartime aims that often diverged sharply from 'winning'.

Colombia's armed conflict has spanned the decades from the mid-1960s to the present day and has seen left-wing guerrillas (principally the FARC) opposing government forces (which have had various degrees of support from a range of paramilitaries). During Colombia's long years of war, the paramilitaries became known for targeting not just guerrillas, but also 'guerrilla collaborators', including trade unionists, human rights workers, organisers of displaced people, and so on.[58] Even where zones had been 'cleared' of guerrillas, selective killing often continued.[59] The paramilitaries enjoyed a great deal of impunity – not least because of a national and international focus on the 'greedy' rebels as the principal (sometimes the only) villain. The civil war was deepened when rebel violence was supplemented by large-scale anti-civilian violence on the part of paramilitaries that were often linked to the military. Particularly with the demise of the Medellin and Cali drugs cartels in 1993–95, the paramilitaries moved strongly into the drugs business; both the paramilitaries and the rebels used violence to protect drugs interests. Many paramilitary leaders were able to use drug money to move into export-oriented agriculture, and in a context of growing international pressure to rein in paramilitary abuses, paramilitary leaders put increasing effort into entering the political mainstream.[60] When the government did turn its attention to demobilising (and even prosecuting) some of the paramilitary actors from 2002, this was a positive development, and the Colombian government went so far as to state on several occasions that the paramilitaries no longer existed.

That would be great news if it were true. Large numbers of paramilitary personnel did indeed go through a demobilisation process. But a 2007 study, focusing on the Middle Magdalena region, noted: 'At the municipal level there is no evidence that the influence of the AUC [the paramilitaries' federation, or United Self-Defence Forces of Colombia] has diminished after the demobilisation of some of its armed structures.[61] A detailed investigation by Human Rights Watch in 2010 showed that a number of 'successor groups' had taken up the reins of criminal operations (notably drug trafficking) that had previously been run by the paramilitaries. This contributed to a renewed increase in internal displacement from 2004 – even though the peace process was supposedly well advanced by this point. Human Rights Watch found it was common for government officials to refuse to register those who said they had been displaced by paramilitaries – on the grounds that the paramilitaries no longer existed![62] The 'successor groups' have themselves followed the bad example of the earlier paramilitaries by attacking human rights workers and trade unionists, as well as displaced people who are often desperate to recover their land. One reason for these continuities is that the successor groups have recruited strongly from demobilised paramilitaries. Another is the continuing demand for drugs (notably from the US). A third is the toleration extended – just as it was earlier to the paramilitaries – by many members of the police and army.[63]

At a deeper level, the paramilitaries and their successors have served a function in propping up a highly unequal class structure. Inequitable land distribution was a key cause of the war in Colombia, and also a key cause of the creation of paramilitaries in the 1980s (partly because landed elites feared a negotiated peace settlement might bring land reform). Yet unequal land distribution remains largely unaddressed; in fact, it has often been exacerbated by the investment – or laundering – of drug profits into export production. As ill-gotten gains were made more 'respectable' in this way (and as human rights pressures rose), there seem to have been increased incentives for limiting outright war and for pursuing political careers, while at the same time retaining the ability to suppress any attempt at land reform or collective bargaining in the labour force through continued individual intimidation and assassinations.[64]

A notable 'permanent emergency' in Asia is the one in Pakistan. Here, the military has been adept, over a very long period, at manipulating a sense of 'emergency' to defend its institutional interests. Though by no means the only source of strongly nationalist sentiments, Pakistan's military is also commonly seen as the biggest obstacle to normalising relations with India (notably over Kashmir), as it is the main beneficiary of continued conflict, which not only justifies its enormous budget, but also provides a pretext for intervening in politics in the name of 'national security'.[65]

In Pakistan, military coups have periodically deposed civilian governments that are seen as not 'performing', and part of the driving force seems to have been to protect the defence budget. If we consider the period 1951–98, Pakistan's defence spending was significantly lower in years immediately preceding military coups than in other years, suggesting that coups served a function in bringing this spending back up to 'acceptable' levels.[66] Even civilian governments often feel a need to 'appease' the military. As one analyst noted, 'Because the [Pakistani] army can destabilize elected governments, most prime ministers or civilian presidents are wary of antagonizing the military by challenging its preferred policies at home or abroad.'[67] Moreover, when mass protests arise (or simply loom on the horizon), Pakistani military officials have sometimes subjected incumbent governments to the threat that soldiers will not confront the protestors.[68]

All this creates a temptation to follow the advice of American political scientist Samuel Huntington, who once suggested that civilian governments could control rogue militaries by letting them 'have their toys' –

in other words, by consenting to large budgets for military hardware. A key problem with this tactic is that, in effect, it rewards extortion. By bolstering the power of the military, it also strengthens the military's hand in any future budgetary 'negotiations'.[69]

Collusion with military power among Pakistani politicians is, in any case, widespread. As another analyst put it, 'Once out of power, political leaders have never hesitated to cut a power-sharing deal with the military, even if that has meant legitimating its institutionalized political role'.[70] Moreover, while military coups in Pakistan are often billed as a response to 'corruption', they also feed it. Very few elected governments in Pakistan have served their full term, and few expect to do so.[71] This sets up some perverse incentives. As Christine Fair put it, 'This expectation conditions party elites to maximize rents during their tenure because thereafter they are likely to spend several years in opposition or, in the event of a military coup, in jail'.[72]

The military's economic interests, having expanded greatly in the 1970s under a policy of industrialisation behind significant tariff barriers, prospered further under privatisation, when military-owned companies bought up public corporations. Some of the businesses of Pakistan's military foundations now dominate their sectors and are able to marginalise competitors.[73]

But if all this is good news for the military, it is not good news for Pakistan. The country's economy remains extremely weak, with low levels of public service, very low taxes, skyrocketing inflation, high unemployment and crippling energy shortages.[74] Yet every year Pakistan spends seven times as much on the military as it does on education. It is a 'luxury' the country cannot afford.

Turkey's military, too, has flourished in conditions of endemic insecurity. And, as in Pakistan, the military has exercised considerable autonomy from civilian governments. With Kurdish separatism seen as a threat, a state of emergency was declared in eleven of Turkey's provinces in 1987.[75] The Turkish army and paramilitary units became involved in the evacuation of some 3,000 villages in south-eastern Turkey, with around 3 million people displaced by the end of 1995.[76] Meanwhile, some soldiers in the Turkish army accused their officers of making money from the conflict.[77] Soldiers and militias became involved in the drugs trade, with large amounts of heroin passing through southeast Turkey on the way from Asia to Europe.[78] There were also large profits from arms procurements.[79] The conflict in south-eastern Turkey helped to boost the military budget; despite a huge rise in public debt through the 1980s and 1990s, and despite major cuts in social spending, military spending actually increased.[80] Turkey's military spending (in US dollars) rose more than fourfold between 1988 and 1999.[81] There was very little civilian oversight of how the defence budget was spent.

Turkey was seen as a key NATO ally by the US government in particular, and international protests over the Kurds were muted. Turkey has for many years been seen in the US as a key base for possible military action in Iraq, Iran and even Syria.[82]

I happened to pass through south-eastern Turkey in 1993 (a memorable trip since our jeep crashed at night-time into a cow). But I was not in Turkey to investigate the local Kurds (or their livestock). I was on my way to northern Iraq, where Save the Children Fund, my employer, was assisting the *Iraqi* Kurds, for whom the UN had established a 'safe haven' (and 'no fly zone') inside Iraq to protect them from Saddam Hussein (and to keep them out of Turkey).[83] The Iraqi Kurds were sometimes referred to by sceptical observers as 'the good Kurds' in contrast to 'the bad Kurds' in allied Turkey. What is not in doubt is that the Kurds in Turkey were suffering severely, or that the US government was actively assisting Ankara with large-scale military aid.[84]

Even in the brief interval between the Cold War and the post-9/11 'war on terror', it was possible to carve out damaging impunity through anti-terrorist and anti-Communist rhetoric. Within Turkey, a negotiated solution was generally seen as taboo and as 'sitting at the table with terrorists'. In fact, those suggesting such a solution were generally imprisoned. Emergency powers were used to ban strikes and control the media.[85] As in Sri Lanka, nationalist parties successfully presented any negotiation or non-military solution as an unacceptable compromise with terrorism – again quite an effective vote-winning strategy (particularly in western and central Turkey). Nationalist parties have turned the funerals of those killed by the PKK rebels into mass protests against any hint of a softer line.[86]

As the PKK violence diminished at the turn of the century, one would have thought that it would be a good opportunity to cut military spending drastically and to spend the money on developing the country. But Turkish military spending (as more recently in Sri Lanka) remained extremely high.[87] The Turkish military also protected its interests via a

range of business enterprises – enterprises that (as in Pakistan) helped
to give the military significant independence from civilian control.[88] In
particular, the military used its pension fund to invest in everything
from supermarkets to real estate, insurance, tourism and car manufac-
ture.[89] The pension fund's profits actually jumped significantly in the
1990s (and significantly more than the stock market average), suggesting
that the military has been a beneficiary of economic liberalisation. This
may also help to explain the strong commitment on the part of successive governments – even after the return to multi-party democracy in
1987 – to an economic reform programme that has greatly increased
public debt, public hardship and income inequality. Also strengthening
the military–business nexus is the fact that many senior officers have
taken up executive positions in large business corporations when they
retire. Meanwhile, growing inequality linked to economic liberalisation
may paradoxically legitimise the military further. While many remain
concerned about the military's political influence, one analyst noted
in 2005:

> The worsening economic performance has radicalized the divide
> between urban and rural, secular and Islamist, and Turkish and Kurdish
> identity groups, and these politicized fault-lines have, in turn, been used
> to justify the expanding role of the military ... As a result, while popular
> confidence in the parliament, political parties and business groups has
> diminished, confidence in the military has increased ...[90]

A particularly interesting case of long-lasting emergency is Egypt, a
country subject to what one observer has aptly described as 'permanent
governance by emergency rule and other exceptional measures'.[91] In a
2007 article, Sadiq Reza noted that Egypt had been in a declared state of
emergency since 1981, and indeed for all but three of the previous fifty
years.[92] Military courts and state security courts have been used extensively – and this practice has been defended as necessary to confront
terrorism and other threats to national security. Meanwhile, a very wide
definition of terrorism has included those 'impairing the national unity
or social peace'.[93] Particularly under Hosni Mubarak, president of Egypt
for almost thirty years until 2011, the state used emergency powers and
military courts to suppress non-violent, as well as violent, political
opposition. This included the intimidation of journalists and other

regime critics. Each extension of emergency legislation was accompanied by promises to repeal it. Yet constitutional amendments, as in 2007, have often entrenched emergency rule.[94] A state of emergency persisted even after the ousting of Mubarak in February 2011.

Significantly, Egypt's highly repressive and undemocratic system has been sustained, in large part, by American aid. In 2009, Chris Hedges reported that Egypt was getting some $3 billion of US aid per year and was required to buy American weapons with $1.3 billion of that.[95] As in many countries, the military's taste for sophisticated weaponry has been nurtured by this process. Meanwhile, Egypt's hugely expensive arms deals have required military middlemen. This has been a major source of private profit, and it represents another incentive for maintaining high levels of military spending.[96]

It is worth noting that military dominance in Egypt has not always been incompatible with social reform. A classic example was the 1952 military coup in Egypt, which actually led to some very radical socioeconomic reforms (including land reform) under Gamal Abdel Nasser. Much more recently, in February 2011, the Egyptian military again showed a degree of radical potential, deposing the Mubarak government in a context of widespread political protest. Partly through this decisive action, Egypt's military was able to avoid a lot of the public hostility that had built up towards the president and his family, who between them had amassed a fortune estimated at $40–70 billion.[97] But while many ordinary soldiers grew to resent the concentration of wealth and brazen corruption under Mubarak, many of the military top brass were benefiting greatly. The interests of the Egyptian military are likely to set limits to the current reform process. The army wants to protect its relationship with the United States – its source of military hardware, training and lucrative kickbacks.[98] Officers in the Egyptian army are keen to protect their subsidies and to insulate themselves from steep inflation.[99]

Economic liberalisation is being presented not only as a way forward for Egypt, but also as something that the country's generals are likely to oppose.[100] The military has often been painted as an implacable opponent of past attempts at privatisation, and some senior officers have indeed spoken out against it.[101] But, as in Pakistan and Turkey, elements of the military have actually positioned themselves very cleverly in relation to substantial privatisation drives that have *already been undertaken*. Today, the Egyptian military has extensive business interests in, for example, construction, gasoline, electronics, household appliances, clothing and food.[102] One informed analyst has noted:

> After relatively short careers in the military high-ranking officers are rewarded with such perks as highly remunerative positions on the management boards of housing projects and shopping malls. Some of these are essentially public-sector companies transferred to the military sector when IMF-mandated structural adjustment programs required reductions in the civilian public sector.[103]

When the Arab Spring sprung, it did not dissolve these interests overnight.

If we turn to the case of Iraq, we see very strongly the vested interests that have grown up around the military in what has been, in effect, a permanent emergency since at least 1974. That was the year of a Kurdish revolt, ruthlessly suppressed by Baghdad, and followed, from 1977, by mass deportations of Iraqi Shia into Iran.[104] Iraq's devastating war with Iran in 1980–88 was followed by Iraq's 1990 invasion of Kuwait and resultant Western attempts to police and punish Iraq in the 1990s. Then there was the US-led invasion in 2003, and the conflict that ensued. Although these various crises are often treated as discrete events, the earlier conflicts actually fed strongly into those that followed. As so often, war begat war. It is a story that shows yet again that, once a huge war machine has been put in place, this machinery can be remarkably difficult to demobilise.

Iraq's army was expanded rapidly in the 1970s, along with the police and the Ba'ath party militia.[105] In his classic book *Republic of Fear*, Kanan Makiya (writing under the pseudonym Samir al-Khalil) argued plausibly that Iraq's machinery of internal repression, once it reached a certain size, seemed to 'demand' an external enemy. Meanwhile, Iraq's population was, for the most part, too terrified to question an arbitrary definition of the enemy handed down from the political leadership. A relatively minor border dispute with Iran rather suddenly assumed an importance that not many people would have guessed at a few years earlier.[106] As Makiya put it:

> Eventually expansion of the means of violence – army, police, security apparatuses, networks of informers, party militia, party and state bureaucracies – underwent the classic inversion: from being a means

to an end, the elimination of opponents and exercise of raw power, they became horrific ends in themselves, spilling mindlessly across the borders that had once contained them. War, any war, it does not matter against whom, is a not unlikely outcome of the unbridled growth of the means of violence, particularly when it is so structured as to compromise literally masses of people in its terror.[107]

After the devastating Iran–Iraq war ended in 1988, a key problem for President Saddam Hussein was what to do with an Iraqi army that had been rapidly inflated to around a million men, from a figure of some 242,000 at the start of the war.[108] When Iraq invaded Kuwait in 1990, this aggression was usually attributed in the West to the 'evil' of Saddam (sometimes called 'the new Hitler').[109] But the logic of a military apparatus that 'demanded' more enemies was apparently still in operation. In addition, Saddam seems to have seen the invasion of oil-rich Kuwait as a way out of the predicament left by a huge army that he could not afford, particularly given the enormous debt that Iraq had run up during the war with Iran.[110] Demobilising such a large army would be extremely risky, especially since it would be hard for soldiers to find another job in a severely damaged economy. Meanwhile, the danger of a military coup was very real, and the rapid expansion of the army during the Iran–Iraq war had introduced a number of elements that were relatively difficult for the ruling Ba'ath party to control.[111] In these precarious circumstances, it seems clear that Saddam's military aggression was intended not only to occupy Kuwait, but also to keep his own army occupied. The invasion also offered to ease Saddam's financial problems – not only by seizing control of additional oil, but also by counteracting Kuwait's bothersome willingness to see prices fall. Iraqi soldiers were incinerated *en masse* by US forces as the Iraqis fled Kuwait.[112] As so often, war was a prelude to insurrection (and further repression). As surviving Iraqi soldiers fled, exhausted and starving, into Basra in southern Iraq, rebellion against Saddam flared up there.[113] It was followed by insurrection in the Kurdish north.[114]

If Saddam was aware of the dangers of sacking soldiers, those dangers were dramatically underlined after he was overthrown. Once a US-led coalition had ousted him in 2003, the new coalition authority simply dismissed the Iraqi army *en masse* and, at least initially, without pensions. Compulsory redundancy was dished out to some 400,000 trained and armed men.[115] The working assumption among the occupying powers seems to have been that Iraqi soldiers would effectively disappear as political and military actors once the Iraqi military was defeated. But this was never realistic. It also rode roughshod over careful negotiations between some US military commanders and Iraqi senior officers – talks that were aimed at contacting and paying some 137,000 Iraqi soldiers and removing the threat they posed.[116] Given the mass sackings, what were the officers and enlisted men of the Iraqi army (trained in violence, inculcated with 'loyalty', and now mostly unemployed and without pensions) expected to do? In the event, many redundant soldiers quickly returned to the fray as 'insurgents' or, in George W. Bush's parlance, 'terrorists'.

The head of the Coalition Provisional Authority, Paul Bremer, said that the decision to disband the Iraqi army was intended to placate Shia and Kurdish demands. It is true that these groups had every reason to be wary of the army, since large numbers of Kurds and Shias had been victims of massive state violence under Saddam. But in practice, the decision to disband not only jeopardised soldiers' livelihoods: it also had a profound effect in alienating Sunni Arabs more generally.[117] At this pivotal time, the loyalties of the Sunni Arabs were actually 'up for grabs', which only underlines the missed opportunities. While the Sunnis were often claimed to be implacable supporters of Saddam, this kind of 'ethnic' analysis (once again) had severe limitations.[118] In fact, most of the coup attempts against Saddam had been led by Sunni officers.[119]

Contributing to the alienation of large numbers of Sunni Arabs was a strong military tradition in, for instance, Mosul, Tikrit, Rawa, Ana, Haditha, Samarra, Baquba and Fallujah. Mosul, for example, became known (with some poetic licence) as 'the city with a million officers'.[120] In Fallujah, where massive US retaliation for the lynching of four American security contractors ended up fuelling the insurgency more generally,[121] large numbers of men had earlier joined the Iraqi armed forces and the Iraqi security services. More generally, when officers and rank-and-file soldiers were dismissed, it provided fertile soil for the Iraqi insurgents.[122] As in many other places (including Sri Lanka and Sudan), the army had offered a kind of outlet and opportunity for many of those who had been marginalised by 'development'. While this system was certainly not a productive, or even an ethical, solution to unemployment or underdevelopment, it could not reasonably or safely be dismantled overnight. One study noted:

> Most of the smaller towns were impoverished in the 1920s and 1930s and the army offered a chance for upward mobility for the disadvantaged Arab Sunnis ... When the military was disbanded, a significant proportion of the male population of these urban centers lost their livelihood. It was no wonder that this area became known as the restive Arab Sunni Triangle after the 2003 war.[123]

In mid-2005, even Iraqi Defence Minister Hazim al-Shaalan observed that Iraq's lawlessness, crime and corruption were the result of the disbandment of Iraq's army.[124] Of course, there were other factors, too. Smuggling and criminal networks had grown up amidst international sanctions and crumbling state services in the 1990s, and these were to prove a lasting source of criminal violence and a useful source of supplies for the insurgents. Paradoxically, the *end* of sanctions also created problems, since it led to a sharp drop in income among influential groups linked to 'sanctions-busting' smuggling operations.[125] In these circumstances, the sacking of soldiers was aptly described by one expert as 'a brutal attack on an already feeble state'.[126] Meanwhile, allied reconstruction efforts failed to fill the vacuum: as Ahmed Hashim has put it, 'All the propaganda about reconstruction notwithstanding, the United States was unable to provide an alternative source of gainful employment or income.'[127]

Given that disbanding the Iraqi army was so counterproductive in terms of defeating the insurgents (and also *predictably* counterproductive), the question arises: why do it? This is a complex issue, but one plausible answer is that 'winning', once again, was less important to Western (and especially American) decision-makers than the psychological satisfaction and perceived domestic political advantages of 'getting rid of the evil ones', a goal that, in Iraq, had originally meant getting rid of Saddam and that was easily extended to Saddam's army, to 'de-Baathification', and to what amounted to an assault on the capacity of the state in general.[128]

When we met in a coffee bar near the US Air Force Academy in Colorado, General James McCarthy was able to reflect on this episode. General McCarthy has served as chair of the US Task Force on Operation

Enduring Freedom Lessons Learned in Afghanistan and Iraq, and he told me:

> In Iraq, we underestimated the enemy and the post-hostilities and those who made the assumption that the Iraqi people would welcome us with open arms were wrong. The assumption was true for those around the policymakers, but [Ahmed] Chalabi [an opponent of Saddam who liaised closely with the Americans on the 2003 invasion] had his own interests and was not representative of the general population. We did not prepare for post-hostilities. I made this point to the administration in 2002. There should have been a shadow government, a set of officials to keep ministries operating, the army intact (with the butchers removed) and used in a constabulary approach and minimal efforts to seek out and kill Iraqi military. The moment they were defeated, that was the primary opportunity to be benevolent. We missed that opportunity. We should have said this is the path and if you're not following, we'll replace you. I didn't say kill, I said replace.

There were precedents for the kind of more cautious approach that General McCarthy was talking about. After an earlier war for 'regime change' that saw the UK deposing a pro-Axis government in 1941, the UK rather *gradually* purged the army of nationalist officers loyal to the ousted 'Four Colonels' junta. This relatively extended process meant that the Iraqi army was still intact, and it helped to maintain a degree of subsequent stability.

As in the cases of Sierra Leone, Rwanda, the former Yugoslavia and elsewhere, one vital lesson from Iraq would seem to be that, once a significant military is in place, it has to be handled with care. You cannot just wish it away.

If many of the sources of instability in Iraq can be traced back to the huge army that was assembled for war with Iran in the 1980s, that catastrophic war also left a legacy of violence *within Iran*.

In post-war Iran, while ordinary Iranian veterans have suffered considerable material neglect, a number of privileged veterans have done extremely well. These include many members of the Revolutionary Guards, a branch of the military heavily involved in internal repression. Members of the Revolutionary Guards moved into a wide range of economic activities, including arms production, construction, the oil and gas sector, telecommunications and smuggling. For those with the right connections, the international sanctions on Iran (in large part reflecting opposition to the country's nuclear weapons programme and first imposed by the US in response to the seizure of American hostages in 1979) have, in many ways, represented an additional opportunity, with increased benefits to be derived from smuggling, thanks to the difference in prices of goods inside and outside the country. Meanwhile, the stand-off with the West legitimised further penetration of the economy by the Revolutionary Guards.[129] So again, there are those who have adapted successfully to 'permanent emergency'.

By the same token, these people are likely losers from any rapprochement with the United States in particular. Moreover, a substantial thaw in international tensions would also mean that reformers could no longer be accused of acting against Iran's national interests.[130] Professor Muhammad Sahimi of the University of Southern California noted in 2009:

> ... better relations with the United States will necessarily imply the lifting of at least some of the economic sanctions imposed by Washington and its allies on Iran. This will threaten the immense economic power of the hard-liners, who control a significant part of Iran's official and underground economy. A few years ago Mr. [Mahdi] Karroubi [former speaker of Iran's Parliament] disclosed that the hard-liners control 63 ports that are outside the government's control. They use these ports to import cheap, low-quality materials and commodities from China and other East Asian nations, greatly hurting Iran's own industrial production, but becoming fabulously rich. If the sanctions are lifted and a more open society emerges, the hard-liners will lose much of their economic power. Moreover, the potential for the emergence of a freer press will most likely reveal the depth of their corruption, bringing with it the loss of their political power.[131]

Observers of Iran have also pointed to the maintenance of a kind of 'war mentality', in which enemies (both internal and external) have been an ever-present (and in many ways useful) spectre. A 'war mentality' has been sustained, in part, by constant media references to the war 'martyrs' (who are also honoured across the physical landscape in cemeteries, memorials and street names), and this has helped to bolster a repressive polity that has proved detrimental for most ordinary Iranians.[132] One study of Iranian politics noted: 'An accusation against the reformists, who want to move beyond the rhetoric of the revolution and deal with the ailing economy and liberalize the political structure, is that they have forgotten the martyrs and their blood.'[133]

It is a process that finds echoes in many countries. In Zimbabwe, for example, the ruling Zanu-PF party has long portrayed political opponents as 'sell-outs' who are working towards some kind of re-imposition of the colonial rule that was ended by the country's war of liberation.[134]

In Eritrea, a 'war mentality' props up an oppressive government. After independence from Ethiopia in 1993, the army was reduced from around 95,000 to less than 50,000. But the 1998–2000 war with Ethiopia (which fuelled a profitable arms race)[135] boosted the army to some 300,000. By 2007, those under some kind of military service numbered 350–420,000.[136] In fact, most of those who were drafted after the Eritrea–Ethiopia war broke out have not been demobilised. A thorough investigation by Gaim Kibreab shows just how pernicious this system has become: Eritrea has somehow become locked into a 'permanent emergency' that has allowed systematic exploitation of conscripts' labour – most notably by the forty or so enterprises (trading, farming, property, and so on) that are controlled by a repressive ruling party whose name – the Eritrean People's Front for Democracy and Justice – has become ever more ironic. The party grew out of the liberation struggle against Ethiopia – a struggle that succeeded in knitting together diverse faith communities and diverse ethnic communities. Conscription has subsequently been pushed as a way of indoctrinating young people with ideas about 'national unity', while helping to maintain a 'siege mentality' even in peacetime. Conscripts' labour has also been used to build villas for senior officers and party officials. Meanwhile, the energies of potentially rebellious young people are absorbed in military service.[137]

At the same time, the human costs have been abhorrent. Eritrea produced about a tenth of Africans seeking asylum in the UK in 2001–07, most of them fleeing conscription (and the Eritrean government has, bizarrely, accused the CIA of luring young people away to weaken the country and further US interests). 'Deserters' have been tortured; relatives of deserters have been arrested (but released if they can pay around

$3,500). State investment has been profoundly distorted and the economy has suffered severely. Kibreab concludes that the use of conscript labour in Eritrea constitutes forced labour or a modern form of slavery.[138]

***

During the Cold War, a sense of permanent crisis legitimised high military spending in the Soviet Union and made strong, repressive government appear 'necessary' if the forces of capitalism were to be resisted and ultimately defeated. In a pattern that generally seems to accompany some of the worst persecution, internal enemies were said to be collaborating with external enemies.

The violence of the Cold War did not simply evaporate when the Berlin Wall fell. Instead, it took on new forms, demonstrating once again the difficulty in dismantling a war machine once it has been set in motion. In fact, the Cold War arms race and the superpowers' various 'proxy wars' left damaging legacies of violence that are routinely ignored by Cold War 'triumphalists'.

One element of the problem was corruption and repression on the part of militaries (like Guatemala's and Indonesia's) that had earlier been nurtured by the Cold War. Even where Cold War military forces were dismantled or dispersed, their potential for violence did not simply disappear. That was shown very starkly in the case of Afghanistan, where the West had backed *mujahadeen* rebels against the Soviet occupiers in the 1980s.

Afghanistan itself lost most of its strategic interest for the West after the Soviet withdrawal in 1989, while the US and other Western countries quickly lost interest in the victorious *mujahadeen* once these fighters had served their purpose against the Soviet Union. The resulting sense of abandonment – combined with a mentality of 'permanent warfare' among many of the *mujahadeen* themselves – was to feed powerfully into anti-Western sentiment, and even ultimately into international terrorism. It started with a growing number of attacks on Western humanitarian agencies trying to help Afghan refugees in Pakistan.[139]

We have seen how governments in Saudi Arabia, Kuwait, Egypt, Tunisia and Algeria encouraged participation in the Afghan *jihad* as a way of shipping out their more troublesome Islamists. After the Soviets left Afghanistan, these restless elements either returned home (where they again posed a domestic threat)[140] or headed off to new wars.[141]

Many Arabs who had fought the *jihad* in Afghanistan went on to fight for the Muslims in Bosnia. Others helped stoke violence in Tajikistan and Chechnya, for example.[142] Still others took the fight to the West, as in the bombing of New York's World Trade Center in 1993 and the terrorist campaign of the Armed Islamic Group of Algeria (GIA) against France in 1995.[143] As French political scientist Gilles Kepel has observed:

> The dispersal all over the world, after 1992, of the [jihadists] formerly concentrated in Kabul and Peshawar [in Pakistan, near the Afghan border], more than anything else, explains the sudden, lightning expansion of radical Islamism in Muslim countries and the West.[144]

Even as far away as the Philippines, a veteran of the *mujahadeen* founded a rebel/terrorist group called Abu Sayyaf.[145] The damaging after-effects of the *mujahadeen* war – and the 'triumph' of the West – were not limited to international terrorism. Another unwelcome by-product was the significant number of *Soviet* veterans of the Afghan war who went into organised crime – using the skills, contacts and even the trading networks that they had developed during the conflict. This was part of a much bigger problem that centred on the (partial) demobilisation of Cold War structures more generally. In particular, the thawing of the Cold War saw many Russian bases being closed and large numbers of military personnel and other security personnel losing their jobs.[146] The collapse of Communism also saw a collapse of employment and social security, and criminality became endemic.[147] In these circumstances, many veterans and serving soldiers positioned themselves either within the criminal underworld or within an emerging 'private security' sector that claimed to protect legitimate businesses from this underworld.[148] Military personnel made large amounts of money from the provision of protection services, from the corrupt privatisation of state assets, from complicity in the drugs trade, from 'kick-backs' relating to continuing arms purchases, and from exploiting the difference between claimed and actual numbers of soldiers (our old friends, the 'ghost soldiers').[149] All of these shadowy activities tended to deepen poverty and endemic disorder within Russia.

Then there were the illegal sales of arms and ammunition left over from the Cold War. Tragically, much of the more conventional Cold War armoury ended up being shipped to developing countries, where it fuelled violence in Africa in particular (a process effectively dramatised in the film *Lord of War* with Nicolas Cage).

Meanwhile, in countries through much of the former Soviet Union, Russian military personnel and national military staff became involved in wide-ranging complicity with arms and drugs smuggling, some of it centring ultimately on the key opium-producing areas of Afghanistan. This has contributed to damaging criminal networks in Ukraine, Tajikistan, Moldova and many other countries, adding to the social problems there. Some of the groups with whom military staff have been complicit have themselves had links to international terrorism of various kinds.[150]

The budget (and status) of the Russian military was cut sharply, and one thing that has puzzled many analysts is why the Russian military would accept this. We have seen just how destabilising such cuts have been in many other contexts.[151] Key factors in this quiescence were the burgeoning criminal activity and the proliferating pay-offs of 'permanent emergency'. Particularly among the most senior ranks, corruption smoothed the path for a partial demobilisation of the Cold War machine. One analyst said of the Russian top brass in the late Yeltsin period, 'If they are allowed to steal, they do not rebel.'[152] More subtly, corruption may also have been tolerated and encouraged as a way for Moscow to control potentially rebellious generals on whom the government holds potentially incriminating information.[153]

Meanwhile, the rising tide of crime was itself a justification for more wars, which in turn provided arguments for retaining some semblance of a strong military. In particular, crime and fear of crime in Russia helped to nurture a resurgent strain of nationalism that blamed Russia's problems on 'alien' elements, notably the Chechens.

The second Chechen war (from 1999) was particularly useful politically and proved crucial in helping Vladimir Putin to gain the presidency.[154] After the bombing of a Moscow apartment block (in circumstances that pointed to the possible involvement of state security agencies),[155] Russia went on the offensive in Chechnya in the name of dismantling 'Chechen criminal networks' and defeating 'Chechen terrorism'. Sergei Kovalev, a biologist and former political prisoner, remembered: 'After the first shock [of the explosions] passed, it turned out that we were living in an entirely different country, in which almost no-one dared talk about a peaceful, political resolution of the crisis with Chechnya.'[156] Human rights organisations and the 'unpatriotic press' were vilified,[157] and this proved to be part of a broader crackdown on civil rights.[158] More generally, the regime of the ex-KGB officer Putin has helped to restore myths dating back to the Soviet era – that the country is surrounded by enemies and infiltrated by a 'fifth column' – in this case NGOs (some foreign-funded), which exert pressure on freedom of information and other human rights issues.

Meanwhile, 'Chechen terrorism' proved a useful scapegoat for structural problems in Russia, including the deepening poverty arising from graft, corrupt privatisation and pervasive criminality.[159] In effect, on *both sides* of the Cold War, the continuing need for an enemy has been reinvented in the form of a 'war on terror'. This has helped produce an uneasy alliance with (largely) hidden victims. As Michael Mann observed in 2003, 'Russia exaggerates the links between Chechen rebels and al-Qaeda to get American blessing for state terrorism.'[160]

***

We have seen how war may serve to divide the opposition; how it may help to build a political constituency; how it may bolster military budgets; and how it may provide cover for corruption and crime. Crucially, many of these benefits may also be promised and conferred by some kind of state of emergency, even in the absence of outright warfare. There are many kinds of violence that can help to preserve a useful language of crisis and a convenient image of 'war'. Perhaps, if we could move beyond a collective obsession with defeating one demon enemy or another, we could then begin to explore – and address – the hidden functions of what seems to be a *continuous* security crisis.

Importantly, if peace does eventually materialise, the political and economic functions of war do not simply disappear. If enemies are useful in wartime, this usefulness does not simply vanish with the advent or declaration of peace. While it may be very useful to claim an *intention* to eliminate some reviled enemy or social problem (as in a war on crime, drugs, terror, etc.), it may be rather less useful to succeed in eliminating it. As in wartime, acts of collusion and corruption need to be seen within this framework. So too, as in war, do aggressive actions that predictably exacerbate the problem. All this helps to explain why genuine peace has proved so elusive in so many countries, and why, once you mobilise for war, it can be surprisingly difficult to *de-mobilise*. A further complication is that war has typically put in place a number of structures that have come to have a vested interest in continued conflict of some kind. No wonder peace is often very violent, while the post-war period turns out, all too often, to be a pre-war period.

Of course, peace can – and does – happen. Wars have become less common since the early 1990s, and battle deaths are sharply down. For once, there is genuinely good news! But we should not forget the hidden and half-hidden violence that has afflicted even countries deemed to be 'at peace'. In fact, a key problem afflicting war-to-peace transitions is that very often it is only the institutionalisation of violence and corruption that makes peace possible. The case of Russia after the Cold War illustrates this well. After civil wars, those who have an interest in continued violence are often well entrenched, not least because a peace process frequently involves – and demands – bringing militarised groups into some kind of deal. For example, in the DRC, after a peace agreement in 2003, transitional government members continued their profitable war by proxy, making use of militias and guerrilla groups in the eastern provinces. In the twelve months following the agreement, more than 650,000 people were displaced by fighting – an *increase* of 22 per cent over the previous year.[161] Those brought into a shady peace deal may subsequently use the threat of violence to make sure their interests are looked after.[162]

In many countries, a war-to-peace transition has been assisted when warlords have acquired resources that are sufficient for them also to acquire an interest in 'law and order' – if only to protect their ill-gotten gains.[163] Antonio Giustozzi has made this argument in relation to Afghanistan, and Philippa Atkinson finds elements of this process in Liberia.[164]

One reason for the above-mentioned reduction in battle deaths may be an increase in the number of democracies. But democratisation can also be destabilising, and abusive military formations have often adapted cleverly to democratisation (just as they have also adapted to economic liberalisation).

In many ways, the policies of Western governments – and of international financial institutions like the World Bank and the IMF – have been based on promoting a set of ideals (notably, democracy, economic liberalisation and sometimes the abolition or rapid downsizing of armies) without giving adequate consideration to those who might wish to subvert, instrumentalise or simply sabotage these processes. The unimpeded orchestration of genocide to derail democracy in Rwanda is the starkest example. Some adaptations have themselves fed into renewed – and sometimes intensified – violence in many countries (as when Uganda and Rwanda built their domestic 'good governance', in part, on foreign predation). A process of adaptation has often helped subtly to undermine or 'hijack' a reform process, whether these reforms aim to promote peace, democracy, economic liberalisation, or some combination of these.

CHAPTER 8

Case Study of a Permanent Emergency: The United States

For those in the academic field of 'development studies' (like myself), the search for 'case studies' normally takes us to Africa, Asia or Latin America – and several examples of 'permanent emergencies' on these continents have been noted. At the same time, the reassuring 'otherness' of these 'faraway' crises can easily reinforce some potentially damaging blind spots closer to home. The current chapter tries to avoid this pitfall by looking at a different case study of 'permanent emergency': the United States.

We are invited to believe that the machinery of war is a mere instrument, to be deployed selectively when politicians see a threat to our national interests. But is this machinery perhaps more accurately regarded as a monster that needs constantly to be fed new victims?

I met Jeff Peskoff, a veteran of the Iraq war, in his house near the military base at Colorado Springs, on the edge of the Rocky Mountains. Jeff told me he spent a great many sleepless nights camped out in the living room. He remembers mortars being lobbed into his compound in the city of Mosul, with three colleagues being killed in these attacks. But this is not another hard-luck story. Peskoff, a lively family man with energy to burn, has turned his 'symptom' into a potential solution, using those restless nights to monitor Congressional voting patterns on cable TV and to write to politicians, urging them to turn away from war and to improve services for veterans. Speaking of the state of Colorado, where the major defence company Lockheed Martin directly employs around 10,000 people, Peskoff does not mince his words:

If the war ends, they will have to lay people off. This town votes 70 per cent Republican.[1] The main reason is that so many are employed by the defence industry – either the military or the defence companies. There are five big companies here ... If you're working at Lockheed Martin making money out of soldiers' deaths, fuck you!

The vast military infrastructure in the US has been dubbed 'the military-industrial complex'.[2] The military budget proposal for financial year 2008 was thirty times higher than all spending on State Department operations and non-military aid combined.[3] The US accounted for close to 40 per cent of arms sales to developing countries between 1992 and 2004.[4] In 2006–07, thirteen of the top twenty-five US arms recipients in the developing world were either undemocratic regimes or regimes that had carried out major human rights abuses.[5]

In 2010, the US government spent $698 billion on defence, fully 43 per cent of defence spending worldwide. The next highest level of spending was China, with an estimated $119 billion, or 7.3 per cent of global spending.[6] According to one careful calculation, the Pentagon absorbs a massive 41.6 per cent of US tax dollars.[7] It has plausibly been argued that the main purpose of US militarism and imperialism is not capturing economic resources abroad, but allowing the Pentagon and military industries to obtain the lion's share of domestic resources.[8]

For a country that proclaims a great distaste of empire, America is not doing too badly. In 2004, Chalmers Johnson reported that the Pentagon had 702 overseas bases in about 130 countries, and another 6,000 bases in the US and its territories. A vast service and leisure industry feeds off these bases. For example, the Pentagon operates 234 golf courses worldwide. Convincing the public that all this is necessary is quite a challenge, but is also an opportunity for a whole new set of beneficiaries: for example, the Pentagon channels $700 million a year to the advertising industry.[9]

All this diverse military spending would look pretty irrational if there were no major threat to confront. While these threats are constantly shifting and mutating, it seems they can never be allowed to disappear. The best guide to this process (once again) may be George Orwell's *Nineteen Eighty-Four*, which was published in 1949, at a time when the fascist threat was suddenly and almost seamlessly being replaced by a Communist threat:

On the sixth day of Hate Week ... when the great orgasm was quivering to its climax and the general hatred of Eurasia had boiled up into such delirium that if the crowd could have got their hands on the two thousand Eurasian war-criminals who were to be publicly hanged on the last day of the proceedings, they would unquestionably have torn them to pieces – at just this moment it had been announced that Oceania was at war with Eastasia. Eurasia was an ally.[10]

At the end of the Second World War, the Soviet Union underwent a transformation from ally to enemy that was almost equally abrupt. On 27 February 1947, in the White House cabinet room, Republican Senator Arthur Vandenberg told President Harry Truman he could have the militarised economy he favoured only if he first 'scared the hell out of the American people' that the Russians were coming.[11] In 1956, the renowned American sociologist C. Wright Mills warned: 'For the first time in the nation's history, men in authority are talking about an "emergency" without a foreseeable end',[12] and in 1957 General Douglas MacArthur recalled:

Our government has kept us in a perpetual state of fear – kept us in a continuous stampede of patriotic fervor – with the cry of a grave national emergency. Always there has been some terrible evil at home or some monstrous foreign power that was going to gobble us up if we did not blindly rally behind it by furnishing the exorbitant funds demanded. Yet, in retrospect, these disasters seem never to have happened, seem never to have been real.[13]

By 1965, the diplomat and writer George Kennan, having earlier highlighted what he saw as Soviet 'expansionism', was noting:

It was perfectly clear to anyone with even a rudimentary knowledge of the Russia of that day that the Soviet leaders had no intention of attempting to advance their cause by launching military attacks with their own armed forces across frontiers.[14]

Worse, many observers felt the Soviet 'threat' – while all too real in terms of the existence of nuclear weapons – had been powerfully stimulated precisely by the huge armaments build-up (and associated Cold War rhetoric) in the United States.

While the Cold War's extended nuclear stand-off meant that one was more than usually unsure of waking up in the morning, the fall of the Berlin Wall in 1989 spelt the end of the Cold War. But this was not to be a time for relaxation.

The year 1992 saw the publication of a document called *Defense Planning Guidance*.[15] Emanating from the Defense Department under Dick Cheney, the document argued for high military spending and urged that the US should maintain its pre-eminence by forestalling the emergence of any military rival, and by preventing the dominance of any strategic region by any 'hostile power'. Noting that the threat from the defunct Soviet Union had diminished, the report observed that 'other threats become more important in the context of defense planning', adding – in a rather circular logic – that this was largely because they 'appear greater relative to the residual Soviet/Russian threat and thus are more likely to drive actual requirements'.[16] While the ideas in *Defense Planning Guidance* plan took a back seat through the 1990s, the attacks of 9/11 propelled them to new prominence. In fact, the policy of pre-emptive war became an explicit cornerstone of foreign policy under President George W. Bush.

Significantly, Bush Jr's policy of pre-emptive war – as well as his Star Wars-style missile defence systems – were originally conceived in corporate-backed think-tanks like the Center for Security Policy and the Project for the New American Century,[17] many of which had defence corporation executives on their boards.[18] The links between the American government and defence companies are extensive and longstanding. Even during the Vietnam War, high-ranking military officers would move easily from war to civilian industry.[19] In 2003, William Hartung and Michelle Ciarrocca noted: '32 major administration appointees … are former executives with, consultants for, or significant shareholders of top defense contractors'.[20] At least one of the martial ties was marital: Lynne Cheney, wife of George W. Bush's vice president, Dick Cheney, served on Lockheed Martin's board of directors from 1994 to 2001.[21]

In this context of a waning Cold War enemy and a politically influential defence sector, we were invited to subscribe to a 'war on drugs' and then a 'war on terror'. I use the word 'invited' loosely, particularly in the latter case, since we were famously informed by President George W. Bush that if we did not join the 'war on terror', we would be considered to have sided with the terrorists.

Revealingly, the sense of rapidly shifting enemies has been replicated even *within* the 'war on terror'. The vicious terror attacks of 9/11, mastheminded and carried out largely by Saudis, were met with an attack on Afghanistan. Then we were told that the essential war was in Iraq. After *that* intervention went badly wrong, we were informed (notably by Barack Obama, during his campaign for the US presidency) that Iraq was actually the 'bad war', while the 'good war' – the war we *really* needed to win to make us safe – was back in Afghanistan. And just when we had adjusted to this latest turn, we began to hear intimations that the key battle with the Taliban lay not so much in Afghanistan as in Pakistan.[22] In line with this, we have seen US unmanned aircraft attacking Pakistan. Then there have been the US air strikes on Somalia.[23] If all that was not war enough, we have been told – on and off – that an attack on Iran may be necessary. And then there was Libya.

As with wars that do not directly involve Western powers, we need to ask what functions are served by this condition of 'permanent emergency'.[24] What ends are served by endless war? The speed with which one enemy replaces another should at least raise the suspicion that someone, somewhere is benefiting. And this suspicion should logically be reinforced by the sheer ineffectiveness of belligerent responses: while the dangers posed by Soviet weaponry, by drugs and by terrorists have not been simply imaginary, there is remarkably little evidence that waging 'war' (or indeed massive preparation for war) is an effective way to counter them.

In the case of the US-led 'war on terror', an important goal other than 'winning' has been finding a justification for the huge military spending (and a role for the enormous military machine) that is a legacy of the Cold War.[25] It is hard to see how a larger military would have prevented 9/11, given the huge size of the existing military and the nature of the terror attacks, which at root involved turning modern technology against itself. Even so, the terrorist strikes spurred a massive rise in defence spending.[26]

Some of the pressure may have come from recession: Hossein-zadeh argues that in the United States military spending props up overall demand when private spending falls.[27] In particular, 'the drastic increases in military spending in the early 1950s, the early 1980s, and the early 2000s all came about on the heels of the respective recessionary cycles of those times'.[28] With the economy slowing down and the so-called 'dot.

com bubble' coming to an end, the George W. Bush regime exploited the shock of 9/11 to push through a massive bonanza for the private sector, based around defence, homeland security and the 'reconstruction' of societies that had been deconstructed, in large part, by the United States.[29] As Naomi Klein noted in 2007, 'Between September 11, 2001, and 2006, the Department of Homeland Security handed out $130 billion to private contractors – money that was not in the economy before and that is more than the GDP [gross domestic product] of Chile or the Czech Republic.'[30] All this was in line with Bush's emphasis on private sector solutions and 'outsourcing': a senior official in the Homeland Security department said: 'We don't make things. If it doesn't come from industry, we are not going to be able to get it.'[31] It was also a chance for big defence firms to diversify: they moved strongly into homeland security after 9/11.[32] Meanwhile, the information technology sector, a key driver of domestic growth in the 1990s, was given a boost by increased Pentagon spending in the early 2000s.[33]

Supplying the troops was also extremely lucrative: the US engineering and construction firm Kellogg, Brown and Root got more than $25 billion in a ten-year contract to supply US troops around the world.[34] Meanwhile, many of the workers got remarkably little pay. For example, Fijian drivers subcontracted to Halliburton in Iraq got just $2.50 an hour and no sick leave when injured.[35] Many of the reconstruction deals were offered secretly, with no competition and minimal oversight, and Naomi Klein provides an eloquent summary of the debacle:

> Halliburton, Bechtel, Parsons, KPMG, RTI, Blackwater and all the other US corporations that were in Iraq to take advantage of the reconstruction were part of a vast protectionist racket whereby the US government had created their markets with war, barred their competitors from even entering the race, then paid them to do the work, while guaranteeing them a profit to boot – all at taxpayer expense.[36]

One US firm, Louis Berger, was getting $1 million per mile of the Kabul–Kandahar highway, with the new road soon visibly crumbling.[37] Louis Berger was one of just two firms that got over half of USAID construction funds for Afghanistan in 2007–09.[38] In Iraq and Afghanistan, a booming private security business provided profits as well as opportunities for Western soldiers to move into a more lucrative line. At the same time, this ate significantly into reconstruction funds.[39] Then there was the huge boost to local Afghan warlords from the massive private contracts for protecting military supply routes, a form of military 'outsourcing' that created a series of perverse incentives (as we saw in chapter 4).

The role of reconstruction companies and bureaucracies in lobbying for war in the first place should not be underestimated, particularly given the influence of key political figures who span both worlds (most notably Vice President Dick Cheney, a former chief executive of Halliburton).[40] Naomi Klein notes that a new branch of the State Department – the Office of Reconstruction and Stabilization – drew up plans for the 'reconstruction' of twenty-five countries (including Venezuela and Iran) that might find themselves subject to a US attack.[41]

The boom in the use of private contractors for dangerous work has important political advantages too. In an incisive June 2011 article in the US-based *Armed Forces Journal*, Colonel T.X. Hammes observes:

> The most highly prized attribute of private contractors is that they reduce troop requirements by replacing military personnel. The Obama administration is struggling to maintain support for 100,000 U.S. troops in Afghanistan. If it had to substitute soldiers for contractors, the number would be more than 200,000. The contractors … also reduce military casualties. During the first six months of 2010, contractor casualties exceeded those of uniformed forces in Iraq and Afghanistan. Contractors provide the ability to initiate and sustain long-term conflicts without the political effort necessary to convince the American people a war is worth fighting.[42]

Two key features of contemporary conflict are, first, that the US has been quick to declare war and, second, that these wars do not end as easily as they started. The rush to private contracting has reinforced both phenomena.

Inside Iraq itself, there was a grave shortage of funding to rebuild Iraqi firms, and very little attempt to involve them in reconstruction projects.[43] The suspicion that reconstruction was largely geared towards American interests was underlined when the major US 'reconstruction' contractors in Iraq showed their preference for using foreign labour rather than Iraqis.[44] With foreign investors buying up Iraqi businesses and foreign imports

flooding in, many Iraqi businesspeople were alienated; some ended up
supporting the insurgents.[45] A chaotic and avaricious reconstruction also
fed into grave shortcomings in basic services over a prolonged period. This
could also fuel insecurity, as when Muqtada al-Sadr organised a kind of
'shadow reconstruction' in Iraq's Shia slums. Al-Sadr recruited young men,
many unemployed, into his Mahdi Army, a combustible paramilitary that
was to contribute greatly to sectarian violence in Iraq.[46]

Meanwhile, the defence and homeland security bonanzas were
certainly good news for the top defence company executives. Between
2001 and 2005, the income of chief executives at the thirty-four top
defence contractors rose by 108 per cent; over the same period, the
income of other chief executives increased by only 6 per cent.[47]

Within the US, I wanted a more local perspective on the war economy,
and the state of Colorado seemed as good a place as any. Colorado is a
friendly and sport-loving state, with beautiful mountains, several major
military bases and a generous share of nuclear weapons. It is the kind of
place where your snack may be named after a bomber ('Drifters burger
bar, Home of the famous B-52 breakfast burrito') and where, if you carry
your three-year-old daughter through a supermarket (as I did), a
middle-aged man will come up to you in a 'Fighter Weapons' T-shirt
and say: 'My little girl is flying fighter jets down in the Persian Gulf. So
hug 'em while you can!'

Over a beer in the sunshine outside an independent bookstore in
downtown Colorado Springs, it was hard to imagine the state's potential
for mass destruction. But local peace activist and former priest, Bill
Sulzman, told me:

> Nuclear weapons, they cut the numbers in half in the early 1990s.
> But there are still forty-nine [Minuteman III intercontinental ballistic
> missiles] in Colorado that are 12–15 times the size of the Hiroshima
> bomb and they can tinker with the warhead to change it – and there
> are 450 in the country.[48]

In line with Naomi Klein's analysis, Sulzman stressed the boom to the
local private sector from exploiting fears around terrorism:

> Inside Schriever and Peterson [air force bases], a lot of the military
> contractors are working alongside the blue suits. The civilians build

these systems. There's a breaking down of what's military and what's civilian. Their PR stuff is using fear. They jumped on the 'war on terror'. The military budget mushroomed since 9/11. Surveillance has increased tremendously ... The military-industrial complex will do a huge pushback. They will raise fear. It's been starting in the last ten years.

From this perspective, increased surveillance has the advantage of re-inforcing fear, even as it claims to reduce threats. On local companies servicing the military, Sulzman added:

I could find 15–20 facilities put in the last ten years or so. Some big corporations are here, but also smaller ones like SI International,[49] SAIC, L-3 communications, Scitor. They've mushroomed in this town, paying high wages and so ingratiating themselves with the local businesses and economic structure.

This growth was in line with a plan that politicians and local officials had evolved for Colorado Springs – a project that involved integrating high-tech military production and high-tech civilian production. Significantly, though, this had not gone quite according to plan. Deindustrialisation – and the growing competitiveness of countries with cheaper labour – has hit Colorado Springs, as it has the rest of America. Loring Wirbel, an activist in Colorado Springs with a special interest in space-based weapons systems, told me:

[Colorado] Springs thought in the nineties that it would balance mili-tary and commercial high-tech. But that commercial high-tech has mostly gone. There's Buckley [Air Force base], near Denver [which includes space-based surveillance and missile-warning facilities] ... A lot of commercial high-tech has disappeared, it's gone to China, Indonesia, Taiwan. There's almost no semi-conductor manufacturing in the US now.

Sulzman was even more emphatic: 'The city is in terrible straits. The public sector is broke.' Sales taxes are down and budget cuts put out more than a third of the city's streetlights.[50] Given the local economic downturn, reliance on the military industries has become all the greater, and, according to Sulzman, it is technology itself that is driving the perception of threats:

> Colorado is very much tied in to drone warfare, computer-controlled. They fly and manoeuvre the whole GPS [Global Positioning System] from Schriever Air Force Base. Schriever also have a space warfare centre – wargaming that's futuristic. They're planning the war after the next war. At Buckley [Air Force Base], there's a lot of signals intelligence. They're going to do a space-based infrared system. The approach is: 'What's coming online? How would we use it? Who would we use it against?'

This raises the scary possibility that, while we may imagine ourselves deploying machinery in order to win wars, the machinery may also be helping to shape the wars we fight. If Sulzman is right, then we are in danger of becoming slaves to our own technology, produced by our own production line.

On the whole, US politicians have performed poorly in resisting these pressures. In fact, they have actively encouraged the militarisation of the economy. Political lobbying around defence contracts in the US is notorious. With advertising and spin increasingly the key to political success, politicians are always looking for campaign funding. Many get generous election contributions from the military-industrial complex.[51] Then there is the political bun-fight over resources: Hossein-zadeh observes that 'all members of the Congress, regardless of their political orientation, vigorously compete with each other to attract defense contracts to their districts'.[52]

Local authorities have joined this unedifying contest with enthusiasm, and experience seems to show that if you don't shell out, you may lose out. Wirbel again:

> Colorado should have got more military intelligence centres and funding. San Antonio [Texas] has space military intelligence. There was heavy plugging from Texas. Maybe they [the federal government] want a quieter and more out of the way place [than Colorado]. Twenty years ago, cities had a bidding war for commercial companies, for example a vacation on taxes for 5–10 years,[53] and now the same is true for military intelligence. San Antonio told the NSA [National

Security Agency]: 'We'll give you an old Sony semi-conductor plant – for the new NSA storage facility – and we'll give you the roads.' The NSA came back to Colorado and said: 'What can you do for us?' But cities here are highly libertarian and there was a reluctance to provide. [Colorado] Springs did a lot of soul-searching recently – why are we losing out to Austin [Texas] and San Antonio?

In the US, pressure to rein in gigantic military spending has periodically gathered steam, and this pressure exists today, particularly since spending on many government services is being cut severely. But the war machine has its own logic that does not lend itself to large budget cuts. That was clear when Jimmy Carter ran for president in 1976. He promised defence spending cuts but, after a well-funded backlash from conservative opinion, Carter went on to implement defence spending *increases*.[54] Similar forces were mobilised under Clinton.[55] Expectations that Democrats might somehow rein in the war machine were raised again in November 2006, when mid-term elections saw the Democrats capture a majority in the US Senate and House of Representatives. But in the summer of 2008, Garett Reppenhagen, a veteran of the Iraq war, gave me his assessments of the Democrats' failure to ramp up the pressure on President Bush:

Democrats were telling me they were not going to fund this war [Iraq war]. Then the next day they do! A lot of politicians are probably linked to people profiting in some way. For example, the VA [Department of Veterans Affairs] is buying huge amounts of pharmaceuticals. That's a money market. Every piece of equipment you use is made by someone. Near here, in Longmont, they're making a special gun – if you run out of ammo, you can use Iraqi ammo, AK47 ammo.

When I spoke to Wirbel in the summer of 2009, he had had a chance to assess the first few months of the Obama administration:

With Obama, it's similar to [former President] Andrew Jackson's idea of 'manifest destiny'. You don't really examine the assumptions. [For Obama] Iraq was the bad war of choice, and Afghanistan the good war of necessity. Obama and Hillary Clinton are in the centrist wing [of the Democratic Party]. I wasn't expecting that much fundamental change from them. It's kind of like expecting to get good gas mileage out of a Hummer – our government is not built for that!

While many on the left have been disappointed with Obama, he himself repeatedly promised to get tougher on America's 'real' enemies in Pakistan and Afghanistan. Perhaps the problem was that this message was not being 'heard'.[56] In 2010, there were 118 US drone attacks in Pakistan – more than double the total during the entire presidency of George W. Bush.[57] If you drive past the US Air Force Academy outside Colorado Springs ('Speed checked by aircraft'), you will catch a distant view of the academy chapel, a striking design in more than one sense, since it seems to be built to resemble a series of razor-sharp missiles pointing at the sky.[58] Just down the road from the academy was where I met General James McCarthy, a former Vietnam bomber pilot who now teaches the air force recruits. General McCarthy, a courteous and friendly man, seemed broadly in agreement with Wirbel on military spending: 'The expectation is it will go down but it isn't going to drop off a cliff.'

In March 2011, the US-based Project on Defense Alternatives charted US defence spending since the Second World War and found peaks during the Korean War, the Vietnam War and the Reagan years. With the end of the Cold War, spending drifted downwards, before surging from around 2001, spurred, in large part, by the response to 9/11.[59] The Project on Defense Alternatives noted: 'All told, the Obama administration plans to spend at least $5 trillion (2010 USD) on defense during 2010–2017, which is 5% more in real terms than the Bush administration authorized for 2002–2009.'[60] That certainly looks suspiciously like Wirbel's 'Hummer', and the report adds: 'US defense spending is now stabilizing at levels significantly above Cold War *peaks* (adjusted for inflation) and far above the Cold War average, in real terms' (emphasis in original).[61]

So what explains this reluctance or inability substantially to cut defence spending? The military economy certainly makes a difference. The marginal states of Ohio and Indiana have important General Electric and Rolls-Royce plants.[62] It is a brave politician who promises to shut them down or who challenges the other vested interests that have grown up around the war machine. In the summer of 2011, I had the chance to meet Shawn McKenna, an engaging and highly intelligent veteran of the Vietnam War who now works with homeless veterans in Colorado Springs. I asked him what he thought of the military's role in the economy of Colorado state and Colorado Springs, in particular. He observed:

> If the military cuts back here, this place is in trouble. This place thrives on war, and fear, and paranoia! We have more vets per capita than most of the western United States. We have government contractors, military contractors, satellite contractors. The economic impact would terrible – and I'm a conservative! Ronald Reagan was my hero, and I voted for Bush! … We had a cutback in the seventies and that was hard. In the nineties, they took the 4th infantry division out and sent it to Fort Hood [Texas]. That was a huge loss … I've come to realise that the US is just as corrupt as any banana republic. But we just hide it a lot better.

Another factor in the resilience of the war machine is that nobody wants to look weak – least of all the Democrats. As Merrill Goozner has noted: 'in this post 9/11 society, few politicians – including a president with a history of opposing the Iraq war – appear willing to run the political risk of challenging military spending levels'.[63] Lawrence Korb, a defence analysis at the Center for American Progress, observed: 'The problem is the Democrats are afraid of being branded soft on defense. All the other downturns in defense spending were done by Republicans'.[64] There seems to be something in this: Eisenhower cut spending, so did Nixon and Ford, and then George H.W. Bush (a path that Bill Clinton continued to pursue).[65] Interestingly, a growing body of *Republican* opinion has recently expressed opposition to foreign wars and massive military spending, reflecting traditional concerns over 'big government' and a feeling that high military spending does little to address violence by non-state actors.[66]

At the home for Colorado's homeless veterans, I asked McKenna why Western publics seem to acquiesce rather readily to 'the next war', the war that, we are told, will finally bring peace. His answer came in a torrent of angry but eloquent words:

> America doesn't want peace! That's not why they fight. Fighting for peace is like fucking for virginity! There never was a time we weren't in

conflict with someone. If not the Brits, then fighting the Indians, then the Brits again, then the pesky Native Americans again, then with the Mexicans in 1848, then the Mexicans again, and joining the European war. There's never been a time when we were at peace. The allure is, we are victims of our own propaganda – that Americans can do anything, that if you mess with us, things will go badly for you. If you say 'We're gonna fight these nasty guys', people will vote for you. In this country, you cannot function being seen as weak. I'm convinced there's something in the White House – when you drink the water, you get an attack of the stupids! Even Obama, we're still not out of Afghanistan!

The influence of the military-industrial complex extends to academia, too. For example, between 2003 and 2008 the Massachusetts Institute of Technology (MIT) and Johns Hopkins University got over $842 million in military contracts.[67] In his 2009 book *Empire of Illusion*, Chris Hedges reports huge funding of research (for example at his university, Penn State) by corporate and Pentagon money. This includes funding for developing machines for surveillance, as well as machines of destruction.[68] That military-academic link also seems to have been strong in Colorado. Sulzman told me: 'They [the military and associated industries] heavily affect the University of Colorado Springs, like the science department, and the university has a degree in homeland security. You can buy influence in the academic community. We try to expose that.'

One of the attractions of high-tech weapons is that they offer the prospect of reducing the loss of American life, especially when the weapons are unmanned. As Wirbel observes: 'Colorado and Texas are involved in the mechanisation of war, running the joysticks of UAVs [unmanned aerial vehicles], so the economic costs go way high but the direct people cost is much lower than a Vietnam situation.' The promotional video for the SWORDS (Special Weapons Observation Reconnaissance Detection System) robot notes:

The robots themselves, these things are amazing. We can have them do anything they want. They don't complain like our regular soldiers do. They don't cry, they're not scared. This robot here has no fear, which is a good supplement to the United States army.[69]

Sulzman sees unmanned aircraft like Predator and Reaper (being used extensively in Pakistan)[70] as a way not only to minimise US casualties, but also to get round a taboo on face-to-face assassination (a taboo that found a prominent exception in bin Laden). Sulzman suggests that the drive to build new 'high-tech' weapons has also been fuelled by inter-service rivalry, including rivalry over recruiting:

> People in New Mexico or Nevada sit at a screen. There's a fascination with science, technology and engineering. On the army drawing boards are robotic tanks, robotic soldiers, helicopters without pilots. The army is working on its own version of Reaper and Predator [which are used primarily by the air force and the CIA] and then they turn around and sell it as 'Wouldn't it be exciting to join the army?'

Sulzman stresses the attractions of 'remote' warfare, in terms of both reducing risk and providing another profit opportunity:

> War has gotten so layered that you still have the brutal face-to-face kick in the door, as in Iraq, but even the army has long-range artillery that can fire 150 miles. They're a very long distance from the result that they cause, and they like this concept of having machines do the face-to-face stuff. But that is expensive. Corporations see a new frontier and a new business opportunity, and war is kind of a permanent thing.

Technology may also provide a beguiling sense that machines, rather than humans, are taking some of the difficult decisions. In *The Betrayal*, General Corson told how a new 'man sniffer', used in the Vietnam War, could pick up ammonia from mammals and indicate how far away they were. The trouble was that it could not distinguish between Viet Cong and civilians (or even between humans and buffalo). Corson refers to a 'mystical belief in depending on the impartiality and preciseness of science to make the basic life-and-death decisions'. Thus, 'if the "man sniffer" tells you there are enemy in the forest you can bomb or napalm them with a clear conscience'.[71]

Can the current levels of military spending be sustained? Sulzman, for one, does not think so: 'I don't think this society will stop doing it till it implodes. Big empires do overreach and finally you just can't pay for

it any more – I don't think it will be a *moral* crisis.' It is an argument that
has been put forward by Paul Kennedy in his book *The Rise and Fall of
the Great Powers*.[72] Empires become overextended; military spending
goes too high; then empires run up huge debts and eventually fall when
no one will lend them any more money.[73]

It is here that China has become pivotal: in effect, Beijing has bankrolled the US and its costly military economy.[74] As Chris Hedges notes:
'The moment China, the oil-rich states, and other international investors stop buying US Treasury Bonds, the dollar will become junk.
Inflation will rocket upward.'[75] In these circumstances, China has even
gone so far as to chastise the US for spending huge sums on a military
that it cannot afford.

China's economic importance has also helped to shape American
definitions of the enemy. In particular, while China was touted by some
US hawks as a promising new enemy in the wake of the Cold War,
economic realities have helped rein in this tendency. Thomas Barnett's
influential book *The Pentagon's New Map* is a particularly interesting
window on this process. The book provides a surprisingly frank insider's account of the Pentagon's search for new enemies as the Cold War
waned. For example, during the second Clinton administration, Barnett
came across the following mock 'personals' ad taped to a wall in a
Pentagon office:

> ENEMY WANTED: Mature North American Superpower seeks
> hostile partner for arms-racing, Third World conflicts, and general
> antagonism. Must be sufficiently menacing to convince Congress
> of military financial requirements. Nuclear capability is preferred;
> however, non-nuclear candidates possessing significant bio-chemical
> warfare resources will be considered ...[76]

A joke, obviously. But Barnett sees this ad as reflecting a dilemma that
the Pentagon took very seriously: what do you do with all that high-tech
weaponry and with those huge military budgets after the collapse of
their primary *raison d'être* – the 'evil empire' that was the Soviet Union?
Trained as a Sovietologist and, in his words, 'abandoned by history',[77]
Barnett adapted quickly to the post-Cold War world. His extensive work
for the US military (and in the related think-tank world) also put him in
a good position to know the thinking inside the Pentagon, and in the

following passage he discusses a group that is worried about the waning of the Cold War (a group he dubs the 'Cold Worriers'):

> ... all this sexy, high-tech military capability that we were buying across the nineties really needed a sexy, high-tech enemy to fight against, right? Absolutely, said the Cold Worriers, and if Russia looked more feeble as the decade unfolded, then, damn it, we would make do with China.[78]

Barnett saw institutional interests as feeding into the construction of enemies (including China) for many years to come:

> ... it takes several years to build a modern aircraft carrier, and that ship's life may span more than half a century. To justify that sort of expenditure, you need to project an awfully big threat deep into the future. The more you do that, budget cycle after budget cycle, the more that sketchy forecast takes on the air of an immutable truth.[79]

In *Obama's Wars*, Bob Woodward also notes that the Pentagon tends to focus on planning and equipping for future wars, and sometimes gives these more attention than the ones that America is actually fighting: 'Many of the Pentagon's endless meetings, schedules and intense debates', he reports, 'seemed to be about some distant, theoretical war.'[80]

The strange 'desire' for a high-tech enemy has been quite persistent (though tempered by a preference for enemies against whom one can easily win). In 2007, an official with USAID gave me this summary of his own interactions with the Pentagon:

> They would really like a war with the Soviet Union or North Korea. They need an adversary. We have a lot of tanks and military hardware that are not that useful. They are looking to civilian agencies [like USAID] with a lot of humility now. How can they get out of this mess? What are the non-kinetic [i.e. non-violent] tools? They really don't want to be in these places – Afghanistan, Iraq.

In his 2005 book *The New American Militarism*, Andrew Bacevich noted that senior US military officers had usually been adamant that they did

not want to get stuck in another Vietnam, but then found themselves
mired in Iraq.[81] One military insider suggested to me:

> Being an F-16 pilot is the sexiest career in the Air Force, not flying
> the C-130s [transport planes] or UAVs [unmanned aerial vehicles],
> which are a better fit for unconventional warfare. So there was a
> feeling in the Air Force, 'Let's get the wars in Iraq and Afghanistan over
> with and move on to preparing for China or Russia' – that's the kind
> of 'winning big battles in a big war' we're configured and equipped
> to fight.

These tensions fed into the June 2008 decision to fire US Air Force
Secretary Michael Wynne and Chief of Staff General Michael Moseley
after Secretary of Defense Robert Gates had expressed irritation at what
he saw as a weak commitment by the US Air Force to UAVs.[82]

In Barnett's view, there are two main problems with the tendency to
select China as the 'enemy of choice'. The first is the high degree of
economic integration with the US (including heavy US imports from
China and major Chinese loans to the US). The second problem is that
a war with China might be tricky because of the small matter of China's
nuclear weapons. We can see here a variation of the thinking behind the
invasion of Iraq: what singles out a country for attack is not so much its
military strength as its weakness.[83] Meanwhile (as when the Saudis were
exempt from reprisals despite the fact that fifteen of the nineteen
September 2001 hijackers were Saudi), economic strength can bestow a
certain immunity.

So what is the solution to the Pentagon's potential unemployment
crisis? According to Barnett, it is taking regular and unilateral military
action in what he calls 'The Gap', helpfully defined by him as 'the places
where people still go medieval on one another'[84] (and elsewhere in the
book as the areas that globalisation has hardly reached). According to
Barnett, the Gap is a zone of impunity for Washington: 'it is not a matter
of the U.S. government acting unilaterally whenever it pleases, just
wherever it needs to inside the Gap'.[85]

Just when we are recovering from this licence to invade, we are
informed that 'since there is no exiting the Gap militarily, there is no
such thing as an exit strategy'.[86] In other words, if your country is suffi-
ciently poor, the US has a right to invade you – and a right to stay on a

permanent basis. For those who worry that Iraq did not have weapons of mass destruction that could justify a US-led invasion, Barnett has some reassuring words: 'Taking down Saddam forced the United States to take responsibility for the security environment in the Gap, and that's why I supported the war.'[87]

Barnett advocates 'a strategy of preemptive war inside the Gap'[88] and wants to reassure his readers (and China) that the strategy of preemption does not extend to what he calls 'the core' (basically, richer countries). In fact, Barnett emphasises the importance of making common cause with China in the global war on terrorism.

But this would seem to be a blueprint for a policy of endless war against poor countries around the world. Barnett's recipe for undying war would not matter too much if he was a crackpot militiaman living in the depths of Montana. Unfortunately, he is the author of bestselling books that are taken very seriously in the Pentagon and are endorsed by a range of dignitaries. An assessment in the *National Review* proclaimed *The Pentagon's New Map* to be 'brilliant and innovative', while Asif Shaikh of International Resources Group noted that Barnett 'puts forward a truly "new paradigm" '. For his part, Dr Peter Schoettle at Washington's prestigious Brookings Institution suggests: 'You will be amazed at the lightbulbs that will go off in your mind as you read his work.'

I am happy to agree with this last comment if we take out 'lightbulbs' and replace it with 'alarm bells'. These bells sound just a little louder when we realise that International Resources Group (of which the enthusiastic Mr Shaikh is chief executive) is a consultancy firm that lists the US Defense Department among its clients.

Barnett wants to suggest that the US should use its military might to spread free markets and democracy around the world. Otherwise, poor countries will turn into threats that will call forth a greater level of destruction from the US. If that sounds pretty crude, it sounds worse in Barnett's own words:

> ... either we use our tremendous power as a nation to make globalization truly global, or we condemn some portion of humanity to an outsider status that will naturally morph – through pain and time – into a definition of the enemy. And once we have named our enemies, we will invariably wage war, unleashing the death and destruction that come with it.[89]

Like a lot of militaristic thinking, this lies somewhere between a prediction and a threat. But there is a soft and cuddly side to Barnett, too. His book has lots of references to poverty and exclusion, though there is no evidence that the author knows anything about these phenomena. In any event, he is much less interested in the problem of exclusion than in the 'solution'. That solution is belligerence: the way to 'make globalization truly global', according to Barnett, is war – and lots of it.

While Bush's policy of pre-emptive war raised fears of endless armed conflicts around the world, Barnett does not share these fears. He describes pre-emption as stopping the bad guys before they can do great harm, adding: 'Frankly, that's the ideal.'[90] Old-fashioned deterrence will not work, according to Barnett, because 'they' are not like 'us':

> When the Bush Administration talks preemption, it is talking about actors and regimes in the Gap that we must prudently assume might be undeterrable, simply because they do not live in the same world or adhere to the same security rule sets that we do.[91]

Barnett is known for his engaging and amusing PowerPoint presentations. 'I have a little trick I like to use when I give my grand-strategy brief on the future of globalization', he confides. He would ask his audience to yell out their worst fears about the Bush administration's foreign policy:

> Someone yells out, 'We're a global cop!' And I reply, '... in the Gap!' Another blurts, 'We're always so unilateral!' And I retort, '... in the Gap!' A third offers grimly, 'We start wars preemptively!' And I follow with, '... in the Gap!' I know it sounds like an infomercial gimmick, but frankly, it works.[92]

Presumably, what Barnett means here is that it works in stirring up an audience. Whether it works for nations invaded by the US is a larger and more complicated problem. In any event, this would seem to be a genuinely terrifying window on what can pass for serious policy consideration in and around the Pentagon.

Meanwhile, the ecstasy in discovering a 'new enemy' that can legitimately be invaded is, for Barnett, hard to contain – particularly since it will justify huge defence spending without alienating the Chinese. Barnett describes how 9/11 brought a flash of awareness:

> Suddenly I don't need the bogeyman of a near-peer competitor to motivate my 'defense transformation', because I realize we simply don't have the military that we need to deal with all this disconnected-ness, all this pain, all these lesser included. Suddenly I understand the danger isn't a *who* but a *where*. *Suddenly my eyes light up ...* (emphasis in original)[93]

That ecstasy was matched by Defense Department officials, according to Barnett, who recalls his own presentation to a Secretary of Defense briefing session (with aides to Rumsfeld) in March 2002:

> Then I click my remote and that big red blob dissolves into view, encompassing all the regions they intuitively realize are now in play for the Defense Department in this global war on terrorism. I say, 'What you are looking at are the battle lines in this war. This is the expeditionary theater for the U.S. military in the twenty-first century.' *Suddenly their eyes light up ... and the Pentagon has a new map.* (emphasis in original)[94]

One way of legitimising intervention is actually to *provoke* aggression. Ideally, for Thomas Barnett, the chosen target can be provoked into violence that will legitimise a war against it. I am not making this up:

> In the case of a regime, you simply keep ratcheting up your demands for compliance, and when the regime cannot comply and cannot be provoked into a precipitating action by your constantly growing mili-tary pressure, you preempt.[95]

But what is it that gives the US the right to launch wars against countries that have not attacked it? Would this right also extend to, say, Iran if the Tehran government thought – and it may well do – that the US was going to attack *it*? Barnett does not begin to ask this question, let alone answer it. But he does ask what gives the US the right to ignore the UN and attack unilaterally. His answer: because the US spends so much money on defence! If other advanced countries want a greater say in who gets attacked, he argues, they will also have to boost their defence spending.[96] Might, in other words, is right. Significantly, Barnett's book has little or nothing to say about international law, which is potentially a major fly in his ointment (as it was for George W. Bush). Barnett, incidentally, claims to be Democrat. But if this is the progressive view, I would not like to see the conservative one. No wonder 'My wife worries that I am secretly becoming a Republican ...'[97]

Alarmingly, Barnett's views also found echoes in British official thinking. For example, in September 2002 British Foreign Secretary Jack Straw suggested that 9/11 might herald:

> ... a future in which unspeakable acts of evil are committed against us, coordinated from failed states in distant parts of the world. [Places like] Somalia, Liberia and Congo invoke the Hobbesian image of a 'state of nature' without order ... And at home it has brought drugs, violence and crime to Britain's streets ...[98]

Criteria for being declared a 'failed state' (and therefore liable to intervention) are rarely set out or based on any clearly expressed indicators.[99] We have seen that Somalia was invaded, with US encouragement, at the point when it was on its way to *recovering* from being a failed state.

In his 2004 book *The Breaking of Nations*, Robert Cooper (an adviser to Blair and a senior European Union official) backed a policy of pre-emptive attacks against those who might acquire nuclear weapons, and then noted that if everyone tried to 'get their retaliation in first',[100] it could lead to chaos. His solution?

> A system in which preventative action is required will be stable only under the condition that it is dominated by a single power or a concert of powers. The doctrine of prevention therefore needs to be complemented by a doctrine of enduring strategic superiority – and this is, in fact, the main theme of the US National Security Strategy.[101]

Of course, that 'strategic superiority' was itself to be maintained by a policy of pre-emption, so we were dancing in crazy circles here. Cooper, named as one of Britain's top 'public intellectuals' by *Prospect* magazine in 2005, was one of a number of prominent analysts who backed the adoption of 'double standards'.[102] In April 2002, Cooper noted:

The postmodern world has to start to get used to double standards. Among ourselves, we operate on the basis of laws and open co-operative security. But, when dealing with old-fashioned states outside the postmodern continent of Europe, we need to revert to the rougher methods of an earlier era – force, pre-emptive attack, deception, whatever is necessary ... Among ourselves, we keep the law but when we are operating in the jungle, we must also use the laws of the jungle.[103]

This passage, which seemed dreadful at the time, appeared even more so after revelations of torture at Abu Ghraib. Paul Kahn, in his book *Sacred Violence*, spells out rather succinctly how fears of terrorism and nuclear proliferation have dovetailed and fed into the 'laws of the jungle': 'Terror threatens to go nuclear,' Kahn writes, 'and the response has been the "rediscovery" of torture.'[104]

***

A sense of 'permanent emergency', then, has legitimised continuously large allocations of resources to the military machine in the West. In fact, powerful interest groups – particularly in the US – have become heavily dependent on this mechanism.

While some threats are real (as 9/11 showed), the best way to respond to a threat – today as always – is an open question. Most of the evidence suggests that war only makes the problem worse. Yet we seem just as enamoured as ever with the endless replication of 'wars for peace'. At least part of this addiction comes from the demands of the war machinery itself – the economic dependence on military production and the various vested interests in war. Meanwhile, any sense that we have collectively gone crazy by allocating such vast resources to killing must, it would seem, be ruthlessly kept at bay. The sheer irrationality of making new ways of killing people can only be rendered a little less 'senseless', it appears, by discovering an endless series of 'threats' and 'targets' that will justify such a huge and continuous expenditure of money, effort and brain-power.

A small but revealing window on these shifting threats and targets has been the strange world of American professional wrestling. During the Cold War, one prominent US wrestler, known as 'Boris Breznikoff', used to bait the crowd by singing the Soviet National Anthem and

waving the Soviet flag. While fifty-two Americans were being held
hostage in Iran in 1979–81, a wrestler going by the name of 'The Iron
Sheikh' would brag of his friendship with Ayatollah Khomeini. He then
reinvented himself as Colonel Mustafa, an Iraqi and close confidant of
Saddam Hussein.[105]

Chris Hedges argues that these staged wrestling matches provide an
outlet for the economic and social frustrations of the mostly working-
class spectators. That seems highly plausible – and foreign policy may
itself provide some kind of 'theatre' in which these frustrations and
aggressions can find an outlet.

There are always other possible enemies, after all, including the finan-
ciers who helped to precipitate global economic crisis from 2008. After
the US housing and stock-market crash, the personalities that wrestling
fans 'loved to hate' came to include investor and author John Bradshaw
Layfield, who played wrestling tycoon JBL and who would arrive at
matches in a giant white limousine, bragging that he made money while
most Americans lost their retirement fund and their children's education fund. Meanwhile, the referee would systematically fail to enforce
the rules – for example, by failing to prevent two wrestlers from ganging
up on one.[106] If that, too, is an outlet for popular frustrations, it also hints
at potentially revolutionary resentments, for which the 'evil enemy'
abroad provides a convenient focus.

CHAPTER 9

Shame and the Psychological Functions of Violence

We have seen how the economic and political functions of war produce powerful interests in the continuation of war. These functions help to explain the prevalence of militarily counterproductive tactics. And they help to explain why post-war violence is so common. But several puzzles remain.

For one thing, the extremity of violence in conflicts – and the evident anger – is not easily explained by some kind of calm and rational calculation of self-interest. Secondly, many of the participants in war and in post-war violence derive remarkably little benefit from it (as we saw in Sierra Leone) – another problem for the 'rational actor' framework. Thirdly, the sheer volatility of violence and the sometimes arbitrary choice of targets do not always sit comfortably with an emphasis on cold, rational calculation.

Academic observers have tended to examine the psychology of violence under a range of headings, like 'revenge', 'obedience', 'brutalisation', and 'frustration.'[1] My intention here is not to survey this broad terrain, but to highlight a neglected psychological function of wartime and post-war violence. Whether we are talking about wars involving Western powers or other wars, a central role has been played by *shame*, and we need to understand the functions of violence in *warding off a threat of shame*. Crucially, the avoidance of shame – and conversely the pursuit of respect – represents another important goal that departs from the commonly assumed aim of 'winning'. Understanding the role of shame can help us to understand why the *choice of targets* – in 'our wars' as well as 'their wars' – is so often indiscriminate, even to the point of making 'winning' much less likely. Understanding shame can also help to explain why violence (and especially indiscriminate violence) promotes more violence, and why it *is* so counterproductive in terms of the expressed aim of winning.

Straying one day into the criminology section at my local bookshop, I was lucky enough to stumble on James Gilligan's fascinating study of violent criminals in the United States, *Violence: Reflections on Our Deadliest Epidemic*.[2] Gilligan's book helped me to interpret some of the bewildering events I had investigated in Sierra Leone, in particular. Gilligan, a renowned psychiatrist and prison reformer, concludes that most violence arises from the impulse to restore self-respect and eliminate a sense of shame – in extreme cases, by physically eliminating the person who is arousing, or re-awakening, feelings of shame that go back to childhood. Usually (though not always), this involves a radical jump or 'disconnect' between the person (or people) causing the original humiliation and the eventual choice of victim. In this model, the point of violence is not to *deter*, nor even to achieve some kind of justice; it is to restore a sense of control and a dubious measure of 'respect' by passing on the humiliation to others. French philosopher René Girard made an observation closely related to Gilligan's humiliation model: 'When unappeased, violence seeks and always finds a surrogate victim. The creature that excited its fury is abruptly replaced by another, chosen only because it is vulnerable and close at hand.'[3]

Social conditions make a big difference to the ease with which people are aroused to violence, Gilligan emphasises. He quotes a study of ghetto areas in Philadelphia: 'There is a general sense that very little respect is to be had, and therefore everyone competes to get what affirmation he can from what is available. The resulting craving for respect gives people thick skins and short fuses.'[4]

Gilligan emphasises that shaming abusers – not least by incarcerating them and humiliating them once in prison – is only likely to reinforce the abuse (and the rate of repeat offending for those emerging from prison is indeed very high).

My own investigations, combined with Gilligan's insights, have led me to the conclusion that shame impacts on wartime and post-war violence in four main ways – ways that apply both in wars directly involving Western countries and in those that do not. First, violence may offer *an immediate 'solution' to feelings of powerlessness and injustice*. In other words, it may offer some kind of psychological release.

This may sometimes be a more powerful motivation for violence than the pursuit of longer-term political solutions for injustice. The satisfactions of violence here are typically limited in duration, but (rather on the model of an addiction) this fleeting quality may not inhibit the behaviour, so much as motivate a repetition.

A second connection between shame and violence centres on the *manipulation* of shame. For example, recruitment of fighters may rest on exploiting and exacerbating shame, while legitimising abusive war systems may depend on *distributing* shame in particular ways. A striking feature of shame and guilt is that perpetrators frequently feel remarkably little of either (seeing their own violence as justified or even righteous), while the victims of violence – including sexual violence – often feel great shame and guilt, even though they have done nothing wrong.

A third mechanism connecting shame and violence arises from violence itself. It seems that the perpetrators of violence frequently *redouble their violence* in the face of criticism (and the associated threat of shame). Where violence becomes part of an exploitative system, this criticism is particularly likely – as is a violent reaction to the criticism.

A fourth way in which shame fuels violence also arises from violence – more specifically, from the shame that violence typically imposes on its *victims*, who may themselves resort to violence to restore a sense of agency, control and respect. This represents a particularly vicious circle that takes us back to the first way in which shame fuels violence: that is, when violence offers an immediate solution to powerlessness and injustice.

***

Consider that first way first. In many wars in poorer countries, a major contributor to violence has been its function in resolving feelings of powerlessness and injustice. During civil war in El Salvador, a sense of pride from participation in rebellion could provide a corrective to years of deference to landlords who disrespected the peasantry.[5]

In Colombia, those who joined the rebels and their opponents in the paramilitaries frequently came from a similar class background (an echo of Sierra Leone).[6] Former paramilitaries said they had been treated with respect when they carried a gun, but that, once demobilised, they risked being just another unemployed young man.[7] Going out with the prettiest women was another attraction of joining the paramilitaries.

Anthropologist Kimberly Theidon notes that part of the context is a glorification of men-with-guns in the Colombian media.[8]

Even where feelings of 'respect' are fleeting, they may still be alluring – even addictive. Such motivations have little to do with 'winning' – and often make winning less likely. They are also closely linked to two of the blind spots discussed earlier in the book: grievances in the insurgency and grievances in the counterinsurgency. While 'greed' (as we have seen) has been put forward as an explanation for civil wars, it is also something that itself needs to be explained. This is part of the value in looking at grievances. As we saw in the case of Guatemala, perceptions of 'disrespect' and 'betrayal' can feed into abuses within the machinery of counterinsurgency – even after a war is over.

Again, the case of Sierra Leone is illuminating. Two main kinds of powerlessness and injustice can be identified in that country: those arising in peacetime and those arising in wartime. In peacetime, resentments against village chiefs, for example, had built up over a long period. A paramount chief from Moyamba district in western Sierra Leone told me:

> So many chiefs were created which did not have popular support. Some of the chiefs who enjoyed the favour of the government ruled very adversely, abused and molested their subjects and connived with the administration, particularly under the APC [All People's Congress], to intimidate and vandalise civilians and villages …

For central government, this system had its advantages. As one team of researchers noted, 'Once you are assured of the loyalty of the chiefs, responsibility towards the rural populace can be abrogated except for carefully targeted patrimonial distributions at election time.'[9]

But the resulting resentments proved highly destructive. During the civil war, young rebels would sometimes humiliate village chiefs and even make them dance or plant swamp rice – a pattern that echoed some of the Khmer Rouge violence in Cambodia's mass killings of the 1970s.[10] Philippa Atkinson and her colleagues reported:

> … the general pattern was to arrive in a village firing in the air, and then immediately to seek out the Chief and village elders. The chief, often old and endowed with great respect and status, would then be

publicly humiliated in front of the rest of the inhabitants. Some were beaten, others made to crawl about on the floor or wait on the invaders. Some were replaced by collaborators or farcical child-chiefs.[11]

In a horrifying twist, Sierra Leone's rebels would sometimes force villagers to 'applaud' atrocities – a further indication that violence was being used to invert the social pyramid and transform a disempowered youth, however briefly, into 'big men'. Like a dream or a violent movie, war offered a reversal – often equally fleeting – of the humiliations and frustrations of everyday life. The 1997 military coup (and the previously noted humiliation of senior officers) also showed how violence could bring an immediate reversal of social hierarchies. One experienced British aid worker with the Council of Churches in Sierra Leone told me: 'By fighting, you're going from being nothing in a village to being Rambo.'[12]

At times, the pursuit of respect bordered on farce: British Major Phil Ashby reported a typical conversation with a teenage rebel.

> Ashby: Hello, what's your name?
> Rebel: I am Dead Body.
> Ashby: Pleased to meet you, Mr Body.
> Rebel: Staff Captain Dead Body!

The rebels sometimes presented recruitment and violence as forms of initiation that would confer the respect due to adults. Work on neighbouring Liberia also suggests that some young men saw war as a way of making a transition (in part, through material acquisition) to the status of adults.[13]

Many of the peacetime frustrations in Sierra Leone stemmed from state failure. The 1980s had been a bad time for those looking to benefit from state services. The IMF pushed successfully for severe cuts and for a drastic currency devaluation that fuelled inflation, reduced the real value of official salaries, and stimulated corruption. Key problems included crumbling health and educational services, as well as the increasingly corrupt system for administering justice through local chiefs.[14] One man, a chemist, told me he fondly remembered the 1960s and 1970s, when 'people went to hospital for a cure, not to die'. Noting the role of poor access to education, a detailed study concluded: 'The vast majority of combatants across factions were uneducated and poor. Many had left school before the conflict started either due to lack of fees or because schools had closed down.'[15]

Elsewhere in the world, the Arab Spring and the case of Sri Lanka remind us of the dangers of education without adequate employment, and the same goes for Sierra Leone. One local worker with Catholic Relief Services emphasised that violence could somehow reverse a loss of face, warding off the shame associated with dropping out of school:

> The educational system has increased rebel and soldier numbers. A lot drop out of school early and these do not have fair job opportunities and, having gone to [secondary] school, they do not want to go back to their villages and till the land. They feel they are a little too enlightened to go back and till the soil! They feel their friends will laugh at them, and say you're still farming even though you went off to school. They saw that being a rebel you can loot at will, then you have a sway over your former master, who used to lord it over you, or the others who might have laughed. You might as well go to the bush and become a rebel. There is no master there. You are master of yourself ... In my time, there were no celebrations at the time of exams. Now they make elaborate parties and the children feel big and then when the results come, they have all failed![16] They cannot get jobs. They cannot go back to school.

This analysis resonates with Kris Hardin's comments on Kono district in the 1980s:

> Individuals who are successful in primary school and then advance to the secondary schools in Koidu and another major town, even if only for a few years, consider themselves too educated to return to farming and what they consider the boredom and poverty of 'village life'.[17]

The dynamic also mirrors some of the difficulties when Vietnamese peasants were generally unable to proceed beyond elementary school and the rebels capitalised on their frustration. As General William Corson put it:

After achieving a certain social status through education – regardless to what level – it is extremely difficult for a Vietnamese to return to the rice fields as a shoulder-pole carrier. The peasant cannot understand why he has to – and the [Viet Cong] cadre is Johnny on-the-spot to tell him.[18]

In Sierra Leone, a reluctance to return to one's village 'empty handed' could also impede post-war 'reconstruction'. Krijn Peters makes this point, and also reminds us that, particularly for ordinary fighters, the promise of riches in wartime was often not matched by the reality:

... many of the younger ex-combatants do not have ready access to land. Often, they feel unable to return home, until they have something to show and the war – contrary to the assumptions of the greed not grievance model – left many poorer than the day they began.[19]

Tackling rural grievances that impede access to land will also be important here.

Significantly, it is not necessarily poverty that causes shame, but the interaction of poverty and wealth, the juxtaposition of 'underdevelopment' and a development effort that somehow manages to exclude huge sections of society. Paul Richards has stressed the 'humiliations' involved in exclusion from modernity in Sierra Leone.[20] Frustrated expectations are a related problem. These dynamics have troubling implications for the 'aid community', where some aid workers' and consultants' comfortable lifestyles – and the insistence that other people 'need to be developed' – can easily feed into an incendiary experience of shame.[21]

In a large house near to one of the spectacular beaches that line the capital Freetown, Amy Smythe, soon to become a minister in the democratic government of Tejan Kabbah, told me in 1995:

People in the communities have a sense of justice and respect for life, but people have been so disempowered and being told they are useless, they are poor, they are illiterate, and they have lost their humanity and are behaving like animals. People are not poor – they are rich in potential ... Before, their self-perception was different.

All the anger welling up in Sierra Leone did not translate into a rebellion with a clear political ideology that could win 'hearts and minds' through practical solutions to peacetime frustrations. While there were some efforts in this direction,[22] deficiencies in the country's educational system were a major obstacle. So was the killing of some of the more educated rebels by an insecure rebel leadership at an early stage in the war. But the rebels' brutality and weakly articulated ideology should not lead us to suppose that grievances were irrelevant.

If peace was a source of many frustrations, war went on to deepen many people's experience of powerlessness and injustice, feeding the violence in a vicious circle.

Part of the reason was the further collapse of state services – including security – in wartime. Given the chronic insecurity (and the particular vulnerability of civilians), signing up to one military faction or another could offer the prospect of survival and even a precarious security. The incentive to join a faction was increased by the risk of being labelled an 'enemy sympathiser', particularly for male youths who had been displaced from home towns and villages.[23]

Also feeding a sense of powerlessness and injustice were endemic neglect and abuse within the various military factions. Most glaringly, young rebel fighters had generally themselves been victims of abduction, and they had sometimes been forced into abuses against their own communities and even their own families. One knowledgeable aid worker described the rebels as the 'human rights abusing products of human rights abuses'.[24]

Significantly, rebels sometimes remembered with relish the abuses they had carried out – almost as if it obliterated the earlier powerlessness and humiliation. One girl who was subjected to multiple rapes was naturally reluctant to tell visiting researchers about it, but much preferred to talk about how she had learned to shoot, how she had become a commando and had killed people taken from passing cars.[25] One woman who researched sexual violence in Sierra Leone reported: 'Many of the girls I talked to mentioned female rebels who were in fact more violent than male rebels.'[26]

As for the government soldiers, Amy Smythe spelt out the links between their abuses (including 'sell game') and their experience of neglect at the hands of the government in Freetown:

A soldier 200 miles into the bush is being told to fight the rebels who are his brothers. He cannot eat. Why should he not compromise? What does the government mean for him – without weapons, food, money? You start exerting the power you have got with other people. It is your brutality which you have imported from the government you are supposed to be representing.

There is a well-known saying: 'Power corrupts, and absolute power corrupts absolutely.' But this was a little different. Soldiers had a combination of power (in relation to civilians) and powerlessness (in relation both to their superiors and to the elusive rebels). It was this combination that seems to have been so conducive to abuse.

The corruption of military supply lines and the government's virtual abandonment of front-line soldiers had helped to precipitate a military coup in 1992. But if anything, the coup added to a sense of abandonment. In fact, members of the new junta, who liked to demonstrate their power and virility by driving their convoys through the streets of Freetown at hair-raising speeds, seemed more intent on enjoying a privileged lifestyle than on helping their comrades-in-arms upcountry. In a manoeuvre worthy of George Orwell's *Animal Farm*, the young coup-makers installed themselves in the opulent palace of former president, Siaka Stevens. The palace quickly acquired a reputation for sex, drugs and rap – along with the popular nickname 'America'. One senior Sierra Leonean civil servant with very good contacts in the military explained to me in 1995 how the coup came to be regarded by many soldiers upcountry:

There's a sabotage system, a lack of commitment. It's a very covert mutiny. The view is, 'We went in support of you [the coup-makers] and you are not looking after us. We still face the same lack of welfare, boots, medicines, food and, importantly, human care and contact. We cannot even meet with you now. You are under escort. Deliberately, you are making it impossible for us to talk to you.' Then the slave mentality comes in. Every time somebody has been enslaved, he will enslave somebody else. You get soldiers behaving like paramount chiefs and harvesting our crops – to balance it up.

We have also seen how the 1997 military coup was fed by a sense of neglect within the army, and how this reignited a destructive cycle of violence within the country.

Having returned to Sierra Leone in 2001 (by which time the war was mercifully winding to a close), I wanted to get a better understanding of the motivations of those who had carried out such awful cruelties – not least in the mad fury of the January 1999 abuses in Freetown. While this did not present any particular physical danger for me, it proved mentally hazardous – and perhaps also morally so. I met a lot of ex-combatants from various factions. My dreams were very disturbing and probably not helped by my Lariam anti-malarial medication. Being awake in the early hours was no better: I was wracked by a strange combination of insomnia, chest pain and delirium, as I struggled to get inside the heads of those who had carried out horrendous acts of violence, including amputations and the massacre of civilians sheltering in churches and mosques. Particularly uncomfortable was what seemed to be a genuine sense of outrage and self-righteousness among many of the young fighters in Sierra Leone. If explaining seemed close to excusing, then any attempt at empathising seemed to risk something worse. How much sympathy for the Devil could a person summon up (I wondered at four in the morning), without becoming one of his number?

Over breakfast, when the mosquitoes had calmed down and I had a chance to look at the often amusing stories in the local papers, things did not seem quite so melodramatic. I had a feeling that if there was something to be risked by my proposed line of enquiry, there was much more to be gained. I wanted to understand the fury of the fighters and the anger that seemed to lie behind extreme atrocity.

While most of my earlier research had concentrated on the mundane benefits of the country's sinister 'war system', it was becoming clear to me that grievances were fermenting in the hearts of perpetrators, as well as of victims. One young man who had taken part in the 1999 attack on the capital had clearly been incensed by the execution of twenty-four soldiers when the junta was deposed. Pointing his finger and making clear that no interruptions would be tolerated, he said: 'Those people they killed, the twenty-four, they are the nucleus of the army. They were wiped off! These so-called people [in Kabbah's civilian regime] were barbaric! We have sacrificed our life for this nation!' Some of his fellow attackers had been dismissed from Sierra Leone's army and wanted reinstatement. Others were angry at the abuses they had been subjected to while still in the army. This anger made a big impression on the local aid worker who was held hostage in June 1999 by the 'West Side Boys' (a key element in the January 1999 attack). The former hostage told me:

> ... within the army, they feel they are not treated fairly, not receiving sacks of rice, and feel they are being used or bullied ... When they find themselves in the bush, they inflict the same injustice on those under them that they are complaining about ... They're finding worth, attention and respect, and they think one way is by bullying those under them.

Whether within the army, within rogue army factions, or within the ranks of the rebels, young fighters often vented their frustrations on easy and unarmed targets. What started as hostility towards 'big men' – whether chiefs or army officers – could easily mutate into atrocity against ordinary civilians. Girard's insight bears repeating: 'When unappeased, violence seeks and always finds a surrogate victim. The creature that excited its fury is abruptly replaced by another, chosen only because it is vulnerable and close at hand.'[27]

It turned out that, just as disrespect could fuel violence, respect – more encouragingly – could have the opposite effect. Reining in the abusive counterinsurgency, as noted, proved to be an important ingredient for peace in Sierra Leone. Commenting on vigorous (if belated) British government efforts to reform the army and police in Sierra Leone, one young man (who had wanted to get into the army but had been denied because he lacked the right connections) observed in 2001:

> The soldiers now have pride in the job, because they have been given the basic things. The British have done well here. The British are providing bread and tea for the police. They are proud. They have mobile phones. If you deprive him, he will become undisciplined. Civilians have started praising the military. You can be naturally peaceful, but the situation can make you behave like an animal. People can change. The environment is the thing.

While each emergency is different, some of the dynamics in the DRC have been very similar to those in Sierra Leone. We have seen that the material benefits of violence help to explain much of the violence: the Congo's rich resources attracted the unwelcome involvement of neighbours and promoted some strange collaborations. Disorder may also have been a useful political instrument for neighbouring powers. But as in Sierra Leone, the sheer ferocity of the violence – including very widespread rape – suggests limits to the explanation of violence as 'economics by other means' or even 'politics by other means'. Again, violence has often been used to reverse feelings of powerlessness and injustice.

Pre-war grievances in the DRC were hugely diverse and hugely important. President Mobutu was notoriously avaricious and wasteful. He ordered the construction of an international airport in his home village and encouraged his senior officials to replicate his own enthusiastic embezzlement of public revenues. In a comprehensive assessment, Georges Nzongola-Ntalaja notes:

> the physical infrastructure of production and distribution decayed thoroughly, the health and educational sectors deteriorated beyond recognition, and children died by the thousands each year of preventable and easily curable diseases such as malaria, measles and dysentery.[28]

Soldiers created insecurity through arbitrary 'tax collection'. Riven by corruption, the security forces were a 'paper tiger' and tended to wilt when confronted with armed groups. This became particularly clear when rebels advanced quickly from the east in 1996–97 and took over the government.

Once outright conflict was under way in the DRC, wartime grievances compounded peacetime problems. As with other war systems, understanding the DRC war system means understanding the abuses *against* the perpetrators of violence. Part of the problem lay in the large-scale diversion of resources intended for ordinary soldiers within the DRC army – something that not only confounded soldiers' expectations of discipline and order within the army, but also contributed to widespread cynicism and opportunism. Falling victim to such diversion, soldiers in many parts of the DRC resorted to looting to feed themselves – an extension of abusive behaviour in 'peacetime'. Neglect could take many forms, and one soldier noted that his commanders had refused to give him money for medicine to treat his son, who was dangerously ill with diarrhoea; when his son died, the soldier resorted to selling weapons in order to pay for the burial.[29] Unpaid and underpaid military personnel are widely seen as a key source of sexual violence.[30]

Congolese soldiers spoke of their desire for an administrative position – for working behind a desk. 'Manhood' was strongly linked to material wealth (not least because it could attract women) rather than being linked to violence *per se*. Many joined the army because they were forced to, or out of poverty, or because they wanted an education. One female soldier linked rape to low pay, saying low pay meant soldiers could not win or keep the loyalty of a woman. She contrasted this low pay with the higher salaries of Zimbabwean soldiers, who were said to be popular with local women.[31]

As Chris Dolan showed in his pioneering work on Uganda, the shame surrounding a diminished ability to provide can easily feed into various kinds of violence: when a relatively benign definition of 'masculinity' proves unworkable, more aggressive self-definitions are often adopted. One of Dolan's informants in eastern DRC observed: 'Each time that the men have lost interest in society they form a separate group and one of the first things they do is to rape the women and the girls.'[32] Some women mentioned a common resort to drinking among men, and another sign of crisis was that many young men were having trouble affording marriage. Weaknesses in the disarmament, demobilisation and reintegration programmes, with many promises unfulfilled, were contributing to these dynamics by failing to help individuals recover their livelihoods; meanwhile, ordinary fighters saw many of their leaders proceed to privileged positions. Some young people went so far as to say that 'the men have become the women', referring to the dependence of many unemployed men (often having had their assets stolen) on women who had become more economically active (for example, with small businesses) during wartime.[33]

Horrendous crimes like rape can surely never be fully 'understood'.[34] The danger that understanding will be seen as excusing is also very real. But Chris Dolan also wants to emphasise the dangers in not *trying* to understand. In a key passage, he observes:

... the lack of understanding of what is going on psychologically for the individual perpetrator (as opposed to the 'rational choice' by military commanders of sexual violence as a weapon of war) makes preventive work extremely difficult, and effective interventions with possible or actual perpetrators virtually impossible.[35]

Meanwhile, weak chains of command – and the high levels of sexual violence even after the ostensible end of war – underline the limits of interpreting rape as simply a weapon of war.[36]

Explanations centring on humiliation also have something to offer in relation to the event that precipitated war in the DRC: the 1994 Rwandan genocide. In general, explanations focusing on 'ethnic hatreds' or on 'greed' do not take us a great distance. So far as 'greed' is concerned, it is true that there was significant desire for land, and that some of the perpetrators of genocide were motivated by the prospect of seizing land from victims or of losing it in the future to Tutsi insurgents.[37] But the lack of valuable natural resources in Rwanda is striking. The political functions of genocide (for the elite) are more notable, though we should observe that the strategy was not, in the end, successful (the government was overthrown by Tutsi rebels, who stopped the genocide). In any case, there remains the puzzle of how so many people could be mobilised into such vicious face-to-face violence. While part of the explanation may be a certain habit of obedience within a small, strong state where disobedience was often dangerous,[38] the scale of the participation is still hard to fathom (as is the level of atrocity).[39]

Once again, the frustrations and humiliations of peacetime would seem to be a vital part of the story. International development agencies often saw Rwanda as a success story, and in this sense the genocide 'came out of nowhere'. But this developmental 'success' was largely a case of growth without widespread benefits. Illiteracy remained high, for example. Forced labour in work gangs was widely used in 'development' projects. Meanwhile, government restrictions made migration from rural areas to the cities virtually impossible, so tensions in rural areas were ratcheted up.[40] When there was a sharp economic downturn from the mid-1980s (including falling coffee prices), it brought widespread hardship and even famine.

Some people, nevertheless, were doing very well indeed. One analyst has referred to an 'ethnic group' that incorporated those Hutu and Tutsi that had acquired an education and a European knowledge (*savoir-faire*), adding: 'All these people denigrate the rural way of living.'[41] Peter

Uvin, an expert on Rwanda who spent time as an aid worker there, notes that this elite, which had access to foreign consumer goods, enjoyed sprinkling its conversation with French words, as if to distinguish itself from the masses, to whom it tended to display 'a condescending, rude and manipulative attitude'.[42] In a significant passage, Uvin notes:

> A large part of the population has internalized these values, accepting this lifestyle as the only 'good' one, and judging its own fate as primitive, inferior and undesirable. Little is left of the pride of the African farmer in his culture. Most farmers, especially the young, consider the need to farm a demonstration of failure and baseness, and would give up farming immediately to become a simple sentry, cook, or, especially, driver, in any development project, and to live in the city.[43]

Yet most of those in rural villages were trapped there, partly because of the government prohibitions on internal migration. The schools system produced large numbers of semi-educated youth, and peasant life brought many a sense of 'personal failure'.[44] Uvin again:

> It is hard for most of us to imagine how tense and frustration-rich a society must be in which the majority is subject to exclusion and prejudice – whether racist prejudice or the 'second prejudice' of the development game, which acts in the name of the poor but excludes them from its benefits, which humiliates rather than strengthens them. It is not surprising that there exists a strong need to scapegoat others and to direct aggression and frustration externally.[45]

When soldiers feared they would lose their jobs in the peace process, this fed (as we have seen) into the participation of many of them in genocide. But the fear was not only of unemployment. When the Rwandan prime minister tried to reassure the troops that they would be employed in development projects during the post-war period, this incensed many Rwandan soldiers all the more. As a Human Rights Watch report noted, 'It was just such menial labour that they thought they had left behind in their new military careers.'[46]

In many countries, the humiliations and stigma of 'underdevelopment' have now been supplemented by the 'securitisation' of underdevelopment.[47] According to this discourse, which has underpinned the project of 'development as counterinsurgency' from Afghanistan to Sri Lanka, poverty is not just a problem but a *threat*. As Susan Rice, a US politician and intellectual, put it in November 2001, 'Much of Africa has become a veritable incubator for the foot soldiers of terrorism … These are the swamps we must drain.'[48] British academic Mark Duffield has compellingly stressed the dangers – and the strong imperial echoes – in the discourse that people's lives in 'underdeveloped' countries are somehow 'incomplete' and that these people have to be rescued from their unfortunate condition in the interests of 'our' security.[49]

If we turn now to 'Western wars', we can see that here, too, violence has routinely offered some kind of immediate (if usually fleeting) solution to feelings of powerlessness and shame. Again, it has pulled violence in directions we would not expect if the aim in a war were simply to win.

Although the terrorists behind 9/11 have often been dismissed as 'evil', some observers have stressed that perceptions of humiliation strongly inform their atrocities. Bin Laden cited historical and current humiliations as the main cause of their violence. In his first public statement after 9/11, he declared: 'What America is tasting now is only a copy of what we have tasted. Our Islamic nation has been tasting the same for more than 80 years of humiliation and disgrace.'[50] Later, attempting to justify 9/11 and the 2004 Madrid bombings, bin Laden asked: 'Which religion considers your killed ones innocent and our killed ones worthless? And which principle considers your blood real blood and our blood water?'[51] In this context, violence is presented as a way of regaining individual and collective self-respect.

The humiliation is seen as demanding more humiliation, and violence becomes – bizarrely – an affirmation of one's humanity. The events of 9/11 were certainly humiliating for many Americans, and seem to have been intended as such.

One American soldier had attended high school in Egypt. After serving in Iraq, he filed as a conscientious objector. He gave researcher Pamela Creed the following sophisticated interpretation of the motives of the 9/11 terrorists:

> They didn't choose a military target but a 'soft' one, a target designed to drive home the idea that we cannot protect our women and children. In many ways, I think the terrorists were attacking the masculinity

and image of our society as much as the society itself. I believe they may have been trying to replicate some of the humiliation they felt themselves, by making America feel weak and helpless just as many of their home countries have felt weak and helpless against America in the past.[52]

That sense of humiliation certainly seems to have been felt by George W. Bush himself, who suggested after 9/11 that the terrorists had come to see the US as a 'materialistic', 'impotent' and 'flaccid' society that was too weak to stand up to their intimidation.[53] Of course, if humiliation is fuelling terrorism,[54] then the problems with waging humiliating wars in response to terrorism are hard to ignore.[55]

A major clue to the central role of humiliation in driving the (humiliating) response to 9/11 was the arbitrary choice of target. The point was to pick on *someone*. Crucially, there was no logical connection between the problem (9/11) and the solution (attacking Iraq). In this sense, the attack had something of the irrationality of a witch-hunt.[56] In the US, there was a determination to find a target for retribution after 9/11, perhaps *any* target. Just after 9/11, President Bush declared: 'Somebody is going to pay.'[57] He told King Abdullah of Jordan: 'There's a certain amount of blood-lust, but we won't let it drive our reaction … We're steady, clear-eyed and patient, but pretty soon we'll have to start displaying scalps.'[58] In the absence of any readily identifiable perpetrators, there was reason to search for a 'surrogate victim' who could take the blame. Iraq was also 'close at hand': in contrast to elusive and suicidal terrorists, 'Iraq' was clearly stamped on the map and wasn't going anywhere.

There are many other similarities to a witch-hunt.[59] One was the attraction of picking on a victim because of the victim's *weakness*. In witch-hunts, the preferred victim has often been an elderly woman who cannot easily fight back. In contrast to countries that actually *had* weapons of mass destruction, Iraq could be attacked with relatively minimal fear of retaliation. After the 2003 attack on Iraq, Indian novelist and activist Arundhati Roy commented: 'We once again witnessed the paranoia that a starved, bombed, besieged country was about to annihilate almighty America. (Iraq was only the latest in a succession of countries – earlier there was Cuba, Nicaragua, Libya, Grenada, Panama.)'[60]

Certainly, Iraq was a more politically convenient target for retaliation than, say, Saudi Arabia (from which, as noted, fifteen out of the nineteen

9/11 hijackers originated). For any retaliation against the Saudis could have drastically affected US security and oil interests. As the 'war on terror' progressed, bin Laden was widely believed to be hiding in Pakistan (and eventually, in May 2011, he was found and killed there). The Pakistani security services were known to be supporting the Taliban.[61] Yet Afghanistan remained the preferred target for retaliation. As David Cameron said (after US special forces killed bin Laden in a large house some 800 metres from Pakistan's military academy), if Britain wants to turn away from Pakistan on the grounds of harbouring terrorists, 'you are left with a nuclear power in danger of massive extremism and massive instability'.[62] If Girard stressed that violence tended to home in on 'surrogate victims' who were 'close at hand', he also emphasised that the target tends to be picked precisely because it *cannot* retaliate. In fact, Girard presented scapegoating and religious sacrifice as vital mechanisms for bringing cycles of retaliation to a close. He saw them as further contributing to social cohesion by producing a kind of unanimity among the persecutors. It is interesting in this respect that, for many critics, the problem with invading Iraq was not that there was no connection to 9/11; it was that there was insufficient *unanimity* among the international community. British Prime Minister Tony Blair said his main fear was that the US would act alone.

Part of the powerlessness feeding into the attack on Iraq was a sense of *ignorance* on how to respond to 9/11. The causes of terrorism were poorly understood and not helped by weaknesses in relevant academic disciplines, like international relations (too much focus on states) and political science (often strangely depoliticised with more numbers than insights). In his book *Religion and the Decline of Magic*, Keith Thomas shows how witchcraft flourished historically when the causes of disease were poorly understood. More generally, witch-hunts have often accompanied disasters that defy ready explanation or cure. Killing witches, in this context, *becomes* the cure.

Given that most people did not know how to *explain* 9/11 (and could not hope to punish the immediate perpetrators), *false certainty* seems to have had a particular appeal. Hannah Arendt's work (especially her *Origins of Totalitarianism*) can help in understanding the strange allure of false certainties – like the false certainty that Jews were destroying Germany.[63] This allure may be stronger after a major setback that cannot easily be explained (whether 9/11 or defeat in the First World War); conditions of *economic uncertainty* may add fuel to the fire.[64]

As in a witch-hunt, the source of evil was personalised – in this case, it was boiled down to the individual known as Saddam Hussein. As in a witch-hunt, there was a focus specifically on evil intentions (Saddam's intention of using weapons of mass destruction), and this ill-will was seen as punishable in itself.[65] Of course, bin Laden was also a personification of evil. When he was eventually killed, the press wasted little time in identifying 'the new bin Laden' – a man called Anwar al-Awlaki, who was quickly targeted by the US in a failed missile attack inside Yemen, and eventually killed in a drone attack in September 2011.

At the risk of appearing entirely bewitched by my own analogy, let me mention one more important element. Witch-hunts are typically accompanied by a range of practices that lend these ludicrous enterprises some bogus measure of plausibility – even in the face of a failure to fix whatever crisis may underpin the persecutions. The same applied to the attack on Iraq (and has been true of the 'war on terror' more generally). If the initial witch-hunt or search for the evil ones has not brought the desired result, the conclusion is not that the witch-hunt is irrational and ineffective, but that more witches must be found (often among critics of the witch-hunt). Similarly, in the 'war on terror', the failure to eliminate 'the terrorists' has repeatedly been accommodated by finding a new target.

Confessions are an obvious way of making a witch-hunt appear grounded in truth. We know that the 'war on terror' has seen torture being widely used on suspected terrorists, and some have confessed to crimes they did not commit.[66] A confession was also demanded of Saddam. In fact, Bush made it clear that the only way to avoid war was for Saddam to give a 'full and complete' declaration of the illicit weapons of mass destruction, which he did not, in fact, possess. It is interesting that UN weapons inspector Hans Blix himself compared the aborted weapons inspection in Iraq to a witch-hunt. When US officials rejected the idea that Iraq could meet specified 'benchmarks' so as to show willingness to cooperate with inspectors and to disarm (a path favoured by Germany and Russia and being considered by the UK), Blix understood the US position to be: 'The witches exist; you are appointed to deal with these witches; testing whether there are witches is only a dilution of the witch hunt.'[67]

In a witch-hunt, certain characteristics might be held to mark out a witch, but again their absence could be accommodated. Keith Thomas commented on historical witch-hunts: 'If she [the accused] were searched for the Devil's mark, her body was certain to offer some suitable mole or excrescence; if not, then she must have cut it off, or perhaps concealed it by magic; it was known that these marks could mysteriously come and go.'[68] When 'weapons of mass destruction' did not materialise, there was talk of Saddam concealing them, destroying them or shipping them abroad. The US and UK governments argued that Saddam may have destroyed his own weapons on the eve of war,[69] while Italian Prime Minister Silvio Berlusconi noted: 'If I was in the position of President Saddam Hussein, I would have made these arms vanish, either by destroying them or sending them out of the country.'[70]

In inter-war Germany, some Nazis argued that the scarcity of evidence about a Jewish conspiracy was only evidence of their skill in concealing it; moreover, since a conspiracy was, by nature, secret, people should not expect concrete evidence of a Jewish conspiracy.[71] One is reminded of Donald Rumsfeld's view, in the context of Iraq and the 'weapons of mass destruction', that 'absence of evidence is not evidence of absence'.[72]

Hannah Arendt, as noted, stressed the usefulness of 'action as propaganda': bold (and often violent) action could, in time, make implausible fascist propaganda appear truer than it did originally. In the wake of 9/11, Iraq was labelled a supporter of al Qaeda. These accusations, which built to a crescendo in early 2003, were able to achieve a kind of retrospective 'truth' and a manufactured plausibility when US military intervention led to the formation of 'al Qaeda in Iraq'. Very few people realised that this organisation had its roots in a jihadist group that was *opposed* by Saddam Hussein (called Tawhid al-Jihad). US citizens who bought into the notion that Iraq was responsible for 'terrorism' and for 'harbouring al Qaeda' were largely unaware of the self-fulfilling nature of George W. Bush's original accusation.

If responses to 9/11 can usefully be seen as a response to powerlessness, they cannot reasonably be regarded as a serious attempt to defeat terrorism. This is largely because the response – as with the counter-insurgencies we have looked at in many countries – predictably created new enemies. This is one respect in which the analogy with a witch-hunt is perhaps *inappropriate*. On Girard's logic, the function of a witch-hunt is to break the cycle of retaliation. But the attack on Iraq has *encouraged* retaliation.

Given the sheer scale of the violence and the large number of casualties, it could not realistically end a cycle of violence. Moreover, if Girard was right that the *unanimity* of persecutors brings a perverse kind of *social harmony*, this unanimity was certainly not present over Iraq. In fact, the international community – and Iraq itself – was extremely divided.

At the level of ordinary recruits to Western armies, peacetime power-lessness seems to be a factor. Arguably, 'failed states' have fuelled violence on *both sides* of the 'war on terror'. A good proportion of recruits to Western militaries are young people who are unable to find a secure life or a respected role outside the ranks of the military. While combat can be dangerous, US military bases at home and abroad can be something of an oasis of good physical security, health care and education.[73] Particularly in the poorer parts of the US, the contrast with surrounding areas may be dramatic, and the state may be failing to provide these things. Corporal Phillip Leal, a US military recruiter in Dallas, said: 'I tell people there's probably a good chance of going [to Iraq], but you have to meet your maker at some point. It could happen here in Dallas, with the crime rate we've got, or it could happen there.'[74] It helps when people's status and citizenship are marginal. For example, many of those who enlist in the area are Latinos who are legal residents and get onto a fast track to citizenship by joining the military.[75]

Slashed state budgets are adding to the problem across the United States, as is the deindustrialisation to which high military spending (by taking away precious investment and 'research and development') has powerfully contributed.[76] (While many have linked deindustrialisation to cheap labour abroad, the productivity of manufacturing equipment is also crucial.)[77] Seymour Melman suggests: 'On the current path, what will be left for young men and women other than to enroll in one of the Pentagon's formations?'[78]

If all this were not bad enough, many of the promises made to would-be recruits are exaggerated and even downright dishonest.[79] Jorge Mariscal, a Vietnam veteran based at the University of California, San Diego, said the military has focused on Latinos:

> They know Latino youth are emerging as their largest target market, and they also know we have very low college attendance rates. There's

a lot of people who say if they don't join the military they're gonna be in gangs, but that's a sad commentary on how we settle for the status quo. If the government wants to provide money for kids to go to college, that's great, but it should be a college fund, not asking people to risk their lives.[80]

Recruiter Staff Sergeant Antonio Salas grew up doing migrant farm work. He joined the United States army at eighteen (this would have been around 1990), when he saw his peers being drawn into gangs and drugs: 'I realized there was only a few things that would happen to me if I stayed at home. I'd either end up in jail or dead. I wanted something better.'[81]

Western soldiers' sense of powerlessness in wartime has also fed violence in various ways – sometimes making winning less likely. Some American soldiers in Vietnam complained that they could not find a mass enemy, but only booby traps and land mines. For some, *redefining* the enemy as civilian sympathisers was one way of making the enemy visible and accessible.[82] Often, a sense of powerlessness among soldiers on the ground was reinforced by hostility to politicians and senior officers, with the latter sometimes putting foot-soldiers in harm's way while remaining back at base camp.[83] (A range of frustrations also fed into attacks on civilians by South Vietnamese troops, as we have seen.) Iraq war veteran Garett Reppenhagen referred to a growing 'rift' with Iraqi civilians perceived as unwilling to help in tracking down insurgents: 'instead of blaming your own command for putting you there in that situation, you start blaming the Iraqi people because you can't abuse your own chain of command and your superiors, but you do have complete power over the average Iraqi person'.[84]

***

A second aspect of the relationship between shame and violence has been the manipulation of shame. While feelings of shame, powerlessness and injustice may arise (so to speak) *naturally* and *spontaneously*, they are also subject to large amounts of orchestration and manipulation.

Whether in wars that directly involve Western powers or in those that do not, organising and sustaining mass violence is likely to depend on the successful manipulation of shame – to obtain recruits, to direct violence in politically and economically convenient directions, and to give the violence an air of legitimacy. Manipulating shame often involves taking advantage of social and cultural definitions of what is shameful – for example, the idea (common to many cultures) that non-violence in the face of a threat is particularly shameful for a man.

War has often been legitimised by loading shame and responsibility onto the shoulders of ordinary combatants and the victims of violence, while those who orchestrate war inhabit a strange and dangerously shameless world, reinforcing their impunity. Often, the distribution of shame within war systems seems to be in inverse proportion to the distribution of resources, with those who make the greatest gains helping to ensure that it is their victims who bear the greatest burden of shame.

The manipulation of shame in 'their wars' is starkly demonstrated by the case of Rwanda. If the puzzle of mass participation in the Rwandan genocide is partly explained by the frustrations and shame associated with 'development', that is only one element of the story. Added to the shame of development were the shame of past domination, the shame of military setbacks, and the shame of impending demobilisation – and all of these were subject to extreme manipulation, notably by a media that often explicitly espoused Hutu supremacism, as well as by extremist Hutu politicians.

A historical and colonial experience of domination by the Tutsis seems to have created among many ordinary Hutu a sensitivity to the idea that this domination might be renewed once the RPF rebels moved into government.[85] On top of this, the August 1993 power-sharing agreement with the invading RPF rebels, seen by many as a humiliation, was turned into a call to persecute the internal enemy, who were held responsible. Mahmood Mamdani comments that the army's leadership:

> held the political opposition responsible for dressing up defeat as power sharing and disguising national betrayal as democratic opposition ... The hour had struck for the most ardent champions of Hutu Power – for those whose patriotic zeal knew no limits – to call the nation to arms against those they considered to have betrayed it. The enemy within were the Tutsi and their objective accomplices, the Hutu political opposition ...[86]

Soldiers' fears around demobilisation were also manipulated. With many soldiers mutinying amidst widespread fears for their jobs,

President Juvénal Habyarimana declared the 1993 Arusha Accords to be no more than 'a scrap of paper'.[87]

Christopher Taylor, who was an aid worker in Rwanda and who married a Rwandan Tutsi, suggests that many Hutus seem to have internalised the common colonial view that Tutsi women were more beautiful (because 'more European-looking'). Taylor links this with a dangerous undercurrent of hostility to Tutsi women, who were depicted by Hutu extremists as dangerous women who led Hutus – and foreigners – astray.[88]

In Sierra Leone, a peacetime experience of powerlessness and disrespect created in many youths a susceptibility to promises of a better life. The rebel leadership promised education, wealth and respect, but these desirable things were usually elusive. The most significant material wealth was usually reserved by the upper ranks.[89] Meanwhile, forcing young recruits into abuses against their own communities (and even their own families) made it much harder for them to leave the ranks of the rebels and face the shame and recrimination arising from their actions.[90] The large-scale rape and sexual abuse of female recruits also placed a powerful barrier of shame between the victims and their communities.[91] Some rapes seem to have been purposely carried out in a very public way, and the RUF rebels actively played on the shame this instilled. As Human Rights Watch reported: 'The rebels instilled fear in their "wives" by telling them that their families would not accept them back.'[92] Tattoos were also used to 'mark' people as rebels and to make reintegration more difficult.

The cases of Sierra Leone and Cambodia suggest that extreme measures (for example, the use of child soldiers and reliance on indoctrination and forced atrocities) may sometimes reflect the difficulty of maintaining 'discipline' in circumstances where economic opportunities make fighters more interested in accumulation than 'victory'.[93]

In the DRC, humiliation has been a common part of the initiation of new recruits. One thirty-one-year-old male soldier said: 'When you enter the centre [for military training] you are civilian and now you must become hard, learn the tough spirit of a soldier. If you do not know that, some beating up is required.'[94] Being called 'a woman' was common during training.[95] There are also numerous accounts of people having been forced into violence against their own families in the DRC.[96] Meanwhile, atrocities against the enemy have also involved a manipulation of shame, as when rape was used as a weapon of war.[97] Rape in wartime has sometimes been interpreted as 'an effort to humiliate (feminise) enemy men by sullying their women/nation/homeland, and proving them to be inadequate protectors'.[98] In the DRC, some aid workers have reported a sense of *political* powerlessness (in relation to both local actors and the international community), and suggest that this, too, may be feeding into sexual violence.

While it may be tempting to imagine that the manipulation of shame is a characteristic of 'their wars', it has – again – been a common technique closer to home. Part of this is the use of humiliation as a weapon in wartime. One of the most horrific examples was the mass rapes by Russian soldiers at the end of the Second World War.[99] The Jews were humiliated in countless ways before millions were killed. Somehow the idea that European wars are more 'civilised' has survived the Holocaust. Subsequently, 'collaborators' with the Nazis were themselves humiliated (for example, by shaving women's heads) at the end of the war. Even the British Home Guards (whose cuddly image as doddery would-be opponents of 'Mr Hitler' was popularised in the British TV series *Dad's Army*) endorsed the use of mutilation to humiliate and demoralise in one manual: 'a shot should never be fired at a single Nazi if he can be disposed of by the bayonet, or a blunt instrument, for the demoralizing effect is great when, next morning, a sentry or a patrol is found mutilated.'[100] At the time of the US-led intervention in Iraq, a US Marine Corps manual noted: 'Do not shame or humiliate a man in public. Shaming a man will cause him and his family to be anti-Coalition … Shame is given by placing hoods over a detainee's head. Avoid this practice. Placing a detainee on the ground or putting a foot on him implies you are God.'[101] Such cultural knowledge, clearly intended by the writer to produce more sensitive interventions, found its shadow side at Abu Ghraib.

More broadly, societal shame has been subject to extreme manipulation, notably by the Nazis and their allies in the business world after the First World War. Societal shame was compounded – and the Nazis' task made easier – when the victors imposed reparations on Germany, effectively pinning all the blame for the war on the Germans.[102] A popular belief that Germany had been 'winning' seems to have added to the sense of treachery.[103] The sense of humiliation in the US after 9/11 also represented a powerful 'resource' that could be mobilised by those with more pragmatic concerns (like oil and finding a role for the massive military machine).[104]

Military recruitment and training in the West have routinely involved the manipulation of shame. As in non-Western wars, those who are most susceptible to recruitment have typically been very young, and some of them have been children.[105] Selling 'our wars' as a kind of glamorous 'video game' is one element of this manipulation (and, oddly, it mirrors the use of videos – including Rambo – as part of recruiting and training in wars in West Africa). Once a young recruit to 'our wars' is signed up, this manipulation typically involves some kind of systematic humiliation during training that will break down the individual spirit and inculcate a willingness to kill on behalf of a nation or an idea.[106] There are people whose brains, as Bob Dylan sang in 'License to Kill', have been mismanaged with a great deal of skill. For many, in the West, a 'rational' and 'normal' war is one where people lay down their lives for a cause or a nation. Giving priority to personal survival or personal gain looks 'bizarre' and 'irrational' from within this framework. But what if it requires organised humiliation to get people to the point where they are willing to kill and die for cause or country? Which is the 'irrational' war now?

One only has to look at the US army's website to get a flavour of the manipulation of shame (and respect). One young recruit is quoted as saying: 'Growing up in a Hispanic household, my parents always taught me dignity and respect. Now that I'm in the army I clearly understand what those words really do mean to me. My parents are very proud of me for what I'm doing and what a man I've become.'[107] Yet that sense of 'becoming a man' is often ambivalent. Iraq war veteran Garett Reppenhagen told me:

In the military commercials, you're told you'll become a man, and be all you can be. The reality is they dress you, they feed you, they tell you when to get up and when to go to the bathroom, how to act. We're humiliated on a constant basis. You feel powerless and hopeless.

A sense of being infantilised can feed into a desire to restore a sense of power through violence. As another young US veteran put it, 'In the military, you sometimes feel like a child – or a man when you're firing a gun. It's confusing!' In fact, humiliation is turned into aggression on a fairly systematic basis, and one psychiatric study of Vietnam veterans noted that on the drill field:

the training officer treats the trainee in the same way that he wants the soldier to treat the enemy in battle. To escape the low and painful status of victim and target of aggression, the mantle of the aggressor is assumed with more or less guilt.[108]

Significantly, violence is not the only way to escape a feeling of power-lessness. Referring to the involvement of many veterans (including himself) in anti-war campaigning, Reppenhagen added: 'In activism, I see a lot of guys getting a lot of that power back.'

Terrorist groups have themselves relied heavily on the manipulation of shame. Referring to local leaders in Yemen, one founding member and field commander of Al Qaeda in the Arabian Peninsula, Qassem al-Raymi, noted:

The biggest shame is for the tribal sheikhs to turn into foot soldiers and slaves of [President] Ali Abdullah Saleh, who is himself a slave to the Saudi riyal and the American dollar. And I say to those sheikhs ... where is the manhood and the magnanimity ... or did it die with your forefathers and you have buried it with them?[109]

Islamist terrorist groups have sometimes subjected new recruits to a stream of videos about the oppression of Muslims worldwide. A very *personal* sense of shame may also be exploited. Swiss intellectual Tariq Ramadan has described the process by which some of his fellow Muslims have been recruited into terror organisations:

Young people are told: everything you do is wrong – you don't pray, you drink, you aren't modest, you don't behave. They are told that the only way to be a good Muslim is to live in an Islamic society. Since they can't do that, this magnifies their sense of inadequacy and creates an identity crisis. Such young people are easy prey for someone who comes along and says, 'there is a way to purify yourself'. Some of these figures even keep the young people drinking to increase their sense of guilt and make them easier to manipulate.[110]

On similar lines, veteran journalist Robert Fisk notes that some Muslims have enjoyed freedoms and pleasures in the West, but feel somehow 'corrupted' for doing so. For a dangerous few, terror attacks might be a way not only of tackling this guilt but of hitting back at the society that had 'corrupted' them.[111]

Extreme Islamist groups may appeal to those who feel themselves peripheral in the Muslim world, as well as in relation to Europe or the US – perhaps in terms of their language and traditional culture. They may see extremism as a short cut to being a true Muslim, better than the lazy or decadent fellow Muslims who may be criticising them. Anatol Lieven observes, 'This is a tremendously appealing thing if you are a young, impoverished de-cultured person, whether in Chechnya, southern Thailand or even Afghanistan.'[112]

Another element in the manipulation of shame is the use of shame to *legitimise* a war.

Particularly where a society feels a degree of shame over a given war, it has repeatedly proved tempting for politicians and publics to pass the blame onto the 'crazy' and 'abusive' soldiers who pursued it. Paul Lerner has documented the view among many German officials and psychiatrists at the end of the First World War that war trauma, usually labelled 'hysteria', was essentially the response of a sick individual to an event (war) that others found invigorating.[113] More recently – whether in Vietnam, in Sierra Leone's civil war or in the US-led attack on Iraq – many lower-level soldiers saw themselves not only as having been placed in an impossible position from a military point of view, but also as receiving the lion's share of the blame when things went wrong.

Noting a longstanding Hollywood obsession with deranged Vietnam veterans, veteran Tim O'Brien has commented: 'The nation seems too comfortable with – even dependent on – the image of a suffering and deeply troubled veteran. Rather than face our own culpabilities, we shove them off onto ex-GIs and let them suffer for us.'[114]

The US failure to win in Korea was traumatic – having helped to overcome Fascism, the US found it was unable to defeat Communism. But rather than blaming failure on the generals and the politicians, many tried to blame it on ordinary soldiers – and particularly on those who had been taken prisoner. Some were court-martialled for cooperating with the enemy. Shortly after the end of the Korean War in 1953, Senator Joseph McCarthy went hunting for 'reds' within the army.[115]

Captain Marc A. Giammatteo, an Iraq veteran who served on a presidential commission that reviewed the treatment of veterans, noted: 'I, and others I have spoken to, felt that we were being judged as if we chose our nation's foreign policy and, as a result, received little if any assist-ance.'[116] Self-blame can also kick in, as one US veteran of Iraq told me: 'The level of guilt soldiers feel coming out of the war is significant. The reason so many vets kill themselves is because they've been fighting what they feel is an unjustified war.'

***

There is a third important way in which shame may feed violence. Violence typically generates criticism, whether from others or from oneself. Violent groups may even be denigrated as less than human. Criticism in turn brings threatening feelings of shame. And insofar as violence has been motivated by a desire for self-respect, any threat to this self-respect may be all the more alarming. Paradoxically, those resorting to violence have routinely used further violence to keep further criticism at bay and to ward off closely associated feelings of shame. This may be done by intimidating critics (or groups perceived as crit-ical). At the extreme, these individuals or groups may be killed. This is another sense in which war is made to look more legitimate by violence itself – and this turns out to be important in wars involving Western powers, as well as in wars that do not.

Gilligan's insights help us to understand how the neglect and disre-spect of ordinary soldiers can feed powerfully into their atrocities, and how criticisms from civilians can also feed into this process and, more generally, into abusive 'war systems'. Where soldiers feel that their cause is just, the determination to ward off shame may be all the greater. This is one of many reasons why it is so difficult to sort out 'the good guys' from 'the bad guys' in a war: the sense that one is 'a good guy' can fuel rage – and associated atrocities – against those who say otherwise.

During Sierra Leone's war, the abuses by various factions naturally prompted civilians to recoil from those factions, and sometimes – as we have seen – to organise militarily against them. This, in turn, prompted increased hostility towards civilians, and in these circumstances what-ever element of idealism the fighters possessed seems only to have added to the sense of having been 'betrayed' by civilians – the most vicious of circles. Many of those government soldiers who had succeeded in main-taining military discipline, even in the face of official neglect, were enraged by civilians' accusations that they had sold out to rebels – and some vented their fury through violence. Referring to the rapid expansion of the army (notably after the 1992 military coup), one very intelligent former rebel told me:

> The 1992 recruitment [into the army] was fluid, irregular. So street boys, highway robbers and known thieves were given guns. So they vandalised their fellow civilians – more than the trained soldiers. But they were all blamed in the army. Soldiers ask, 'Why do the civilians reject us?'

Early in the war, RUF rebels were increasingly dismissed at home and abroad as mindless thugs, even as animals or devils. Meanwhile, particularly by 1994–95, government soldiers were increasingly accused by civilians of behaving like rebels.

A local aid worker said of the rebels and rogue soldiers who made the May 1997 coup and then invaded Freetown in January 1999: 'They felt that the civilians had gone against them, so they started killing the civilians indiscriminately. They thought they were unimportant in the eyes of the civilians. So they were finding every way to find recognition.'

By the late 1990s, even the civil defence forces and ECOMOG peacekeepers were attracting significant criticism from civilians (and some international observers and officials) – not only for pursuing economic agendas, but also for instances of physical abuse against civilians. Despite the importance of 'sell game' within ECOMOG, there was also significant resistance and quite a high casualty rate. Adekeye Adebajo has written about the sense of ingratitude among the West African peacekeepers in Sierra Leone.[117] This also seems to have fed into abuses by ECOMOG troops, particularly during the January 1999 rebel attack on Freetown. A variety of factions (rebels, government soldiers, civil defence fighters and ECOMOG) were incensed when civilians labelled them – not without cause – as 'greedy'.

For individuals in precarious situations, showing respect could be a useful survival strategy. Although my interviews covering Sierra Leone's story took me from dilapidated hotels to diamond mines and camps for displaced people in that country, one of the most revealing unfolded in 'The Horse and Jockey', a comfortable pub in north Oxford, England. Here, a young Sierra Leonean studying at Oxford Brookes University told me about his survival tactics when rebels and rogue government soldiers occupied his neighbourhood of Waterloo, in the suburbs of Freetown, in January 1999. Of the attackers he said:

> They worry about betrayal to the army or the *kamajors*. One wrong move would have meant death or amputation for me and my family … By running away from him [the rebel], this is going to make things worse. Hence the [rebel] slogan: 'Why are you running from us, and you don't run away from ECOMOG? What do you see in us that you don't see in them?' So sometimes running away is going to exacerbate more cruelty. You have to say 'OK, I'm with you. I support you. There's nothing wrong with you' … I was able to use this tool to survive.

Even good intentions could feed into extreme violence. In Sierra Leone, fighters on both 'sides' were routinely indoctrinated into believing that their cause was righteous, and any challenge to this belief was frequently met with fury – and escalating violence.[118]

Whenever the named enemy proved elusive or enjoyed some significant or unexpected success, there was a strong temptation to blame civilians for acts of 'betrayal', including the passing of secrets to 'the other side'. Highlighting reprisals against those supporting the military–RUF regime that ruled in Sierra Leone from May 1997 to February 1998, one former RUF fighter observed: 'Unarmed civilians have killed so many just by pointing.' For their part, government soldiers often found it difficult to distinguish rebels from civilians.

Significantly, after the May 1997 coup, the rebel RUF broadcast an 'Apology to the Nation'. It included the statement: 'We did not take to the bush because we wanted to be barbarians, not because we wanted to be inhuman, but because we wanted to state our humanhood …'[119]

As earlier in the war, even the most atrocious violence was sometimes accompanied by attackers insisting on their own humanity. A fifty-year-old police officer recalled how he was tied and beaten in the face and abdomen: a rebel commander calling himself 'Major S'

> put me in the corner of my house. He threw me on the ground so I was sitting, tied on the ground about a yard from Major S and he said, you think we should remain in the bush don't you, but the bush is made for animals.[120]

As before, the more brutal the rebels' behaviour, the more civilians perceived them to be 'brutes' or less than human.[121] Explaining why he wants to extract his 'pound of flesh' in Shakespeare's *The Merchant of Venice*, the moneylender Shylock observes: 'Thou call'dst me dog before thou hadst a cause; But since I am a dog, beware my fangs.'

The man held virtual hostage at Waterloo described the situation of the rebels (who included rogue government soldiers) with an unusual degree of insight and even empathy:

> They still don't want to accept that their philosophy does not appeal, so they want to do it by force … They unleash punishment, which makes the civilians shy away or treat them as enemies. At the same time, they want some kind of recognition from the civilians because they have some kind of ideology and beliefs …

I asked if that need for recognition gave him any leverage in his attempt to survive the rebel occupation of Waterloo: 'Yes, this did give me a little bit of power. I could offer recognition. As well as a number of practical things they needed. Of course, they had most of the power!'

Junior officers behind the May 1997 coup seem to have felt humiliated both by the army and by civilians. At a conference in 1996, soldiers complained that civilians were ungrateful and that accusations of collaboration were humiliating.[122] The *kamajors'* alliance with the mercenary company Executive Outcomes had also been a humiliation for the army – the prominence of both groups was effectively a very public recognition that the army could not do its job.

When I had the opportunity to ask coup leader Johnny Paul Koroma about the reasons for the coup, he told me: 'When a soldier is killed, the government will not do anything. When a *kamajor* is injured, a soldier is taken straight to Pademba Road [prison].' Koroma clearly perceived the rise of the *kamajors* as a source of shame: 'The Kamajors … proceeded to the next degrading step of imposing a 6 o'clock curfew on all soldiers in Southern and Eastern provincial towns and cities … no self-respecting Army would tolerate such humiliation indefinitely.'[123]

As so often before, perceived humiliation fed into further humiliating acts. Brigadier General Mitikishe Khobe, the head of the West African force that ejected the junta, observed:

The failure of the senior officers to carry out needed reforms and improve upon the professional training and welfare of soldiers plus active subversion by political opponents of the elected Government led to the mutiny of 25 May 1997. The mutiny completely destroyed any semblance of order within the Armed Forces. Its own soldiers daily humiliated the entire Officer Corp.[124]

Part of this was junior soldiers simply ordering senior officers to salute them and to pay them compliments.[125]

Discussing the 'Never Again' peace campaign, in which ActionAid was a key actor, one worker with the agency said:

> When you go to ex-combatants and say you must demonstrate remorse, they will kill you. You have to time it. As far as he is concerned, he has done the right thing. You have to gauge the mood before you go in. When they have evidence of their colleagues being reintegrated and their colleagues have not been in jail and have schools, jobs, they can use that as a basis to trust. So they can talk more openly and feel remorse.

A surprising number of ex-combatants express very idealistic career aims,[126] and the ActionAid worker's emphasis on reintegration would seem to accord with John and Valerie Braithwaite's distinction between 'stigmatising' shaming and reintegrative shaming. Stigmatising shame makes crime worse. By contrast, there is evidence that crime can be reduced when individuals are treated as a good person who has carried out a bad act.[127]

Soldiers' perceptions of civilians' 'disrespect' also fed violence in the DRC. Maria Eriksson Baaz and Maria Stern point to soldiers' feeling that civilians did not respect them and saw them as 'worthless people'.[128] Soldiers and police were often referred to as *miyibi* (or 'thieves').[129] There was 'a negative spiral of increasing civilian-military hostility'.[130] One soldier complained:

> We are the ones who have to come to them [civilians] and beg for food … they fear us. But also, they don't understand what we are doing. We are fighting and suffering for the country, to protect the nation and them and their things. Many die, and many, many get injured. But nobody cares for them. Not the Army and not the civilians …[131]

Turkish security personnel in the predominantly Kurdish south-east, one 2007 study notes, 'are acutely sensitive to local resentment over [the] bloody past. Alienation from their operational environment has fed an ultra-nationalistic culture among them'.[132]

In her study of war widows and the Guatemalan civil war, Judith Zur notes how the chiefs (*jefes*) of the abusive civil patrol units have had a strong fear of the words of women (and war widows in particular). Part of this has been fear of physical and legal retribution, which the condemnation of women was seen to make more likely. Zur also noted a strong fear of spiritual retribution and fear of the women's ridicule and laughter: '*jefes* (and men generally) are bewildered and offended by the women's laughter, their "lack of respect", and wonder what they will do next'.[133] The perpetrator's fear of his victim may be a cause of redoubled violence, and Zur notes that Mayan Indians' reputation for magic led to dangerous paranoia among the *ladino* (usually meaning mestizo or mixed race) 'about the harm the uncontrolled Indian could do to them'.[134]

Turning now to 'our wars', civilian criticism has often been similarly incendiary.

After the first English civil war (1642–46) Parliamentarian soldiers were worried not only about pay and conditions, but also about civilians' antipathy towards them. Conrad Russell notes: 'the army had acquired since 1645 a general suspicion of civilian hostility towards them, and wanted a supreme authority which would protect them against it'.[135] That was part of the impetus for the rule of Oliver Cromwell.

An important underpinning for the Nazi movement was a feeling among many First World War veterans that civilians had let them down and then compounded the betrayal by shaming soldiers at war's end. In the journal of the Deutscher Offizierbund, a major organisation for former officers, it was noted: 'The German army returned home in 1918 after doing its duty for 4½ years and was shamefully received. There were no laurel wreaths; hate-filled words were hurled at the soldiers. Military decorations were torn from the soldiers' field-grey uniforms.'[136] Adding to the sense of disrespect was the Weimar government's refusal to issue war medals, on the grounds that these smacked of the previous 'imperialist' regime of Kaiser Wilhelm II.[137]

Faced with the potential shame of defeat, the Nazis (many of them veterans) tried to locate the shame elsewhere, blaming particular elements that were seen as having corrupted society and as having

betrayed the heroic body of soldiers. Particularly prominent here was
Ernst Röhm, who came to see himself as a representative of the so-called
'front generation'. Röhm was a leading figure in the Nazi movement
until he was ruthlessly murdered at the instigation of his one-time friend
Adolf Hitler in 1934. He wanted his comrades in arms to receive the
respect and recognition that he felt they had been denied by the post-
war Weimar government. Röhm articulated a sense of political exclusion on the part of the German soldiery, stating: 'The goal of my politics
is to obtain by fighting for the German front soldier the share in leadership due to him and also to ensure that the ideal and spirit of the front
line prevails in politics.'

In a sense, the aim of Nazi veterans like Adolf Hitler and Ernst Röhm
was actually to reintegrate society into the (allegedly superior) 'soldierly'
values and experiences that they said were embodied by the veterans.
Here, it was the society – and, even more so, certain elements within it
– that was pathologised, rather than the veterans. Wolfgang Schivelbusch
made a similar point when he contrasted the German soldiers' return
with more traditional cultures, where rituals of return:

> require that warriors who have spilled blood undergo purification
> rituals before being allowed back into the community. In Germany, by
> contrast, the warriors were to carry the knowledge of fire back to the
> home front, which would then be purified as well.[138]

Coming more up to date, one of the things I found most interesting
about talking to US veterans from Iraq was their evident sense of
idealism, and how this very idealism could feed into anger and abuse via
a sense that the Iraqis were 'ungrateful'. A young US veteran of Iraq
described the effects on himself and his fellow soldiers:

> Even over a year, it became less 'Let's help these people!' than 'Let's get
> me and my buddies home!' There's a temptation – before, you used
> a rifle to shoot a suspected rebel and now I'm going to use a grenade
> and call in an air strike! It goes from 'Let's help these people!' to 'Let's
> help ourselves!' You're tired, you're hungry, you're dehydrated. It's
> like, 'We're here for them. They don't want us, so why should I help
> them?' Some snap sooner than others. But we all have a point where
> we will snap.

This veteran chose to go AWOL (and to serve time in prison); he made the decision, he told me, in order to avoid 'losing his soul' in the brutal-ising process that he had observed all too often in Iraq. After inter-viewing fifty combat veterans from Iraq, Chris Hedges and Laila al-Arian observed:

> Being surrounded by a hostile population makes simple acts such as going to a store to buy a can of Coke dangerous. The fear and stress pushes troops to view everyone around them as the enemy. The hostility is compounded when the real enemy, as in Iraq, is elusive, shadowy, and hard to find. The rage soldiers feel after a roadside bomb explodes, killing or maiming their colleagues, is one that is easily directed over time to innocent civilians, who are seen to support the insurgents.[139]

A tendency on the part of many US soldiers in Iraq to consider everyone as the enemy has been quite widely remarked upon.[140] A court martial was often regarded as unlikely and less scary than immediate death. As a popular example of graffiti in the 'Porta-John' toilets observed: 'Better to be judged by twelve than carried by six.'[141]

Sergeant Camilo Mejia, who applied to be a conscientious objector, commented on his time in Iraq: 'The frustration that resulted from our inability to get back at those who were attacking us led to tactics that seemed designed simply to punish the local population that was supporting them.'[142] One soldier said: 'I felt like there was this enormous reduction in my compassion for people. The only thing that wound up mattering is myself and the guys that I was with. And everybody else be damned …'[143] Denigration of Iraqi culture – 'haji food', 'haji homes' and 'haji music' – could feed into this.[144] This denigration could also be instrumentalised, as when Specialist Fernando Braga was told during training that a 'haji kid' in front of a convoy should simply be run over: it would reduce the risk to the convoy from stopping and 'He [the commander] said the reason was that we shouldn't hesitate because of the way they would treat their children. They don't value human life like we do and they don't share our same Western values.'[145] A war that was often said to be defending and exporting Western values perhaps lends itself to such brutal rationalisations.

***

A fourth way in which shame fuels violence is via the shame that violence typically imposes on its *victims*. We have seen that this can contribute to the spurious 'legitimacy' of war. Further, these victims may themselves resort to violence to restore a sense of agency, control and respect – a vicious circle feeding back into our first mechanism (violence as a short-term solution for powerlessness and injustice). Given this, we might expect an endless repetition and escalation of violence. Explaining why this is often avoided is a complex task, but the victims of violence may lack the *means* of violence, they may choose to eschew violence, and they may also be *inhibited* by feelings that violence against them is somehow their fault.

Significant research on conflict in Uganda and Guatemala has shown how displacement and loss of livelihood can fuel further violence, particularly when men and teenage boys try to revive a sense of control, respect and self-respect through the use of violence. This can take the form of domestic violence, as well as joining armed groups.[146] In Guatemala, soldiers would accompany *jefes* (or civil patrol chiefs) to their villages and instigate atrocities that drove a wedge between the *jefes* and their own people and therefore obliged the *jefes* to remain loyal to the army. Those who joined the civil patrols had often suffered the humiliation of being unable to provide for their families: some had seen their villages destroyed in army bombardments; others had to work as patrollers a long way from home and lost touch with their normal liveli-hood. The abusive civil patrols provided a new space for the assertion of male identity and for the adoption of a measure of suspect 'self-respect' for patrollers, who had often resented the control and abuse meted out to them by the army, but who now identified with the dominant mili-tary/*ladino* race.[147] Zur comments: 'the immediate power of a rifle and the ability to evoke fear in fellow villagers is a more than satisfactory compensation for all the years of disrespect … By casting his lot with the army, the *jefe* can see himself as "more" human than his fellow villagers.'[148]

We have seen that many perpetrators in 'their wars' are also, in some sense, victims. In addition, sustaining and legitimising violence in 'their wars' has involved distributing guilt and shame to the victim, while shielding the perpetrators from this guilt and shame.[149] This is often reinforced by regimes of punishment and impunity. In Guatemala, General Rios Montt seized power in 1982 and presided over some of the worst human rights abuses in the war. Yet Montt has pursued a successful

political career in post-war Guatemala, clinging on despite an international arrest warrant issued in Madrid. Prosecutions for sexual violence
in the DRC have focused on lower-ranking soldiers, not senior military
figures.[150]

Two prominent analysts of shame and violence have argued that the
shame of oppressed indigenous minorities – and of women who are victims
of domestic violence – can help in understanding why it is that these groups
continue to be dominated.[151] Victims tend to internalise shame, telling
themselves that they are being bullied because there is something wrong
with them as a person or group.[152] Cultural factors can be important here.
In Guatemala, some of those attacked said, 'We must have committed a
very bad sin. What sin could that be?'[153] Somewhat similarly, Buddhist
beliefs about 'karma' can make an individual feel at least partly responsible for any suffering they have experienced.[154]

Importantly, it is not just violence that causes shame, but the
complexion that society puts on violence after the event. (The clearest
example of this is rape, where the trauma of the physical act has routinely
been compounded by the shame – even sometimes *responsibility* – that
society subsequently imposes on the victim.)[155]

In Uganda, official propaganda blamed the Acholi for Uganda's
suffering.[156] This also seems to have been internalised by the Acholi to
quite a large extent, and indeed to have been seen by some as a reason
why God singled them out for salvation through the Holy Spirit
Movement (forerunner of the Lord's Resistance Army rebels). One study
found that Acholi soldiers returning home from the mid-1980s were
seen as having become unclean as a result of their killing. Many soldiers
were regarded as bringing with them the spirits of those they had killed,
and as responsible for the misfortune that had befallen the Acholi; the
rebel Holy Spirit Movement (forerunner of the LRA) offered to wash
away some of this shame – sometimes through more bloodshed.[157] In Sri
Lanka, Tamil communities have sometimes reacted to experiences of
imprisonment and torture with forms of ritualised self-harm that seem
to give some relief, perhaps partly by restoring some sense of control.[158]

If there is an assumption that the world is basically 'just' – or even that
governments have legitimacy – then this can reinforce assumptions
about the guilt of victims.

Hannah Arendt observed in the context of the Nazi holocaust:
'Common sense reacted to the horrors of Buchenwald and Auschwitz

with the plausible argument: "What crime must these people have committed that such things were done to them!"[159] President George W. Bush's close adviser Karl Rove said of the 'war on terror': 'Everything will be measured by results. The victor is always right. History ascribes to the victor qualities that may not actually have been there. And similarly to the defeated.'[160]

Attempts to redistribute shame after a war are likely to be heavily contested. For the perpetrators of violence, the threat of shame and of practical recrimination tends to carry over into peacetime.

In many of 'our wars', significant blame and shame have often been loaded onto veterans, as we have seen. One problem with this tendency to blame veterans – and to label veterans 'crazy' – is that veterans themselves may react strongly, either as individuals or as a group. Well-documented individual responses have included crime, addiction and mental health problems. Collective responses have included the role of angry veterans in the rise of Nazism.[161]

While those subjected to violence may indeed become perpetrators, there are also dangers in highlighting this: paradoxically, it can impose yet more shame on the victims of violence. Vanessa Pupavac has criticised the idea that a resumption of conflict can be achieved with sufficient therapy – a solution that has been widely advocated (and strongly funded) as a means of ending what some call a 'cycle of violence'. Pupavac notes: 'Disturbingly, [the] model of cycles of emotional dysfunctionalism proposes that brutal experiences entail brutalisation, thus pathologising survivors as future perpetrators of brutal acts.'[162] It seems to me that there is a great deal of evidence that falling victim to violence *does* *indeed* increase the likelihood of committing future violence, though usually within a broader system where the violence of the abused is manipulated by those who are orchestrating matters in a more calculating way. Pupavac's point about the danger of compounding victims' shame – and misallocating responsibility for violence – remains a compelling one.

***

We can see, then, that shame has powerfully shaped 'their wars' and 'our wars', and the manipulation of shame has helped to generate violence and to legitimise it. Of course, atrocities and mass violence can never be fully understood. But the psychological functions of this violence –

along with the more mundane economic and political functions – help to explain why winning is so often a low priority. When 'solutions' to violence – the bombing of Cambodia, the killing and internment of Tamils in Sri Lanka, the mass displacement now in Pakistan – involve large-scale humiliation, there is no realistic prospect of their ending a cycle of violence. Since these solutions are adopted nonetheless, we must deduce that they are serving other, less loudly proclaimed, purposes.

Conclusion

What is war? What functions does it serve? Who benefits? This book has tried to challenge the traditional and 'common sense' model of war as a contest between two (or more) 'sides' aiming to win. It has examined the variety of functions (economic, political, psychological) that are served by wartime strategies that have very little to do with winning (and very often make victory less likely). And it has looked at the functions of exactly this idea that war *is* a contest to win, an image of war that has all too often lent spurious legitimacy to some very murky and self-interested agendas.

Even though there are wars where winning remains an important objective for one or both sides, there are also a great many where winning, for a range of influential actors, has taken a back seat. Typically, in these latter cases (where 'war systems' may be a better term than 'war'), there are usually major incentives for a number of parties to claim that war is a moral and existential imperative – that it is 'all about winning', surviving, and 'defeating the evil ones'. Indeed, these claims – often made with the full force of state-controlled media and with local and foreign journalists systematically excluded from conflict zones – have greatly distorted our perceptions about the nature and purposes of violence.

The French philosopher Michel Foucault, who was interested in the hidden functions of apparently failing policies, once described the prison system as 'the detestable solution, which one seems unable to do without'.[1] (One hidden function, for Foucault, was creating a 'criminal class' whose subsequent monitoring would provide a focus for police activity.) War also seems to have something of this 'detestable' and strangely 'indispensable' quality. We are aware (at some level) of the horrendous costs of war. We know (at some level) that civilians have often borne the brunt of violence. And we know (again at some level) that violence breeds more violence. But war remains the evil option that we appear chronically unable to reject; the hateful solution beloved of powerful interests; the nightmare for which we sometimes vote and with which we are still seemingly half in love.

Civil wars in poorer countries have usually been seen as conflicts between rival ethnic groups, or between a government and its rebel opponents. But whether a war is internal or international, many important and hidden conflicts are likely to be disguised by these rather traditional understandings. Avoiding the temptations of depicting war as 'contest', as 'chaos', or as an accumulation of 'mistakes', this book attempts to plot an alternative path. It focuses on *war systems* – wars that actually serve complex functions for a variety of groups. A declared war against a 'demon' enemy turns out to be an 'excellent' context in which a wide variety of violent, profitable and politically advantageous strategies can be pursued with a great deal of impunity. Many of these strategies are irrelevant to 'winning', and many actively impede this endeavour. Powerful interests have emerged in the continuation of conflict. And if by some means peace is finally declared, war systems will frequently mutate, rather than disappear altogether.

In a civil war, seeing war as 'government' versus 'rebels' takes critical attention away from the agendas and actions – often deeply damaging – of those who position themselves within a particular counterinsurgency effort. It is much too easy to get mesmerised by a particular group of rebels as the key problem that needs to be dealt with. Quite apart from the political and economic functions of such a distorted view, it also seems to serve a kind of 'projection' function: it takes the shame out of the problem of violence by presenting it as arising not from 'us' but from 'them'.

As the examples of Sierra Leone and Colombia strongly suggest, the solution to civil war often lies in restraining the *counterinsurgency* rather than in focusing exclusively on the insurgency. By the same logic, the best way to address terrorism may be to curb the *counterterrorism* operations. That means a change in the behaviour of those who decide policy in Washington and London, for example. It also means reining in the abuses of a wide range of governments – from Israel and Pakistan to China, Ethiopia, Eritrea and Sri Lanka – that justify internal repression (sometimes even massacres) in the name of 'counterterrorism'.

Of course, achieving these various behaviour changes is much easier said than done. But what seems particularly unhelpful in promoting such change is the insistence that a particular enemy (notably, today, 'Islamist' terrorism) is so evil and so intractable that all those who claim to oppose it will be given virtually unconditional support. We have seen how overlapping war systems – notably, a civil war wrapped unhelpfully in a global war – have routinely generated impunity, and part of the mechanism here is the mutual reinforcement of national and international definitions of the enemy. Both the Cold War framework and the 'war on terror' framework have regularly given rise to a category of 'illegitimate civilians', whose suffering (and perhaps ultimately elimination) is assumed to be necessary for a more just or secure international order.[2] Indeed, if sacrifice at the individual level has sometimes been seen as 'healing',[3] the same would seem to apply to the sanctioned sacrifice of these populations.[4] The current 'war on terror' is, in many ways, reinventing the old policies of 'backing your friends' that produced so much impunity – and stored up so many combustible grievances – during the Cold War.

Behind the loudly proclaimed war against some named and reviled enemy – the Soviet Union or the US during the Cold War, the Revolutionary United Front rebels in Sierra Leone, the Lord's Resistance Army in Uganda, the FARC rebels in Colombia, al Qaeda or the Taliban in the 'war on terror' – we typically find a complex, but perhaps ultimately comprehensible, set of economic and political interests and agendas, many of which actually thrive on continued conflict. While the 'two sides' in a war often seem to agree that a war is a case of 'us versus them' or 'government versus rebels' or 'the Free World versus Communism' or even 'the United States versus Islamic fundamentalists', both 'sides' in a war may have important vested interests in such a definition – not least the legitimacy it bestows on their resort to force and the leeway it may grant to exploiting and controlling a variety of groups beyond the named enemy (including their 'own people'). Meanwhile, civilians themselves will often give a different account of the fault-lines of conflict, frequently emphasising the division between those who have arms and those who do not.

When we look closely, the 'rational' and 'proper' wars waged by the West actually seem to be infused with a good measure of 'irrationality' (for example in the choice of targets and tactics, and in the use of humiliation to break down the new recruit). Meanwhile, the apparently irrational violence of 'their wars', while often similarly vicious, may be actually strongly informed by rational self-interest (such as avoiding danger and acquiring wealth).[5]

Some people – a minority, but often a devastatingly influential one – have been making money directly from the suffering of war and war-related famine. Others have had an economic interest in keeping society on a militarised footing – not least because of resources flowing in from outside. Still others have been profiting politically from some kind of 'state of emergency' – for example, by stalling on elections and by rebranding opposition as 'treachery'. In these circumstances, actions that might defeat the enemy may be neglected or even intentionally shunned, while predictably counterproductive tactics – like attacking innocent parties, whether states or civilians – are routinely tolerated or even actively encouraged. At some level, while the war system claims to be eliminating the enemy, it actually depends on *reproducing* the enemy.

The enemy, we should remember, is often not nearly as powerful or organised as has been claimed: the fact that children make up a large proportion of many reviled armed factions in Africa gives us a clue. But while reviled foes have often been weak and disorganised, the actions of the counterinsurgents or counterterrorists may help to transform and strengthen the enemy to a significant degree. Indeed, both 'sides' may end up proclaiming (with a dread that is tinged with the pleasure of 'being right' and is laced with a variety of more practical benefits): 'Yes, the enemy is just as powerful as we always said it was!'

If the fault-lines in any given conflict cannot be reduced to those between 'ethnic groups' or between the main armed factions, what form *do* they take? We have seen that there may be very fundamental tensions (and outright violence) between, for example, civilians and armed groups, between men and women, between young and old, between different geographical regions, and between different socio-economic classes (which may cut across so-called 'ethnic hatreds'). It follows that a compromise between the armed factions or between the leaders of different ethnic groups will not, in itself, be a recipe for peace, since the other fault-lines and tensions are likely to remain in place. The fact that peace has been declared does not mean, moreover, that violence (including criminal violence and violence to sustain a repressive state) has lost its usefulness. Moreover, hidden fault-lines may even be *exacerbated* by a peace agreement, as when those excluded try to fight their way to the negotiating table. For all these reasons, a formal peace agreement is only the beginning of what needs to be a much longer peace process.

Those in charge of international interventions have often expressed the need for peace, justice, liberalisation and democracy. In seeking an end to any given war, the expressed aim has generally been to 'end the madness', restore some kind of sanity, and resume the process of 'development'. But what if war and other kinds of mass violence are not actually madness but the result of actions by diverse groups with diverse interests, for whom violence is in some sense functional? What if these violent actions have been spurred by *previous* attempts at 'development' (which it would be folly to resume)? What if democratisation – or the prospect of criminal trials – has itself been a trigger for violence (as in Rwanda)? What if liberalisation has eroded the political support for peace, as in Sri Lanka? And what if peace, when it does finally arrive, is not simply the 'dawn of good sense' but a kind of 'dirty bargain' between those who previously had an interest in war and have now decided, for whatever reasons, that they have an interest in peace?

Mapping these diverse and shifting interests is a very different approach from calling for 'an end to the madness' or indeed from attempting to prescribe all those good things – peace, justice, democracy, economic liberalisation – that are widely said to go together and to reinforce each other. Yet such mapping is essential: peace is a hard-headed calculation that actually cannot be divorced from – or understood in isolation from – the benefits of war.

Among the factors that can encourage a shift towards less violent behaviour (though rarely towards an *absence* of violence) are: the severe depletion of resources that had previously attracted looting;[6] a desire on the part of 'warlords' to protect their 'ill-gotten gains';[7] a change in the behaviour of governments or rebel groups in neighbouring countries;[8] a substantial – or threatened – decrease in the quantity of international aid; the arrival of an international peacekeeping/aid regime, particularly one that offers a large amount of patronage in relation to the size of the country;[9] and the implementation of a far-reaching reform of the security sector.[10] But however it is achieved, the end of a civil or regional war is unlikely to be very 'pure' or 'nice': it is more likely to institutionalise corruption. In fact, if it did not institutionalise corruption in some form, those who had previously been violent would be unlikely to accept it.[11]

If the 'dirty bargain' theory holds – and there is plenty of evidence to suggest that it does[12] – then the various elements of a conventional Western or 'Washington' solution (whether justice, democracy, economic liberalisation or peacekeeping missions themselves) cannot be assumed to be helpful; rather, they need to be evaluated in terms of their likely impact on such a bargain and their likely impact on the calculations of those with access to the means of violence. Focusing on peacekeeping missions in particular, Alex de Waal makes the enlightening suggestion that there will be a 'market' for loyalty, with rebels and warlords often using violence (and sometimes votes or withdrawing economic cooperation) to extract a better price for their loyalty. The various bargains with a national government will also be affected by bargains that local elites may make with other governments in the region. Now in these circumstances, de Waal argues, international peacekeeping missions may significantly distort this 'political marketplace' – either by throwing their weight behind the government or behind rebels/warlords. Arguably, a peace agreement built on such a bargain is unlikely to hold unless the peacekeeping mission continues indefinitely – hence, the title of de Waal's insightful article, 'Mission without end?'.

After the overthrow of the Taliban government in 2001, the 'political settlement' was very profoundly shaped by international actors, and those interests linked to the Taliban were substantially excluded. Perhaps a huge and speedy international effort at state-building – and a tolerance of 'moderate' Taliban interests – might have stabilised this arrangement. But the reality was a rather weak state-building effort and a continuous exclusion of the 'terrorist' Taliban. The resulting political settlement would appear extremely dependent on the continued injection of outside resources and troops. This in turn would seem to be a recipe for either state collapse or permanent external intervention – or even, possibly, for both.

This book has shown that violence may be much easier to ignite than to defuse; and when a war ends, many of its horrors are just beginning. The permanence of the emergency in somewhere like Afghanistan contrasts with international eagerness to declare the situation 'post-conflict' (as after 2001), a declaration that falsely implied victory (with all the short-term political rewards that an appearance of victory can bring). Even if it could be shown that a particular planned or impending war was 'just', the predictable legacy of violence in the long years that follow a war (as with the terrorism of some 'Arab Afghans') should surely create a powerful presumption against a resort to war. While a belief persists that violence can somehow solve the problem of violence – that one more war will somehow set us free – the evidence in this book suggests overwhelmingly that this is not the case.

The book has looked not only at war, but at the reproduction of war: the way that enemies are defined and redefined, invented and re-invented, whether in wartime or peacetime; the way that greed and grievance interact (for example when the greedy manipulate the griev-ances of others);[13] the way that wars mutate and proliferate; and the way that brutality frequently flourishes in what we sometimes optimistically call 'peace'. Making and sustaining peace in these circumstances is not just about securing victory over this or that enemy; nor is it simply about getting two sides to be reconciled with each other; more than this, it involves systematically questioning and challenging the definitions of enmity that create – and re-create – mass violence. It also requires rethinking our understanding of 'war' itself and uncovering the complex functions that are served by particular (and often shifting) definitions of the enemy. By focusing on *war systems*, we can begin to get away from the pitfalls of imagining that war is a contest in which the overriding goal is military victory. In other words, we begin to realise that there is more to war than winning.

Violence has a strange quality of 'sneaking up on us', so that suddenly – and perhaps with the 'best of intentions' – we may find that we have become perpetrators (or at least that we have *voted* for a perpetrator). Many of us have been ready to tolerate, or even promote, violence against those who seem somehow to stand in the way of 'progress', whether this progress takes the form of socialism, democracy, free markets, freedom from terror, or whatever. This is known, in Tony Blair's world, as 'fighting for our values'. But just when we become convinced that justice is on our side, some of the greatest perils creep into play. Of course, humanitarian and human rights law is supposed to protect us from our more ruthless inclinations: not every means to an end is permitted. But the record here is not good. One problem is ignoring the law; another is that law is itself permissive of quite wide-ranging violence.[14]

A related difficulty is that even the categories we use for the purposes of 'protection' carry subtle dangers. Thus, even as we congratulate ourselves on the 'civilised' and 'humane' idea that a certain group must be protected (civilians, 'innocent civilians', women and children, those in 'safe areas', refugees, the 'internally displaced', our fellow nationals or ethnic or religious group – or indeed humans in general), we may already be sharpening our knives for those who do not fall into this protected category. While the dangers inherent in prioritising one's own nation, ethnic group or religious community are relatively obvious, the problem goes well beyond this.

If civilians are to be protected, for example, does that imply that soldiers can legitimately be killed? And does such 'legitimate' killing extend, for example, to the destruction of Iraqi soldiers fleeing from US and allied forces during the Gulf War – soldiers who were attacked with a 'fuel-air' explosive that created a fireball effect and incinerated or asphyxiated everything and everyone around it?[15] If we stress the need to protect '*innocent* civilians', does this imply that somewhere there exist civilians who are rather less than innocent (perhaps ambiguously linked to rebels or *genocidaires*) who do not quite deserve the same protection?[16] Such a view would be extremely dubious from a legal point of view, but this nevertheless seems to have been the attitude towards Hutu civilians in the DRC after the Rwandan genocide, and towards many groups of civilians who found themselves on the 'wrong side' of the Cold War or the 'war on terror'. If we focus (naturally enough) on the protection of women and children, does that somehow tacitly imply that men are fair game (or even, when *our* women and children are not success-fully protected in practice, that it is necessary to exact revenge on *their* women and children)? If civilians in 'safe areas' are to be protected, does this imply (as the Sri Lankan government insisted in 2009) that those outside these areas are legitimate targets? If refugees are entitled to special international protection, does that help expose the internally displaced (as in Sudan in 1988) to unmitigated violence and to hunger without relief? And if the internally displaced are then brought under the 'protection' umbrella, what about those who never moved at all? Finally – and I am not a vegetarian, but the question nevertheless suggests itself – if humans are to be protected, does that imply a licence to kill animals (and even, in the fantasy world of the ethnic nationalist, a licence to kill those humans who have been *redefined* as animals)? Perhaps one can take this line of thinking too far. But the hidden victims of a righteous war are also victims of a system where many governments and aid agencies claim to provide 'protection' (a protection that somehow did not quite extend to these victims).[17] To what extent do aid agencies themselves rank among the beneficiaries of conflict, surviving and prospering by exaggerating the degree to which they can bring solutions?

Adding to the complexity of war is the tendency for fault-lines to shift as time passes, with violence perhaps displaced from its original target. Sometimes the original target has been difficult or even impossible to reach (as with Sierra Leone's elusive rebels or the suicidal terrorists of 9/11), and this has encouraged a search for new targets. Sometimes violence has been directed towards those resembling the original target in some way (perhaps ethnically), or towards critics of the original violence, or towards an internal 'fifth column' ('the Jews', 'the Tutsis') that is held to be responsible for military setbacks. A powerful regime will typically reserve the right to shift or expand its category of 'enemies',[18] exercising social control by feeding the individual's fear that he or she will soon fall into the 'enemy' category. If you oppose an officially approved persecution, or question the approved 'fault-lines' in a conflict, you too may soon be called an enemy – a witch, rebel, terrorist, collaborator or accomplice. Again, if you are not 'with us', you are 'against us'. Among those who have generally been rather effectively controlled in this way are international aid agencies (including within the UN system), which have often remained silent about large-scale abuse – for a range of legitimate reasons (like fear of expulsion), as well as less legitimate ones (like desire for profile, desire to spend one's budget, and the influence on UN executive boards of governmental representatives who are themselves complicit in the violence).[19]

Although 'rebel greed' has recently become a fashionable explanation for civil war, this book has suggested that we need to give increased attention to the role of 'greed' – or, more neutrally, of economic agendas – within the *counterinsurgency*. More broadly, we need to comprehend the myriad ways in which a rebellion may be 'hijacked' and turned to political and economic advantage – notably by actors associated with a regime that is involved in 'counterinsurgency'. We also need to understand how counterterror can be 'hijacked'. Part of this involves understanding the role of international aid in exacerbating abuses and exploitation by groups linked to the counterinsurgency or counterterror.

Current conventional wisdom has it that security is necessary for development, and development is necessary for security. In the context of counterinsurgency (for example, in Afghanistan), development and state-building are seen as an essential part of promoting security. It is commonly believed that this kind of intervention can help to win 'hearts and minds' in a context where military force alone is increasingly recognised as ineffective. But we need to take local power dynamics seriously, rather than simply assuming them away. Particularly where it is poorly directed and poorly monitored, aid can reinforce vested interests in continued conflict. It can reinforce government corruption and make rebels look attractive by comparison. And it can also help to fund rebel groups. The same goes for all the resources associated with resupplying international troops. Some of the scepticism about aid in civil and regional wars needs to be taken more seriously in the context of wars involving Western powers. When victory proves elusive (as now in Afghanistan), those who have advocated war (or war-plus-aid) on such terrain should not be allowed to turn around and claim that unforeseen corruption and other unanticipated 'problems of implementation' have unfortunately derailed their good intentions.[20]

Considerable outrage, for example, has recently been expressed in the West at Pakistan's 'double game' in relation to the 'war on terror' – and in some ways this outrage is understandable. But why are we so surprised that Pakistan – and various actors within it – are looking after their own interests? How long are Western politicians in particular going to go on being surprised that other people do not think exactly as they do? This would seem to be imperialism's Achilles' heel: that it imperiously assumes others will follow its lead. It should hardly need stating that you cannot abolish other people's wills and agendas simply by declaring that your own agenda is paramount. Using money to persuade the reluctant has its own problems, not least the perverse incentives to keep a conflict going.

Western governments have a strong preference – evident in the 'war on terror' and earlier, during the Cold War – for fighting wars within poor countries (rather than on their own territories) and for using local troops as much as possible. Given this, in practice the 'aims', even in these wars, will largely be defined locally. In fact, just as the aims in a civil war may often be determined by local actors within a weak state, so, too, the aims in a global war are likely to be powerfully shaped by local actors. Assuming that Western governments *desire* to eliminate the enemy (an assumption that has itself been questioned here), these governments' *ability* to do so is limited by two problems operating in tandem. First, Western governments cannot dictate terms to their allies, who may have other priorities and who may, moreover, be more interested in reaping the economic and political benefits of conflict (including international aid) than in bringing it to a close.[21] Secondly, even assuming that these allies desire to win their respective wars, they may be unable to control the behaviour of key elements within their own societies – militia leaders, warlords, traders, even army officers – who may themselves have surprisingly little or no interest in successful counterinsurgency. The 'weak state' in-country is clearly central to this second problem. While there is a growing acknowledgement that the limits to state power have helped to shape civil wars in poor countries, we seem particularly reluctant to acknowledge how much they have also shaped wars in which Western governments have been prominent participants.

In addition to devoting more attention to regional actors, regime 'greed' and local warlords, we should also take very seriously the complex grievances that have infused the violence of combatants and ex-combatants. Again, this means listening. Such is the dominance today of a numerically oriented 'political science' that we are in danger of equating objectivity with algebra, while listening is sometimes tarred with the brush of being 'unscientific'. Paul Collier has gone so far as to argue that there is no point in asking rebels about the reasons for their rebellion, since they will always seek to present themselves as altruistic and ideologically driven.[22] He is certainly right that humans have a tendency to varnish the truth;[23] but the sincerity of rebels – and, importantly, of other relevant actors – can always be tested by comparing words with actions and by soliciting a range of interpretations of war, most notably the interpretations of civilians. The point is to talk rather than to denigrate talking.

Without an understanding of when and why rebel groups are found to be useful or even necessary, it is almost impossible to think of ways of rendering these groups *unnecessary*. In other words, these groups are difficult or impossible to counter when we are blind to the many functions (finding security, excitement, self-respect in the face of repeated foreign invasion and occupation, and so on) that they may serve. Labelling such groups 'evil' stands in the way of this, since evil cannot reasonably be seen as serving a function. When we are blind to the functions of war (and the functions of rebel groups), this can feed into policies – especially aid policies – that end up making the situation worse.

Meanwhile, the victims of violence are typically made to feel ashamed. If we assume that the world is, in some sense, fair and just, then guilt may be widely inferred from punishment. At the same time, those orchestrating (and benefiting from) war tend to escape both shame and punishment.

In the West, we have been subjected to the politics of the bowling-alley: no sooner has one enemy been toppled than another pops up in its place; and if the original target stubbornly refuses to fall, another is lined up just in case. In these noisy and scary circumstances, the only way to avoid a state of chronic, permanent and anxious confusion, perhaps, is to mimic the short-term memory of TV news, forgetting the last enemy as soon as a new one comes to prominence.

At the moment, wars seem to be treated like fashions – the hope is that we will adopt them on a whim, and that when we discard them, we will buy another one. As one surprisingly frank advertising campaign in London's Selfridges store put it: 'You want it, you buy it, you forget it.' Perhaps aware of the opportunities created by this kind of serial amnesia, President George W. Bush's secretary of defence, Donald Rumsfeld, once observed that many journalists had 'the attention span of gnats'.[24]

Most of the evidence suggests that our endless wars, while wreaking massive destruction overseas, do not even make us safer.[25] But, as with the failed promises of consumerism, this is not necessarily a problem. After all, it creates more demand. All that is necessary for this dysfunctional system to function smoothly is that we should forget just how badly the last 'solution' worked, so that we can embrace the next one.[26] But can we somehow lengthen – and deepen – our own attention span? Can we rein in our sense of confusion and begin to comprehend the seemingly endless succession of home-made wars-for-peace in which the enemy *du jour* succeeds its predecessor with indecent and mystifying haste? Can we somehow understand – and even resist – the official definitions of who it is that we are supposed to be fighting at any particular moment? Can we begin to address the systematic impunity arising from simplistic definitions of an 'evil enemy'? And can we do a better job of protecting 'illegitimate civilians' from the pernicious inter-action of local and global definitions of the 'enemy'? These tasks are surely not beyond us. Setting aside our preconceptions about the nature of war – and the primacy of winning – would seem to be a good start.

Endnotes

Introduction

1. The attack was on Saama, near Tongo.
2. Human Rights Watch (2003: 31–2).
3. See also an autobiographical account in Beah (2007).
4. See, for example, IRIN/OCHA (2000).
5. The rebel Revolutionary United Front's initial hostility towards local chiefs and government officials quickly gave way to more indiscriminate attacks on civilians.
6. Compare Nordstrom (1999; 2004).
7. International Rescue Committee (2008).
8. Richani (2007: 403).
9. See also Menkhaus (2004).
10. See, for example, ibid.
11. See, notably, Suhrke and Berdal (2011). An interesting related discussion is Rodgers (2006).
12. See, for example, Sheehan (1990); Bilton and Sim (1993).
13. Kiernan (2002: 16).
14. ibid.: 23.
15. ibid.; see also Shawcross (1980).
16. Peceny and Stanley (2010).
17. Drury, Ballinger and Shipman (2010); Bergen and Cruickshank (2007).
18. BBC2, *Afghanistan: War Without End* (22 June 2011).
19. See, for example, Kaplan (1994).
20. See, particularly, Kalyvas (2004).
21. Kaplan (1994).
22. Campbell (2002: 32).
23. *Daily Telegraph*, 16 December 1995. In fairness, the text of the advertisement was actually more informative than most.
24. Melvern (2001).
25. Arendt (1971).
26. Kalyvas (2004).
27. We may note that this was a state where elite economic interests have been accommodated.

Chapter 1: Resource Wars

1. A more detailed account can be found in Keen (2005a).
2. Catholic Relief Services (1995).
3. Taylor's motives also included hostility to a Sierra Leonean government which provided a base for West African 'peacekeepers' who were fighting Taylor's Liberia. See Keen (2005a).
4. One study, which looked at variations across different units within the rebel RUF and the civil defence forces, has suggested that where armed groups rely on material incentives to recruit, and where there is weak disciplinary action, armed groups are likely to be particularly abusive. See Humphreys and Weinstein (2006).
5. Keen (2005a); Gberie (1997; 2005); Peters (2006; 2011).
6. For example, Khobe (1998); Gberie (1997).
7. Keen (2005a: 209). Cf. also Kaldor (2007: 57) on Bosnia-Herzegovina: '... the mafia economy was built into the conduct of warfare, creating a self-sustaining logic to the war both to maintain lucrative sources of income and to protect criminals from legal processes which might come into effect in peacetime'.
8. See, for example, Shawcross (1996).
9. Keen (2005a).
10. Kabbah (2003).
11. Hirsch (2001: 57).
12. UN Secretary-General (1997: 7); Fithen (1999); Bangura (1997: 239).
13. Although army discontent was clearly rising in early 1997, Kabbah's government reportedly turned down a plan by Executive Outcomes to provide a 500-man anti-riot force together with two South Africans based at military headquarters in Freetown, whose job would be to warn of any coup plots (Pech and Hassan, 1997).
14. Sierra Leone Police Force (1998: 12); see also Khobe (1998: 19).
15. Gberie (1997: 150). Some reports said more than 5,000 RUF fighters quickly arrived in Freetown. Others put it at 2,000 (Hirsch, 2001: 120).
16. *For Di People* newspaper, cited in Gberie (1997: 150).
17. Peters (2006; 2011).
18. Relief and Rehabilitation Committee (2000: 7).
19. Rupert (1999); Article 19 and Forum of Conscience (2000: 10); *Africa Confidential*, 22 January 1999; field research in Sierra Leone, 1995.
20. Panel of Experts (2000: para 248); see also International Crisis Group (2001).
21. See Adebajo (2002).
22. Richards (2001: 45–46).
23. Britain agreed to provide 10,000 self-loading rifles to the government army (Norton-Taylor and McGreal, 2000). Some British arms ended up with the West Side Boys; some children in the Sierra Leone army were carrying British-given arms (Renton, 2000).
24. Collier (2009).
25. See, for example, Albrecht and Jackson (2009); Keen (2005a).
26. Keen (2005a).
27. De Waal (2009).
28. De Beers executive director Gary Ralfe spelled out the logic in 1997: 'UNITA ... has over the recent few years been responsible for most of the production in Angola. One of the essential jobs that we at De Beers carry out worldwide is to ensure that diamonds coming onto the markets do not threaten the overall price structure and therefore although we have no direct relationship with UNITA, there is no doubt that we buy many of those diamonds that emanate from the UNITA-held areas in Angola, second-hand on the markets of Antwerp and Tel Aviv' (Le Billon, 2001a: 75–6). When rebel leader Jonas Savimbi was killed in 2002 and a ceasefire was

agreed, companies holding diamond concessions in Angola saw their value fall, suggesting that the market saw this peace as bad news. A key reason seems to have been that UN sanctions had forced UNITA to do diamond deals that were very favourable to the buyers (Guidolin and Le Ferrara, 2005/2006: 1–22).

29. On this, see particularly Global Witness (2003).
30. Panel of Experts (2000).
31. Neil Cooper (2002); also Pugh and Cooper (2004); Malone and Nitzschke (2005).
32. Keen (1998); Kaldor (2007).
33. Astill (2002); Panel of Experts (2001; 2002).
34. Shawcross (1996).
35. Le Billon (2001a).
36. Davis (1988).
37. Stoll (1992: 103).
38. Dolan (2009).
39. Remarks by Anatol Lieven, in Middle East Policy Council (2005); Lieven (1999); Kovalev (1997).
40. Stewart, Brown and Langer (2008: 295).
41. Bacik and Balamir Coskun (2011: 254).
42. Bacik and Balamir Coskun (2011: 257).
43. Keen (2008).
44. International Crisis Group (2003: 19).
45. International Crisis Group (2004).
46. De Waal (2005).
47. Keen (2008).
48. Keen (2008); see also Baas (2012).
49. Keen (2008).
50. Panel of Experts (2001; 2002).
51. Panel of Experts (2001: para 180).
52. ibid.
53. ibid.
54. Tangri and Mwenda (2003).
55. Panel of Experts (2001).
56. Astill (2002); see also Panel of Experts (2002).
57. Panel of Experts (2001, para 130).
58. ibid.: para 114.
59. An uneven line from Pweto to Mbandaka.
60. Panel of Experts (2001).
61. Panel of Experts (2002: paras 65–66).
62. ibid.: para 66.
63. ibid.: para 68. For a discussion of Congolese soldiers' reluctance to confront the genocidaires groups, see, for example, Autesserre (2007).
64. Behrend (1998). Some Acholi joined the rebel Ugandan People's Democratic Army, which later gave way to rebels known as Holy Spirit Movement and the Lord's Resistance Army.
65. Dolan (2009: 54).
66. See discussion in Dolan (2009). Also Beber and Blattman (2011).
67. Dolan (2009).
68. Dowden (2010).
69. Mwenda (2010: 48).
70. ibid.: 52.
71. ibid.: 57.
72. Schomerus (forthcoming).

73. ibid.
74. ibid.
75. For example, Spencer (2008); Rajasingham-Senanayake (1999).
76. As Mats Berdal (2003) has pointed out, a faction's interest in economic resources may be related to the need to reward and sustain its own followers; see also Giustozzi (2009).
77. See, for example, Rajasingham-Senanayake (1999).
78. Wikileaks, available in www.guardian.co.uk/world/us-embassy-cables-documents/ 108763, 18 May 2007.
79. Rajasingham-Senanayake (1999).
80. Wikileaks, in www.guardian.co.uk/world/us-embassy-cables-documents/108763), 18 May 2007 (information is attributed by the US embassy to 'informants', including 'a US-based NGO'). See also Rajasingham-Senanayake (1999).
81. Beeson (2008).
82. Klein (2003).
83. Nixon (2004).
84. McCulloch (2003).
85. McCulloch (2003).
86. Beeson, Bellamy and Hughes (2006).
87. Human Rights Watch (2006: 1).
88. ibid.; see also McCulloch (2003).
89. International Crisis Group (2011a: 29).

Chapter 2: Aiding Resource Wars?

1. Collier's work did help to put economic agendas on international radar screens. The contributions by Collier and his fellow Oxford University researcher Anke Hoeffler (for example, Collier and Hoeffler, 1999) came in the context of a large body of qualitative work on the political economy of war (see, for example, Duffield, 1994b; Ellis, 1995; Kaldor, 2007; Reno, 1995; de Waal, 1997). But this body of qualitative work was largely ignored (an exception being my own work on Sudan, cited in Collier, 1995). Collier and Hoeffler produced a set of numbers that showed (or at least seemed to show) that civil wars have been driven, in large part, by rebel 'greed'. They found a number of proxies for 'greed' and for 'grievance' and produced evidence that the former were much more closely associated with outbreaks of civil war. The technical problems with this work have spawned a large number of criticisms. One problem is the way 'greed' and 'grievance' were measured. This kind of work involves finding something you can measure that will serve as a 'proxy' for something – like 'greed' or grievance' – that you cannot directly measure. While this process has an air of science and objectivity about it, a great deal hinges on how the 'proxies' are chosen and assigned. In this case, proxies were assigned to 'greed' and 'grievance' in a rather arbitrary way. For example, low literacy levels were taken to be a proxy for 'greed' (on the logic that there would be a lot of young people with few economic alternatives to looting); but we know that low literacy has also generated significant grievances. If we switched the allocation, it would point to the importance of grievance not greed. Greed and grievance are often hard to separate, with each fuelling the other (see, for example, Keen, 2008). Even looting, easily labelled as 'greed', may stem from very different motivations. There are differences, for example, between looting rebel supporters, looting the rich, and looting the general population (Bakonyi, 2010). There are also major political problems with the Collier/Hoeffler approach. In particular, their interpretation of 'greed' analysis focused almost exclusively on rebel groups; dangerously pushed aside here were all the economic agendas that have been associated with counterinsurgencies.

Meanwhile, the grievances that have informed both rebel and government violence also went missing. Particularly in his recent work, Collier also links civil war prevention to a strong counterinsurgency (preferably with foreign support) (Collier, 2007; 2009) and he tends to delegitimise rebellion, since his emphasis on rebel greed implies that insurgents are self-interested 'rebels without a cause' (see Duffield, 2001). On a more general bias towards the sceptical analysis of insurgencies rather than counterinsurgencies, see Berman (1976). The unfortunate thing about this form of myopia was that it matched rather precisely the biases in many previous misunderstandings and interventions: a blind eye to governmental abuses and a blind eye to the grievances informing abuses on both sides. In fact, it can plausibly be argued that the politically convenient nature of the Collier/Hoeffler approach contributed powerfully to its popularity in policy circles. Ross (2004) finds that 'lootable' resources (like alluvial diamonds) are conducive to non-separatist wars in which government soldiers engage in predation as well as rebels.

2. See, for example, UNDP (1995: 3).
3. See, for example, Cole (1995: 17); Allen (1995: 102–3).
4. Compare Chari and Verdery (2009).
5. Sesay (1995: 165–182, 185–6); Keen (2005a).
6. Bank of Sierra Leone (1995: 68).
7. Bradbury (1995: 32); Fyle (1994).
8. Compare Edkins (1996) on famine discourses that marginalise violence.
9. For example, Bradbury (1995).
10. Kandeh (1996: 397).
11. Keen (2008: 189).
12. For pioneering work on the beneficiaries of famine, see Rangasami (1985).
13. Karim et al. (1996).
14. Vlassenroot and Raeymaekers (2009).
15. See Marriage (2006b).
16. Emizet (2000); Stockton (1998).
17. Emizet (2000: 183).
18. Panel of Experts (2001: para 138).
19. ibid.: para 188. Rwanda and Uganda were not the only acquisitive actors in the region. For example, Zimbabwe's military cooperation with the former DRC government had been encouraged by the granting of mining concessions (in Katanga and Kasai regions) to Zimbabwean companies (Panel of Experts, 2001).
20. Tangri and Mwenda (2003: 1).
21. Malone and Nitzschke (2005).
22. Autesserre (2007: 427).
23. Mamdani (2007); see also Neil Cooper (2002) on the blind spots of the international community in relation to the DRC.
24. See, for example, Reeves (2009).
25. Stockton (2003).
26. ibid.: 21.
27. Marriage (2006b).
28. Many aid workers have suggested that the international community took inadequate steps to break down the command and control of warlords in the DRC. As in other contexts like Afghanistan, whatever leverage the international community has in relation to warlords will be hard to bring to bear without some degree of unity.
29. Autesserre (2007); see also Group of Experts (2009).
30. International Crisis Group (2006a: 25–6).
31. Tangri and Mwenda (2003).
32. Dolan (2009).
33. ibid.: 231.

34. ibid.: 243.
35. Internal Displacement Monitoring Centre (2008).
36. Berdal (2003).
37. See also, for example, Guáqueta (2007).
38. Gutiérrez Sanin (2008); Richani (2007).
39. Gutiérrez Sanin (2008).
40. Theidon (2009); Richani (2007).
41. See, for example, Fajardo (2003); see also Restrepo and Spagat (2005).
42. Theidon (2009).
43. Restrepo and Spagat (2005).
44. Carlton (1994: 285) notes: 'Just as the parliamentarians vented their frustrations on Irish prisoners so the royalists increasingly went in for plunder. For them – unlike the roundheads – it grew into a necessity, with the decline of their supply lines: unable to control plunder, the royalists lost the first civil war.'
45. See, particularly, Neil Cooper (2002); also Pugh and Cooper (2004).
46. Anderson (1999).

Chapter 3: Vietnam: Useful enemies and useless allies

1. Corson (1968: 97). Provincial and village forces – expanded from 1967 – also responded slowly or not at all to reports of Communist activity (D. Hunt, 2010).
2. Much of this more recent literature emerged from the study of Africa.
3. Corson (1968: 207).
4. ibid.: 208–9.
5. See, for example, Shawcross (1980: 259).
6. Corson (1968: 109).
7. ibid.: 97–8.
8. Sheehan (1990: 510). This stance earned the colonel a reputation in some quarters as a Communist agent. But Sheehan comments: 'Chinh was too cruel to the peasantry, targeting hamlets for air strikes and shelling them with point-detonating ammunition that did blow up houses and blast away people, to have been a genuine Communist sympathizer.'
9. ibid.
10. Kalyvas (2004: 132).
11. ibid.
12. D. Hunt (2010).
13. Sheehan (1990: 542).
14. Lewy, quoted in D. Hunt (2010: 39).
15. Corson (1968: 68–9).
16. D. Hunt (2010).
17. ibid.: 38.
18. Corson (1968).
19. See, for example, Tilman (1966); Barakat, Deely and Zyck (2010).
20. Vann worked first as a 'pacification representative' of the US Agency for International Development (USAID) in Hau Nghia province (which had largely been ceded to the Viet Cong) and from the end of 1966 as head of USAID's pacification programme in the districts surrounding Saigon.
21. Sheehan (1990); Kalyvas (2004; 2006).
22. Bilton and Sim (1993).
23. Kalyvas (2004); Peceny and Stanley (2010). It is true that, under particular conditions, indiscriminate violence may have some effect in 'pacifying' a population. In Guatemala's civil war, for example, rebel groups were often unable to provide protection to civilians. So in this case the vicious and often indiscriminate

counterinsurgency produced a relatively weak incentive for civilians to defect to the rebels. However, in most cases rebels can offer at least some degree of protection and, in these circumstances, the counterproductive effects of indiscriminate counterinsurgency are likely to be very strong. On these dynamics, see Kalyvas (2004; 2006).

24. Sheehan (1990).
25. Corson (1968: 278).
26. Sheehan (1990: 512); see also Race (1972).
27. Sheehan (1990).
28. Race (1972: 199–200). The pattern of recruitment into government jobs also ensured that officials were drawn from social elements that were least able to empathise with the rural population (Race, 1973).
29. Corson (1968).
30. D. Hunt (2010: 36).
31. Race (1972).
32. Corson (1968).
33. Sheehan (1990).
34. Corson (1968).
35. ibid.: 124.
36. Sheehan (1990).
37. See, for example, Sheehan (1990).
38. Race (1972).
39. Corson (1968: 160).
40. Lewy, quoted in D. Hunt (2010: 42–3).
41. Sheehan (1990: 524).
42. ibid.
43. R. Hunt (1995: 49).
44. D. Hunt (2010: 50).
45. ibid.
46. ibid.: 49–50.
47. Sheehan (1990: 515).
48. Corson (1968).
49. ibid.: 126.
50. ibid.: 174.
51. ibid.
52. Sheehan (1990).
53. D. Hunt (2010).
54. Sheehan (1990).
55. ibid.
56. Corson (1968: 102). This was a 'feudal' characteristic of many weak states, from Sierra Leone in the present age back to pre-Revolutionary France.
57. D. Hunt (2010).
58. Corson (1968).
59. D. Hunt (2010); see also Scott (2011).
60. Sheehan (1990: 510).
61. ibid.
62. D. Hunt (2010).
63. Corson (1968).
64. D. Hunt (2010: 36).
65. Corson (1968: 71).
66. D. Hunt (2010).
67. Corson (1968: 125).
68. ibid.: 216.

69. ibid.: 126.
70. ibid.: 216.
71. Sheehan (1990).
72. D. Hunt (2010).
73. Sheehan (1990); Gelb and Betts (1979).
74. Corson (1968: 117).
75. Trullinger (1994: 150–6).
76. See, for example, Trullinger (1994: 98).
77. ibid.: 163.
78. Barakat, Deely and Zyck (2010).
79. Corson (1968).
80. D. Hunt (2010).
81. D. Hunt (2010: 52).
82. Corson (1968: 101–3).
83. Race (1973).
84. Sheehan (1990).
85. Corson (1968: 104).
86. ibid.: 285.
87. Race (1973: 231).
88. ibid.: 232.
89. Gelb and Betts (1979: 1).
90. Corson (1968); see also Shawcross (1980).
91. Arendt (1971).
92. Shawcross (1980).
93. Arendt (1971).
94. ibid.
95. Corson (1968: 81).
96. Gelb and Betts (1979: 18).
97. Corson (1968: 81).
98. Arendt (1971).
99. Corson (1968).
100. ibid.
101. See, for example, Race (1973).
102. In USAID, a lot of time and energy was spent in preparing reports showing visible progress.
103. D. Hunt (2010: 38); see also Faludi (1999).
104. See, notably, Faludi (1999: 331–2) and Bourke (1999: 217).
105. Sheehan (1990: 510–11).
106. Corson (1968: 75, 80).
107. Shawcross (1980: 210).
108. Corson (1968: 80).
109. Lifton (1974: 350).
110. ibid.: 351; also Shawcross (1980).

Chapter 4: Afghanistan

1. Kilcullen (2009: 43).
2. ibid.: 44.
3. Egnell (2011); Kilcullen (2009). See also remarks by Michael Scheuer, in Middle East Policy Council (2005).
4. Kilcullen (2009).
5. ibid.
6. ibid.

7. Egnell (2011).
8. Ledwidge (2011: 105).
9. International Crisis Group (2011c: 2).
10. Kilcullen (2009: 49).
11. Rubin (2007: 65).
12. Rashid (2007).
13. For example, Borger (2011).
14. See, for example, Barakat and Zyck (2010).
15. The US has generally opposed negotiation with senior Taliban leaders, but has increasingly favoured some 'reintegration' of lower-level fighters.
16. Rubin (2007).
17. Jonathan Goodhand (2008: 171); see also Johnson and Mason (2007: 71–89).
18. Johnson and Mason (2007: 85); see also Bhatia, Lanigan and Wilkinson (2004).
19. On the presence of foreign troops as a reason for joining the Taliban, see Gordon (2011) and Lafraie (2009).
20. Goodhand and Sedra (2010).
21. See, for example, Rubin (2007); Human Rights Watch (2004).
22. See, for example, Gordon (2010).
23. Egnell (2011).
24. Egnell (2011); Farrell and Gordon (2009); Bird and Marshall (2011); Ledwidge (2011).
25. Galbraith (2010); Chaudhuri and Farrell (2011).
26. Chaudhuri and Farrell (2011); see also Woodward (2010).
27. See, for example, Hastings (2010).
28. Johnson and Mason (2007: 87).
29. Flynn, Pottinger and Batchelor (2010: 8).
30. Kilcullen (2009).
31. See, for example, Gordon (2011); Goodhand (2008).
32. Gordon (2011).
33. Rubin (2007).
34. Gordon (2011); Ghufran (2009).
35. See, for example, Simon and Stevenson (2009); Lieven (2009); Ghufran (2009).
36. Ghufran (2009).
37. Woodward (2010: 166). The increase in military action against the Taliban has displaced insurgents into other parts of Afghanistan, notably the north (Chaudhuri and Farrell, 2011).
38. Simon and Stevenson (2009: 60).
39. Chaudhuri and Farrell (2011); see also Rubin (2007).
40. Chaudhuri and Farrell (2011).
41. See, for example, BBC2, *Secret Pakistan: Double Cross* (26 October 2011).
42. Chaudhuri and Farrell (2011: 291).
43. See, for example, Rubin (2000: 1794).
44. Chaudhuri and Farrell (2011); see also remarks by Michael Scheuer, in Middle East Policy Council (2005).
45. In addition, public opinion in Pakistan makes it hard for the state authorities to turn against the Afghan Taliban. In these unpromising circumstances, Chaudhuri and Farrell (2011: 296) refer to 'a strategy of hope in which key strategic impediments are implausibly expected to fall in line with ISAF [International Security Assistance Force] campaign objectives.' See also Rubin (2007).
46. Rubin (2007: 69).
47. A useful overview is Corn (2010).
48. Wilder (2009). See also Fishstein and Wilder (2011).
49. Anderson (1999).

50. Keen (2008; 2005a); Woodward (1995); Joint Evaluation of Emergency Assistance to Rwanda (1996); Stockton (2003).
51. Goodhand and Sedra (2010: S79).
52. Kepel (2002).
53. See, for example, Johnson and Mason (2007).
54. Giustozzi (2009).
55. Rubin (2000).
56. Giustozzi (2009: 80–1).
57. ibid.
58. Rubin (2000: 1794).
59. Giustozzi (2009).
60. Giustozzi (2007: 7).
61. International Crisis Group (2011c).
62. Chaudhuri and Farrell (2011); Barakat and Zyck (2010); International Crisis Group (2010c). Tajik over-representation in the army reflects, in part, a reluctance of many Pashtuns to serve in the army. Tajik over-representation among officers includes the (largely Pashtun) south (International Crisis Group, 2010c). See also Lieven (2009). Moreover, a high percentage of those Afghan army officers who *are* Pashtun actually served with the Moscow-backed Afghan Communist forces fighting the *mujahadeen*, a further source of tension (Burke, 2011).
63. International Crisis Group (2010c: 2).
64. Kilcullen (2009).
65. International Crisis Group (2011c).
66. Goodhand and Sedra (2010).
67. Chaudhuri and Farrell (2011).
68. ibid.: 278.
69. Rubin (2007: 67).
70. Bird and Marshall (2011).
71. See, for example, Goodhand and Sedra (2010); Donini (2010).
72. Goodhand (2008); Giustozzi (2009).
73. Goodhand and Sedra (2010); Forsberg (2010).
74. Gordon (2011); see also Bhatia (2007).
75. Rubin (2007: 66).
76. Chayes (2003).
77. The administration in Kabul controls the appointment of provincial governors and district officials. Cf. Reno (1995).
78. Kilcullen (2009).
79. Scott (2011); Giustozzi (2009); Goodhand (2008).
80. Rashid (2007: 19). The largest ethnic group, the Pashtuns, tended to be marginalised (notwithstanding the installation of a Pashtun president).
81. Forsberg (2010).
82. International Crisis Group (2010c: 6).
83. Gordon (2011); Goodhand (2008).
84. Thompson (2010).
85. Wilder (2009); see also Rubin (2007).
86. Wilder (2009); Thompson (2010).
87. Wilder (2009).
88. Marlowe (2010).
89. Gordon (2011).
90. Wilder (2009). Multiple sub-contracting creates lots of profits all the way along the chain (see Bird and Marshall, 2011).
91. Wilder (2009); International Crisis Group (2011c).
92. Thompson (2010); Kilcullen (2009).

93. Kilcullen (2009); Rubin (2007).
94. Goodhand and Sedra (2010).
95. Rubin (2007: 76).
96. Forsberg (2010).
97. ibid.: 65.
98. ibid.: 7. Even among those sub-tribes that have provided the dominant political and commercial networks, large elements remain excluded.
99. ibid.
100. ibid.
101. ibid.: 27.
102. Police chiefs have also complained that their own units often report not to them but to local power figures. Commanders have sometimes attached their men to several police units at once, so the men can draw multiple salaries (ibid.).
103. ibid.
104. ibid.: 7.
105. ibid.; see also Chaudhuri and Farrell (2011).
106. Forsberg (2010).
107. ibid.: 23.
108. See, for example, Andreas (2004).
109. Forsberg (2010: 51).
110. Bird and Marshall (2011). 'Iraqis often used American troops to settle family disputes, tribal rivalries, or personal vendettas' (Hedges and al-Arian, 2008: 59).
111. Reno (1995); see also Keen (2005a; 2008).
112. Forsberg (2010: 64).
113. ibid.
114. International Crisis Group (2011c).
115. Theros and Rosen (2011).
116. Tierney (2010: 37).
117. ibid.: 38.
118. Riechmann and Lardner (2011), citing interviews and US task force documents obtained by Associated Press.
119. Wilder (2009).
120. Galbraith (2010).
121. Tierney (2010: 34–5).
122. For example, Watan Risk Management (ibid.).
123. ibid.; Roston (2009).
124. Tierney (2010: 34).
125. Roston (2009).
126. Haji Fata, chief executive of Mirzada Transport Company in Kabul, quoted in Green and Bokhari (2009).
127. Tierney (2010: 35).
128. Wilder (2009).
129. Thompson (2010: 13).
130. ibid.; see also Oxfam (2011); Goodhand and Sedra (2010).
131. Goodhand and Sedra (2010).
132. International Crisis Group (2011c); Johnson and Mason (2007).
133. Goodhand and Sedra (2010).
134. See, for example, ibid.
135. Donini (2010: 3).
136. ibid.
137. See, for example, Watson Institute for International Affairs (2004).
138. Donini (2010: 3).
139. See, for example, Stockton (2003); Macrae and Leader (2000).

140. Goodhand and Sedra (2010); Gordon (2010); Dorronsoro (2009).
141. Johnson and Mason (2007: 87).
142. See, for example, Mirsky (2000).
143. Egnell (2011).
144. Gordon (2011).
145. Egnell (2011: 305).
146. Wilder (2009).
147. ibid.; see also Thompson (2010).
148. Goodhand and Sedra (2010).
149. Rubin (2007: 71).
150. Donini (2010); Thompson (2010).
151. Donini (2010); Polman (2010).
152. Donini (2010: 4).
153. See, for example, Rieff (2010).
154. Egnell (2011: 302).
155. BBC2, *Afghanistan: War Without End* (22 June 2011). See also Johnson and Mason (2007) on the lack of development and reconstruction in Paktika province.
156. Gordon (2010).
157. ibid.
158. Goodhand and Sedra (2010: S95).
159. ibid.; see also Thompson (2010). Some progress has been made in extension of medical services and education (personal communication, Stuart Gordon).
160. Personal communication, Stuart Gordon.
161. See, for example, Dilanian (2009).
162. See, for example, Dilanian (2009).
163. Thompson (2010); Goodhand and Sedra (2010). 'Priority should be given to assessing stabilisation effects of projects, rather than assuming impact based on amounts of money spent or the number of projects implemented ... The pressure to spend too much money too quickly ... is having many harmful and destabilising effects' (Thompson, 2010: 3–4). See also Theros and Rosen (2011).
164. For one critique, see Oxfam (2011).
165. ibid.: 10.
166. Corson (1968: 109).
167. Galbraith (2010).
168. In this connection, Forsberg mentions the militias of Abdul Razak in Spin Boldak district (Forsberg, 2010).
169. Theros and Rosen (2011).
170. B. Woodward (2002: 295).
171. ibid.: 137.
172. On the history of this assumption (and its many pitfalls), going back to the US intervention in the Philippines in 1898–1902, see particularly Barakat, Deely and Zyck (2010).
173. Chaudhuri and Farrell (2011: 287).
174. Gordon (2011: 53).
175. See Fawaz Gerges' excellent book *The Far Enemy* (2005); see also Gerges (1999); Human Security Report Project (2008); Said (2011); Juergensmeyer (2002).
176. BBC2, *Afghanistan: War Without End* (22 June 2011).
177. Cf. de Waal (2009).

Chapter 5: The Political Functions of War

1. On the Cold War period, see Chomsky (2006).
2. Peter Applebome, 'Sense of pride outweighs fears of war', *New York Times*, 24 February 1991, quoted in Marvin and Ingle (1999: 236).

3. Marvin and Ingle (1999).
4. Marvin and Ingle (1996: 772).
5. Kahn (2008: 43).
6. ibid.: 148–9.
7. Slim (2007: 131–2).
8. ibid.
9. Mansfield and Snyder (1995: 34).
10. On the role of democratisation, see Mansfield and Snyder (2005).
11. Schivelbusch (2001: 205).
12. Whalen (1984).
13. Lerner (2003: 48).
14. ibid.
15. ibid.: 45.
16. ibid.: 48.
17. ibid.
18. Whalen (1984: 17).
19. See, for example, Bartov (2000).
20. Keen (2008).
21. See, for example, de Waal (2007); Keen (2008).
22. See, for example, Metz (2007).
23. Duffield (1994a).
24. Baas (2012).
25. ibid.: 58.
26. ibid.: 65.
27. ibid.
28. International Crisis Group (2004).
29. De Waal (2007).
30. On the paradox of 'failure' and stability, see particularly ibid.
31. ibid.; see also Keen (2008). On the political functions of anti-Western rhetoric in much of the Arab world, see Mansfield and Snyder (2005).
32. See, for example, Moro (2008); de Waal (2009).
33. Srinisivan (2010). In the 2008 census that was used for the 2010 elections '… most of the estimated 2.6 million internally displaced (IDPs) living in camps, as well as people from groups hostile to the NCP [ruling National Congress Party] living in "insecure" neighbourhoods of cities and the population of rebel-controlled areas were not counted' (International Crisis Group, 2010a: 1).
34. De Waal (2009).
35. On the numbers who moved and the varying estimates, see Emizet (2000).
36. Acemoglu, Robinson and Verdier (2004).
37. For more on this argument more generally, see Mansfield and Snyder (1995; 2005); Snyder and Mansfield (1995).
38. African Rights (1994).
39. Prunier (1995: 101–2).
40. ibid.: 108–9.
41. Mamdani (2001: 210).
42. See, for example, African Rights (1994); Bartov (2000).
43. Human Rights Watch/International Federation of Human Rights (1999: 61).
44. ibid.
45. Hara (2002).
46. See, for example, World Bank (2004).
47. See, for example, Power (2002).
48. See Taylor (1999).

49. Kaldor (2007: 44), quoting Živanović, whom she describes as 'an independent-minded liberal'.
50. ibid.: 59.
51. ibid.
52. Turton (1997); Ignatieff (1993).
53. Research in Belgrade, summer 1999; Woodward (1995). Sanctions eased in 1995 but were tightened again in 1998 over Serb abuses in Kosovo.
54. Glenny (1992).
55. In constant 1988 prices.
56. Kaldor (2007: 47).
57. ibid.: 47.
58. ibid.: 48.
59. ibid.
60. ibid.
61. Andreas (2004); Bougarel, Helms and Duijzings (2006).
62. Research in Belgrade, 1999; Woodward (1995).
63. Venugopal (2008).
64. International Crisis Group (2007: 7–8).
65. Venugopal (2009b).
66. ibid.: 35.
67. International Crisis Group (2007: 7–8).
68. Venugopal (2009a).
69. ibid.
70. ibid.
71. ibid.
72. Venugopal (2009b); International Crisis Group (2007).
73. Venugopal (2009b).
74. Spencer (2008).
75. ibid.: 614.
76. ibid.: 619.
77. See, for example, Weissman (2011a).
78. See, for example, University Teachers for Human Rights (2009).
79. ibid.: 58.
80. A UN Panel of Experts noted: 'A number of credible sources have estimated that there could have been as many as 40,000 civilian deaths' (Panel of Experts, 2011: 41).
81. In the DRC, some respondents said politicians fund armed groups in the hope that a continued state of war will delay or prevent the next round of elections (Dolan, 2010).
82. On the use of disorder as a political instrument, see particularly Chabal and Daloz (1999).
83. Russell (1971: 379).
84. ibid.: 379.
85. See, for example, Royle (2004).
86. Russell (1971: 386).
87. T. Hunt (2002).
88. ibid.: 253.
89. Remarks by Michael Scheuer, in Middle East Policy Council (2005: 5). Scheuer added that the same process (sending militants to foreign wars) was probably occurring in Iraq.
90. In South Africa, the energies of potentially disruptive soldiers who had worked for the Apartheid government were partially absorbed by recruitment into mercenary companies fighting on the African continent. While this became illegal from 1998, fines were generally low (Goering, 2004).

91. Peters (2006: 49); see also Amos (2011).
92. This strategy may be complementary to a strategy of divide and rule.
93. Davis (1988: 24).
94. Report of the Commission for Historical Clarification (1999: para 24).
95. ibid.: para 25.
96. ibid.
97. ibid.: para 31.
98. ibid.
99. Guáqueta (2007). Decentralisation may have made this worse (Richani, 2007).
100. Guáqueta (2007).
101. Dolan (2009).
102. Kahn (2008: 176).
103. Mwenda (2010).
104. ibid.: 54.
105. Berman (1976).
106. ibid.: 170.
107. See, notably, Turton (1997).
108. de Waal (2007).

Chapter 6: Wars Within Wars

1. Bradbury (1995: 26).
2. Atkinson et al. (1991: 12).
3. These are well dramatised in Miller (1996); see also Nordstrom (2004).
4. Quoted in Kalyvas (2003: 485). Paul and Demarest (1992: 154) go on to note: 'San Pedro has been moving in the direction of greater democracy, while the Guatemalan government has been moving in the opposite direction. Increasing divergence between the two tendencies, the local and the national, can be seen as a source of the affliction that befell San Pedro.' See also Kabera and Muyanja (1994: 98); Kriger (1992).
5. Weissman (2004); see also Stockton (1998).
6. See, in particular, Byman (2006).
7. See, for example, Barakat, Deely and Zyck (2010).
8. Vaux (2001); Keen (2008).
9. Keen (2008).
10. Martinez (1998).
11. ibid.: 168.
12. See, for example, de Waal (2007).
13. Silverstein (2005). See also Prunier (2005: 138–9).
14. Prendergast and Thomas-Jensen (2009: 213); see also Keen (2008).
15. See, for example, Prunier (2005).
16. For an enlightening analysis, see Flint (2010).
17. Martinez (2006).
18. ibid.
19. *Guardian* (2011).
20. Mackay (2002).
21. Martinez (2006: 153).
22. On this struggle, see Ronin (2002).
23. Adebajo (2011).
24. Martinez (2006).
25. Samatar (2011).
26. Bryden (2011: 1).
27. Samatar (2011).

28. ibid.; see also Menkhaus (2010); Leduc and Neuman (2011).
29. Verhoeven (2009).
30. ibid.
31. Menkhaus (2010).
32. Samatar (2011).
33. International Crisis Group (2011d: 2).
34. Bradbury (2010: 6).
35. Verhoeven (2009).
36. ibid.: 417; see also Bradbury (2010).
37. Menkhaus (2010).
38. Leduc and Neuman (2011).
39. Dempsey (2008: 2); see also International Crisis Group (2008a).
40. Menkahus (2010; 2011).
41. Leduc and Neuman (2011).
42. Menkhaus (2010).
43. ibid.
44. ibid; Leduc and Neuman (2011).
45. Arendt (1979).
46. Menkhaus (2010); Bradbury (2010: 1–24).
47. Bradbury (2010: 12–13).
48. Menkhaus (2010).
49. See, for example, Human Rights Watch (2010b).
50. Allie (2011: 12); Binet (2011).
51. Binet (2011).
52. Bradbury (2010).
53. See discussion in Mirsky (2000).
54. Schomerus (forthcoming).
55. ibid.
56. Mwenda (2010).
57. Rampton and Stauber (2003: 117).
58. Fajardo (2003).
59. See, for example, Sadeh (2001).
60. See, notably, Pieterse (1985).
61. Wyatt (2010).
62. ibid.
63. Baudrillard (1995).
64. Bouillon (2004).
65. Klein (2007).
66. Bouillon (2004).
67. Phillips (2011).
68. ibid.
69. For example, Whitaker (2010).
70. ibid.
71. ibid.
72. ibid.
73. Lacharité (2011: 46–7).
74. ibid. A diplomatic intervention by Qatar in 2007 – and stories appearing on the Qatar-based Al Jazeera television station – helped bring increased attention to the Houthi conflict in Yemen.
75. cf. Bauer (1971); de Waal (1997).
76. Phillips (2011: 99–100).
77. ibid.: 107.
78. ibid.

79. ibid.
80. ibid.: 107.
81. Cohen (2010).
82. Bird and Marshall (2011).
83. Wright (2011).
84. Cohen (2010: 141).
85. Shah (2003).
86. Bird and Marshall (2011); Schmidt (2009).
87. Bird and Marshall (2011); Schmidt (2009).
88. Wright (2011).
89. Rashid (2007: 18).
90. Wright (2011).
91. Fair (2011); Shah (2003); see also Woodward (2010: 3–4).
92. Cohen (2010).
93. Shah (2011).
94. ibid.
95. See, for example, Bird and Marshall (2011).
96. ibid.
97. Oxfam (2011).
98. Fair (2011).
99. Schmitt and Sanger (2010); Fair (2011).
100. Hedman (2009a).
101. ibid.
102. Hedman (2009b: 4).
103. ibid. It has plausibly been argued, for example, that US provision of military assist-
     ance to the Philippines and Indonesia to counter 'terrorism' without tying this to
     security sector reform makes it harder for reformist voices to be heard within
     South East Asian governments (Beeson et al., 2006).
104. This was in 1996 (European Commission) and 1997 (US).
105. Bradbury (2010: 12–13).
106. Anderson (2011).
107. ibid. This is reported by Anderson, but interestingly it is not in the printed version
     of the defence minister's speech.
108. Wikileaks (2007).
109. Anderson (2011); see also Goodhand (2010).
110. Channel 4, *Sri Lanka's Killing Fields* (14 June 2011).
111. Goodhand (2010: S359).
112. Weissman (2011b).
113. Channel 4, *Sri Lanka's Killing Fields* (14 June 2011).

Chapter 7: The Politics of Permanent Emergency

1. Mark Duffield wrote about 'permanent emergencies' in, for example, Duffield
   (1994a); see also Duffield (2001).
2. Liberation Tigers of Tamil Eelam.
3. Weissman (2011a).
4. On this role, see, for example, Goodhand (2010).
5. It had already framed military advances in the east in 2006–07 as 'humanitarian',
   with the aim of 'liberating Tamil civilians' (Goodhand, 2010). On government
   policy in the Vanni in 2008, see, for example, Human Rights Watch (2008).
6. Human Rights Watch (2009b: 19–20).
7. Weissman (2011a: 28).
8. Channel 4, *Sri Lanka's Killing Fields* (14 June 2011).

9. See, for example, Goodhand (2010).
10. Weissman (2011a).
11. ibid.
12. Allie (2011: 1).
13. Shashikumar (2009).
14. Weissman (2011b).
15. MSF reports that it undertook not to release information on service provision. Weissman (2011a).
16. See also Human Rights Watch (2009b).
17. The term Vanni refers to the northern mainland, but not the Jaffna Peninsula.
18. Human Rights Watch (2008: 17).
19. Beeson et al. (2006).
20. ibid.
21. Keen (May 2009).
22. Goodhand (2010).
23. Quoted in ibid.: S346.
24. See, for example, Korf (2006).
25. International Crisis Group (2011b).
26. Anderson (2011).
27. ibid.
28. International Crisis Group (2011b: i).
29. Goodhand (2010); International Crisis Group (2008b).
30. International Crisis Group (2008b: 30).
31. International Crisis Group (2011b: i).
32. Welikala (2008: 237).
33. See also International Crisis Group (2010b).
34. Venugopal (2009b).
35. International Crisis Group (2011b).
36. See, for example, Wood (2009).
37. International Crisis Group (2011b).
38. Wickramatunga (2009).
39. ibid.
40. Anderson (2011: 42).
41. Zur (1998).
42. Schirmer (1999); see also Preti (2002).
43. Schirmer (1999).
44. Briscoe and Rodriguez Pellecer (2010); see also Keen (2003).
45. Keen (2003); Schirmer (1999).
46. Stanley and Holiday (2002); see also Snyder and Jervis (1999).
47. See also Smyth (2005).
48. Schirmer (1999).
49. Even in the absence of outright civil war, certain groups of people may be highly vulnerable to state violence (see, for example, Scheper-Hughes, 1993).
50. Cruz and Diamint (1998: 116).
51. See for example, Dreyfus (1999); Simpson (1994).
52. Cruz and Diamint (1998).
53. Associated Press (2011).
54. See, for example, O'Day (2001).
55. Cruz and Diamint (1998); see also Pachico (2011).
56. Zur (1998: 4).
57. Cruz and Diamint (1998).
58. See, for example, Gutiérrez Sanin (2008); Restrepo and Spagat (2005).
59. Vargas (2010).

60. Richani (2007).
61. ibid.: 412.
62. Human Rights Watch (2010a).
63. ibid.
64. Richani (2007).
65. Fair (2011); Shah (2003).
66. Ibrahim (2009).
67. Fair (2011: 577).
68. ibid.
69. Shah (2003: 38); see also Cruz and Diamint (1998).
70. Shah (2003). This phenomenon has also been observed in Africa – for example, in Sierra Leone (Kandeh, 1996; 1999).
71. Fair (2011).
72. ibid.: 576.
73. Mani (2007).
74. Shah (2011).
75. Bacik and Coskun (2011).
76. ibid.; see also Human Rights Watch (1994).
77. Mater (1999).
78. See, for example, Cam (2006).
79. Tirman (1997).
80. Demir (2005).
81. Akça (2010).
82. Fernandes (2006).
83. Keen (1993).
84. See, for example, McDowall (1997: 438).
85. Bacik and Coskun (2011).
86. ibid.
87. Akça (2010).
88. On this issue more generally, see Mani (2007) and Human Rights Watch (2006).
89. Demir (2005).
90. ibid.: 674.
91. Reza (2007: 1).
92. ibid.
93. ibid.: 543.
94. ibid.
95. Hedges (2009).
96. Armbrust (2011).
97. Goldstone (2011).
98. Karawan (2011); Armbrust (2011).
99. Karawan (2011).
100. Kirkpatrick (2011).
101. See, for example, Kirkpatrick (2011); Goldstone (2011).
102. Bumiller (2011).
103. Armbrust (2011).
104. al-Khalil (1989).
105. ibid.
106. ibid.
107. ibid.: 271.
108. The figure at the start of the war is from al-Khalil (1989: 33); also see Marine Corps Historical Publication (1990).
109. See, for example, Macdonald (2002).
110. Marine Corps Historical Publication (1990).

111. ibid.
112. See, for example, al-Khalil (1989).
113. al-Khalil (1989).
114. See, for example, Keen (1993).
115. Dodge (2009).
116. ibid.
117. This was a decision that was supported by senior British officials, according to the US head of the Coalition Provisional Authority, Paul Bremer (Bowcott, 2010).
118. See, notably, Dodge (2007).
119. al-Marashi and Salama (2008).
120. ibid.: 204.
121. See, for example, Allawi (2007).
122. See, for example, Hashim (2006); Dodge (2009).
123. al-Marashi and Salama (2008: 204); see also US Committee on Foreign Relations, testimony of Dr Toby Dodge (Dodge, 2004).
124. al-Marashi and Salama (2008).
125. Dodge (2009); Allawi (2007); Hashim (2006); Andreas (2004).
126. Dodge (2009: 10).
127. Hashim (2006: 26).
128. See, notably, Dodge (2009).
129. See, for example, Alfoneh (2007).
130. Sahimi (2009). Compare also the anti-Western rhetoric in much of the Arab world.
131. ibid.
132. Alfoneh (2008).
133. Gerami (2003: 268).
134. Those who acted on official encouragement to seize land from white farmers were often referred to as 'war veterans', but most were too young to be actual war veterans. Nevertheless, they were conceived by the government as participants in an ongoing struggle against white colonialism (e.g. Kriger, 1992). Violence of various kinds has offered a 'lifeline' to Mugabe in conditions of economic austerity and political unrest. Work by Teddy Brett shows how economic liberalisation in Zimbabwe helped to set up political pressures which Mugabe then attempted to resolve with a series of dangerous and often violent measures, including not just the redistribution of land to war veterans but also payment of compensation to veterans (which in turn threatened fiscal stability). These projects culminated in Zimbabwe invading the DRC – something that yielded benefits for army officers and key politicians (Brett, 2006).
135. International Crisis Group (2005).
136. Healy (2007).
137. Kibreab (2009).
138. ibid.
139. Kepel (2002: 218).
140. ibid.
141. ibid.
142. ibid.
143. ibid.: 298.
144. ibid.: 298.
145. Hedman (2009b).
146. See, for example, Castells (1998).
147. See, for example, ibid.
148. See, for example, ibid.
149. See, for example, ibid.; Bukkvoll (2008).

150. See, for example, Chledowski (2005).
151. Taylor (1999).
152. Oksana Antonenko, in Bukkvoll (2008).
153. Bukkvoll (2008).
154. See, for example, Soros (2000); Kovalev (2000); Mansfield and Snyder (2005).
155. See, for example, Gentleman and McDonald.
156. Kovalev (2000: 6).
157. ibid.
158. Kovalev (2007).
159. Castells (1998).
160. Mann (2003: 174).
161. Englebert and Tull (2008).
162. Compare de Waal (2009).
163. Compare also Preston (2004) on the potential for peace that may arise when a gulf opens between an acquisitive leadership and a disgruntled following.
164. Atkinson (2011).

Chapter 8: Case Study of a Permanent Emergency: the United States

1. In a study of the 2004 presidential election, Colorado Springs emerged as the most conservative major city in the country, with over 67 per cent of voters choosing conservative candidates (Bay Area Center for Voting Research).
2. Given the growing links with the gaming industry in particular, some have also referred to the military-industrial-entertainment complex. Stahl (2006: 116): 'In the 1990s ... Sega game systems developed simulator software for Lockheed Martin. Lockheed returned the favor by manufacturing chips for Sega game modules.' In the 1990s, the military commissioned modified commercial games as quickly as they could be developed (ibid.). Sony's new PlayStation2 was considered by the Japanese government to be powerful enough to use as an actual missile guidance system, and its export accordingly required a special licence (ibid.).
3. Hossein-zadeh (2007).
4. Perkins and Neumayer (2010).
5. New American Foundation (2008).
6. SIPRI (2011).
7. Hossein-zadeh (2006: 14). This excludes the Social Security Trust Fund from the federal budget.
8. See, notably, Hossein-zadeh (2006).
9. Stahl (2006).
10. Orwell (1949/2009).
11. Vidal (2002: 158).
12. Bacevich (2005: 33).
13. General Douglas MacArthur, 1957, quoted in Gravel and Lauria (2008: 131).
14. George Kennan, May 1965, in Hossein-zadeh (2006: 78).
15. Hossein-zadeh (2006).
16. Principal Deputy Under Secretary of Defense (1992). Also Tyler (1992) – bizarrely, this has passages that were later deleted in the Defense Department document that was declassified fifteen years later.
17. Hartung and Ciarrocca (2003).
18. ibid.
19. Corson (1968).
20. Hartung and Ciarrocca (2003).
21. ibid.
22. Woodward (2010).

23. See, for example, Stratton (2008).
24. Compare Duffield (1994a).
25. For example, Keen (2006). Examining a decline since 1990 in the desire to be recruited into the military, one study noted that this was a problem, in part, because, 'Over time, a shortage of military personnel may result in base closures that may cause economic hardships for their host cities' (Brown and Rana, 2005: 260).
26. See, for example, discussion in Keen (2006).
27. Hossein-zadeh (2006).
28. ibid.: 9.
29. Klein (2007).
30. ibid.: 301.
31. ibid.: 300.
32. Hartung and Ciarrocca (2003).
33. Custers (2010).
34. Chatterjee (2009: x).
35. ibid.: xiii.
36. Klein (2007: 355).
37. Bird and Marshall (2011: 135).
38. International Crisis Group (2011c: 19).
39. See, for example, Shepherd (2008).
40. See, notably, Klein (2007); see also Keen (2006); Barakat, Deely and Zyck (2010).
41. Klein (2007).
42. Hammes (2011).
43. Klein (2007).
44. ibid.
45. ibid.
46. ibid.
47. ibid.
48. A Congressional Research Service report noted in 2008 that there were 450–500 Minuteman III ICBMs in the US (Woolf, 2008). See also Colorado Coalition (2011).
49. SI International was taken over by Serco in December 2008.
50. Booth (2010).
51. Hossein-zadeh (2006).
52. ibid.: 14.
53. Cf. Frank (2004).
54. Scott (2011).
55. ibid.
56. McCrisken (2011).
57. ibid.: 793.
58. The reader can find it on Google images.
59. Project on Defense Alternatives (2011).
60. Conetta (2010: v).
61. ibid.: 1.
62. Goozner (2011).
63. ibid.
64. ibid.
65. ibid.
66. ibid.
67. Hossein-zadeh (2006); Hedges (2009).
68. Hedges (2009).
69. BBC Radio 4, RoboWars, episode 2 (8 February 2010).
70. Simon and Stevenson (2009).
71. Corson (1968: 250). Cf. Lifton (1974: 353–4).

72. Kennedy (1989).
73. ibid.; Hossein-zadeh (2006).
74. For an excellent analysis, see Wade (2008).
75. Hedges (2009: 188).
76. Barnett (2004: 108).
77. ibid.: 5.
78. ibid.: 100–1.
79. ibid.: 115.
80. Woodward (2010: 20).
81. Bacevich (2005).
82. See, for example, Gasparre (2008).
83. Cf. Roy (2004).
84. Barnett (2004: 150).
85. ibid.: 176.
86. ibid.: 173.
87. ibid.: 155.
88. ibid.: 143.
89. ibid.: 124.
90. ibid.: 171.
91. ibid.: 171.
92. ibid.: 169.
93. ibid.: 153–4.
94. ibid.: 154.
95. ibid.: 175. That might sound Machiavellian and even rather far-fetched, but minor provocations have sometimes proved enough for a major response. General Corson, for one, questions the wisdom of ordering 'systematic bombing of North Vietnam on the flimsy pretext of "armed attack"' by 'over-age' North Vietnamese boats against US destroyers in the Tonkin Gulf in 1964 (Corson, 1968: 3). It is doubtful whether these attackers actually fired torpedoes. See also discussion in Mirsky (2000). The scale of a North Vietnamese 'invasion' of South Vietnam was also exaggerated (Corson, 1968).
96. Barnett (2004: 175–6).
97. ibid.: 167.
98. Quoted in Verhoeven (2009: 410).
99. See, for example, Verhoeven (2009).
100. Cooper (2004: 64).
101. ibid.: 65.
102. See also Kagan (2002: 16), who stated that the US 'must live by a double standard'.
103. R. Cooper (2002).
104. Kahn (2008).
105. Hedges (2009).
106. ibid.

Chapter 9: Shame and the Psychological Functions of Violence

1. See, for example, Elizur and Yishay-Krien (2009), Glover (1999) and Zimbardo (2008) on brutalisation, and Browning (1992) and Cramer (2006) on obedience.
2. Gilligan (1999). For another interesting exploration of the links between violence and shame, see Scheff (1994).
3. Girard (1977: 2).
4. Quoted in Gilligan (2003: 1161).
5. Wood (2001).
6. Theidon (2009).

7. ibid.
8. ibid.
9. Fanthorpe, Jay and Kamara (2002: 15–16).
10. Bradbury (1995: 41). The public humiliation and execution of chiefs and imams is also noted by Muana (1997: 79). Cf. Kiernan (1996).
11. Atkinson et al. (1991: 11). Of course, the abuses of the Khmer Rouge were on a different scale. But again, there are echoes here of the Khmer Rouge practice of according significant powers of judgement and accusation to children, who were often seen as immune from the corruption preceding 'Year Zero'. In her work on warfare in early twentieth-century China, Diana Lary (1985: 89) mentions ordinary soldiers' 'lust for revenge against a world in which they had been impotent as civilians, even before they went into the army'.
12. See also Richards (1996).
13. Utas (2005).
14. Keen (2005a).
15. Humphreys and Weinstein (2004: 2).
16. Naturally, one must sometimes allow for an element of exaggeration.
17. Hardin (1993: 81).
18. Corson (1968: 141).
19. Peters (2006: 132).
20. Richards (1996).
21. On this issue, see Hancock (1989); Polman (2010).
22. Keen (2005a); Peters (2011).
23. Keen (2005a).
24. Lord (2000: 15).
25. Coalition to Stop the Use of Child Soldiers (1999: 65–6).
26. Tina Aarvold, personal communication.
27. Girard (1977: 2).
28. Nzongola-Ntalaja (2002: 150–1).
29. Eriksson Baaz and Stern (2008).
30. Dolan (2010).
31. Eriksson Baaz and Stern (2008).
32. Dolan (2010: 19).
33. ibid.
34. One helpful discussion is Wood (2009).
35. Dolan (2010: 59).
36. ibid.
37. See, for example, McDoom (2008).
38. See, for example, Straus (2006).
39. African Rights (1994).
40. Uvin (1998; 2000).
41. Uvin (2000: 173), citing A. Destexhe.
42. ibid.
43. ibid.: 173, citing J.-C. Willam.
44. Uvin (1998: 116–17).
45. Uvin (2000: 174).
46. Human Rights Watch/International Federation of Human Rights (1999: 60).
47. Duffield (2007).
48. Quoted in Verhoeven (2009: 418).
49. Duffield (2007).
50. Gilligan (2003: 1162).
51. Slim (2007: 150).
52. Creed (2009: 218–19).

53. Bob Woodward (2002: 38–9).
54. See, for example, Stern (2004).
55. For a fuller discussion of this point, see Keen (2006).
56. Thomas (1978).
57. Bob Woodward (2002: 17).
58. ibid.: 168.
59. For a more extended discussion, see Keen (2006).
60. Roy (2004: 105). Scott et al. (2009: 461) note: '... only two military actions since World War II fall cleanly into the "conventional war against a near-peer military of another nation" category – the Korean War and Gulf War'.
61. Waldman (2010); see also BBC2, *Afghanistan: War Without End* (22 June 2011).
62. Daily Mail online (2011).
63. Arendt (1979).
64. The message that we can have everything if we want it badly enough can quickly turn into self-blame. See Bageant (2007), Arendt (1979) and Hedges (2009).
65. For a more detailed discussion, see Keen (2006).
66. See, for example, Danner (2004).
67. Blix (2004: 202).
68. Thomas (1978: 658).
69. This would certainly be unusual behaviour, to put it mildly, prior to a major conflict.
70. *Time* (2003: 8).
71. For an enlightening discussion of the Jews as an 'elusive enemy', see Bartov (2000).
72. Again, there is a fuller discussion in Keen (2006).
73. See, for example, discussion in Hedges (2009: 101). Hedges notes, for example, that most of his working-class family in Maine were veterans: 'You serve in the military because it is one of the few jobs in which you can get health insurance and a decent salary. College is not an option.'
74. Feldman (2007).
75. ibid.
76. Melman (1985; 2008).
77. Melman (1985; 2008).
78. Melman (2008).
79. Conversations with various Iraq veterans in Colorado Springs.
80. Feldman (2007).
81. ibid. One detailed study in the UK found that: 'The armed forces draw non-officer recruits mainly from among young people with low educational attainment and living in poor communities. A large proportion join for negative reasons, including the lack of civilian career options; a survey in the Cardiff area in 2004 found that 40% of army recruits were joining as a last resort' (Gee, 2007: 2). The study also found that negative publicity over the 'war on terror' and improvements in educational opportunities had led to intensified efforts at recruitment, particularly among the very young. In the financial year 2006–07, one third of new non-officer recruits to the UK armed forces were children (ibid.: 21). In 2005, the UK Ministry of Defence stated: 'The Services need to attract those under 18 in order to compete effectively in an increasingly competitive employment market ... Once individuals attain the age of 18 years they are more difficult to attract as recruits' (ibid.: 22).
82. Faludi (1999).
83. ibid.
84. Hedges and al-Arian (2008: 103).
85. Mamdani (2001); Prunier (1995).
86. Mamdani (2001: 203).
87. Human Rights Watch/International Federation of Human Rights (1999: 60–1); see also Mamdani (2001).

88. Taylor (1999).
89. Humphreys and Weinstein (2004); see also Keen (2005a).
90. See, for example, Richards (1995: 158). This also happened in Mozambique's civil war (ibid: 139).
91. For example, Tina Aarvold, personal communication.
92. Human Rights Watch (2003: 44). Human Rights Watch (2003: 52) also reported that rape survivors feared their communities would not accept them back, but that such fears often proved unfounded.
93. See Le Billon (2001b: 571).
94. Eriksson Baaz and Stern (2008: 67). Cf. also Kelly (2010).
95. Eriksson Baaz and Stern (2008).
96. Dolan (2010).
97. See, for example, International Alert/Réseau des Femmes pour un Développement Associatif (2004).
98. Summary of perspectives in Eriksson Baaz and Stern (2008: 67).
99. See, for example, Beevor (1999).
100. Bourke (1999: 92).
101. Danner (2004).
102. Schivelbusch (2001).
103. See discussions in Bartov (2000), and Schivelbusch (2001).
104. Even during the Cold War, some – like Jerry Falwell in 1980 – expressed the view that a Communist enemy would take advantage of a nation with weak morals (Bacevich, 2005). Meanwhile, those in the very masculine world of nuclear strategising used a language – vertical erector launches, thrust-to-weight ratios, deep penetration, spasm attacks – that seemed to attach great virility to the arms build-up (Cohen, 1987).
105. As noted, minors (aged 16 and 17) continue to be recruited into the UK army (Gee, 2007). See also Coalition to Stop the Use of Child Soldiers (2008).
106. See, for example, Bourke (1999); Grossman (1995). Grossman emphasises the natural reluctance to kill and the role of new training techniques in raising the number of US soldiers willing to kill in Vietnam compared with the Second World War.
107. http://www.goarmy.com/flindex.jsp?#?channel=&video=
108. Osiel (1999: 195).
109. Phillips (2011: 103).
110. Vallely (2005).
111. Fisk (2005).
112. See, for example, remarks by Anatol Lieven, in Middle East Policy Council (2005: 8).
113. Lerner (2000; 2003).
114. O'Brien (1979: 100). See also Bacevich (2005: 39). Myra MacPherson (1988: 209) noted of the Vietnam War: '... some veterans sift over and over again the merits of the war, clutching at or violently rejecting "noble cause" straws, seeking answers, seeking comfort, seeking to place blame elsewhere. Where that blame justifiably belongs is with leaders who devised and strategized this war but somehow they have escaped the tainted scapegoatism of the veteran. Kissinger and his like cavort in the highest circles, are assured of media and political camp followers, and generally cleanse themselves in self-justifying memoirs.'
115. Severo and Milford (1990).
116. Minear (2007: 58).
117. Adebajo (2002).
118. Keen (2005a).
119. Sierra Leone Broadcasting Service (1997).
120. Human Rights Watch (1999: IV, 15).

121. In May 2000, Mustafah Kamara, who played a key role in the capture of Foday Sankoh, said: '… we stripped him. He is an animal so he should be naked like an animal' (McGreal, 2000: 1). Interestingly, the captor was also keen to dehumanise himself – in the form of a dangerous animal. His adopted persona of a scorpion was reminiscent of the labels – Tigers, Cobras – adopted by several groups within the Sierra Leonean army, and of Bockarie's assumed name, 'Mosquito'.
122. Pemagbi (1999).
123. Letter from Johnny Paul Koroma to ECOWAS, August 1997.
124. Khobe (2000: 62).
125. ibid.
126. For example, a 16-year-old girl captured by the RUF said she had helped to chop off people's hands; now she wanted to become a nurse (interviewed by Ambrose James, in Lord, 2000: 48).
127. Braithwaite and Braithwaite (2001).
128. Eriksson Baaz and Stern (2008: 62).
129. ibid.: 65.
130. ibid.: 66.
131. ibid.: 74.
132. Uslu (2007: 163).
133. Zur (1998: 123).
134. ibid.: 36.
135. Russell (1971: 388).
136. Whalen (1984: 34). Seeing conflict as essentially between 'two sides', the victors at the time of the 1919 Versailles Treaty believed that a lasting peace could be promoted by ensuring that the enemy remained as weak as possible. But internal conflicts were just as important – and a harsh peace exacerbated them. The German right popularised the idea that veterans were abused when they returned home. Hermann Goering described how 'very young boys, degenerate deserters, and prostitutes tore the insignia off our best front line soldiers and spat on their field gray uniforms' (Richard Hamilton, *Who Voted for Hitler?*, cited in Lembcke, 1998: 86). This seems to have been a distortion of something that did happen: for soldiers in revolt had sometimes ripped insignia from the uniforms of their officers (Lembcke, 1998: 86).
137. Diehl (1987).
138. Schivelbusch (2001: 235).
139. Hedges and al-Arian (2008: xiii). Hedges and al-Arian contacted Military Families Speak Out, Veterans for Peace, Vote Vets and Iraqi Veterans Against the War, noting that the last mentioned was especially helpful in finding veterans for them to talk to.
140. See, for example, Scott et al. (2009).
141. ibid.: 472.
142. Hedges and al-Arian (2008: xxiv).
143. ibid.: xiii, quoting Sgt Ben Flanders.
144. ibid.
145. Hedges and al-Arian (2008).
146. Dolan (2009); Zur (1998).
147. Zur (1998).
148. ibid.: 107–8.
149. For a fuller discussion, see Keen (2003).
150. Human Rights Watch (2009a).
151. Braithwaite and Braithwaite (2001: 4).
152. ibid.; see also Fanon (2001).

153. As retold to the author by human rights worker, Guatemala City, 2002; see also Manz (1988).
154. Summerfield (1998).
155. See, for example, Human Rights Watch (2003).
156. Behrend (1998); Dolan (2009).
157. Behrend (1998).
158. Derges (2009).
159. Arendt (1979: 446). Bartov (2000: 99) writes of the search, in Germany after the First World War, for 'an enemy ... whose very persecution would serve to manifest the power and legitimacy of the victimizer'.
160. Bob Woodward (2002: 338).
161. See, for example, Whalen (1984).
162. Pupavac (2004: 163).

Conclusion

1. Foucault (1977: 232).
2. See, particularly, Weissman (2004).
3. Girard (1977); Allen (1997).
4. Weissman (2004).
5. For an interesting related discussion, see Dexter.
6. Atkinson (2011).
7. Giustozzi (2009).
8. Keen (2005a).
9. De Waal (2009).
10. Keen (2005a).
11. Keen (2001); Le Billon (2003).
12. Keen (2001); de Waal (2009); see also North, Wallis and Weingast (2009); and Di John and Putzel (2009).
13. On this interaction, see for example Cramer (2002).
14. Kahn (2008).
15. al-Khalil (1989).
16. See Slim (2007); Keen and Lee (2009).
17. See particularly DuBois (2009); Pantuliano and O'Callaghan (2006).
18. Bartov (2000); Arendt (1979).
19. Among the most interesting recent discussions is Magone, Neuman and Weissman (2011).
20. Cf. Schaffer (1984).
21. One exploration of this is Byman (2006).
22. Collier (2000).
23. See, particularly, Mkandawire (2002) on perpetrators' need to rationalise their actions.
24. Bob Woodward (2002: 283).
25. See, for example, Keen (2006).
26. ibid.

Bibliography

Aarvold, Tina, '"Rebel girl": An Exploration into the Role of Girls Abducted during the War in Sierra Leone', MSc, Dept of Human Sciences, Brunel University (2002)

Acemoglu, Daron, James Robinson and Thierry Verdier, 'Kleptocracy and Divide-and-Rule: A Model of Personal Rule', Alfred Marshall Lecture, *Journal of the European Economic Association*, 2:2-3 (April–May 2004), pp. 162–92

Adebajo, Adekeye, 'Building Peace in West Africa: Liberia, Sierra Leone, and Guinea-Bissau', International Peace Academy Occasional Paper Series, Boulder: Lynne Rienner (2002)

——, 'Gaddafi: The man who would be king of Africa', *Guardian*, 26 August 2011

Africa Confidential, 22 January 1999

African Rights: Death, Despair and Defiance, London: African Rights (1994)

Akça, Ismet, 'Military-Economic Structure in Turkey: Present Situation, Problems, and Solutions', Turkish Economic and Social Studies Foundation, Istanbul (July 2010), pp. 1–36

Albrecht, Peter and Paul Jackson, 'Security System Transformation in Sierra Leone, 1997–2007', UK government Global Conflict Prevention Pool/Global Facilitation Network for Security Sector Reform/International Alert (February 2009)

Alfoneh, Ali, 'How Intertwined Are the Revolutionary Guards in Iran's Economy?', *Middle Eastern Outlook* (22 October 2007)

——, 'Iran's Parliamentary Elections and the Revolutionary Guards' Creeping Coup d'Etat', *Middle Eastern Outlook* (21 February 2008)

Allawi, Ali A., *The Occupation of Iraq: Winning the War, Losing the Peace*, New Haven and London: Yale University Press (2007)

Allen, R., 'Strasser ousted in palace coup', *West Africa* (22–8 January 1995), pp. 102–3

Allen, Tim, 'The Violence of Healing', *Sociologus*, 47: 2 (1997), pp. 101–28

Allie, Marie-Pierre, 'Acting at Any Price', in Claire Magone, Michael Neuman and Fabrice Weissman (eds.), *Humanitarian Negotiations Revealed: The MSF Experience*, London: Hurst and Co. (2011)

Amos, Julia, 'Non-Profits of Peace: Two West African Case Studies of Mediation by Conflict-Resolution NGOs', D. Phil., Oxford University (2011)

Anderson, Jon Lee, 'Death of the Tiger: Sri Lanka's brutal victory over its Tamil insurgents', *New Yorker* (17 January 2011)

Anderson, Mary, *Do No Harm: How Aid Can Support Peace – Or War*, Boulder, Colorado: Lynne Reinner (1999)

Andreas, Peter, 'Criminalized Legacies of War', *Problems of Post-Communism*, 51:3 (May/June 2004), pp. 3–9

Arendt, Hannah, *The Origins of Totalitarianism*, Harvest (1979, first published in 1951)

——, 'Lying in Politics: Reflections on The Pentagon Papers', *New York Review of Books* (18 November 1971)

Armbrust, Walter, 'A Revolution against Neoliberalism', al Jazeera (last modified 24 February 2011)

Article 19 and Forum of Conscience/Jon Lunn and John Caulker, 'Moments of Truth in Sierra Leone: Contextualising the Truth and Reconciliation Commission' (August 2000)

Associated Press, 'Mexican authorities disband Veracruz police force in bid to stem corruption', *Guardian* (22 December 2011)

Astill, James, 'Rwandans wage a war of plunder', *Observer* (4 August 2002)

Atkinson, Philippa, 'Stationary and Roving Banditry: An alternative historical perspective on the Liberian conflict', PhD, London School of Economics and Political Science (2011)

Atkinson, Philippa, Anabel Hoult and David Mills, *Sierra Leone – A security crisis: '99% of your life is ours'*, Oxford: Refugee Studies Programme (1991)

Autesserre, Séverine, 'DR Congo: Explaining Peace Building Failures, 2003–2006', *Review of African Political Economy*, 34: 113 (2007), pp. 423–41

Baas, Saskia, *From Civilians to Soldiers and from Soldiers to Civilians: A micro-approach to disarmament, demobilisation, and reintegration (DDR) in Sudan*, Amsterdam: Amsterdam University Press (2012)

Bacevich, Andrew, *The New American Militarism: How Americans are Seduced by War*, Oxford and New York: Oxford University Press (2005)

Bacik, Gokhan and Bezen Balamir Coskun, 'The PKK Problem: Explaining Turkey's Failure to Develop a Political Solution', *Studies in Conflict and Terrorism*, 34 (2011), pp. 248–65

Bageant, Joe, *Deer Hunting with Jesus: Dispatches from America's Class War*, New York: Crown Publishers, 2007

Bakonyi, Jutta. 'Between protest, revenge and material interests: a phenomenological analysis of looting in the Somali war', *Disasters*, 34:S2 (2010), pp. S238–55

Bangura, Yusuf, 'Reflections on the Abidjan Peace Accord', *Africa Development*, 22:3 and 4 (1997), pp. 217–42

Bank of Sierra Leone, 'BSL Bulletin', Freetown (April 1995)

Barakat, Sultan, Sean Deely and Steven Zyck, ' "A tradition of forgetting": stabilisation and humanitarian action in historical perspective', *Disasters*, 34:S3 (2010), pp. 297–319

Barakat, Sultan and Steven Zyck, 'Afghanistan's Insurgency and the Viability of a Political Settlement', *Studies in Conflict & Terrorism*, 33 (2010), pp. 193–210

Barnett, Thomas, *The Pentagon's New Map: War and Peace in the Twenty-First Century*, London: Penguin (2004)

Bartov, Omer, *Mirrors of Destruction: War, Genocide and Modern Identity*, Oxford: Oxford University Press (2000)

Baudrillard, Jean (trans. Paul Patton), *The Gulf War Did Not Take Place*, Bloomington: Indiana University Press (1995)

Bauer, Peter, *Dissent on Development: Studies and Debates in Development Economics*, Harvard University Press (1971)

Bay Area Center for Voting Research, 'The Most Conservative and Liberal Cities in the United States', http://alt.coxnewsweb.com/statesman/metro/081205libs.pdf (n.d.)

BBC Radio 4, *RoboWars*, Episode 2 (8 February 2010)

BBC2, *Afghanistan: War Without End* (22 June 2011)

BBC2, *Secret Pakistan: Double Cross* (26 October 2011)

Beah, Ishmael, *A Long Way Gone: Memoirs of a Boy Soldier*, London: Fourth Estate (2007)

Beber, Bernd and Christopher Blattman, 'The Logic of Child Soldiering and Coercion', http://chrisblattman.com/documents/research/2011.LogicOfChildSoldiering.pdf? 9d7bd4 (July 2011)

Beeson, Mark, 'Civil-Military Relations in Indonesia and the Philippines: Will the Thai Coup Prove Contagious', *Armed Forces and Society*, 34:3 (April 2008), pp. 474–90

Beeson, Mark, Alex Bellamy and Bryn Hughes, 'Taming the tigers? Reforming the security sector in Southeast Asia', *Pacific Review*, 19:4 (2006), pp. 449–72

Beevor, Antony, *Stalingrad*, London: Penguin (1999)

Behrend, Heike, 'War in Northern Uganda' in Christopher Clapham, ed, *African Guerrillas*, Bloomington, Ind.: Indiana University Press (1998)

Berdal, Mats, 'How "New" are "New Wars"? Global Economic Change and the Study of Civil War', *Global Governance*, 9:4 (2003), pp. 477–502

Bergen, Peter and Paul Cruickshank, 'The Iraq Effect: War has increased terrorism sevenfold worldwide', *Mother Jones* (1 March 2007)

Berman, Bruce, 'Bureaucracy and Incumbent Violence: Colonial Administration and the Origins of the "Mau Mau" Emergency in Kenya', *British Journal of Political Science*, 6:2 (April 1976), pp. 143–75

Bhatia, Michael, 'The Future of the Mujahideen: Legitimacy, Legacy and Demobilization in Post-Bonn Afghanistan', *International Peacekeeping*, 14:1 (January 2007), pp. 90–107

Bhatia, Michael, Kevin Lanigan and Philip Wilkinson, 'Minimal Investments, Minimal Results: The Failure of Security Policy in Afghanistan', Afghanistan Research and Evaluation Unit briefing paper (June 2004), pp. 1–22

Bilton, Michael and Kevin Sim, *Four Hours in My Lai*, London: Penguin (1993)

Binet, Laurence, 'Ethiopia: A Fool's Game in Ogaden', in Claire Magone, Michael Neuman and Fabrice Weissman (eds.) *Humanitarian Negotiations Revealed: The MSF Experience*, London: Hurst and Co. (2011)

Bird, Tim and Alex Marshall, *Afghanistan: How the West Lost its Way*, New Haven and London: Yale University Press (2011)

Blix, Hans, *Disarming Iraq: The search for weapons of mass destruction*, Bloomsbury (2004)

Booth, Michael, 'Colorado Springs cuts into services considered basic by many', *Denver Post* (31 January 2010)

Borger, Julian, 'Afghanistan faces $4 billion defence shortfall', *Guardian* (1 December 2011)

Bougarel, Xavier, Elissa Helms and Ger Duijzings (eds.), *The New Bosnian Mosaic: Identities, Memories and Moral Claims in a Post-War Society*, Aldershot: Ashgate (2006)

Bouillon, Markus E., 'The Failure of Big Business: On the Socio-economic Reality of the Middle East Peace Process', *Mediterranean Politics*, 9:1 (Spring 2004), pp. 1–28

Bourke, Joanna, *An Intimate History of Killing: Face-to-face killing in twentieth-century warfare*, London: Granta (1999)

Bowcott, Owen, 'British officials "backed disbanding of Iraqi army"', says US ambassador', *Guardian* (28 May 2010)

Bradbury, Mark, 'Rebels Without a Cause? An Exploratory Report on the Conflict in Sierra Leone', CARE International (April 1995)

——, 'State-building, Counterterrorism, and Licensing Humanitarianism in Somalia', Feinstein International Center, Tufts University (September 2010), pp. 1–24

Braithwaite, John and Valerie Braithwaite, 'Shame and Shame Management', in Eliza Ahmed, Nathan Harris, John Braithwaite and Valerie Braithwaite (eds.), *Shame Management Through Reintegration*, Cambridge: Cambridge University Press (2001)

Branch, Daniel, 'Footprints in the Sand: British Colonial Counterinsurgency and the War in Iraq', *Politics and Society*, 38:1 (2010), pp. 15–34

Branch, Daniel and Elisabeth Wood, 'Revisiting Counterinsurgency', *Politics and Society*, 38:3 (2010), pp. 3–14

Brett, E. A. 'State Failure and Success in Ugandan and Zimbabwe: The Logic of Political Decay and Reconstruction in Africa', Crisis States Programme, LSE, working paper 78, series 1 (February 2006)

Briscoe, Ivan and Martin Rodriguez Pellecer, 'A state under siege: elites, criminal networks and institutional reform in Guatemala', Netherlands Institute of International Relations Clingendael (September 2010)

Brown, Ulysses and Dharam Rana, 'Generalised Exchange and Propensity for Military Service: The moderating effect of prior military exposure', *Journal of Applied Statistics*, 32:3 (2005), pp. 259–70

Browning, Christopher, *Ordinary Men: Reserve Police Battalion 101 and the Final Solution in Poland*, New York: HarperPerennial (1992)

Bryden, Matt, 'Somalia's Famine is Not Just a Catastrophe, It's a Crime', *Enough* (October 2011)

Bukkvoll, Tor, 'Their Hands in the Till: Scale and Causes of Russian Military Corruption', *Armed Forces and Society*, 34:2 (January 2008), pp. 259–75

Bumiller, Elisabeth, 'Egypt Stability Hinges on a Divided Military', *New York Times* (5 February 2011)

Burke, Jason, *The 9/11 Wars*, London: Allen Lane (2011)

Burnham, Gilbert, Riyadh Lafta, Shannon Doocy and Les Roberts, 'Mortality after the 2003 invasion of Iraq: a cross-sectional cluster sample survey', *The Lancet*, 368 (October 2006), pp. 1421–8

Byman, Daniel, 'Friends Like These: Counterinsurgency and the War on Terrorism', *International Security*, 31:2 (Fall 2006), pp. 79–115

Byman, Daniel, Michael Scheuer, Anatol Lieven and W. Patrick Lang, 'Iraq, Afghanistan and the War on "Terror"', *Middle East Policy*, 12:1 (Spring 2005), pp. 1–24

Cam, Surhan, 'Institutional Oppression and Neo-Liberalism in Turkey', working paper 81, Cardiff School of Social Sciences (2006)

Campbell, Greg, *Blood Diamonds*, Boulder: Westview Press (2002)

Carlton, Charles, *Going to the Wars: The Experience of the British Civil Wars, 1638–1651*, London and New York: Routledge (1994)

Castells, Manuel, *1998: End of Millennium*, Malden, MA, and Oxford: Blackwell Publishers (1998)

Catholic Relief Services, 'Chronology of Events Leading to the Closure of the ULIMO Demobilization Project', Freetown (1995)

Chabal, Patrick and Jean-Pascal Daloz, *Africa Works: Disorder as Political Instrument*, Oxford: James Currey (1999)

Channel 4, *Sri Lanka's Killing Fields* (14 June 2011)

Chari, Sharad and Katherine Verdery, 'Thinking between the Posts: Postcolonialism, Postsocialism, and Ethnography after the Cold War', *Comparative Studies in Society and History*, 51:1 (2009), pp. 6–34

Chatterjee, Pratap, *Halliburton's Army: How a Well-Connected Texas Oil Company Revolutionized the Way America Makes War*, New York: Nation Books (2009)

Chaudhuri, Rudra and Theo Farrell, 'Campaign disconnect: operational progress and strategic obstacles in Afghanistan, 2009–2011', *International Affairs*, 87:2 (2011), pp. 271–96

Chayes, Sarah, 'Dangerous liaisons', *Guardian* (7 July 2003)

Chledowski, Stephen, 'Military Corruption and Organized Crime in Eastern Europe and the Caucasus', *Journal of Military and Strategic Studies* (Spring 2005), pp. 1–31

Chomsky, Noam, *Deterring Democracy*, London: Vintage (2006)

Coalition to Stop the Use of Child Soldiers, 'The Use of Children as Soldiers in Africa: A country analysis of child recruitment and participation in armed conflict', London (1999)

——, 'Child Soldiers: Global Report 2008', London (2008)

Cohen, Carol, 'Sex and Death in the Rational World of Defense Intellectuals', *Signs*, 12:4 (Summer 1987), pp. 687–718

Cohen, Stephen, 'How a Botched US Alliance Fed Pakistan's Crisis', *Current History*, 109:726 (April 2010), pp. 138–43

Cole, Bernadette, 'A Taxing Issue', *West Africa* (9–15 Jan 1995), p. 17

Collier, Paul, 'Civil War and the Economics of the Peace Dividend', Centre for the Study of African Economies, working paper series no. 26 (1995)

——, 'Doing Well out of War: An Economic Perspective', in Mats Berdal and David Malone (eds.), *Greed and Grievance: Economic Agendas in Civil Wars*, Boulder: Lynne Rienner/International Peace Academy (2000)

——, *The Bottom Billion: Why the Poorest Countries are Failing and What Can Be Done About It*, Oxford: Oxford University Press (2007)

——, *Wars, Guns, and Votes: Democracy in Dangerous Places*, New York: HarperCollins (2009)

Collier, Paul, V. L. Elliott, Havard Hegre, Anke Hoeffler, Marta Reynal-Querol and Nicholas Sambanis, *Breaking the Conflict Trap: Civil War and Development Policy*, World Bank policy research report, vol. 1 (2003)

Collier, P. and A. Hoeffler, 'Justice-Seeking and Loot-Seeking in Civil War', World Bank (1999)

Colorado Coalition, 'Fact Sheet for a Resolution to Congress' (January 2011)

Conetta, Carl, 'An Undisciplined Defense: Understanding the $2 Trillion Surge in US Defense Spending', Cambridge, MA and Washington DC: Project on Defense Alternatives. Briefing Report 20 (January 2010)

Cooper, Neil, 'State Collapse as Business: The Role of Conflict Trade and the Emerging Control Agenda', *Development and Change* 33:5 (2002), pp. 935–55

Cooper, Robert, 'Why we still need empires', *Observer* (7 April 2002)

——, *The Breaking of Nations: Order and Chaos in the Twenty-First Century*, London: Atlantic Books (2004)

Corn, Tony, 'COIN in Absurdistan: Saving the COIN Baby from the Afghan Bathwater (and Vice-Versa)', *Small Wars Journal* (July 2010)

Corson, William, *The Betrayal*, New York: W. W. Norton and Co. (1968)

Cramer, Christopher, 'Homo Economicus Goes to War: Methodological Individualism, Rational Choice and the Political Economy of War', *World Development*, 30:11 (2002), pp. 1845–964

——, *Civil War is Not a Stupid Thing: Accounting for Violence in Developing Countries*, London: Hurst and Co. (2006)

Creed, Pamela, 'Myth, Memory and Militarism: The Evolution of an American War Narrative', PhD, George Mason University (2009)

Cruz, Consuelo and Rut Diamint, 'The New Military Autonomy in Latin America', *Journal of Democracy*, 9:4 (1998), pp. 115–27

Custers, Peter, 'Military Keynesianism today: an innovative discourse', *Race and Class*, 51:4 (2010), pp. 79–94

Daily Mail online, 'First the tears, then the anger', *Daily Mail* (4 May 2011)

Danner, Mark, 'The Logic of Torture', *New York Review of Books* (24 June 2004)

Danssaert, Peter and Thomas, Brian, 'Greed and Guns: Uganda's Role in the Rape of the Congo', Antwerp: International Peace Information Service (n.d.)

Davis, Shelton, 'Introduction: Sowing the Seeds of Violence', in Robert Carmack (ed.) *Harvest of Violence: The Maya Indians and the Guatemalan Crisis*, Norman and London: University of Oklahoma Press (1988), pp. 3–36

Demir, Firat, 'Militarization of the Market and Rent-Seeking Coalitions in Turkey', *Development and Change*, 36:4 (2005), pp. 667–90

Dempsey, Thomas, 'Evaluating U.S. Policy Objectives and Options on the Horn of Africa', Hearing before the Subcommittee on African Affairs, US Committee on Foreign Relations (11 March 2008)

Derges, Jane, 'Eloquent Bodies: Conflict and ritual in northern Sri Lanka', *Anthropology & Medicine*, 16:1 (April 2009), pp. 27–36

Dexter, Helen, 'New War, Good War and the War on Terror: Explaining, Excusing and Creating Western Neo-Interventionism', *Roundtable*, 38:6 (2007), pp. 1055–71

Di John, Jonathan and James Putzel, 'Political Settlements', Issues Paper, Governance and Social Development Resource Centre (June 2009)

Diehl, James, 'Victors or Victims? Disabled Veterans in the Third Reich', *Journal of Modern History*, 59:4 (1987), pp. 705–36

Dilanian, Ken, 'Short-staffed USAID tries to keep pace', *USA Today* (1 February 2009)

Dodd, Vikram, 'Terrorism policy flaws "increased risk of attacks", says former police chief', *Guardian* (7 July 2010)

Dodge, Toby, testimony to US Committee on Foreign Relations on 'The Iraq Transition' (20 April 2004)

——, 'State Collapse and the Rise of Identity Politics', in Markus Bouillon, David Malone and Ben Rowswell (eds.) *Iraq: Preventing a New Generation of Conflict*, Boulder: Lynne Rienner (2007)

——, 'The changing political economy of Iraq: sanctions, invasion, regime change, civil war and beyond', paper delivered at 'Power after Peace: The Political Economy of Post-Conflict State Building', King's College London (10 December 2009)

Dolan, Chris, *Social Torture: The Case of Northern Uganda, 1986–2006*, New York: Berghahn Books (2009)

——, '"The War is Not Yet Over": Community Perceptions of Sexual Violence and its Underpinnings in Eastern DRC', London: International Alert, www.international-alert.org/sites/default/files/publications/1011WarIsNotYetOverEng.pdf (September 2010)

Donini, Antonio, 'Afghanistan: Humanitarianism Unraveled?' Feinstein International Center, Tufts University, briefing paper (May 2010)

Dorronsoro, Gilles, 'The Taliban's Winning Strategy in Afghanistan', Carnegie Endowment for International Peace (2009), pp. 1–32

Dowden, Richard, 'Bitter legacy of Uganda's civil war', BBC news (30 September 2010)

Dreyfus, Pablo, 'When all the Evils Come Together: Cocaine, Corruption, and Shining Path in Peru's Upper Huallanga Valley, 1980–1995', *Journal of Contemporary Criminal Justice*, 15:4 (November 1999), pp. 370–96

Drury, Ian, Lucy Ballinger and Tim Shipman, 'MI5 boss says Blair's War on Terror has left Britain more at risk', *Daily Mail* online (21 July 2010)

DuBois, Marc, 'Protection: The New Humanitarian Figleaf', www.rsc.ox.ac.uk/pdfs/endnotemarkdubois.pdf (2009)

Duffield, Mark, 'Complex Emergencies and the Crisis of Developmentalism', *IDS Bulletin*, 25:4 (1994a), pp. 1–14

——, 'The Political Economy of Internal War', in Joanna Macrae and Anthony Zwi (eds.) *War and Hunger: Rethinking International Responses to Complex Emergencies*, London: Zed Books and Save the Children (1994b)

——, 'Post-modern Conflict: Warlords, Post-adjustment States and Private Protection', *Civil Wars*, 1:1 (Spring 1998), pp. 65–102

——, *Global Governance and the New Wars: The Merging of Development and Security*, London: Zed Books (2001)

——, *Development, Security and Unending War: Governing the World of Peoples*, London: Polity (2007)

——, 'Global Civil War: The Non-Insured, International Containment and Post-Interventionary Society', *Journal of Refugee Studies*, 21:2 (2008), pp. 145–65

Edkins, Jenny, 'Legality with a Vengeance: Humanitarian relief in complex emergencies', *Millennium Journal of International Studies*, 25:3 (1996), pp. 547–75

Egnell, Robert, 'Lessons from Helmand, Afghanistan: What now for British counterinsurgency?', *International Affairs*, 87:2 (2011), pp. 297–315

Elizur, Y. and Yishay-Krien, N., 'Participation in Atrocities among Israeli Soldiers during the First Intifada: A Qualitative Analysis', *Journal of Peace Research*, 46:2 (2009), pp. 251–67

Ellis, Stephen, 'Liberia 1989–1994: A Study of Ethnic and Spiritual Violence', *African Affairs*, 94 (1995), pp. 165–97

Emizet, Kisangani, 'The Massacre of Refugees in the Congo: A case of UN peacekeeping failure and international law', *Journal of Modern African Studies*, 38:3 (2000), pp. 163–202

Englebert, Pierre and Denis Tull, 'Post-Conflict Reconstruction in Africa: Flawed Ideas about Failed States', *International Security*, 32:4 (2008), pp. 106–39

Eriksson Baaz, Maria and Maria Stern, 'Making Sense of Violence: Voices of soldiers in the Congo (DRC)', *Journal of Modern African Studies*, 46:1 (2008), pp. 57–86

Fair, Christine, 'Why the Pakistan army is here to stay: prospects for civilian governance', *International Affairs*, 87:3 (2011), pp. 571–88

Fajardo, Luis Eduardo, 'From the Alliance for Progress to the Plan Colombia: A retrospective look at U.S. aid to Colombia', Crisis States Research Centre working papers series 1, no. 28, Crisis States Research Centre, LSE (2003)

Faludi, Susan, *Stiffed: The Betrayal of the Modern Man*, London: Chatto and Windus (1999)

Fanon, Frantz, *The Wretched of the Earth*, Harmondsworth: Penguin (2001, first published 1961)

Fanthorpe, Richard, Alice Jay and Victor Kalie Kamara, 'Chiefdom Governance Reform Programme (formerly Paramount Chiefs Restoration Programme), Project Evaluation and Recommendations', September, 2nd draft (for DFID) (2002)

Farrell, Theo and Stuart Gordon. 'COIN Machine: The British Military in Afghanistan', *RUSI Journal*, 154:3 (June 2009), pp. 18–25

Fearon, James, 'Ethnic Mobilization and Ethnic Violence', in Barry Weingast and Donald Wittman (eds), *Oxford Handbook of Political Economy*, Oxford: Oxford University Press (2006)

Feldman, Megan, 'Yo Soy el Army: Uncle same wants you – especially if you're Latino', *Dallas Observer* (8 February 2007)

Fernandes, Desmond, 'Turkey's US-backed War On Terror: A Cause For Concern?', *Variant*, 27 (Winter 2006), pp. 33–6

Fishstein, Paul and Andrew Wilder, 'Winning Hearts and Minds? Examining the Relationship between Aid and Security in Afghanistan', Tufts University (2011)

Fisk, Robert, 'Something Happened Between "I Love You" and the Click of the Phone', CounterPunch.org (23–4 July 2005)

Fithen, Caspar, 'Diamonds and war in Sierra Leone: Cultural strategies for commercial adaptation to endemic low-intensity conflict', PhD, University College London (1999)

Flint, Julie, 'The Other War: Inter-Arab Conflict in Darfur', Small Arms Survey, Geneva (October 2010)

Flynn, Major Gen. Michael, Captain Matt Pottinger and Paul Batchelor, 'Fixing Intel: A Blueprint for Making Intelligence Relevant in Afghanistan', Center for a New American Security, Washington DC (2010)

Forsberg, Carl, 'Politics and Power in Kandahar', Afghanistan report 5, Institute for the Study of War, Washington DC (April 2010)

Foucault, Michel (ed. C. Gordon), *Power/Knowledge: Selected Interviews and Other Writings*, Brighton: Harvester Press (1972–7)

Foucault, Michel (trans. Alan Sheridan), *Discipline and Punish: The Birth of the Prison*, London: Penguin (1977)

Frank, Thomas, *What's the Matter with America? The resistible rise of the American Right*, London: Secker and Warburg (2004)

Fyle, C. M., 'The Military and Civil Society in Sierra Leone: The 1992 Coup d'Etat', *Africa Development*, 18:2 (1994), pp. 141–2

Galbraith, Peter, 'Petraeus vs. the Mafia', The Daily Beast, www.thedailybeast.com/articles/2010/06/24/david-petraeus-cant-win-in-afghanistan-because-of-hamid-karzai.html (24 June 2010)

Gasparre, Richard, 'Less Ego, More UAVs', *Airforce Technology*, 17 July 2008, www.airforce-technology.com/features/feature2104/

Gberie, Lansana, 'The May 25 Coup d'Etat in Sierra Leone: A Militariat Revolt?', *Africa Development*, 22:3&4 (1997), pp. 149–70

——, *A Dirty War in West Africa: The R.U.F. and the Destruction of Sierra Leone*, London: Hurst and Co. (2005)

Gee, David, 'Informed Choice? Armed Forces recruitment practice in the United Kingdom', Joseph Rowntree Charitable Trust (2007)

Gelb, Leslie and Richard Betts, *The Irony of Vietnam: The System Worked*, Brookings Institution (1979)

Gentleman, Amelia and Henry McDonald, 'Alarm as Dublin trains "KGB"', *Observer* (4 March 2001)

Gerami, Shahin, 'Mullahs, Martyrs and Men: Conceptualizing Masculinity in the Islamic Republic of Iran', *Men and Masculinities*, 5:3 (2003), pp. 257–95

Gerges, Fawaz, 'The Decline of Revolutionary Islam in Algeria and Egypt', *Survival*, 41:1 (Spring 1999), pp. 113–25

——, *The Far Enemy: Why Jihad Went Global*, Cambridge University Press (2005)

Ghufran, Nasreen, 'Pushtun Ethnonationalism and the Taliban Insurgency in the North West Frontier Province of Pakistan', *Asian Survey*, 49:6 (November/December 2009), pp. 1092–114

Gilligan, James, *Violence: Reflections on Our Deadliest Epidemic*, London: Jessica Kingsley Publishers (1999)

——, 'Shame, Guilt and Violence', *Social Research*, 70:4 (Winter 2003), pp. 1149–80

Girard, Rene (trans. Patrick Gregory), *Violence and the Sacred*, 2nd edn, Baltimore: Johns Hopkins University Press (1977)

Giustozzi, Antonio, 'Respectable Warlords? The politics of state-building in post-Taliban Afghanistan', working paper 33, Crisis States Programme, DESTIN, LSE (2004)

——, *Koran, Kalashnikov and Laptop: The Neo-Taliban Insurgency in Afghanistan, 2002–2007*, New York: Columbia University Press (2007)

——, *Empires of Mud: Wars and Warlords in Afghanistan*, London: Hurst and Co. (2009)

Glenny, Misha, *The Fall of Yugoslavia: The Third Balkan War*, London: Penguin (1992)

Global Witness, 'For a Few Dollars More: How al Qaeda moved into the diamond trade', London (April 2003)

Glover, Jonathan, *Humanity: A Moral History of the Twentieth Century*, London: Jonathan Cape (1999)

Goering, Laurie, 'S. Africa strains to keep lid on mercenaries', *Chicago Tribune* (online edition), (19 March 2004)

Goldstone, Jack, 'Understanding the Revolutions of 2011: Weakness and Resilience in Middle Eastern Autocracies', *Foreign Affairs*, 90:3 (May–June 2011)

Goodhand, Jonathan, 'From War Economy to Peace Economy? Reconstruction and State Building in Afghanistan', *Journal of International Affairs*, 58:1 (Fall 2008), pp. 155–74

——, 'Stabilising a Victor's Peace? Humanitarian action and reconstruction in eastern Sri Lanka', *Disasters*, 34:S3 (2010), pp. S342–67

Goodhand, Jonathan and Mark Sedra, 'Who Owns the Peace? Aid, reconstruction, and peacebuilding in Afghanistan', *Disasters*, 34:S1 (2010), pp. S78–102

Goozner, Merrill, 'Why Obama Won't Cut Defense and Reap and Peace Dividend', *Fiscal Times* (23 February 2011)

Gordon, Stuart, 'The United Kingdom's Stabilisation Model and Afghanistan: The impact on humanitarian actors', *Disasters*, 34:S3 (2010), pp. S368–87

——, 'Winning Hearts and Minds? Examining the Relationship between Aid and Security in Afghanistan's Helmand Province', Boston: Tufts University (April 2011)

Gravel, Mike and Joe Lauria, *A Political Odyssey: The rise of American militarism and one man's fight to stop it*, New York: Seven Stories Press (2008)

Green, Matthew and Farhan Bokhari, 'Highs costs to get NATO supplies past Taliban', *Financial Times* (13 November 2009)

Grossman, Dave, *On Killing: The Psychological Cost of Learning to Kill in War and Society*, Boston: Little, Brown and Co. (1995)

Group of Experts, Final report of the Group of Experts on the Democratic Republic of the Congo, S/2009/603, UN Security Council (2009)

Guáqueta, Alexandra, 'The Way Back In: Reintegrating illegal armed groups in Colombia then and now', *Conflict, Security and Development*, 7:3 (October 2007), pp. 417–56

Guardian, 'US Embassy Cables: Sri Lankan government accused of complicity in human rights abuses' (16 December 2010)

Guardian, 'EU arms exports to Libya: who armed Gaddafi?', Datablog (2 March 2011)

Guidolin, Massimo and Eliana Le Ferrara, 'Diamonds Are Forever, Wars Are Not. Is Conflict Bad for Private Firms?', Research Division, Federal Reserve Bank of St Louis, working paper 2005-004C (January 2005, revised October 2006)

Gutiérrez Sanin, Francisco, 'Telling the Difference: Guerrillas and Paramilitaries in the Colombian War', *Politics and Society*, 36:1 (March 2008), pp. 3–34

Hafez, Mohammed, '*Jihad* after Iraq: Lessons from the Arab Afghans', *Studies in Conflict and Terrorism*, 32 (2009), pp. 73–94

Hammes, T. X., 'Contract Terms', *Armed Forces Journal* (June 2011)

Hancock, Graham, *Lords of Poverty: The Power, Prestige and Corruption of the International Aid Business*, Papermac (1989)

Hara, Fabienne, 'Hollow Peace Hopes in Shattered Congo', *Observer* (7 July 2002)

Hardin, Kris L., *The Aesthetics of Action: Continuity and Change in a West African Town*, Washington: Smithsonian Institution (1993)

Hartung, William and Michelle Ciarrocca, 'The Military Industrial Think Tank Complex: Corporate think tanks and the doctrine of aggressive militarism', *Multinational Monitor*, 24:1–2 (January–February 2003)

Hashim, Ahmed, *Insurgency and Counter-insurgency in Iraq*, London: Hurst and Co. (2006)

Hastings, Michael, 'The Runaway General', *Rolling Stone* (22 June 2010)

Healy, Sally, 'Eritrea's Economic Survival', summary record of a conference held on 20 April 2007, Chatham House, London

Hedges, Chris, *Empire of Illusion: The End of Literacy and the Triumph of Spectacle*, New York: Nation Books (2009)

Hedges, Chris and Laila al-Arian, *Collateral Damage: America's War Against Iraqi Civilians*, New York: Nation Books (2008)

Hedman, Eva-Lotta, 'Deconstructing Reconstruction in Post-tsunami Aceh: Governmentality, Displacement and Politics', *Oxford Development Studies*, 37:1 (2009a), pp. 63–76

Hedman, Eva-Lotta, 'The Philippines: Conflict and Internal Displacement in Mindanao and the Sulu Archipeligo', Writenet, commissioned by UNHCR (2009b)

Hirsch, John L., 'Sierra Leone: Diamonds and the Struggle for Democracy', International Peace Academy, Occasional Paper Series, Boulder: Lynne Rienner (2001)

Hossein-zadeh, Ismael, *The Political Economy of U.S. Militarism*, Basingstoke: Palgrave Macmillan (2006)

——, 'Escalating US Military Spending: Income Redistribution in Disguise', Society of Heterodox Economists, University of New South Wales, working paper 2007–10 (2007)

Human Rights Watch, 'Turkey: Forced Displacement of Ethnic Kurds from Southeastern Turkey' (1994)

——, 'Sierra Leone: Getting Away with Murder, Mutilation, Rape' (1999)

——, '"We'll Kill You If you Cry": Sexual Violence in the Sierra Leone Conflict' (2003)

——, '"Enduring Freedom": Abuses by U.S. Forces in Afghanistan' (2004)

——, 'Too High a Price: The Human Rights Cost of the Indonesia Military's Economic Activities' (2006)

——, 'Besieged, Displaced, and Detained: The Plight of Civilians in Sri Lanka's Vanni Region' (2008)

——, 'Soldiers Who Rape, Commanders Who Condone: Sexual Violence and Military Reform in the Democratic Republic of Congo' (2009a)

——, 'War on the Displaced: Sri Lankan Army and LTTE Abuses against Civilians in the Vanni' (2009b)

——, '"Paramilitaries' Heirs": The New Face of Violence in Colombia', (2010a)

——, 'Development without Freedom: How Aid Underwrites Repression in Ethiopia' (2010b)

Human Rights Watch/International Federation of Human Rights, 'Leave None to Tell the Story: Genocide in Rwanda' (1999)

Human Security Report Project, *Human Security Brief 2007*, Vancouver: Simon Fraser University (2008)

Humphreys, Macartan and Jeremy Weinstein, 'What the Fighters Say: A Survey of Ex-Combatants in Sierra Leone', in partnership with Pride, Freetown, www.columbia.edu/~mh2245/Report1_BW.pdf (June 2004)

——, 'Handling and Manhandling Civilians in Civil War', *American Political Science Review*, 100:3 (2006), pp. 429–47

Hunt, David, 'Dirty Wars: Counterinsurgency in Vietnam and Today', *Politics and Society*, 38:1 (2010), pp. 35–66

Hunt, R., *Pacification: The American Struggle for Vietnam's Hearts and Minds*, Boulder: Westview (1995)

Hunt, Tristram, *The English Civil War at First Hand*, London: Phoenix (2002)

Huntington, Samuel, *The Clash of Civilizations and the Remaking of World Order*, London: Touchstone (1998)

Ibrahim, Amina, 'Guardian the State or Protecting the Economy? The Economic Factors of Pakistan's Military Coups', Development Studies Institute, LSE, 9:92 (February 2009)

Ignatieff, Michael, *Blood and Belonging: Journeys into the new nationalism*, London: BBC Books/Chatto and Windus (1993)

——, *Human Rights as Politics and Idolatry*, Princeton, NJ: Princeton University Press (2001)

Internal Displacement Monitoring Centre, 'Uganda: Uncertain future for IDPs while peace remains elusive' (24 April 2008)

International Alert/Réseau des Femmes pour un Développement Associatif, 'Women's Bodies as a Battleground: Sexual Violence Against Women and Girls During the War in the Democratic Republic of Congo, South Kivu (1996–2003)' (2004)

International Crisis Group, 'Sierra Leone: Time for a New Military and Political Strategy' (2001)

——, 'Sudan: Towards an Incomplete Peace', Africa Report 73 (2003)

——, 'Sudan: Now or Never in Darfur', Africa Report 80 (2004)

——, 'Ethiopia and Eritrea: Preventing War', Africa Report 101 (2005)

——, 'Security Sector Reform in the Congo' (2006a)

——, 'Sri Lanka: The Failure of the Peace Process' (2006b)

——, 'Sri Lanka: Sinhala Nationalism and the Elusive Southern Consensus' (2007)

——, 'Somalia: To Move Beyond the Failed State', Africa Report 147 (2008a)

——, 'Sri Lanka's Eastern Province: Land, Development, Conflict', Asia Report 159 (2008b)

——, 'Rigged Elections in Darfur and the Consequences of a Probable NCP Victory in Sudan', Africa Briefing 72 (2010a)

——, 'Sri Lanka: A Bitter Peace', Asia Briefing 99 (2010b)

——, A Force in Fragments: Reconstituting the Afghan National Army', Asia Report 190 (2010c)

——, 'Popular Protest in North Africa and the Middle East (VI): The Syrian People's Slow Motion Revolution', Middle East/North Africa Report 108 (2011a)

——, 'Reconciliation in Sri Lanka: Harder than Ever', Asia Report 209 (2011b)

——, 'Aid and Conflict in Afghanistan' (2011c)

——, 'Somalia: The Transitional Government on Life Support', Africa Report 170 (2011d)

——, 'Popular *Protest in North Africa and the Middle East (V)*: Making Sense of Libya', Middle East/North Africa Report 107 (2011e)

International Rescue Committee, 'Mortality in the Democratic Republic of Congo: An Ongoing Crisis' (January 2008)

IRIN/OCHA, 'Sierra Leone: IRIN Briefing on the civil war', http://reliefweb.int/node/64702 (31 May 2000)

Johnson, Thomas and M. Chris Mason, 'Understanding the Taliban and Insurgency in Afghanistan', *Orbis*, 51:1 (Winter 2007), pp. 71–89

Joint Evaluation of Emergency Assistance to Rwanda, Copenhagen: Danida (1996)

Juergensmeyer, 'Religious Terror and Global War', Orfalea Center for Global and International Studies, University of California, Santa Barbara, paper 2 (2002)

Kabbah, Ahmad Tejan, 'Testimony Before the Truth and Reconciliation Commission, Sierra Leone', www.sierra-leone.org/TRCDocuments.html, 5 August 2003

Kabera, J. B. and C. Muyanja, 'Homecoming in the Luwero Triangle', in Tim Allen and Hubert Morsink (eds.) *When Refugees Go Home*, UNRISD/James Currey/Africa World Press (1994)

Kagan, Robert, 'Power and Weakness', Carnegie Endowment for International Peace, www.ceip.org/files/print/2002-06-02-policyreview.htm (June 2002)

Kahn, Paul, *Sacred Violence: Torture, Terror, and Sovereignty*, Ann Arbor: University of Michigan (2008)

Kaldor, Mary, *New and Old Wars: Organized Violence in a Global Era*, Stanford, CA: Stanford University Press (new edition 2007)

——, 'This Week's Theme: Human Security in Practice', openDemocracy, 20 January 2011

Kalyvas, Stathis, 'The Ontology of "Political Violence": Action and Identity in Civil Wars', *Perspectives on Politics*, 1:3 (2003), pp. 475–94

——, 'The Paradox of Terrorism in Civil War', *Journal of Ethics*, 8:1 (2004), pp. 97–138

——, *The Logic of Violence in Civil War*, Cambridge University Press (2006)

Kandeh, Jimmy D., 'What Does the "Militariat" Do When it Rules? Military Regimes: The Gambia, Sierra Leone and Liberia', *Review of African Political Economy*, 23:69 (1996), pp. 387–404

——, 'Ransoming the State: Elite Origins of Subaltern Terror in Sierra Leone', *Review of African Political Economy*, 26:81 (September 1999), pp. 349–66

Kaplan, Robert, 'The Coming Anarchy', *Atlantic Monthly* (February 1994), pp. 44–74

Karawan, Ibrahim, 'Politics and the Army in Egypt', *Survival*, 53:2 (2011), pp. 43–50

Karim, Ataul, Mark Duffield, Susanne Jaspars, Aldo Benini, Joanna Macrae, Mark Bradbury, Douglas Johnson, George Labri and Barbara Hendrie, 'OLS: Operation Lifeline – a Review', Geneva: Department for Humanitarian Affairs (July 1996)

Keen, David, 'A disaster for whom? Local interests and international donors during famine among the Dinka of Sudan', *Disasters*, 15:2 (1991), pp. 58–73

——, 'The Kurds in Iraq: How Safe is their Haven Now?' Save the Children (1993)

——, *The Benefits of Famine: A Political Economy of Famine and Relief in Southwestern Sudan, 1983–89*, Princeton University Press (1994)

——, 'The Economic Functions of Violence in Civil Wars', Adelphi paper no. 319, Oxford: Oxford University Press and International Institute for Strategic Studies (1998)

——, 'War and Peace: What's the Difference?' in Adekeye Adebajo and Chandra Lekha Sriram (eds.), *Managing Armed Conflicts in the 21st Century*, Special Issue of *International Peacekeeping*, 7:4 (2001), pp. 1–22

——, 'Demobilising Guatemala', Crisis States Research Centre working paper series 1, 37, LSE (2003)

——, *Conflict and Collusion in Sierra Leone*, Oxford: James Currey/International Peace Academy (2005a)

——, 'Liberalization and Conflict', *International Political Science Review*, 26:1 (2005b), pp. 73–89

——, *Endless War: Hidden Functions of the 'War on Terror'*, London: Pluto (2006)

——, *Complex Emergencies*, Cambridge: Polity (2008)

——, 'Compromise or Capitulation: Report on WFP and the Humanitarian Crisis in Sri Lanka', in *Humanitarian Assistance in Conflict and Complex Emergencies*, conference report and background papers, World Food Programme (June 2009)

——, 'Economic Initiatives to Tackle Conflict: Bringing Politics Back In', Crisis States Research Centre, occasional paper 9 (May 2009)

Keen, David and Vivian Lee, 'Civilian status and the new security agendas', in Sarah Collinson, James Darcy, Nicholas Waddell and Anna Schmidt (eds.), *Realising protection: The uncertain benefits of civilian, refugee and IDP status*, Humanitarian Policy Group report 28, London: Overseas Development Institute (September 2009), pp. 11–20

Kelly, Jocelyn, 'Rape in War: Motives of Militia in DRC', Special Report, United States Institute of Peace (June 2010), pp. 1–15

Kennedy, Paul, *The Rise and Fall of the Great Powers*, London: Vintage (1989)

Kepel, Gilles, *Jihad: The Trial of Political Islam*, London: I. B. Tauris (2002)

Khalaf, Samir, *Civil and Uncivil Violence: A History of the Internationalization of Communal Conflict in Lebanon*, New York: Colombia University Press (2002) al-Khalil, Samir, *Republic of Fear*, London: Hutchinson Radius (1989)

Khobe, Brigadier-General Mitikishe Maxwell, 'Anatomy of the Sierra Leonean Conflict and its Resolution by ECOWAS', paper presented to the ECOWAS Regional Forum on Conflict Management and Resolution, Ougadougou, Burkina Faso (7–11 July 1998)

——, 'One Year after Lome', CDD Strategy Planning Series, conference on the peace process, London: Centre for Democracy and Development (15 September 2000)

Kibreab, Gaim, 'Forced Labour in Eritrea', *Journal of Modern African Studies*, 47:1 (2009) pp. 41–72

Kiernan, Ben, *The Pol Pot Regime: Race, Power, and Genocide in Cambodia under the Khmer Rouge, 1975–79*, New Haven and London: Yale University Press (1996)

Kilcullen, David, *The Accidental Guerrilla: Fighting small wars in the midst of a big one*, London: Hurst and Co. (2009)

King, Samantha, 'Offensive Lines: Sport-State Synergy in an Era of Perpetual War', *Cultural Studies – Critical Methodologies*, 8:4 (2008), pp. 527–39

Kirkpatrick, David, 'Egyptians Say Military Discourages an Open Economy', *New York Times* (17 February 2011)

Klein, Naomi, 'Stark Message of the Mutiny', *Guardian* (15 August 2003)

Klein, Naomi, *The Shock Doctrine: The Rise of Disaster Capitalism*, New York: Henry Holt and Company (2007)

Korf, Benedikt, 'Functions of Violence Revisited: Greed, pride and grievance in Sri Lanka's civil war', *Progress in Development Studies*, 6:2 (2006), pp. 109–22

Kovalev, Sergei, 'Russia After Chechnya', *New York Review of Books* (17 July 1997)

——, 'Putin's War', *New York Review of Books* (13 January 2000)

——, 'Why Putin Wins', *New York Review of Books* (22 November 2007)

Kriger, Norma, *Zimbabwe's Guerrilla War: Peasant Voices*, Cambridge: Cambridge University Press (1992)

Lacharité, Michel-Olivier, 'Yemen: Low Profile', in Claire Magone, Michael Neuman and Fabrice Weissman (eds.), *Humanitarian Negotiations Revealed: The MSF Experience*, London: Hurst and Co. (2011)

Lafraie, Najibullah, 'Resurgence of the Taliban Insurgency in Afghanistan: How and why?', *International Politics*, 46:1 (2009), pp. 102–13

Lary, Diana, '"Warlord Soldiers": Chinese Common Soldiers 1911–1937', Cambridge: Cambridge University Press (1985)

Le Billon, Philippe, 'The Political Ecology of Transition in Cambodia, 1989–1999: War, Peace and Forest Exploitation', *Development and Change*, 31 (2000), pp. 785–805

——, 'Angola's Political Economy of War: The Role of Oil and Diamonds, 1975–2000', *African Affairs*, 100 (2001a), pp. 55–80

——, 'The Political Ecology of War: Natural resources and armed conflicts', *Political Geography*, 20 (2001b), pp. 561–84

——, 'Buying Peace or Fuelling War: The role of corruption in armed conflicts', *Journal of International Development*, 15:4 (2003), pp. 413–26

Le More, Anne, 'Killing with Kindness: Funding the demise of a Palestinian state', *International Affairs*, 81:5 (2005), pp. 981–99

Leduc, Benoit and Michael Neuman, 'Somalia: Everything is open to negotiation', in Claire Magone, Michael Neuman and Fabrice Weissman (eds.), *Humanitarian Negotiations Revealed: The MSF Experience*, London: Hurst and Co. (2011)

Ledwidge, Frank, *Losing Small Wars: British Military Failure in Iraq and Afghanistan*, New Haven and London: Yale University Press (2011)

Lembcke, Jerry, *The Spitting Image: Myth, Memory and the Legacy of Vietnam*, New York University Press (1998)

Lenin, Vladimir, *Imperialism: The Highest State of Capitalism*, International Publishers, 1997 (first published 1917)

Lerner, Paul, 'Psychiatry and the Casualties of War in Germany, 1914–18', *Journal of Contemporary History*, 35:1 (2000), pp. 13–28

Lerner, Paul, *Hysterical Men: War, Psychiatry and the Politics of Trauma in Germany, 1890–1930*, Cornell University Press (2003)

Lieven, Anatol, *Chechnya: Tombstone of Russian Power*, New Haven and London: Yale University Press (1999)

——, 'The War in Afghanistan: Its background and future prospects', *Conflict, Security and Development*, 9:3 (October 2009), pp. 333–59

Lifton, Robert, *Home from the War: Vietnam Veterans – Neither Victims nor Executioners*, London: Wildwood House (1974)

Lord, David, *Paying the Price: The Sierra Leone Peace Process*, London: Conciliation Resources (2000)

Lunn, Jon, 'The Power of Justice, Justice as Power: Observations on the Trajectory of the International Human Rights Movement'. Crisis States Development Research Centre, DESTIN, LSE, discussion paper no. 12 (September 2005)

Macdonald, Scot, 'Hitler's Shadow: Historical Analogies and the Iraqi Invasion of Kuwait', *Diplomacy and Statecraft*, 13:4 (2002), pp. 29–59

Mackay, Neil, 'UK sells chemical weapons to the world', *Sunday Herald* (22 December 2002)

MacPherson, Myra, *Long Time Passing: Vietnam and the Haunted Generation*, London: Sceptre (1988)

Macrae, Joanna and Nicholas Leader, *The Politics of Coherence: Humanitarianism and Foreign Policy in the Post-Cold War Era*, Humanitarian Policy Group, HPG Briefing no. 1, London: ODI (July 2000)

Magone, Claire, Michael Neuman and Fabrice Weissman (eds.), *Humanitarian Negotiations Revealed: The MSF Experience*, London: Hurst and Co. (2011)

Malone, David M. and Heiko Nitzschke, 'Economic Agendas in Civil Wars: What We Know, What We Need to Know', discussion paper no. 2005/07, WIDER, United Nations University (2005)

Mamdani, Mahmood, *When Victims Become Killers: Colonialism, Nativism, and the Genocide in Rwanda*, Princeton, N.J. : Princeton University Press (2001)

Mamdani, Mahmood, 'The Politics of Naming: Genocide, Civil War, Insurgency', *London Review of Books* (8 March 2007)

Mani, Kristina, 'Militaries in Business: State-Making and Entrepreneurship in the Developing World', *Armed Forces and Society*, 33:4 (July 2007), pp. 591–611

Mann, Michael, *Incoherent Empire*, London: Verso (2003)

Mansfield, Edward and Jack Snyder, 'Democratization and the Danger of War', *International Security*, 20:1 (Summer 1995), pp. 5–38

——, *Electing to Fight: Why Emerging Democracies Go to War*, MIT Press (2005)

Manz, Beatriz, *Refugees of a Hidden War: The Aftermath of Counterinsurgency in Guatemala*, State University of New York Press (1988)

Al-Marashi, Ibrahim and Sammy Salama, *Iraq's Armed Forces: An Analytical History*, Abingdon: Routledge (2008)

Marine Corps Historical Publication, 'Lessons Learned: Iran-Iraq War', FMFRP 3–203, www.fas.org/man/dod-101/ops/war/docs/3203 (10 December 1990)

Marlowe, Ann, 'Dying for the Karzai Cartel', *National Review Online* (20 May 2010)

Marriage, Zoe, *Not Breaking the Rules, Not Playing the Game: International Assistance to Countries at War*, London: Hurst and Co./Palgrave Macmillan (2006a)

——, 'Defining Morality: DFID and the Great Lakes', *Third World Quarterly*, 27:3 (2006b), pp. 477–90

Martinez, Luis, *The Algerian Civil War, 1990–1998*, London: Hurst and Co. (1998)

——, 'Libya: The Conversion of a "Terrorist State"', *Mediterranean Politics*, 11:2 (July 2006), pp. 151–65

Marvin, Carolyn and David Ingle, 'Blood Sacrifice and the Nation: Revisiting Civil Religion', *Journal of the American Academy of Religion*, 46:4 (1996), pp. 767–80

——, *Blood Sacrifice and the Nation: Totem Rituals and the American Flag*, Cambridge: Cambridge University Press (1999)

Mater, Nadire, 'Soldiers' Tales', *Index on Censorship* 5 (1999), pp. 156–68

McCrisken, Trevor, 'Ten Years On: Obama's war on terrorism in rhetoric and practice', *International Affairs*, 87:4 (2011), pp. 781–801

McCulloch, Lesley, 'Greed: The Silent Force of the Conflict in Aceh', University of Deakin (2003)

McDoom, Omar, 'The Micro-Politics of Mass Violence: Authority, Security, and Opportunity in Rwanda's Genocide', PhD, LSE (2008)

McDowall, David, *A Modern History of the Kurds*, London: I. B. Tauris (1997)

McGreal, Chris, 'I Am a Scorpion. I Captured the Lion', *Guardian* (18 May 2000)

Melman, Seymour, *The Permanent War Economy: American Capitalism in Decline*, New York: Touchstone (1985, first published 1974)

—— (ed. Ben Abrams and Patrick Deer), *War, Inc.*, Vanderbilt University, http://ejournals/library/vanderbilt/edu/ameriquests (2008)

Melvern, Linda, 'The Security Council: Behind the scenes', *International Affairs*, 77:1 (2001), pp. 101–11

Menkhaus, Ken, 'A "Sudden Outbreak of Tranquility": Assessing the New Peace in Africa', *Fletcher Forum of World Affairs*, 28:2 (2004), pp. 73–90

——, 'Stabilisation and Humanitarian Access in a Collapsed State: The Somali Case', *Disasters*, 34:S3 (2010), pp. S320–41

——, 'A Diplomatic Surge to Stop Somalia's Famine', Policy Briefing, The Enough Project (September 2011)

Messiant, Christine, 'Angola: Woe to the Vanquished', in *In the Shadow of 'Just Wars': Violence, Politics and Humanitarian Action*, London: Hurst and Co. (2004)

Metz, Steven, 'New Challenges and Old Concepts: Understanding 21st Century Insurgency', *Parameters* (Winter 2007), pp. 20–32

Middle East Policy Council, 'Symposium: Iraq, Afghanistan and the War on "Terror"', *Middle East Policy*, 12:1 (Spring 2005)

Miller, Arthur (ed. Gerald Weales), *The Crucible: Text and Criticism*, London: Penguin (1996)

Minear, Larry, 'The U.S. Citizen-Soldier and the Global War on Terror: The National Guard Experience', Feinstein International Center (September 2007)

Mirsky, Jonathan, 'The Never-Ending War', *New York Review of Books* (25 May 2000), pp. 54–63

Mkandawire, Thandika, 'The Terrible Toll of Post-colonial "Rebel Movements" in Africa: Towards an Explanation of the Violence against the Peasantry', *Journal of Modern African Studies*, 40:2 (2002), pp. 181–215

Moore Jr, Barrington, *Social Origins of Dictatorship and Democracy: Lord and Peasant in the Making of the Modern World*. Harmondsworth: Penguin (1974; first published 1966)

Moro, Leben, 'Oil, Conflict and Displacement in Sudan', D. Phil., Oxford University (2008)

Muana, Patrick K., 'The Kamajoi Militia: Violence, Internal Displacement and the Politics of Counter-Insurgency', in *Africa Development*, 22:3&4 (1997). pp. 77–100

Mwenda, Andrew, 'Uganda's Politics of Foreign Aid and Violent Conflict: The political uses of the LRA rebellion', in Tim Allen and Koen Vlassenroot (eds), *The Lord's Resistance Army: Myth and Reality*, London: Zed Books (2010)

Nadarajah, Suthaharan, 'Prejudice, Asymmetry and Insecurity', in *Incentives, Sanctions and Conditionality*, Conciliation Resources, London, www.c-r.org/our-work/accord/incentives/asymmetry.php (2008)

Nathan, Laurie, 'The Frightful Inadequacy of Most of the Statistics: A Critique of Collier and Hoeffler on Causes of Civil War', discussion paper II, Crisis States Development Research Centre, LSE (2005)

New American Foundation, 'U.S. Weapons at War 2008' (December 2008).

Nixon, Rod, 'Indonesian West Timor: The political-economy of emerging ethno-nationalism', *Journal of Contemporary Asia*, 34:2 (2004), pp. 163–85

Nordstrom, Carolyn, 1999, 'Girls and War Zones: Troubling Questions' in Doreen Indra (ed.), *Engendering Forced Migration: Theory and Practice*, New York: Berghahn Books (1999), pp. 63–82

——, *Shadows of War: Violence, Power and International Profiteering in the Twenty-First Century*, University of California Press (2004)

North, Douglass, John Wallis and Barry Weingast, *Violence and Social Orders: A Conceptual Framework for Interpreting Recorded Human History*, Cambridge University Press (2009)

Norton-Taylor, Richard and Chris McGreal, 'Sierra Leone Children carry British Guns', *Guardian* (25 May 2000)

Nzongola-Ntalaja, Georges, *The Congo from Leopold to Kabila*, London: Zed Books (2002)

O'Brien, Tim, 'The Violent Vet', *Esquire* (December 1979), pp. 96–104

O'Day, Patrick, 'The Mexican Army as Cartel', *Journal of Contemporary Criminal Justice*, 17:3 (2001), pp. 278–95

Orwell, George, *Nineteen Eighty-Four*, London: Penguin (2009, first published 1949)

Osiel, Mark, *Obeying Orders: Atrocity, Military Discipline, and the Law of War*, Picataway: Transaction (1999)

Oxfam, 'Whose Aid Is It Anyway? Politicizing aid in conflicts and crises', 145 Oxfam Briefing Paper (10 February 2011)

Pachico, Elyssa, 'Former Top Bolivian Drug Czar Arrested in Panama', insightcrime.org (28 February 2011)

Panel of Experts, Report of the Panel of Experts, Appointed Pursuant to UN Security Council Resolution 1306 (2000) in relation to Sierra Leone (December 2000)

Panel of Experts, Report of the Panel of Experts on the Illegal Exploitation of Natural Resources and Other Forms of Wealth of the Democratic Republic of the Congo (2001)

Panel of Experts, Final Report of the Panel of Experts on the Illegal Exploitation of Natural Resources and Other Forms of Wealth in the Democratic Republic of the Congo, UN Security Council (16 October 2002), pp. 1–57

Panel of Experts, Report of the Secretary-General's Panel of Experts on Accountability in Sri Lanka (31 March 2011)

Pantuliano, Sara and Sorcha O'Callaghan, 'The "Protection Crisis": A review of field-based strategies for humanitarian protection in Darfur', HPG Discussion paper, ODI, London (December 2006)

Paris, Roland, *At War's End: Building Peace After Civil Conflict*, Cambridge: Cambridge University Press (2004)

Pastor, Manuel and James Boyce, 'El Salvador: Economic Disparities, External Intervention, and Civil Conflict', in E. Wayne Nafziger, Frances Stewart and Raimo Vayrynen (eds.), *War, Hunger, and Displacement: The Origins of Humanitarian Emergencies*, vol. 2, New York: Oxford University Press (2000)

Paul, Benjamin and William Demarest, 'The Operation of a Death Squad in San Pedro la Laguna', in Robert Carmack (ed.), *Harvest of Violence: The Maya Indians and the Guatemala Crisis*, University of Oklahoma Press (1988), pp. 119–54

Peceny, Mark and William Stanley, 'Counterinsurgency in El Salvador', *Politics and Society*, 38:1 (2010), pp. 67–94

Pech, Khareen and Yusuf Hassan, 'Sierra Leone's Faustian Bargain', *Weekly Mail and Guardian* (30 May 1997)

Pemagbi, Joe, 'The State of Civil Military Relations', Centre for Democracy and Development, 'Engaging Sierra Leone: Round-Table on Reconciliation and State-Building, Lome, Togo, 21–22 June and Other Activities on Sierra Leone', London (1999)

Perkins, Richard and Eric Neumayer, 'The organized hypocrisy of ethical foreign policy: Human rights, democracy and Western arms sales', *Geoforum*, 41 (2010), pp. 247–56

Peters, Krijn, 'Footpaths to Reintegration: Armed Conflict, Youth and the Rural Crisis in Sierra Leone', Proefschrift, PhD, Wageningen University (2006)

——, *War and the Crisis of Youth in Sierra Leone*, Cambridge: Cambridge University Press, and London: International African Institute (2011)

Phillips, Sarah, 'Al-Qaeda and the Struggle for Yemen', *Survival*, 53:1 (2011) pp. 95–120

Physicians for Human Rights (PHR), 'War-related Sexual Violence in Sierra Leone', with UNAMSIL, Boston/Washington DC (2003)

Pieterse, Jan Nederveen, 'Israel's Role in the Third World: exporting West bank expertise', *Race and Class*, 26:9 (1985), pp. 9–30

Polman, Linda, *War Games: The Story of Aid and War in Modern Times*, London: Viking (2010)

Power, Samantha, *'A Problem from Hell': America and the Age of Genocide*, New York: Basic Books (2002)

Prendergast, John and Colin Thomas-Jensen, 'Sudan: A State on the Brink?', *Current History*, 108:718 (May 2009), pp. 208–13

Preston, Matthew, *Ending Civil War: Rhodesia and Lebanon in Perspective*, London: I. B. Tauris (2004)

Preti, Alessandro, 'Guatemala: Violence in Peacetime – A Critical Analysis of the Armed Conflict and the Peace Process', *Disasters*, 26:2 (2002), pp. 99–119

Principal Deputy Under Secretary of Defense, 'FY 94–99 Defense Planning Guidance Sections for Comment', Washington DC (February 1992)

Project on Defense Alternatives, 'The Pentagon and Deficit Reduction', Briefing Memo 47, Cambridge, MA, and Washington DC (1 March 2011)

Prunier, Gérard, *The Rwanda Crisis, 1959–1994: History of a Genocide*, London: Hurst and Co. (1995)

——,. *Darfur: The Ambiguous Genocide*, London: Hurst and Co. (2005)

Pugh, Michael and Neil Cooper, *War Economies in a Regional Context: Challenges of Transformation*, Boulder, Colorado: Lynne Rienner (2004)

Pupavac, Vanessa, 'War on the Couch: The Emotionology of the New International Security Paradigm', *European Journal of Social Theory*, 7:2 (2004), pp. 149–70

Race, Jeffrey, *War Comes to Long An: Revolutionary Conflict in a Vietnamese Province*, Berkeley: University of California Press (1972)

Rajasingham-Senanayake, Darini, 'The Dangers of Devolution: The Hidden Economies of Armed Conflict', in R. Rotberg (ed.), *Creating Peace in Sri Lanka: Civil War and Reconciliation*, Brookings Institution (1999), pp. 57–69

——, 'The Political Economy of Aid, Conflict and Peace Building in Sri Lanka', *Polity*, 3:5 (October–December 2006), pp. 7–13

Rampton, Sheldon and John Stauber, *Weapons of Mass Deception: The Uses of Propaganda in Bush's War on Iraq*, London: Constable and Robinson, 2003

Rangasami, Amrita, 1985. 'Failure of Exchange Entitlements' Theory of Famine: A Response', *Economic and Political Weekly*, XX:41&42 (12 and 19 October 1985), pp 1747–51, 1797–1800

——, *Taliban: Islam, Oil and the New Great Game in Central Asia*, London: I. B. Tauris (2000)

Rashid, Ahmed, 'Letter from Afghanistan: Are the Taliban Winning?', *Current History* (January 2007), pp. 17–20

Reeves, Eric, 'Whitewashing Darfur', *Guardian* (June 14 2009).

Relief and Rehabilitation Committee, Report on Unacceptable Behaviour of CDF in the Southern Region (August 2000)

Reno, William, *Corruption and State Politics in Sierra Leone*, Cambridge: Cambridge University Press (1995)

Renton, Alex, 'Our Guns Arm the Children', *Evening Standard* (24 May 2000)

Report of the Commission for Historical Classification, 'Guatemala: Memory of Silence', conclusions and recommendations, http://shr.aaas.org/guatemala/ceh/report/english/toc.html (1999)

Restrepo, Jorge and Michael Spagat, 'Colombia's Tipping Point?', *Survival*, 47:2 (2005), pp. 131–52

Reza, Sadiq, 'Endless Emergency: The Case of Egypt', *New Criminal Law Review*, 10:4 (2007), pp. 532–53

Richani, Nazih, 'Caudillos and the Crisis of the Colombian State: Fragmented sovereignty, the war system and the privatisation of counterinsurgency in Colombia', *Third World Quarterly*, 28:2 (2007), pp. 403–17

Richards, Paul, 'Rebellion in Liberia and Sierra Leone: A Crisis of Youth?' in Oliver Furley (ed.), *Conflict in Africa*, London: I. B.Tauris (1995)

——, *Fighting for the Rain Forest: War, Youth and Resources in Sierra Leone*, Oxford: James Currey (1996)

——, 'War and Peace in Sierra Leone', *Fletcher Forum of World Affairs*, 25:2 (2001), pp. 41–50

Riechmann, Deb and Richard Lardner, 'U.S. $360M lots to corruption in Afghanistan', *Army Times*/Associated Press (16 August 2011)

Rieff, David, 'Hillary Clinton's Naïve, Muddled Approach to Development', *New Republic* (23 August 2010)

Roberts, Hugh, *The Battlefield: Algeria 1988–2002: Studies in a Broken Polity*, London: Verso (2003)

Rodgers, Dennis, 'Living in the Shadow of Death: Gangs, Violence and Social Order in Urban Nicaragua, 1996–2002', *Journal of Latin American Studies*, 38, (2006), pp. 267–92

Ronin, Yehudit, 'Qadhafi and Militant Islamism: Unprecedented Conflict', *Middle Eastern Studies*, 38:4 (2002), pp. 1–16

Rosen, Nir, 'The Occupation of Iraqi Hearts and Minds', (www.truthdig.com) (27 June 2006)

Ross, Michael, 'What Do We Know About Natural Resources and Civil War?', *Journal of Peace Research*, 41:3 (2004), pp. 337–56

Roston, Aram, 'How the US army protects its trucks – by paying the Taliban', *Guardian* (13 November 2009)

Roy, Arundhati, *The Ordinary Person's Guide to Empire*, London: Harper Perennial (2004)

Royle, Trevor, *Civil War: The Wars of the Three Kingdoms, 1638–1660*, London: Abacus, (2004)

Rubin, Barnett, 'The Political Economy of War and Peace in Afghanistan', *World Development*, 28:10 (2000), pp. 1789–1803

——, 'Saving Afghanistan', *Foreign Affairs*, 86:1 (January–February 2007), pp. 57–78

Rupert, James, 'Diamond Hunters Fuel Africa's Brutal Wars', *Washington Post Foreign Service* (16 October 1999)

Russell, Conrad, *The Crisis of Parliaments: English History 1509–1660*, Oxford: Oxford University Press (1971)

Sadeh, Sharon, 'Israel's Beleaguered Defense Industry', *Middle East Review of International Affairs*, 5:1 (March 2001)

Sahimi, Muhammed, 'Iran's power struggle', letter, *International Herald Tribune* (29 April 2009)

Said, Edward, *Peace and its Discontents: Essays on Palestine in the Middle East Peace Process*, New York: Vintage (1996)

Said, Yahia, 'The Iraq surge 2007–2008: what does Human Security have to say about it?', openDemocracy, 15 January 2011

Samatar, Abdi Ismail, 'Genocidal politics and the Somali famine', 30 July 2011, Aljazeera. net, reposted at AfricaFocus Bulletin (5 August 2011) (http://www.africafocus.org/docs11/som1108.php)

Schaffer, Bernard, 'Towards Responsibility', in Edward Clay and Bernard Schaffer (eds), *Room for Manoeuvre: An Exploration of Public Policy in Agriculture and Rural Development*, London: Heinemann Educational Books (1984)

Scheff, Thomas, *Bloody Revenge: Emotions, Nationalism, and War*, Boulder: Westview Press (1994)

Scheper-Hughes, Nancy, *Death Without Weeping: The Violence of Everyday Life in Brazil*, University of California Press (1993)

Schirmer, Jennifer, 'The Guatemalan Politico-Military Project: Legacies for a violent peace?', *Latin American Perspectives*, 26:2 (March 1999), pp. 92–107

Schivelbusch, Wolfgang, *The Culture of Defeat: On National Trauma, Mourning, and Recovery*, Granta Books (2001)

Schmidt, John, 'The Unravelling of Pakistan', *Survival*, 51:3 (June–July 2009), pp. 29–54

Schmitt, Eric and David Sanger, 'US offers Pakistan army a 2 billion aid package', *New York Times* (22 Oct 2010)

Schomerus, Mareike, 'They forget what they came for: Uganda's army in Sudan', *Journal of Eastern African Studies* (forthcoming)

Scott, Peter, 'Obama and Afghanistan: America's Drug-Corrupted War', *Critical Asian Studies*, 43:1 (2011), pp. 111–138

Scott, Wilbur, David McCone and George Mastroianni, 'The Deployment Experience of Ft. Carson's Soldiers in Iraq: Thinking about and Training for Full-Spectrum Warfare', *Armed Forces and Society*, 35 (2009) pp. 460–76

Sesay, Max, 'State Capacity and the Politics of Economic Reform in Sierra Leone', *Journal of Contemporary African Studies*, 13:2 (July 1995), pp. 165–82

Severo, Richard and Lewis Milford, *The Wages of War: When America's Soldiers Came Home – From Valley Forge to Vietnam*, New York: Simon and Schuster (1990)

Shah, Aqil, 'Getting the Military out of Pakistani Politics: How Aiding the Army Undermines Democracy', *Foreign Affairs*, 90:3 (May–June 2011), pp. 69–82

——, 'Pakistan's "Armored" Democracy', *Journal of Democracy*, 14:4 (2003), pp. 26–40

Shashikumar, V. K., 'Lessons from the War in Sri Lanka', *Indian Defence Review*, 24:3 (July–September 2009)

Shawcross, William, *Sideshow: Kissinger, Nixon and the Destruction of Cambodia*, London: Fontana (1980; first published in 1979)

Shawcross, William, 'Tragedy in Cambodia', *New York Review of Books* (14 November 1996), pp. 41–6, and (19 December 1996), pp. 73–74

Sheehan, Neil, *A Bright Shining Lie: John Paul Vann and America in Vietnam*, New York: Picador (1990)

Sheehan, Neil, Hendrick Smith, E. W. Kenworthy and Fox Butterfield, *The Pentagon Papers: The Secret History of the Vietnam War*, New York Times, 1971

Shepherd, Bob, 'The Iraqi Dogs of War: An ex-SAS veteran reveals the antics of "security experts" helping to lose the war on terror', *Daily Mail*, 2 May 2008

Sierra Leone Broadcasting Service, 18 June 1997

Sierra Leone Police Force, Statement taken from Alfred Abu Sankoh (alias Zagallo), (27 March 1998)

Silverstein Ken, 'Official Pariah Sudan Valuable to America's war on terrorism', *Los Angeles Times* (29 April 2005)

Simon, Steven and Jonathan Stevenson, 'Afghanistan? How Much is Enough?', *Survival*, 51:5 (2009), pp. 47–67

Simpson, John, *In the Forests of the Night: Encounters in Peru with Terrorism, Drug-running & Military Oppression*, London: Arrow (1994)

SIPRI (Stockholm International Peace Research Institute), SIPRI Yearbook 2011: Armaments, Disarmament and International Security – summary (http://www.sipri.org/yearbook/2011/files/SIPRIYB11summary.pdf)

Slim, Hugo, *Killing Civilians: Method, Madness and Morality in War*, London: Hurst and Co. (2007)

Smyth, Frank, 'The Untouchable Narco-State: Guatemala's military defies the DF[A]', *The Texas Observer* (18 November 2005), pp. 6–20

Snyder, Jack and Edward Mansfield, 'Democratization and War', *Foreign Affairs*, 74:3 (1995), pp. 79–97

Snyder, Jack and Robert Jervis, 'Civil War and the Security Dilemma', in Barbara F. Walter and Jack Snyder (eds), *Civil Wars, Insecurity and Intervention*, New York: Columbia University Press (1999) pp. 15–37

Soros, George, 'Who Lost Russia?', *New York Review of Books* (13 April 2000), pp. 10–16

Spencer, Jonathan, 'A Nationalism without Politics? The illiberal consequences of liberal institutions in Sri Lanka', *Third World Quarterly*, 29:3 (2008), pp. 611–29

Srinivasan, Sharath, *War by Other Means: The Politics of Peace Negotiations in Sudan*, D. Phil., Oxford University, 2010

Stahl, Roger, 'Have You Played the War on Terror?', *Critical Studies in Media Communication*, 23:2 (2006), pp. 112–30

Stanley, William and David Holiday, 'Broad Participation, Diffuse Responsibility: Peace Implementation in Guatemala', in Stephen Stedman, Donald Rothchild and Elizabeth Cousens (eds), *Ending Civil Wars: The Implementation of Peace Agreements*, Boulder: Lynne Rienner (2003)

Steele, Jonathan and Suzanne Goldenberg, 'What is the real death toll in Iraq?', *Guardian* (19 March 2008)

Stern, Jessica, *Terror in the Name of God: Why Religious Militants Kill*, HarperCollins (2004)

Stewart, Frances, 'The root causes of humanitarian emergencies', in E. Wayne Nafziger, Frances Stewart and Raimo Vayrynen (eds), *War, Hunger and Displacement: The origins of humanitarian emergencies*, Oxford: Oxford University Press (2004)

Stewart, Frances (ed.), *Horizontal Inequalities and Conflict: Understanding Group Violence in Multiethnic Societies*, New York: Palgrave Macmillan (2008)

Stewart, Frances, Graham Brown and Arnim Langer, 'Major Findings and Conclusions on the Relationship between Horizontal Inequalities and Conflict', in Frances Stewart (ed.), *Horizontal Inequalities and Conflict: Understanding Group Violence in Multiethnic Societies*, New York: Palgrave Macmillan (2008)

Stockton, Nicholas, 'In Defence of Humanitarianism', *Disasters*, 22:4 (1998), pp. 352–60
——, 'Humanitarianism Bound: Coherence and Catastrophe in the Congo, 1998–2002', mimeo. (April 2003)
Stoll, David, 'Evangelicals, Guerrillas and the Army: The Ixil Triangle under Rios Montt', in Robert Carmack (ed.), *Harvest of Violence: The Maya Indians and the Guatemalan Crisis*, Norman and London: University of Oklahoma Press (1992; first published 1988)
Stratton, Allegra, 'US air strike targets Somalian extremists', *Guardian* (3 March 2008)
Straus, Scott, *The Order of Genocide: Race, Power and War in Rwanda*, Cornell University Press (2006)
Suhrke, Astri and Mats Berdal (eds.) *The Peace In Between: Post-war violence and peace-building*, London and New York: Routledge (2011)
Summerfield, Derek, 'The Social Experience of War and Some Issues for the Humanitarian Field', in Patrick Bracken and Celia Petty (eds.), *Rethinking the Trauma of War* London: Save the Children/Free Association Books (1998)
Tangri, Roger and Andrew Mwenda, 'Military Corruption and Ugandan Politics since the late 1990s', *Review of African Political Economy*, 98 (2003), pp. 539–52
Taylor, Christopher, *Sacrifice as Terror: The Rwandan Genocide of 1994*, Oxford and New York: Berg (1999)
Theidon, Kimberly, 'Reconstructing Masculinities: The Disarmament, Demobilization, and Reintegration of Former Combatants in Colombia', *Human Rights Quarterly*, 31 (2009), pp. 1–34
Theros, Marika and Nir Rosen, 'Afghanistan: losing the Afghan people', openDemocracy (16 January 2011)
Thomas, Keith, *Religion and the Decline of Magic*, London: Penguin Books, (1978)
Thompson, Edwina, Report on Wilton Park Conference 1022, Winning 'Hearts and Minds' in Afghanistan: Assessing the Effectiveness of Development Aid in COIN Operations, 11–14 March 2010 (1 April 2010)
Tierney, John, 'Warlord, Inc.: Extortion and Corruption along the U.S. Supply Chain in Afghanistan', Report of the Majority Staff, Subcommittee on National Security and Foreign Affairs, Committee on Oversight an Government Reform, US House of Representatives (June 2010)
Tilman, Robert, 'The Non-Lessons of the Malayan Emergency', *Asian Survey*, 6:8 (August 1966), pp. 407–19
Time magazine, '10 questions for Silvio Berlusconi' (28 July 2003)
Tirman, John, *Spoils of War: The Human Cost of America's Arms Trade*, New York: Free Press (1997)
Torjesen, Stina and Neil MacFarlane, 'R before D: the case of post conflict reintegration in Tajikistan', in *Conflict, Security and Development*, 7:2 (June 2007), pp. 311–32
Trullinger, James, *Village at War: An Account of Conflict in Vietnam*, Stanford University Press (1994)
Tull, Denis and Andreas Mehler, 'The Hidden Costs of Power-Sharing: Reproducing Insurgent Violence in Africa', *African Affairs*, 104:416 (2005), pp. 375–98
Turton, David. 'Introduction: War and Ethnicity', in David Turton (ed.), *War and Ethnicity: Global Connections and Local Violence*, University of Rochester Press (1997)
Tyler, Patrick, 'U.S. Strategy Plan Calls for Insuring No Rivals Develop', *New York Times* (8 March 1992)
UN Inter-Agency Mission, 'Report on Inter-Agency Mission to Sierra Leone and the Sub-Region' (5 September 1995)
UN Secretary-General, 'Report of the Secretary-General on Sierra Leone', report to Security Council (26 January 1997)

UNDP, 'The Humanitarian Emergency in Sierra Leone: First Quarter Summary, January–March', Freetown (1995)

University Teachers for Human Rights, 'Let Them Speak: Truth about Sri Lanka's Victims of War', Jaffna, www.uthr.org/SpecialReports/Special%20rep34/Uthr-sp. rp34.htm (13 December 2009)

Uslu, Emrullah, 'Turkey's Kurdish Problem: Steps Toward a Solution', *Studies in Conflict and Terrorism*, 30 (2007), pp. 157–72

Utas, Mats, 'Building a Future? The reintegration and re-marginalisation of youth in Liberia', in Paul Richards (ed.), *No Peace, No War: An Anthropology of Contemporary Armed Conflicts*, Oxford: James Currey (2005)

Uvin, Peter, *Aiding Violence: The Development Enterprise in Rwanda*, West Hartford, CT: Kumarian Press (1998)

——, 'Rwanda: The Social Roots of Genocide', in E. Wayne Nafziger, Frances Stewart and Raimo Väyrynen, *War, Hunger, and Displacement: The Origins of Humanitarian Emergencies*, vol. 1, WIDER/Oxford University Press (2000), pp. 159–86

Vallely, Paul, 'We Muslims need to get out of our intellectual and social ghettos', *Independent* (25 July 2005)

Vargas, Gonzalo, 'Explaining Violence against Civilians: Insurgency, counterinsurgency and crime in the Middle Magdalena Valley, Colombia (1996–2004)', Ph.D, LSE (2010)

Vaux, Tony, *The Selfish Altruist: Relief Work in Famine and War*, London: Earthscan (2001)

Venugopal, Rajesh, 'Cosmopolitan Capitalism and Sectarian Socialism: Conflict, Development and the Liberal Peace in Sri Lanka', D. Phil. thesis, University of Oxford (2008)

——, 'The Making of Sri Lanka's Post-Conflict Economic Package and the Failure of the 2001–2004 Peace Process', CRISE working paper no. 64, Oxford University (2009a)

——, 'Sectarian Socialism: The Politics of Sri Lanka's Janatha Vimukthi Peramuna (JVP)', *Modern Asian Studies*, 44:3 (2009b), pp. 1–36

Verhoeven, Harry, 'The self-fulfilling prophesy of failed states: Somalia, state collapse and the Global War on Terror', *Journal of Eastern African Studies*, 3:3, (2009), pp. 405–25

Vidal, Gore, *Perpetual War for Perpetual Peace*, Forest Row: Clairview (2002)

Vines, Alex, *Renamo: Terrorism in Mozambique*, London: James Currey (1991)

Vlassenroot, Koen and Timothy Raeymaekers, 'Kivu's Intractable Security Conundrum', *African Affairs*, 108:432 (2009), pp. 475–84

de Waal, Alex, *Famine Crimes: Politics and the Disaster Relief Industry in Africa*, Oxford: James Currey (1997)

——, 'Who are the Darfurians? Arab and African Identities, Violence and External Engagement', *African Affairs*, 104:415 (2005), pp. 181–205

——, 'Sudan: The Turbulent State', in Alex de Waal (ed.), *War in Darfur – and the Search for Peace*, Justice Africa (2007), pp. 1–38

——, 'Mission without End? Peacekeeping in the Africa political marketplace', *International Affairs*, 85:1 (2009), pp. 99–113

Wade, Robert, 'The First-World Debt Crisis of 2007–2010 in Global Perspective', *Challenge*, 51:4 (July/August 2008), pp. 23–54

Waldman, Matt, 'The Sun in the Sky: The Relationship between Pakistan's ISI and Afghan Insurgents', Crisis States Research Centre, LSE, discussion paper 18 (2010)

Watson Institute for International Affairs, 'Interview with UN Veteran Antonio Donini on Lessons Learned in Afghanistan and Elsewhere', www.watsoninstitute.org/news_ detail.cfm?id=175 (4 March 2004)

Weissman, Fabrice, 'Sri Lanka: In All-Out War', in Claire Magone, Michael Neuman and Fabrice Weissman (eds.), *Humanitarian Negotiations Revealed: The MSF Experience*, London: Hurst and Co. (2011a)

——, 'Silence Heals … From the Cold War to the War on Terror, MSF Speaks Out: A Brief History', in Claire Magone, Michael Neuman and Fabrice Weissman (eds.), *Humanitarian Negotiations Revealed: The MSF Experience*, London: Hurst and Co. (2011b)

Weissman, Fabrice (ed.), *In the Shadow of 'Just Wars': Violence, Politics and Humanitarian Action*, London: Hurst and Co. (2004)

Welikala, Asanga, 'A State of Permanent Crisis: Constitutional Government, Fundamental Rights and States of Emergency in Sri Lanka', Centre for Policy Alternatives, Colombo (2008)

Whalen, Robert, *Bitter Wounds: German Victims of the Great War, 1914–1939*, Cornell University Press (1984)

Whitaker, Brian, 'Yemen, where dead men eat lunch', *Guardian* (19 January 2010)

Wickramatunga, Lansantha, 'Letter from the Grave', *New Yorker* (12 January 2009)

WikiLeaks, www.guardian.co.uk/world/us-embassy-cables-documents/108763 (18 May 2007)

Wilder, Andrew, 'A "weapons system" based on wishful thinking', *Boston Globe* (16 September 2009)

Willett, Susan, 'Defence Expenditures, Arms Procurement and Corruption in Sub-Saharan Africa', *Review of African Political Economy*, 121 (2009), pp. 335–51

Wood, Elisabeth, 'The Emotional Benefits of Insurgency in El Salvador', in Jeff Goodwin, James Jasper and Francesca Polletta (eds), *Passionate Politics: Emotions and Social Movements*, Chicago University Press (2001), pp. 267–302

——, 'Armed Groups and Sexual Violence: When is Wartime Rape Rare?', *Politics and Society* 37 (2009), pp. 131–6

Woodward, Bob, *Bush at War*, London: Simon and Schuster (2002)

——, *Obama's Wars*, London: Simon and Schuster (2010)

Woodward, Susan, 'Balkan Tragedy: Chaos and Dissolution After the Cold War', Washington D.C.: Brookings Institution (1995)

——, 'Economic Priorities for Successful Peace Implementation', in Stephen Stedman, Donald Rothchild and Elizabeth Cousens (eds), *Ending Civil Wars: The Implementation of Peace Agreements*, Boulder, Colorado: Lynne Rienner (2003)

Woolf, Amy, 'U.S. Strategic Forces: Background, Developments, and Issues', Congressional Research Service (24 January 2008)

World Bank, 'Rwanda: Country Assistance Evaluation', Report 27568 (5 January 2004)

Wright, Lawrence, 'The Double Game: The unintended consequences of American funding in Pakistan', *New Yorker* (16 May 2011)

Wyatt, Ian, 'Where a Raging Bull Lives', Wyatt Investment Research, 25 June 2010

Yannis, Alexandros, 'Kosovo: The Political Economy of Conflict and Peacebuilding', in Karen Ballentine and Jake Sherman (eds), *The Political Economy of Armed Conflict: Beyond Greed and Grievance*, Boulder, Colorado: Lynne Rienner (2003)

Yousif, Bassam. 'Coalition Economic Policies in Iraq: Motivations and outcomes', *Third World Quarterly*, 27:3 (April 2006), pp. 491–505

Zimbardo, Philip, *The Lucifer Effect: How Good People Turn Evil*, London: Rider (2008)

Zur, Judith, *Violent Memories: Mayan War Widows in Guatemala*, Boulder: Westview Press (1998)

Index